I0762392

TAKING THE FEAR OUT OF

WATERCOLOUR

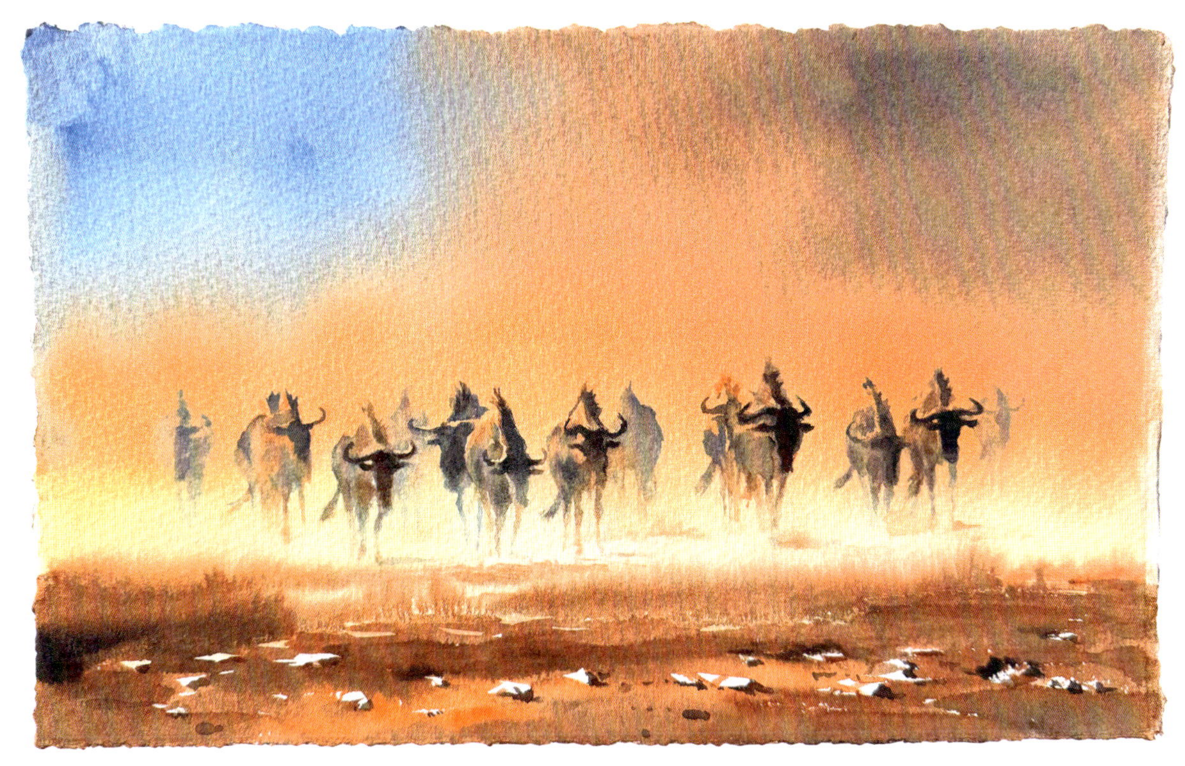

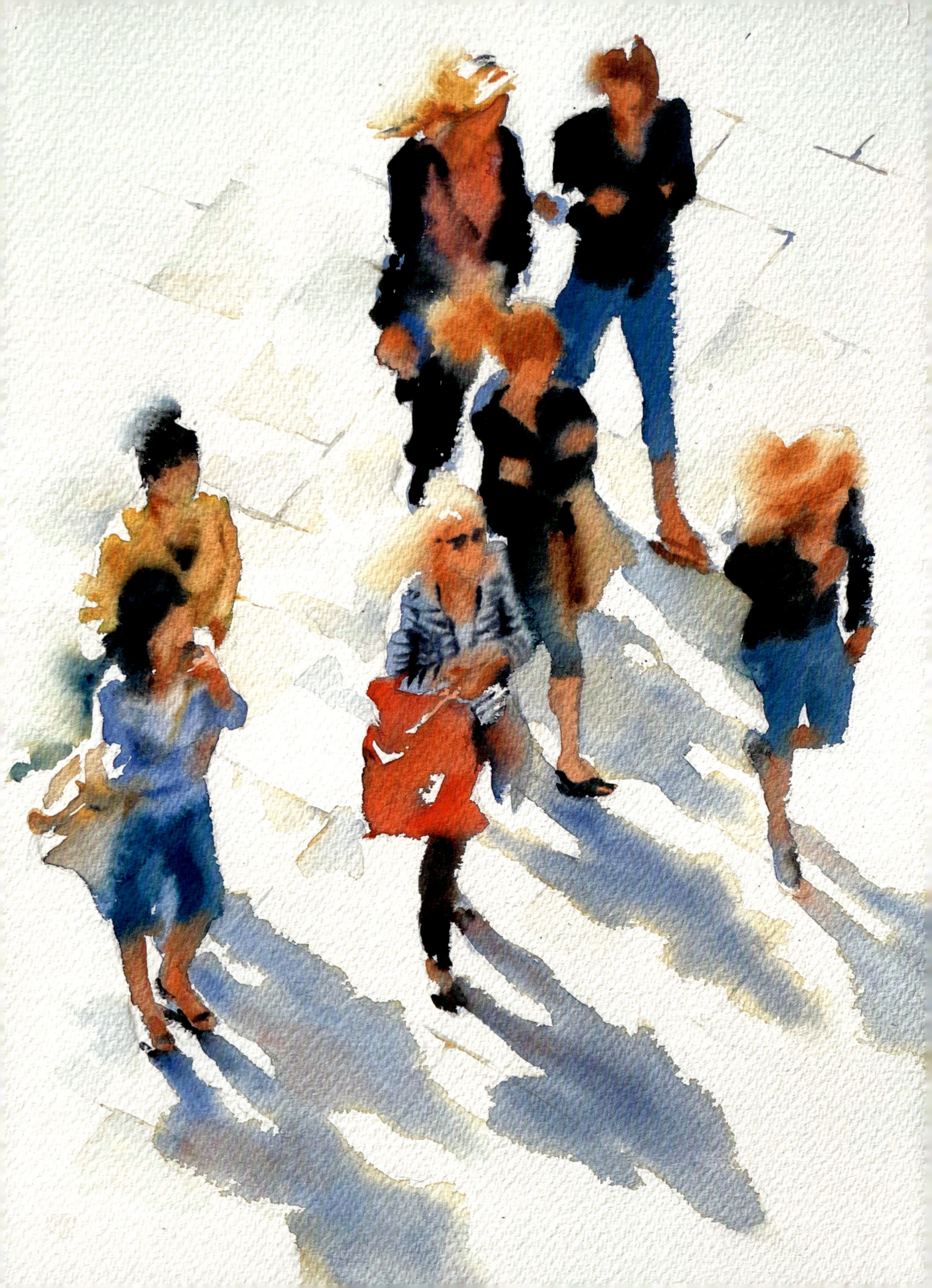

TAKING THE FEAR OUT OF
WATERCOLOUR

PAINT WITH COURAGE AND CONFIDENCE

Hazel Soan

BATSFORD

To my family, friends and followers.

Page 1 **Oncoming,** *23 x 38cm (9 x 15in)*

Page 2 **Girls' Day Out,** *56 x 38cm (22 x 15in)*

▶ **A Slice of Light, Santorini,** *28 x 15cm (11 x 6in)*

First published in the United Kingdom in 2026 by
Batsford
43 Great Ormond Street
London WC1N 3HZ

An imprint of B. T. Batsford Holdings Limited

Copyright © B. T. Batsford Ltd 2026
Text and images copyright © Hazel Soan 2026

All rights reserved. No part of this publication may be copied, displayed, extracted, reproduced, utilised, stored in a retrieval system or transmitted in any form or by any means, electronic, mechanical or otherwise, including but not limited to photocopying, recording or scanning, without the prior written permission of the publishers.

ISBN 978 1 84994 971 2

A CIP catalogue record for this book is available from the British Library.

10 9 8 7 6 5 4 3 2 1

Reproduction by Rival Colour Ltd, UK
Printed by Dream Colour, China

This book can be ordered direct from the publisher at www.batsfordbooks.com or try your local bookshop.

Distributed throughout the UK and Europe by Abrams & Chronicle Books, 1st Floor, 22-24 Ely Place, London EC1N 6TE and 57 rue Gaston Tessier, 75166 Paris, France

www.abramsandchronicle.co.uk
info@abramsandchronicle.co.uk

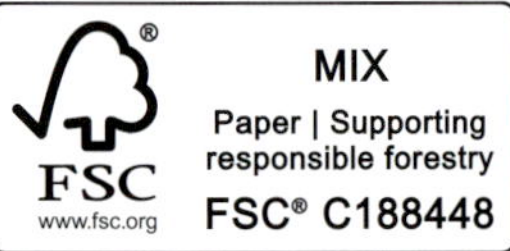

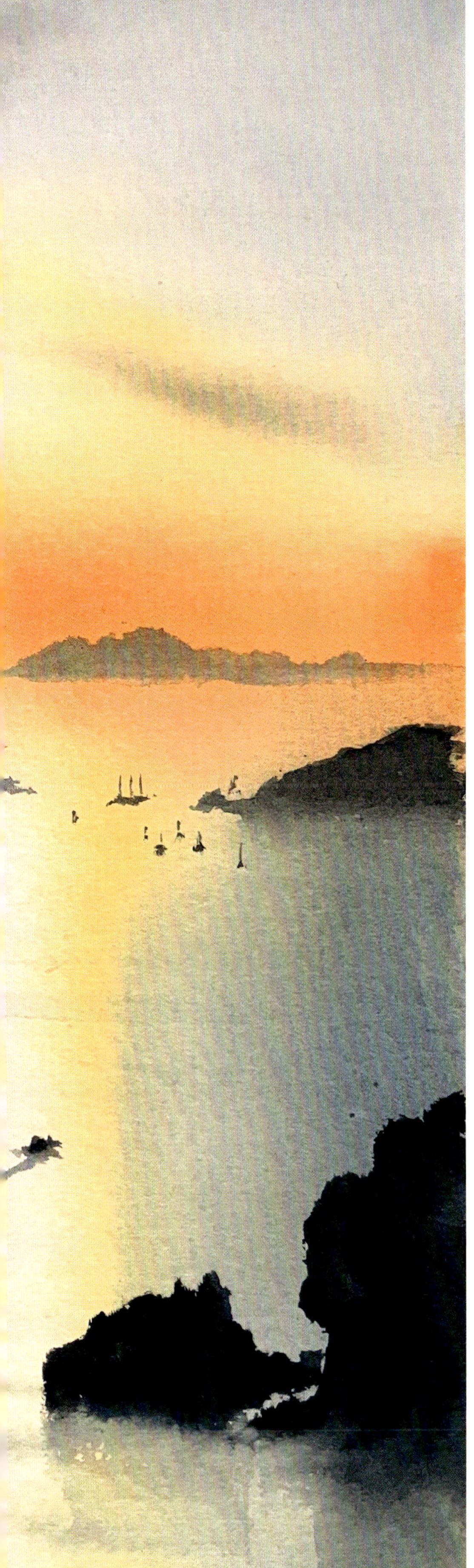

Contents

Introduction

To an outsider, it might sound bizarre that the seemingly gentle art of watercolour painting could engender fear and trepidation, but we who practise it know that it can!

This beautiful and beguiling medium, delightfully mobile with a translucent luminous character, comes with a unique set of challenges to accompany its heady appeal. When these challenges thwart the painting process, they become hard to overcome and generate degrees of anxiety. Even the gleaming white paper can cause trepidation before the first brushstroke, for fear the paper will be wasted.

Have you started a painting with high hopes, excited to paint, but are frustrated by the results or the finished article falling short of expectation? Something tends to go wrong, endorsing watercolour's reputation as an unforgiving medium. As confidence recedes, hesitancy steps in, leading to a vacuum of decision-making: Will I wreck this watercolour? Am I overworking it? Is it okay as is, or does it need more? Is this colour too strong, too dark? Those of you who have experienced this overthinking will know its paralyzing effect and agree I am not exaggerating. I know, because I've been there too!

Watercolour painting is a risky endeavour, but it's the best adrenaline rush I know and comes without risk of physical danger.

▶ **Explosion from the Bush,**
38 x 28cm (15 x 11in)

The beauty of the watercolour medium is that it is uniquely mobile and need not be confined even by the brushstroke, but its very mobility can also cause alarm.

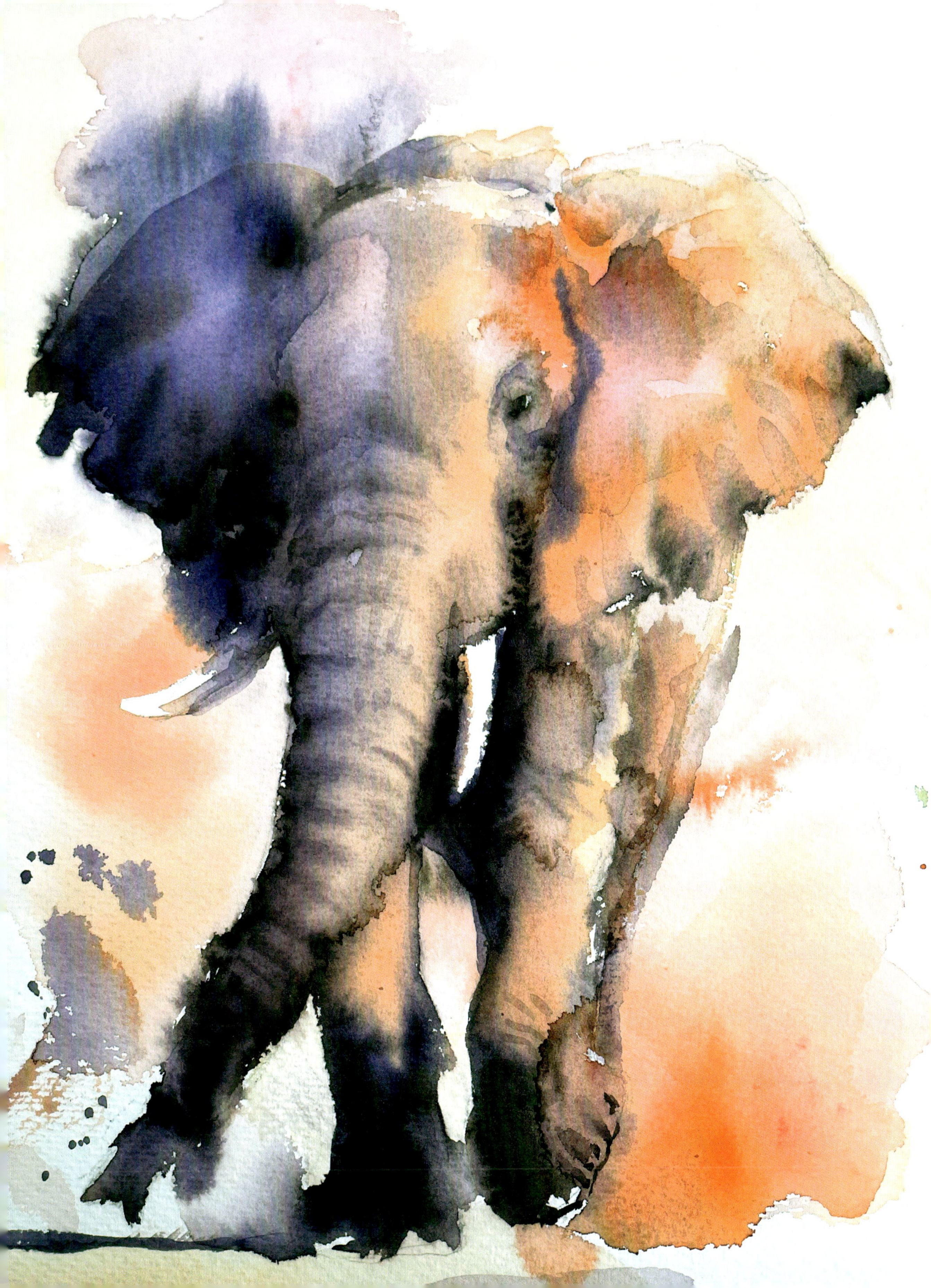

Up for the Challenge

I love that watercolour is a challenge, and have a healthy respect for this tantalizing medium – after all, if it were easy, it would not be considered an art.

But if fear holds us back from fulfilling our potential then we need to overcome it, so I have written this book to help you do just that. I aim to encourage you to approach watercolour by thinking more about keeping the medium itself happy as you paint, and to become one with the materials. We will face up to the common pitfalls, find means of recovery, or learn when it is better to abandon a piece and start again. I will show you that watercolour can be more forgiving than you might think.

▼ **Into the Wind,**
23 x 30.5cm (9 x 12in)
Watercolour is an attractive medium in and of itself. It is a medium of minimums in which single layers of transparent colour can convey whole narratives.

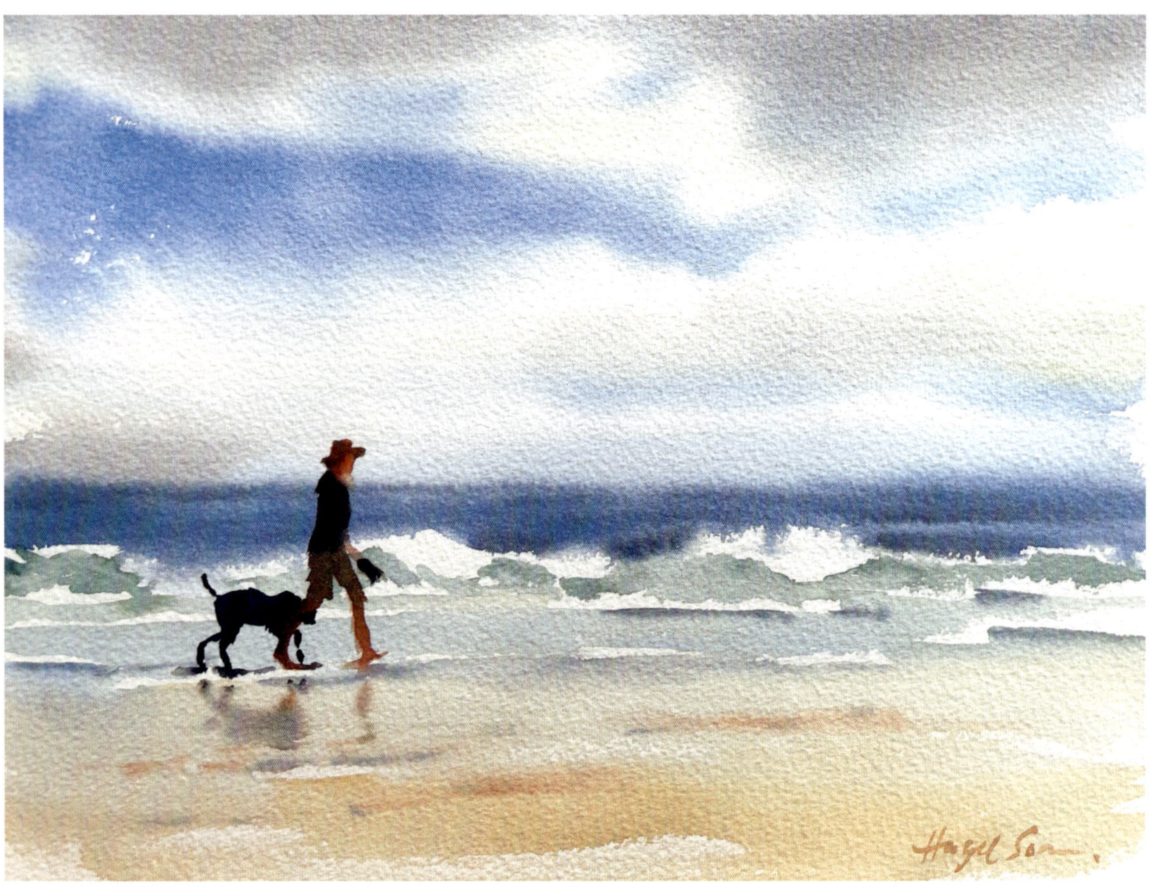

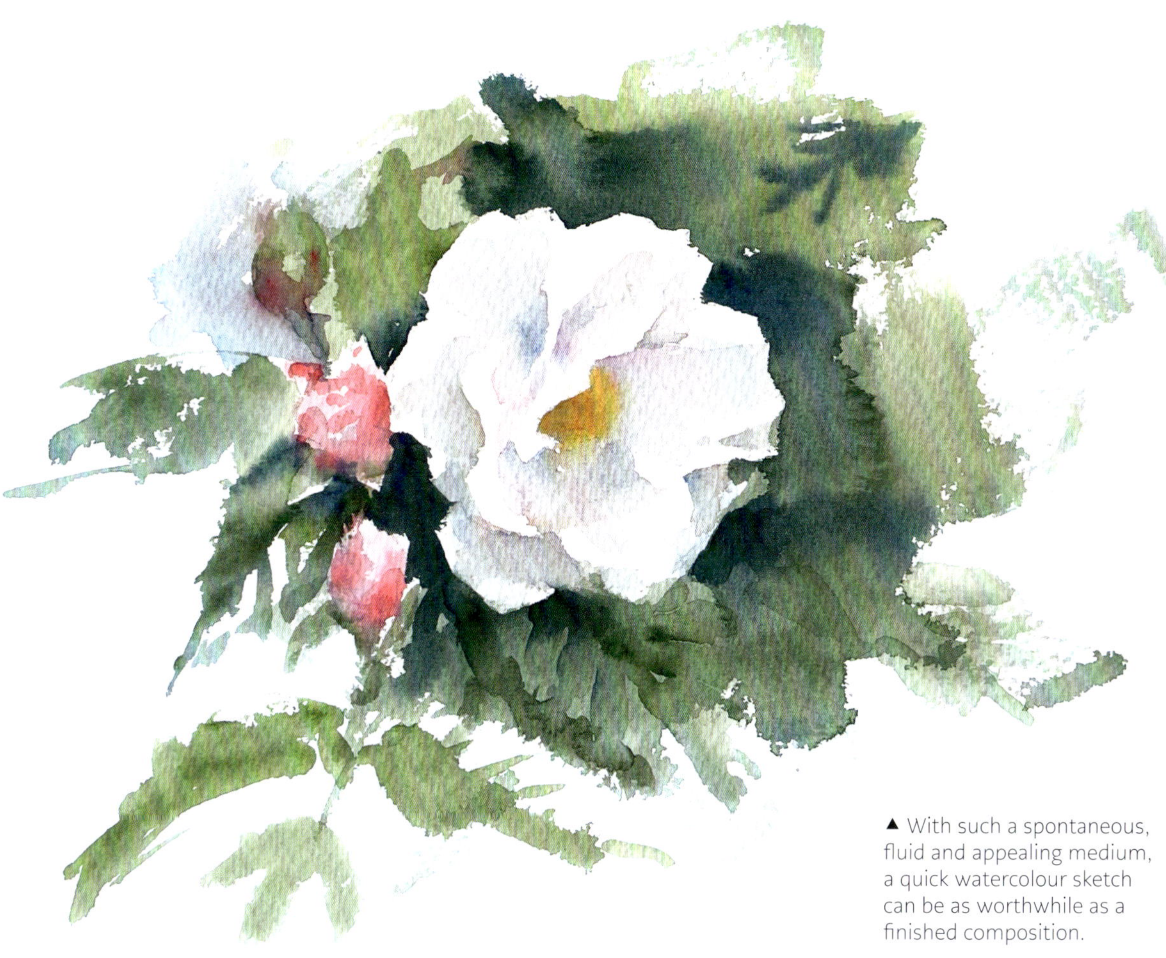

▲ With such a spontaneous, fluid and appealing medium, a quick watercolour sketch can be as worthwhile as a finished composition.

About this Book

The main aim of this book is to dispel the fear and calm the anxiety that hampers watercolour painting by giving you ways of recovery and knowledge about what to expect. While each chapter is dedicated to different challenges, there is inevitable crossover between the chapters, plus practice suggestions and troubleshooting advice. As you understand more about the medium and the materials, you will learn how watercolour behaves, and how to avoid the common pitfalls. Sometimes a solution will be found in letting go rather than taking control.

In a mobile medium, the unexpected can and will happen, so you need to learn how to read what's happening in the palette and on the paper, harness the uncertainty and gain confidence in this lovely medium's innate ability to deliver its own magic. My aim is to equip you to manage the risks so you can embrace the combination of order and randomness that make this dance of water and pigment an endless joy to pursue.

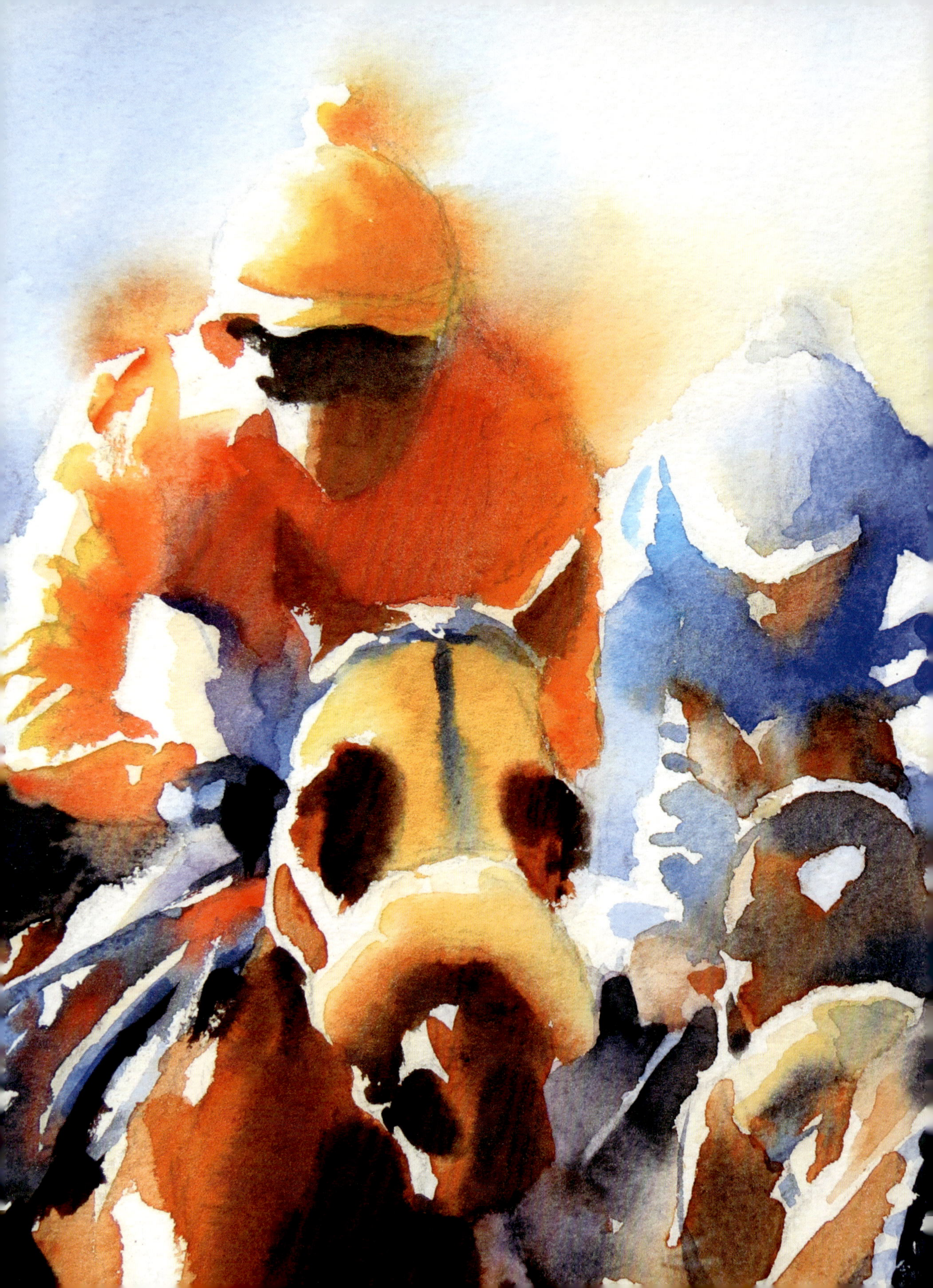

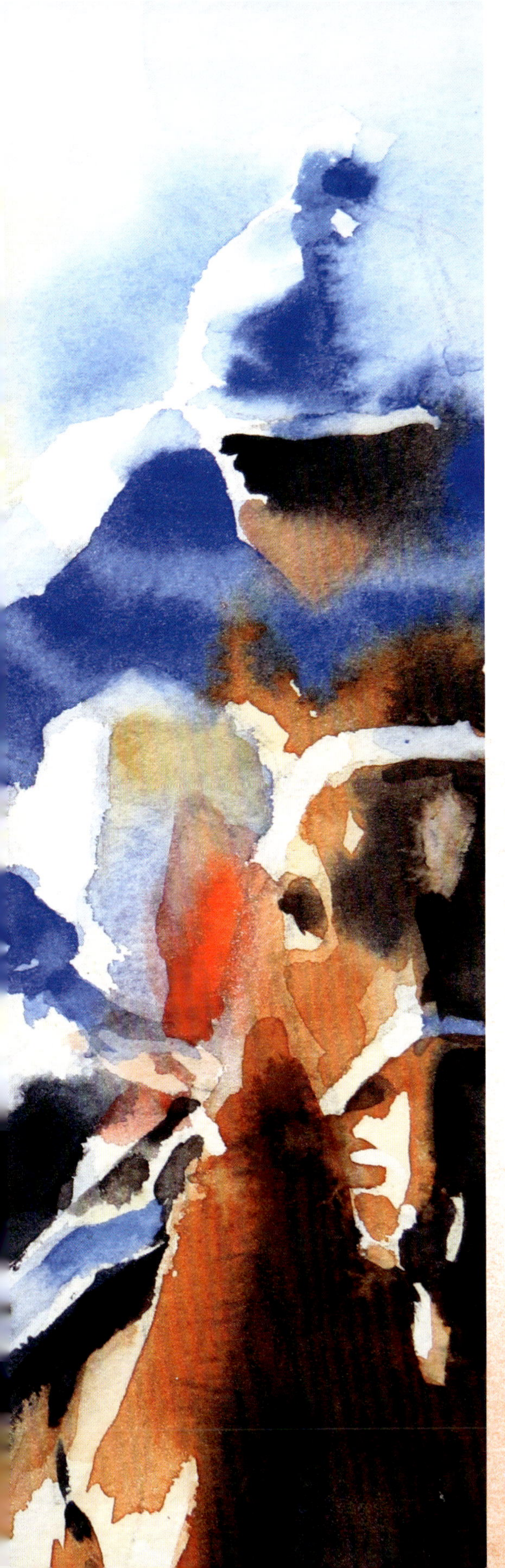

CHAPTER 1

Why is Watercolour Scary?

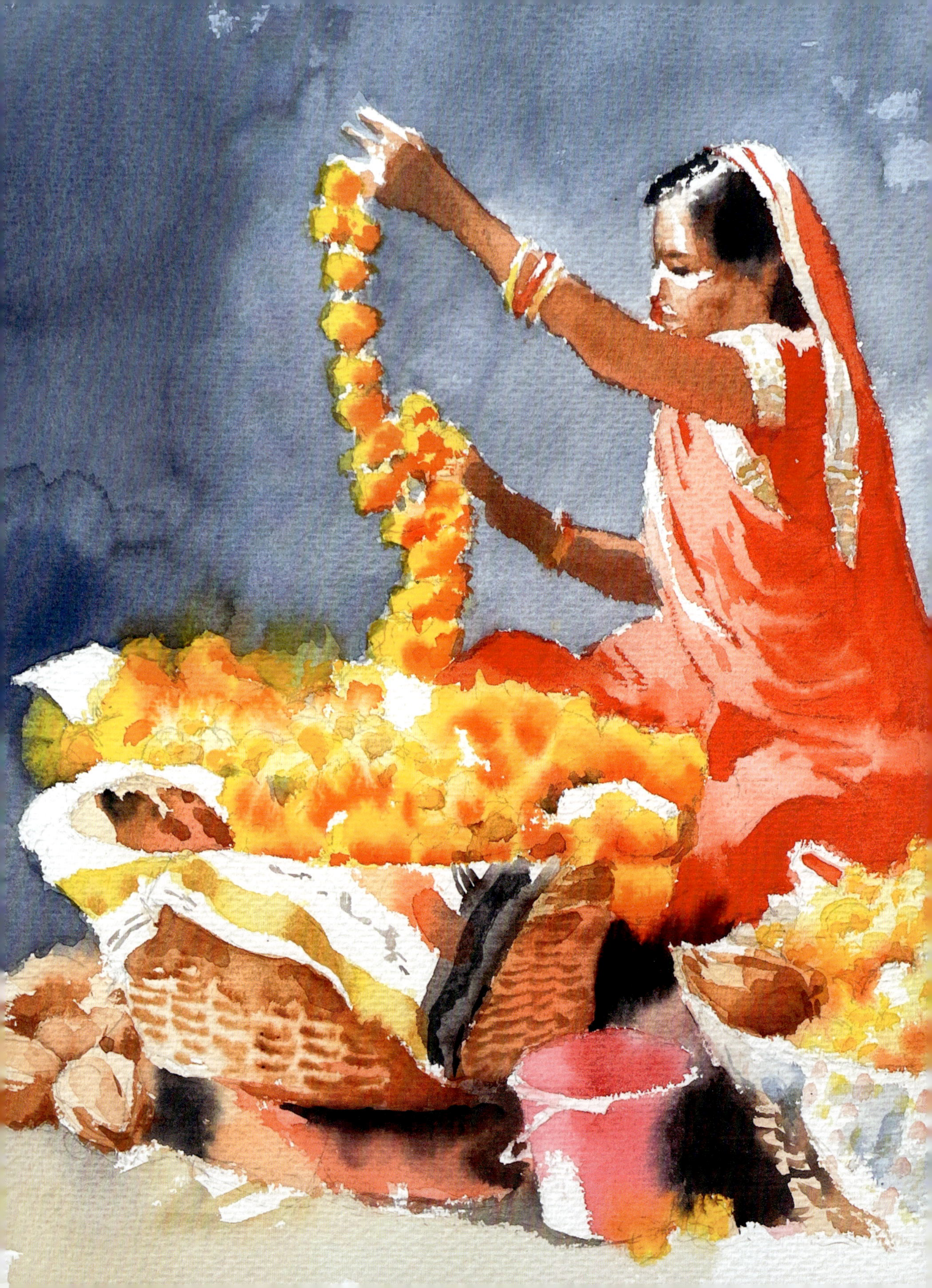

What Can Go Wrong?

Even though I have been painting with watercolour all my adult life, I still feel the adrenaline rising when I paint. I am often not sure what to do and I know how intimidating the next brushstroke can be; people who paint in watercolour understand that painting can indeed be scary!

There is a magical quality to watercolour painting that no other medium can emulate due to it being uniquely mobile. However, this very fluidity, and the uncertainty and unpredictability that accompanies it, is one of the reasons why watercolour is considered a more difficult painting medium than, say, oils or acrylics.

Another reason to fear watercolour is that the white paper represents the light; as such, the light cannot be painted with white paint as it can in oils and acrylic. Instead, it has to be left out as untouched white paper. When painting, **not** painting something (i.e. leaving negative space) is much harder than painting something. Watercolourists can tint the light but mainly paint the shade and, while doing so, are always at risk of losing the light. Therefore, most of the problems discussed on the following pages relate to managing watercolour's liquidity or the loss of light.

To remove the fear and fix the frustration that plagues this exciting pursuit, let's first recognize the challenges this unique medium presents. This chapter presents an overview of the issues that affect every watercolourist, whether beginner, intermediate, amateur or professional. At first sight, the list might make watercolour appear even more daunting, but please carry on to the end if you want to learn to paint watercolour without fear!

◀ **Primary Colour,**
38 x 28cm (15 x 11in)

So long as a watercolour maintains its freshness and is not overworked, uneven washes, background blemishes and unintended backruns need not spoil a composition, and indeed often enhance the character of the painting.

Losing the Light

Being a transparent medium, watercolour relies on the light of the white paper for its translucency. Since representational painting involves painting an impression of the light and shade onto a flat surface in such a way as to persuade the viewer that three dimensions are represented, watercolours are traditionally painted from light to dark. This is a sensible method to retain the light for as long as possible, but it is all too easy to lose the light.

It is the light inherent in watercolour paintings that makes them so special and makes a painting appear vibrant and lively. If the light is lost, a painting becomes dull and lifeless, and the lost light may be difficult or even impossible to retrieve. Maintaining the light in a watercolour and preserving the white space can therefore be a challenge, and its loss is the cause of many common problems.

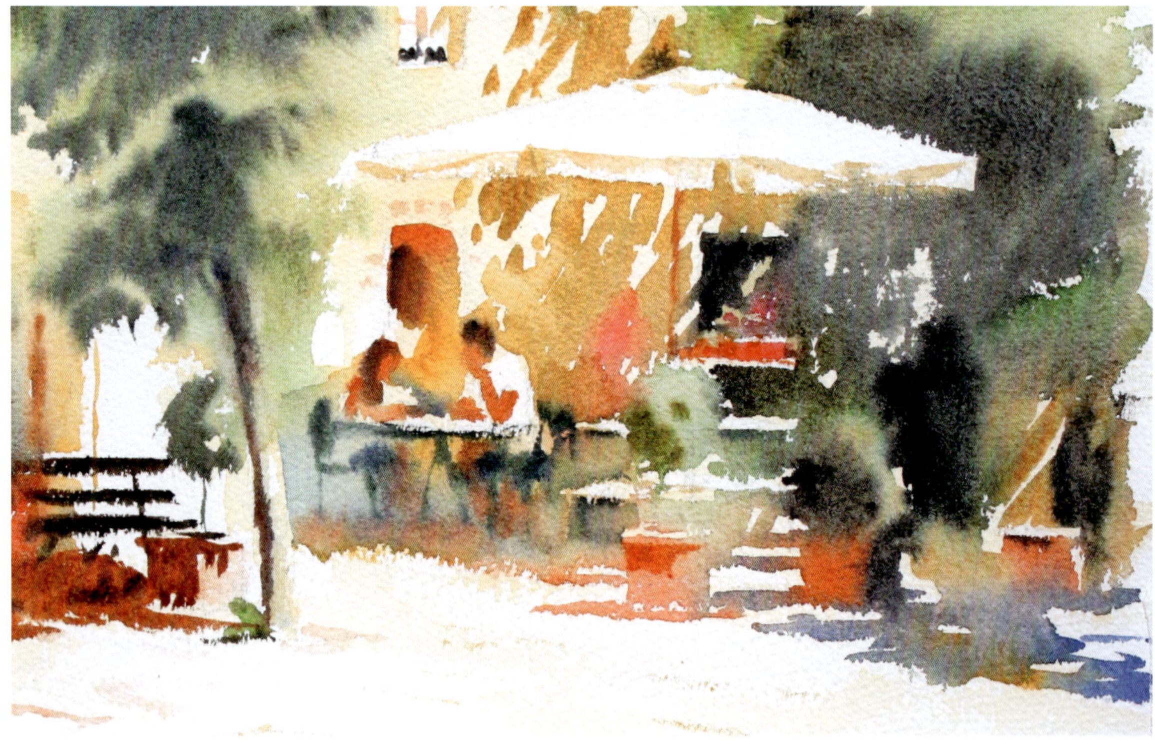

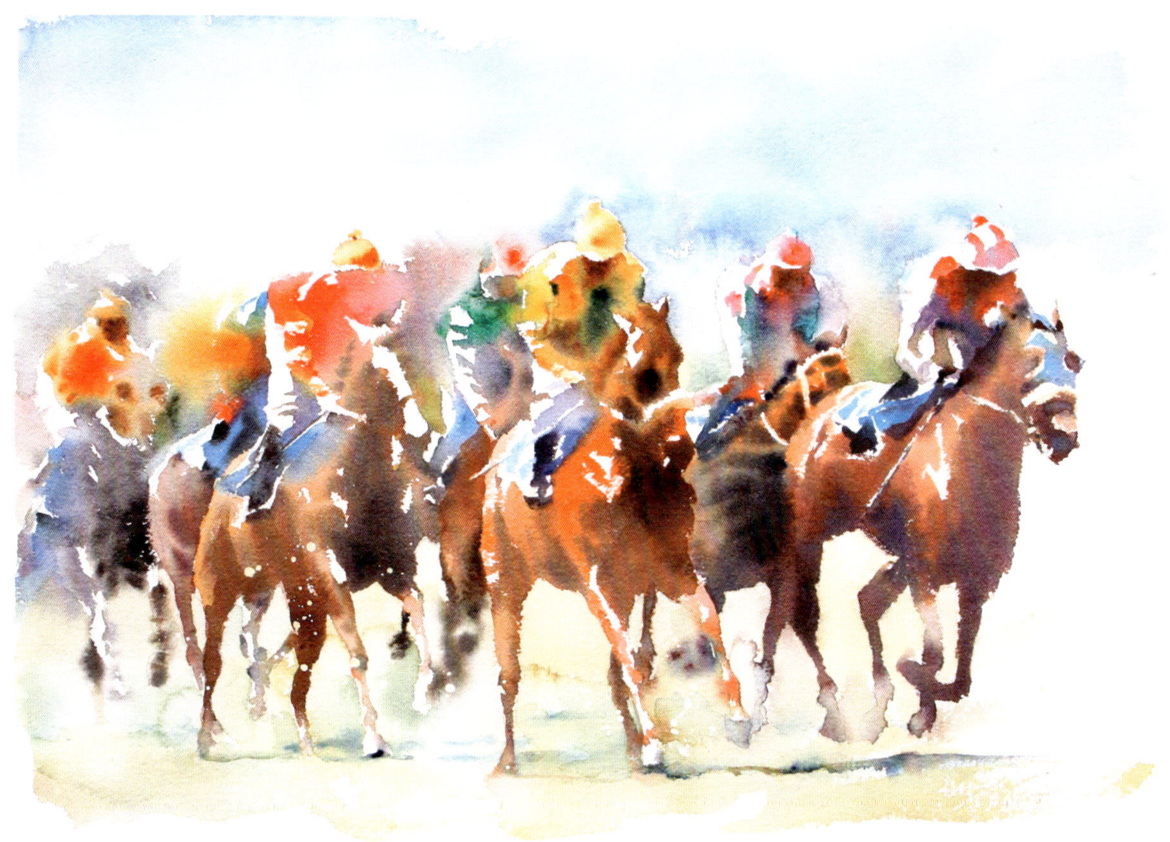

Controlling the Water

▲ **The Race is On,**
35.5 x 51cm (14 x 20in)
Being a fluid medium, watercolour can readily suggest movement. To create blur and lose definition to suggest speed, the pigment is encouraged to bleed and spread by adroit control of the water.

◀ The gleam of the white paper highlights left untouched between washes to represent the light are one of the heady appeals of the watercolour medium.

Watercolour paint is mixed with water. Too much water causes pooling, unpredictable blooms or warping of paper, whereas too little water results in streaky or uneven washes. Weak, washed-out colouring and inadvertent 'cauliflowers' – the backruns that form when wet paint flows backward into already dry paint, stalls and forms a frilly pattern resembling a cauliflower floret – are the chagrin of many a watercolourist, while smeared and striped passages of colour deny watercolour its luminescent charm.

Achieving the right ratio of water to pigment in any given mix is essential for laying the smooth washes, precision brushmarks and wet-in-wet blends for which watercolour is celebrated. This inevitably improves with practice, but achieving the right balance between the water and the pigment is an ongoing challenge and the cause of many missteps and much angst in watercolour painting.

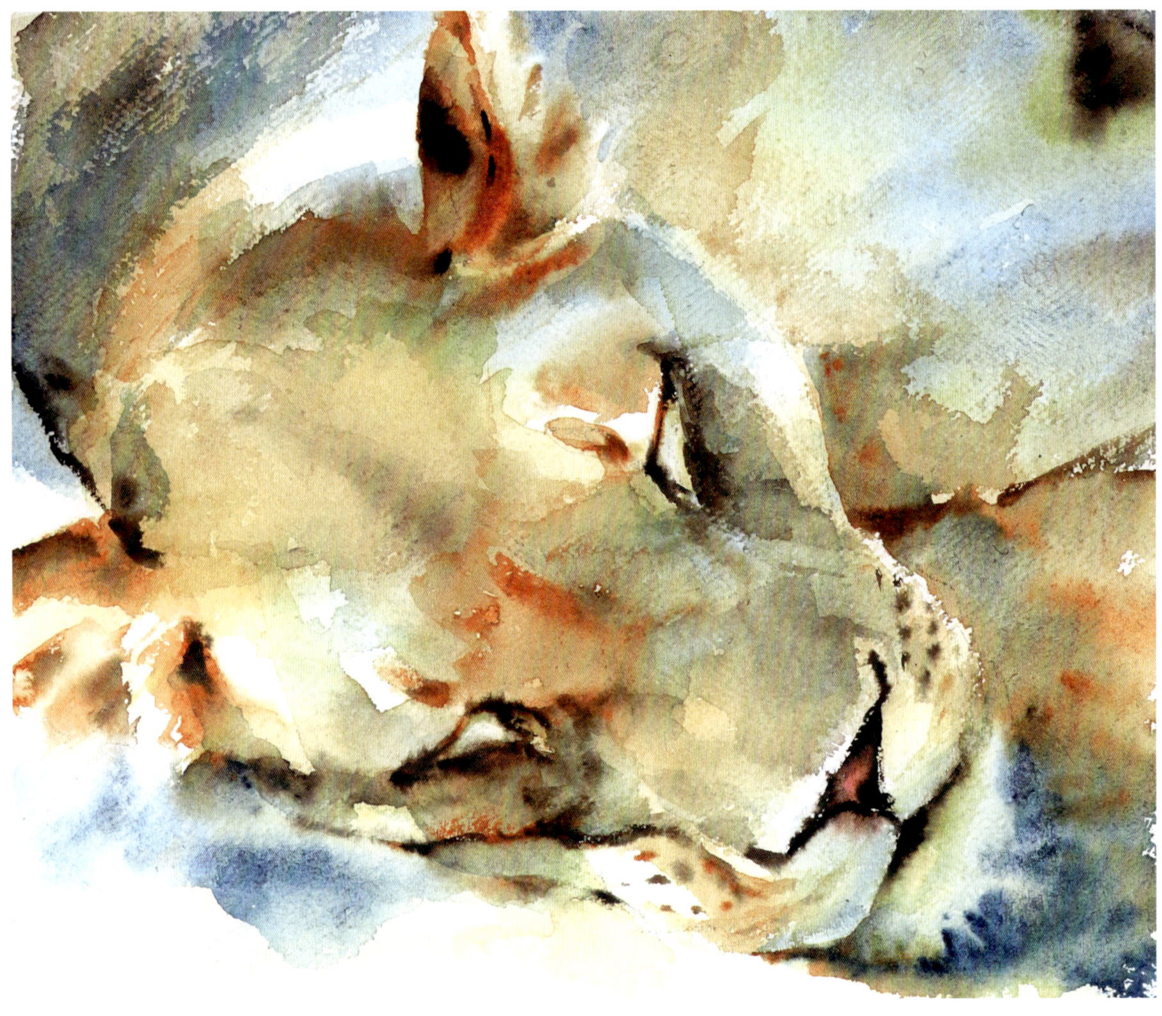

Timing and Drying

The unpredictability of drying time is one of watercolour's constant challenges and affects the outcome of most watercolours and every individual passage of colour. When areas are not fully dry, colours accidentally run into each other or washes dry too fast, causing unintended seams. If wet paint is added over a supposedly dry wash that isn't actually dry, the new colour awkwardly blooms outward, ruining the appearance of the previous wash or unintentionally diluting rather than darkening the shade.

Environmental factors may be beyond our control – we cannot alter humidity or temperature – but we can turn them into our accomplices and learn how to monitor and manage the drying process.

◄ **Sleeping on Sand,**
28 x 33cm (11 x 13in)

Timing is everything when adding detail wet into wet around the eyes, nose and mouth. If the under-wash is too wet, the dense pigment will spread uncontrollably; if it is too dry, the line will be static and hard-edged.

Paper Behaving Badly

The exquisite materials of watercolour – the paint, brushes and paper – are part of the pleasure involved with painting in this remarkable medium. Watercolour paper, with its creamy white tint and range of textures, is a particularly lovely surface to work on, but can also come with its own set of challenges. Wet paper can buckle uncontrollably; warping or even tearing can occur; and overworking the brushwork and colours affects the cherished surface. Preventing problems with paper is one of the most straightforward issues to solve.

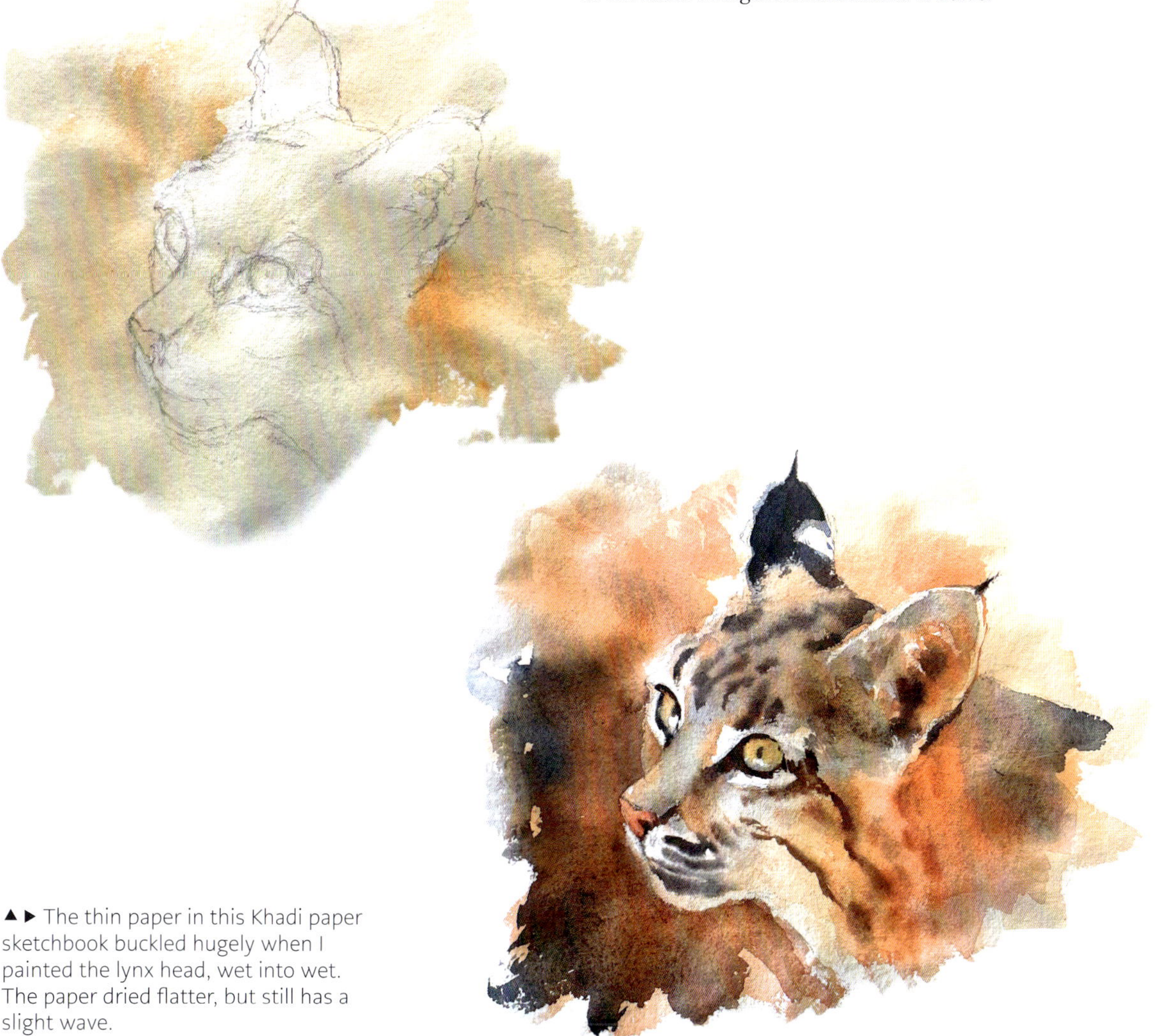

▲► The thin paper in this Khadi paper sketchbook buckled hugely when I painted the lynx head, wet into wet. The paper dried flatter, but still has a slight wave.

Making Mud

Muddy colouring is undoubtedly one of the most common issues to beset watercolour painters. Colour mixing is a challenge common to all painting media, but in the transparent medium of watercolour, the properties of each individual pigment have a greater impact upon the end result than in opaque media such as oils or acrylics. Selecting which colours to use is often accompanied by dilemma and frustration. Managing colour mixing and maintaining the luminosity of the medium through blending and layering becomes easier once you understand more about the properties of the pigments: you will be better prepared to predict their behaviour on the paper and avert the incidence of muddy colouring.

▼ **Jack's Camp,** *18 x 28cm (7 x 11in)*

By mixing the black from the Quinacridone Red, Indian Yellow and Prussian Blue already used in the sky, the silhouettes remain a vibrant colour black, in harmony with the rest of the painting.

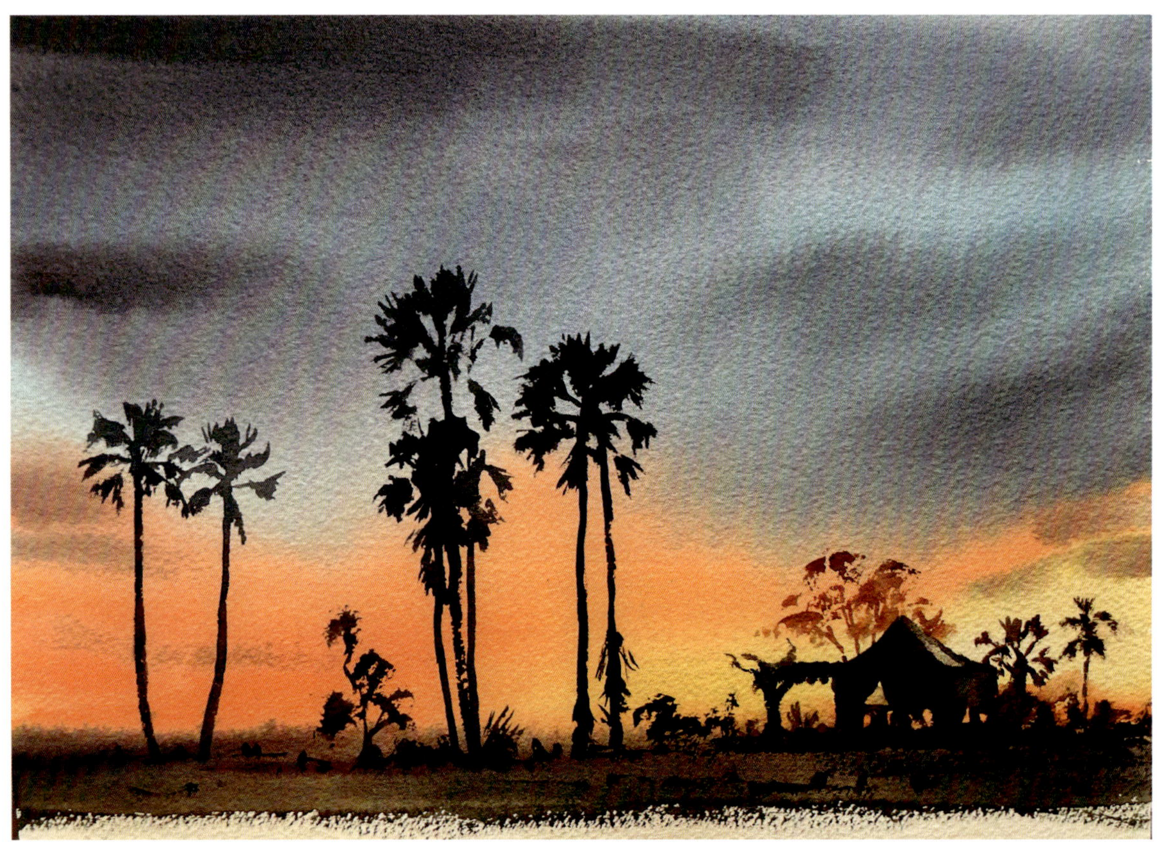

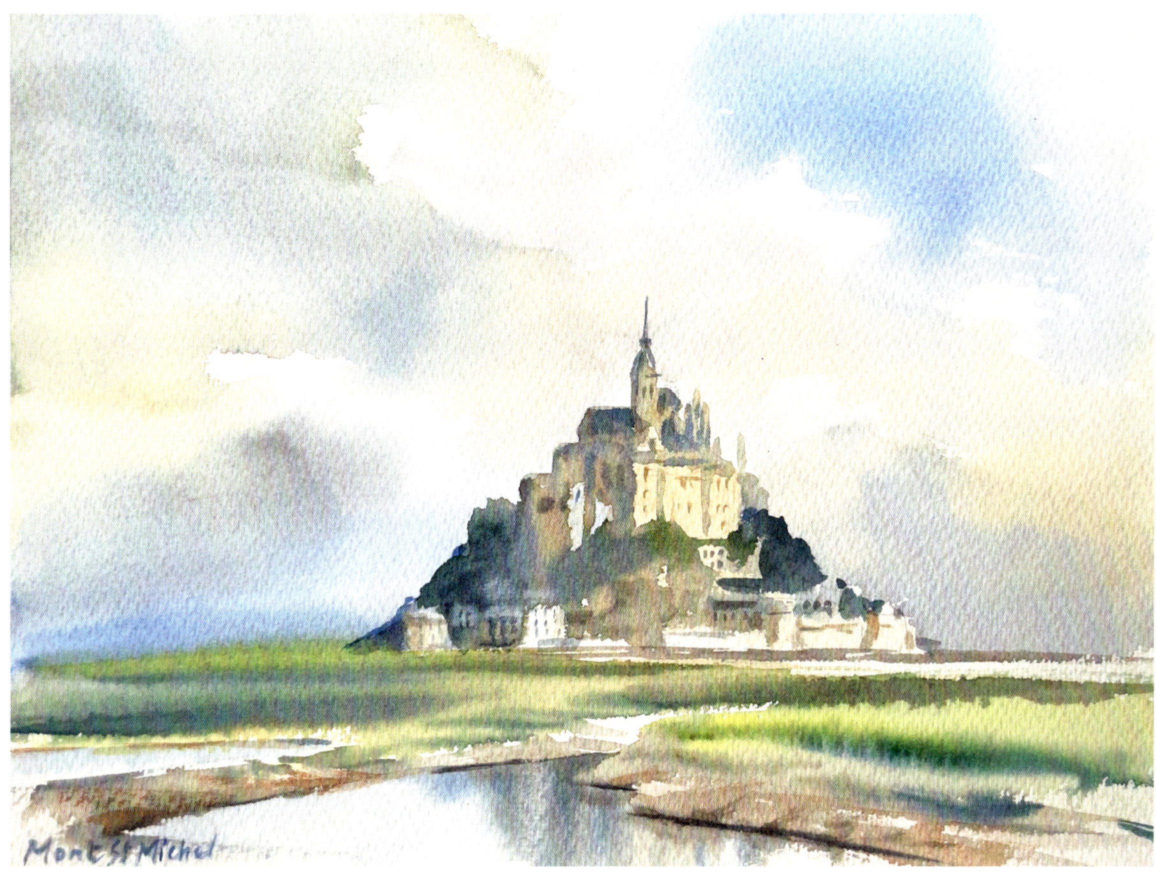

Overworking

Maintaining spontaneity and avoiding lifeless or overworked watercolours is a constant challenge in a medium where freshness is key. Watercolour can be a fast-happening method: sometimes areas of a painting come together unexpectedly quickly, and the temptation to continue painting can be hard to avoid. Too much layering is often the cause of a dull or muddy watercolour. Even when watercolourists know this, the temptation to overwork is the bane of the medium.

When is a watercolour finished? What is unnecessary detail? The tendency to overwork a watercolour is an issue all artists contend with, and watercolour painting is so enjoyable, why would one even want to stop?

▲ **Mont-Saint-Michel,**
28 x 39cm (11 x 15in)
It was tempting to add more detail when in front of such an interesting subject, but once the essence of Mont-Saint-Michel and the foreground marshes appeared complete upon the paper, I guessed it was time to stop.

Unwanted Edges

In a transparent medium, the edges of brushmarks and brushstrokes laid on the paper remain visible and count towards the end result. Hard edges form when the paint dries unexpectedly early, and soft edges are lost when wetted areas evaporate faster than planned. Many background washes have been marred by unintended seams when the wash dried quicker than expected. Mastering lost and found edges for both definition and flow is one of the most appealing aspects of watercolour painting. It can also be a real challenge. Controlling the edges of passages of colour is a skill that can be mastered, and sometimes corrected, if you know the properties of the pigments involved.

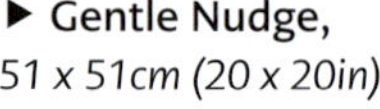

▶ **Gentle Nudge,**
51 x 51cm (20 x 20in)

By contrasting the softness and definition of edges, a lively movement is created between the elephants. Lit edges are largely defined, but in the shadows and in the mud, passages of colour are lost in ambiguity.

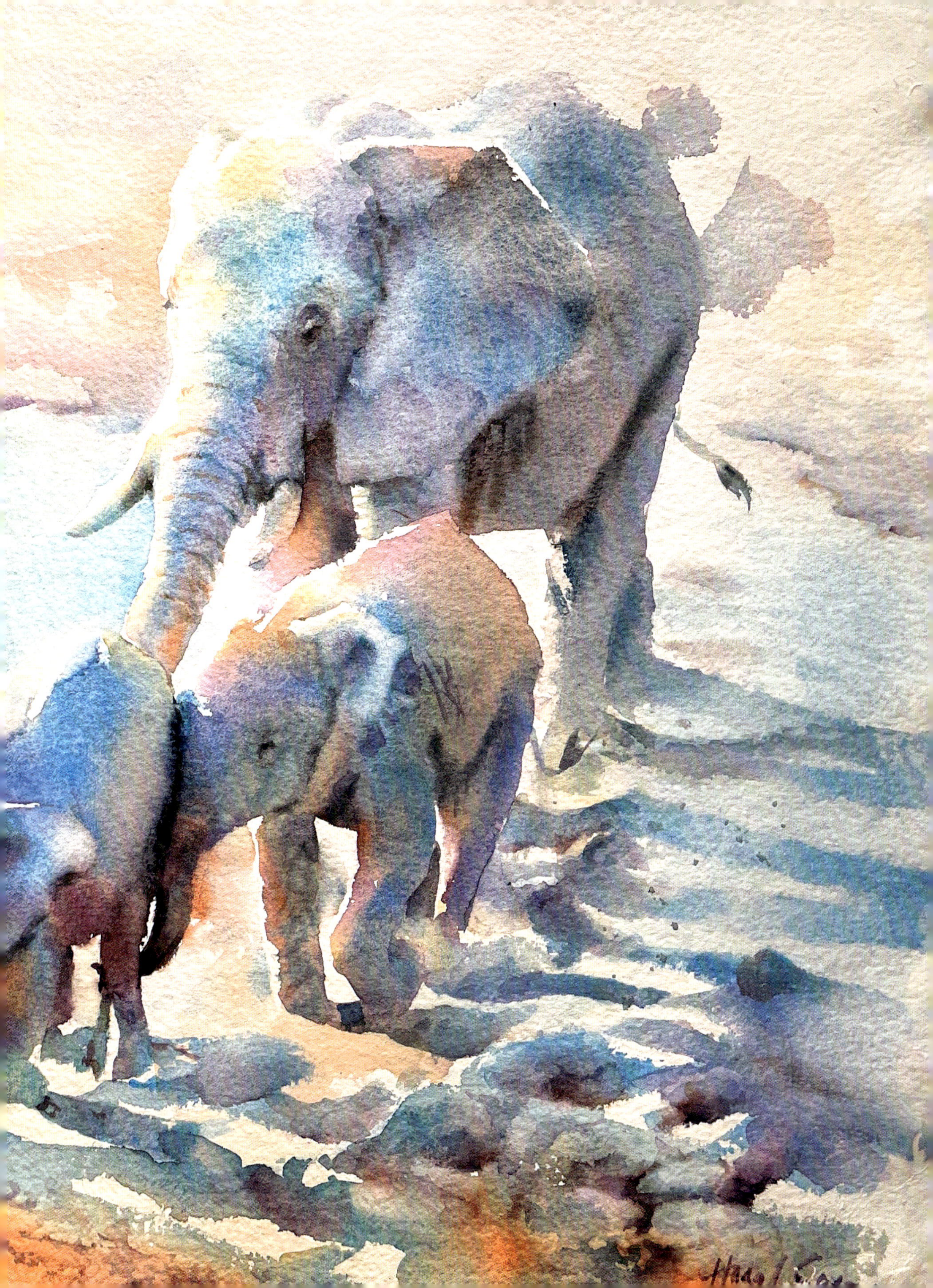

Fear of the Dark

Hesitancy in laying the darks has been the cause of many a dull or overworked watercolour painting. Inexperienced watercolour painters usually take the (supposedly) safer route of building up to dark colours gradually, or err on wishy washy colouring, but a bolder initial approach can often yield better results.

▼ **Baby Gorilla, Rwanda,** *20 x 20cm (8 x 8in)*

Speed was of the essence here: by going straight in with dark concentrated Indigo, the eyes were painted first, and the colour gradually diluted around them for the lighter tones on the face and hair, speeding up the process of representation.

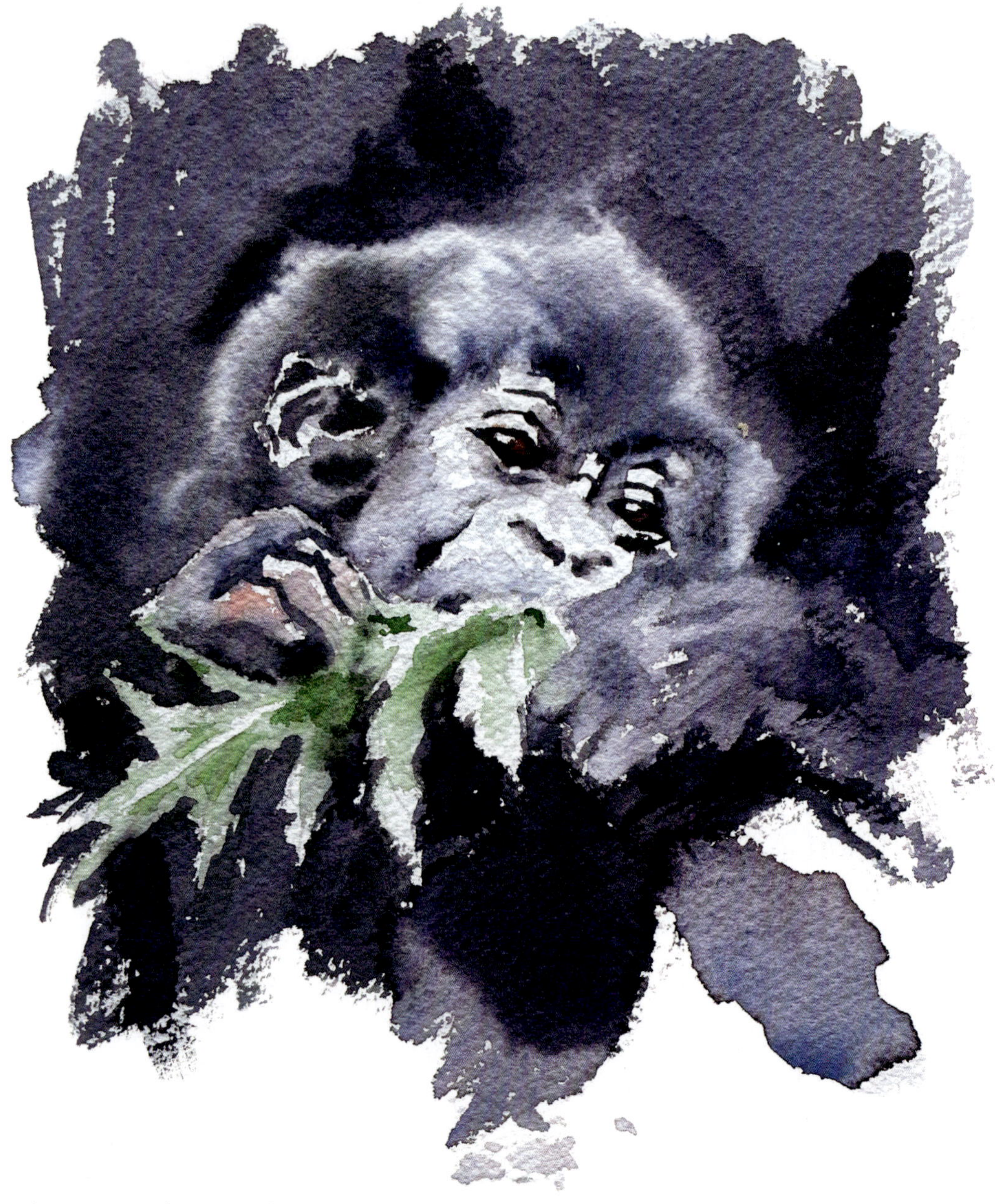

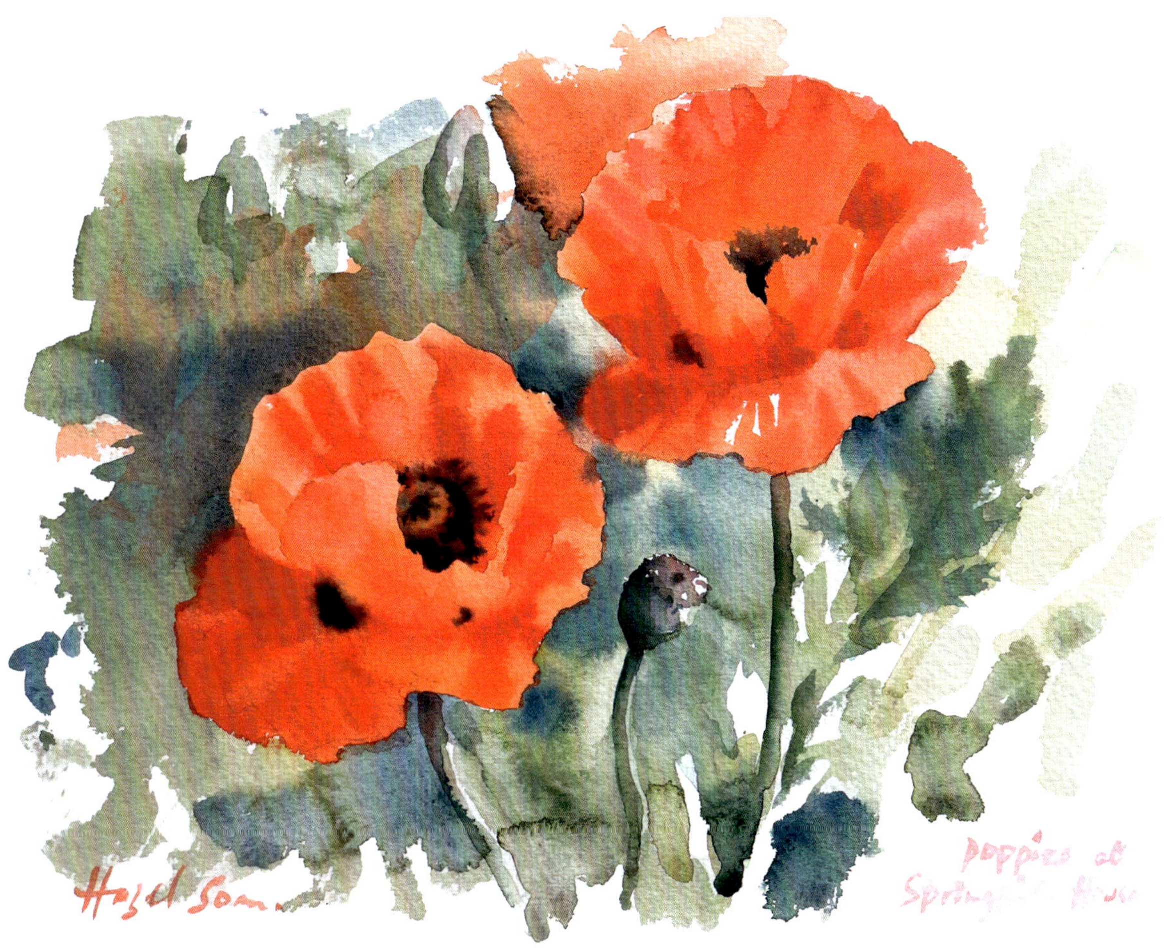

▲ **Springfield Poppies,**
28 x 38cm (11 x 15in)
Knowing I could lift out the Cadmium Red to some degree if the colour looked too bright enabled me to be bold in the first layers, ensuring maximum transparency with this fully opaque red.

Distract and Conquer

Watercolour may be known as an unforgiving medium, but there are actually many ways to fix or even disguise 'mistakes'. Solutions are often down to simply understanding the nature of the pigments. Knowing whether there is a good chance to remedy the issue or a limited ability to correct it, puts you back in control. If an error cannot be fixed, distraction may be the answer. Knowing there are ways to repair or revive a watercolour goes a long way towards conquering the fear, paralysis and even regret that can accompany the finishing stages of a watercolour.

Practice, Practice, Practice

Familiarity Breeds Confidence

Being an agile and lightweight medium, watercolour is used by painters to respond with immediacy to new subjects and circumstances. Each time we paint, a product (the painting) is created. This is one of the beneficial aspects of the medium, but it can sometimes make watercolour painters unwittingly presumptuous when it comes to results. Instead of thinking of each painting as research, practice and exploration, we expect a finished result. We start a new painting full of hope and excitement and end up disappointed when it does not work out as well as we had originally hoped.

But why should it work out? If the subject is unfamiliar, why should we think we can make a satisfying representation at first try? All other artistic disciplines require practice: an actor rehearses before a play; a musician plays a piece multiple times before performing it in front of an audience; writers edit their manuscripts through countless iterations; and in sport, a golfer, for example, practises their swing before hitting their ball; so why does a watercolourist expect to make a successful painting at first attempt?

Colours:

Ultramarine Finest/Blue

Transparent/Burnt Sienna

Sap Green

Schmincke Violet

Yellow Raw Ochre

Brushes:

Size 8 round brush

Size 10 round brush

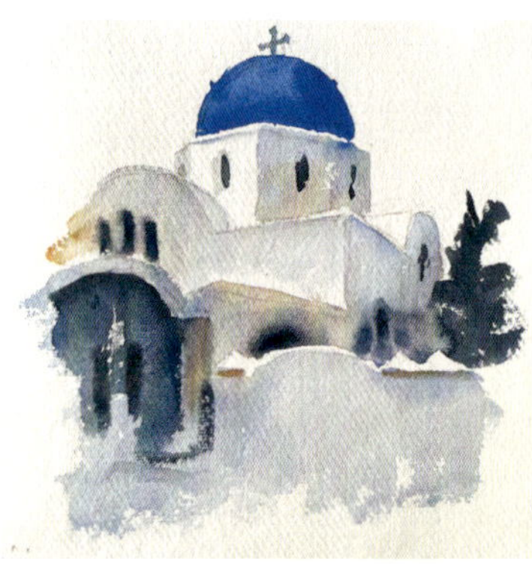

▲ I had always wanted to paint the blue and white churches on Santorini. My first attempt at painting the blue dome of this church was from a low angle. It was painted in my Khadi paper sketchbook.

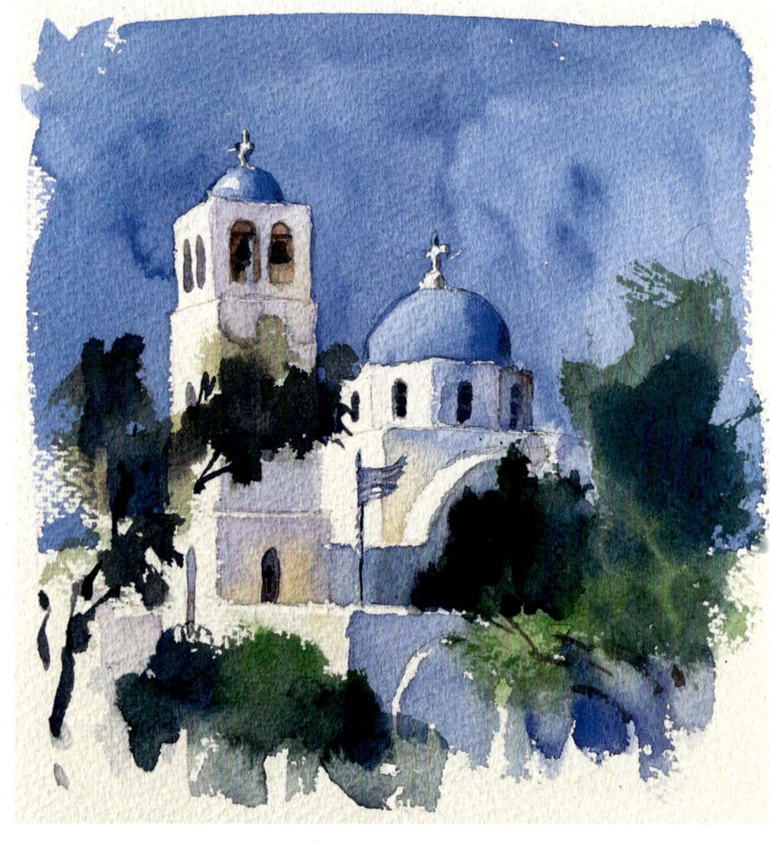

▶ The second version was painted in late afternoon, from a better angle, giving me a view of the dome on top of the tower and the contrast of foliage against the white walls in light and shadow. I enjoyed the composition very much and went back the next morning to paint from the same spot.

Lower your expectations

Inspiration is not the same as execution. Being excited by a subject does not necessarily translate directly into a successful painting straight off the bat (although sometimes fortuitously it does!).

All my paintings, unless they are commissions, are explorative: I am discovering through observation with my brush what is going on, working out light and shade, the main shapes and a suitable set of colours. I often paint the same subject over and over, but as the light changes it is always new. I try to distil the visual information and find the essentials. Sometimes my first effort is successful, but I never assume that it will be, and I never expect to paint the 'perfect' painting at first attempt. In fact, I see every painting as an experiment and as research towards future painting and paintings.

Because the effects of light change quickly and the pattern created is often the inspiration for the painting, there is by default a sense of urgency and priority to the first attempt, but painting the same subject several times is the way to learn to paint. Getting it wrong is not failure: it is normal painting practice!

> Before it becomes a noun, every painting is a verb. The important thing is to enjoy the process: the painting itself is a happy (or unhappy) by-product. In this way, no time or paper is ever wasted.

▲ Morning light comes from the opposite side, offering a new pattern of light and shade. I used the same colours: Ultramarine Blue, Transparent Sienna and Sap Green.

▶ In this third watercolour version, also painted in morning light, I introduced some Schmincke Violet to the original three colours. I just loved painting this church.

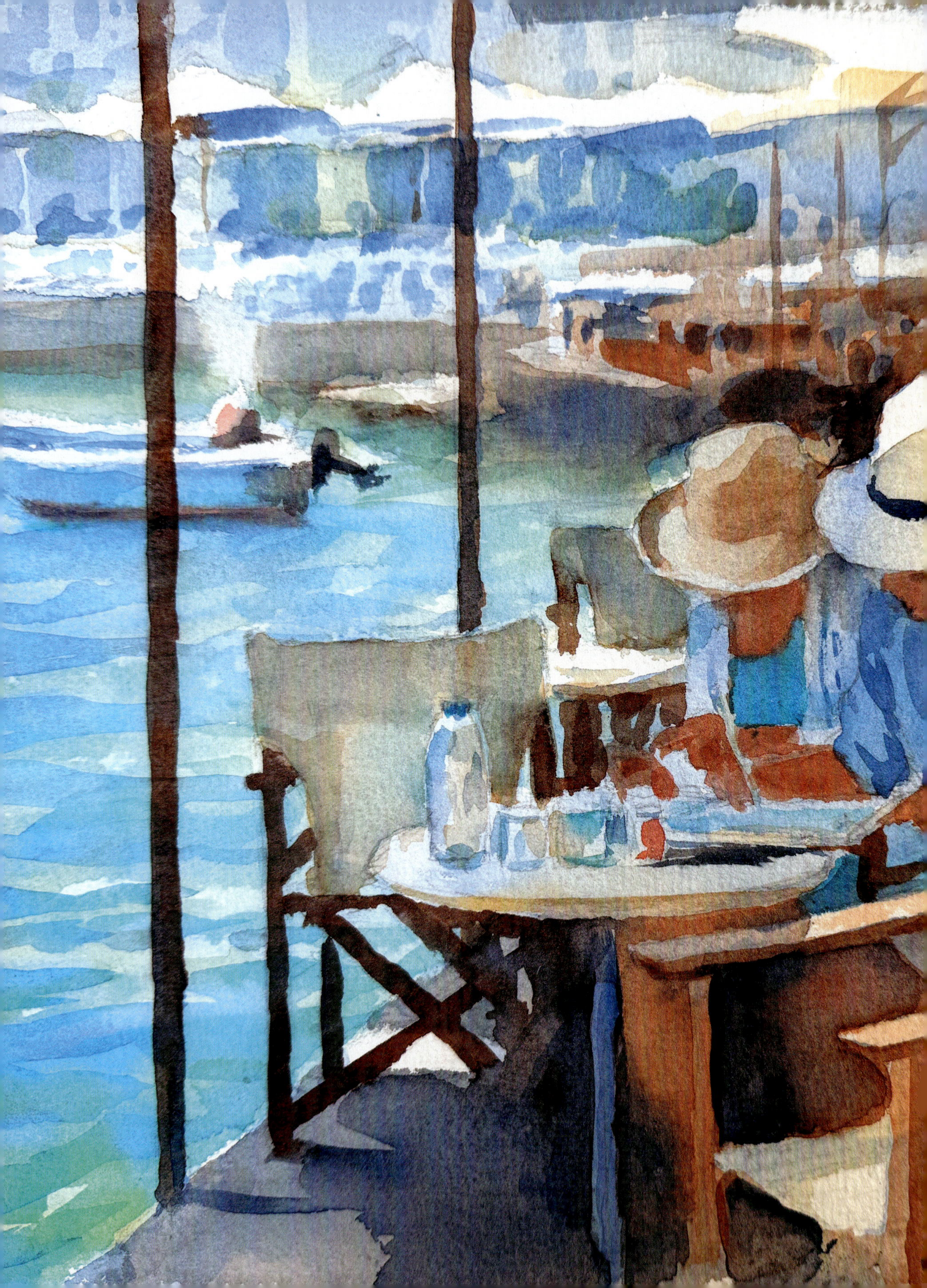

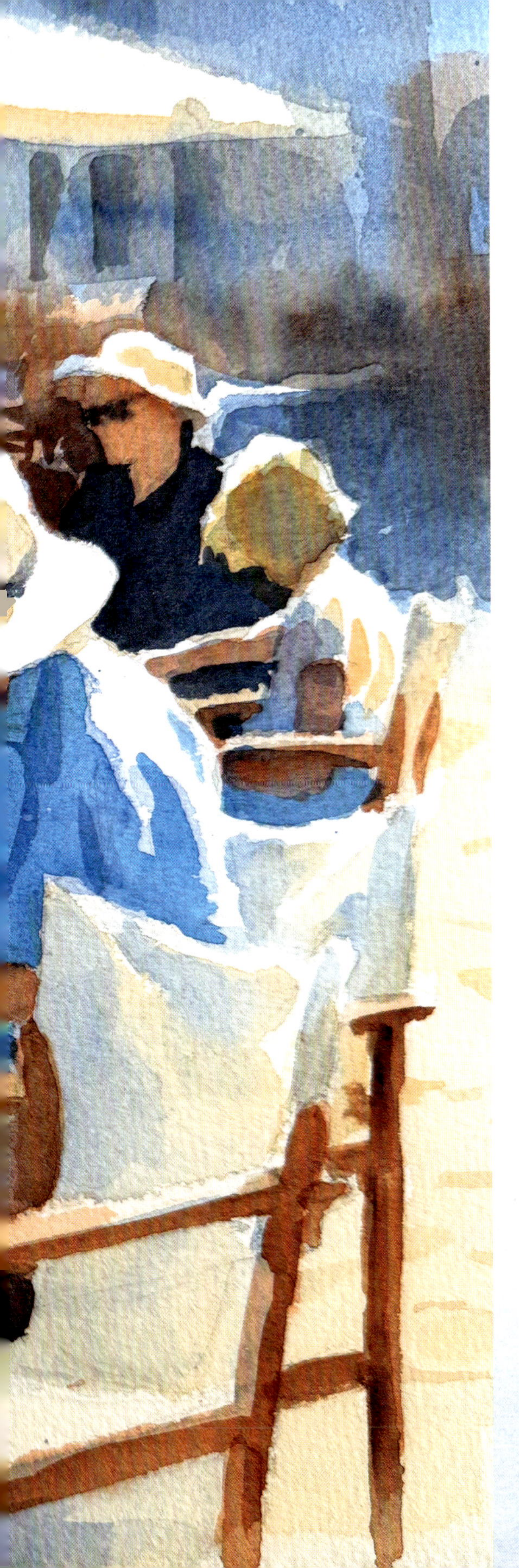

CHAPTER 2

Watercolour: The Transparent Medium

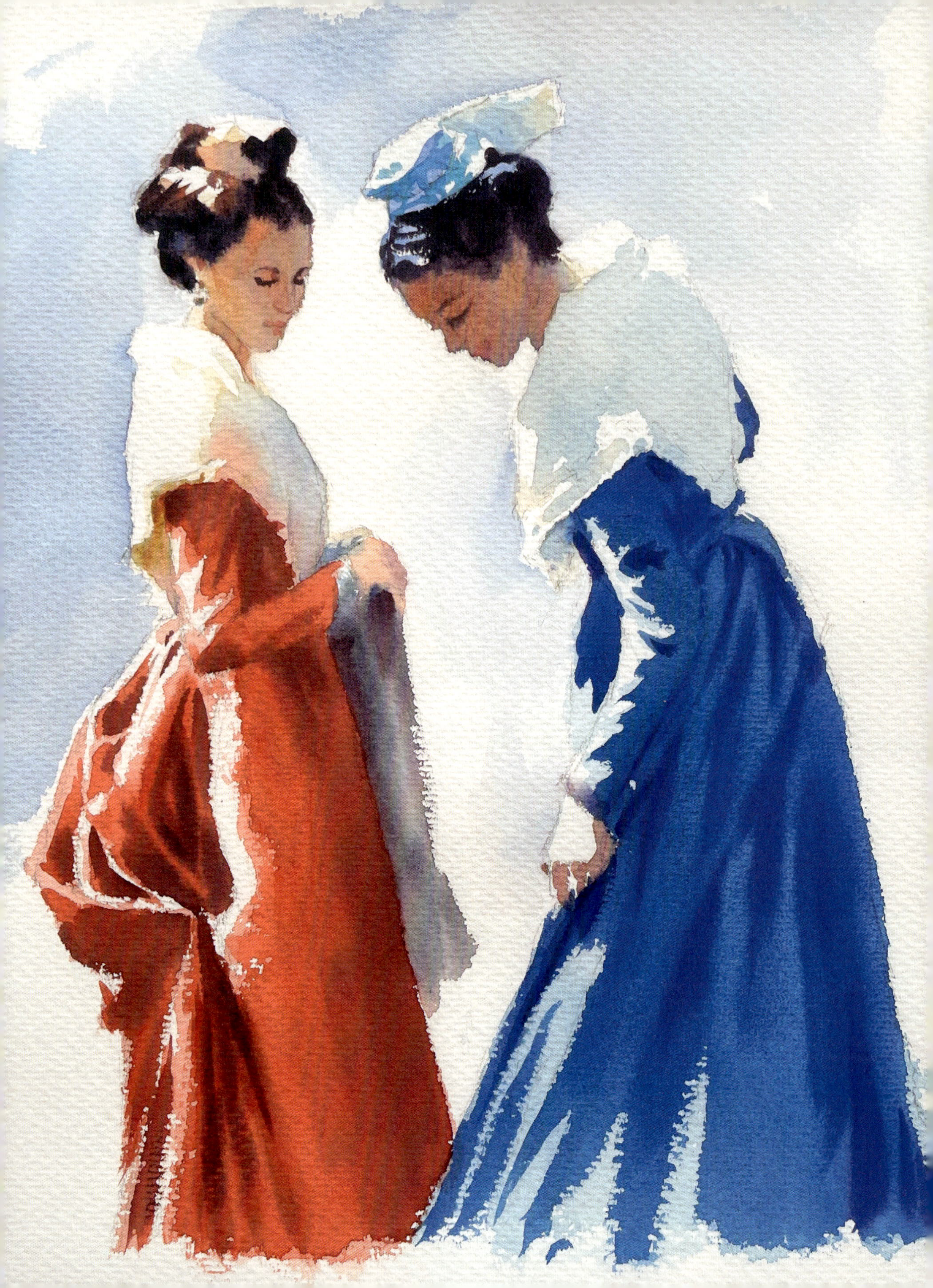

Knowing Your Watercolours

Many of the challenges outlined in the previous chapter can be avoided, averted, resolved or overcome with more knowledge about the properties of the individual pigments and what to expect from them. Some common problems are caused simply by a lack of knowledge as to how watercolour works on paper and how the different colours and their pigments behave.

The watercolours in your paintbox are not just a particular hue: they are made from different physical pigments, organic, mineral and metal, and these pigments have individual properties and characteristics that cause them to act in differing ways on paper and in mixing. These properties include transparency, opacity, staining, lifting, granulating, warmth and coolness. Choosing a set of colours for a painting is less about colour matching and more about finding the right set of properties in the colours chosen for a desired result.

▶ Burnt Sienna and Ultramarine Blue, the colours blended to paint this jackal, have lifting properties, which means they can be easily removed from the paper if readjustment is necessary – an ideal property for painting an animal on the move.

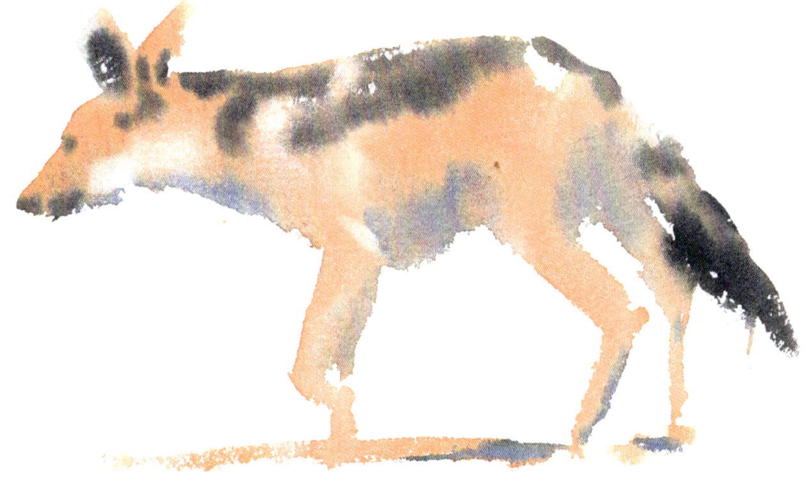

◀ **Dressed in Satin,**
30.5 x 20cm (12 x 8in)
The sheen and shadows of these satin dresses require a wide range of tonal values from light to dark. The transparent colours used here – Brown Madder, Alizarin Crimson and Phthalo Blue – have this property.

How Watercolour Works

Watercolour is a uniquely mobile medium. Fine particles of pigment are floated across the paper suspended in a binder diluted with water. If allowed to settle without undue interference, the water evaporates and the pigment sets in place, creating attractive fields of transparent colour through which light can emanate. Gum arabic is the usual binder, and acts as the 'glue' to adhere the pigment particles to the paper once dry. Watercolour paint comes concentrated into pans or tubes and is mixed with water on the palette to dissolve the binder (gum arabic) before being applied to the paper.

When mixed with water, the pigment particles do not dissolve: they are held in suspension. The more water added to the paint, the paler and more transparent the colour becomes. The less water added, the more vibrant and rich the colour remains.

Typically, watercolour is painted onto paper specially prepared to receive the paint. This paper is commonly made from wood chip or cotton fibres that have been soaked in size (glue) to make the paper surface less absorbent. The colours sit on and between, or seep into the top layer of fibres, staining the paper to differing degrees.

Use artist-quality paint. The tubes or pans of pigment-rich paint go a lot further than cheaper alternatives and will give you better results – you may be surprised how little paint is needed, and any unused paint is reusable.

▶ Pale colours, like the shirt here, need to be diluted with much more water than the small amount needed for the deep, rich colour of the girl's hair.

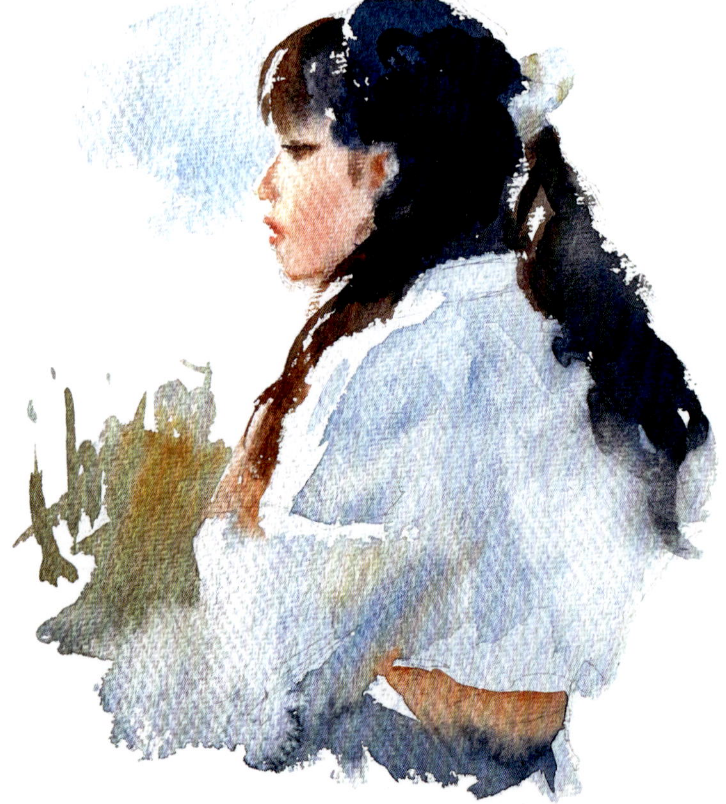

The Light

The light in a watercolour comes from the paper. Light from above illuminates the surface of the paper, and reflects back through the transparent films of colour, giving the luminosity for which watercolour is famed. Because it is transparent, watercolour can be used in multiple layers, traditionally starting with light layers and building towards the darks.

It helps to imagine the pigment particles like zillions of tiny pixels on a screen. In a dilute colour, the pigment is watered down, so there are fewer particles per square inch of paper and therefore more space between the particles for light to filter back to the viewer. The converse is true in more concentrated colour mixes: here, the particles are more tightly packed together, allowing less space in between. Therefore, less light can bounce back from the white paper. This is a neat way to think about it. However, there is more to consider...

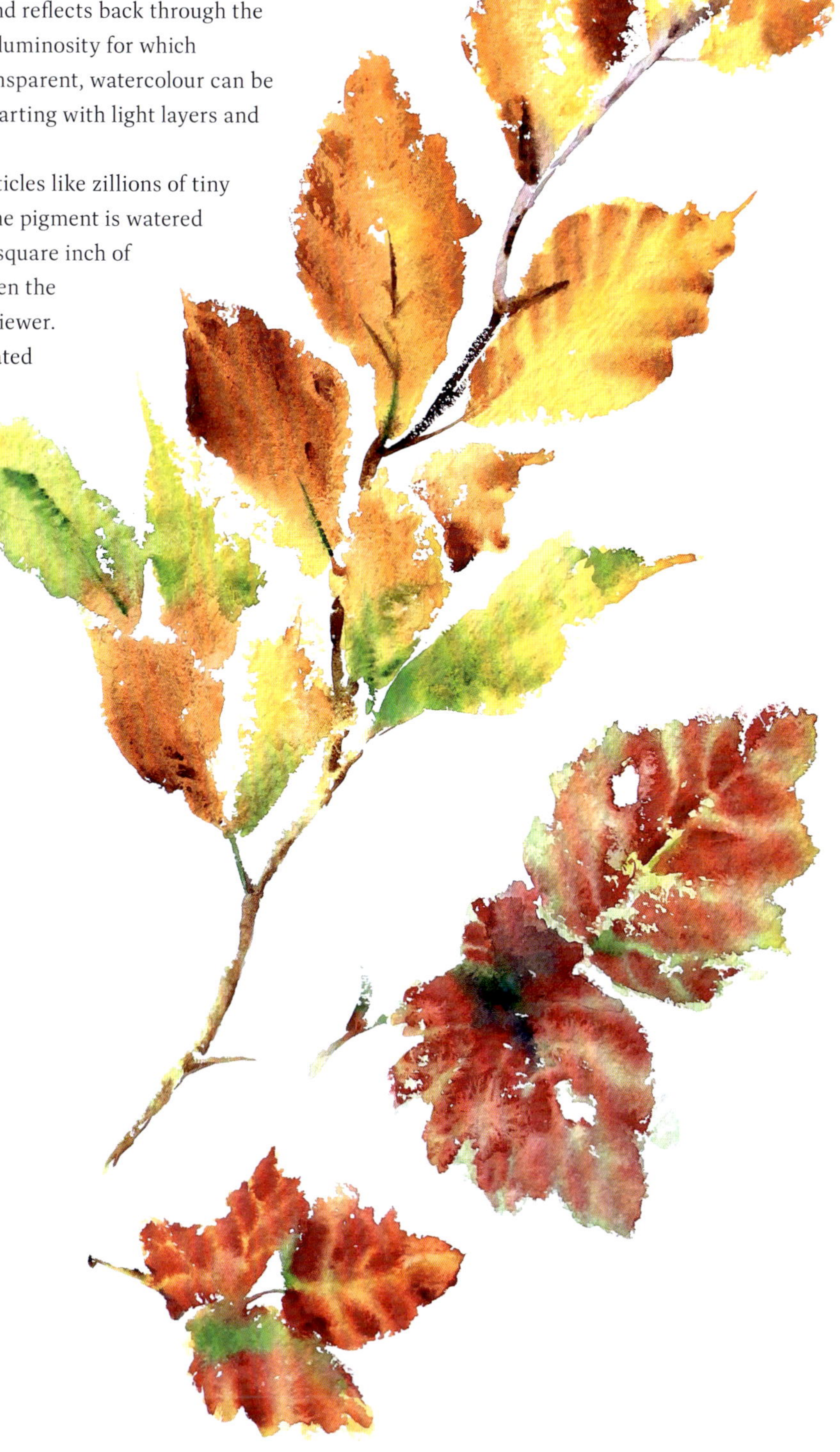

▶ The transparent nature of watercolour pigments allows colours to maintain transparency both when diluted and when laid in rich, concentrated hues. The deep browns and reds in these autumn leaves are as vibrant and transparent as the paler yellows and greens.

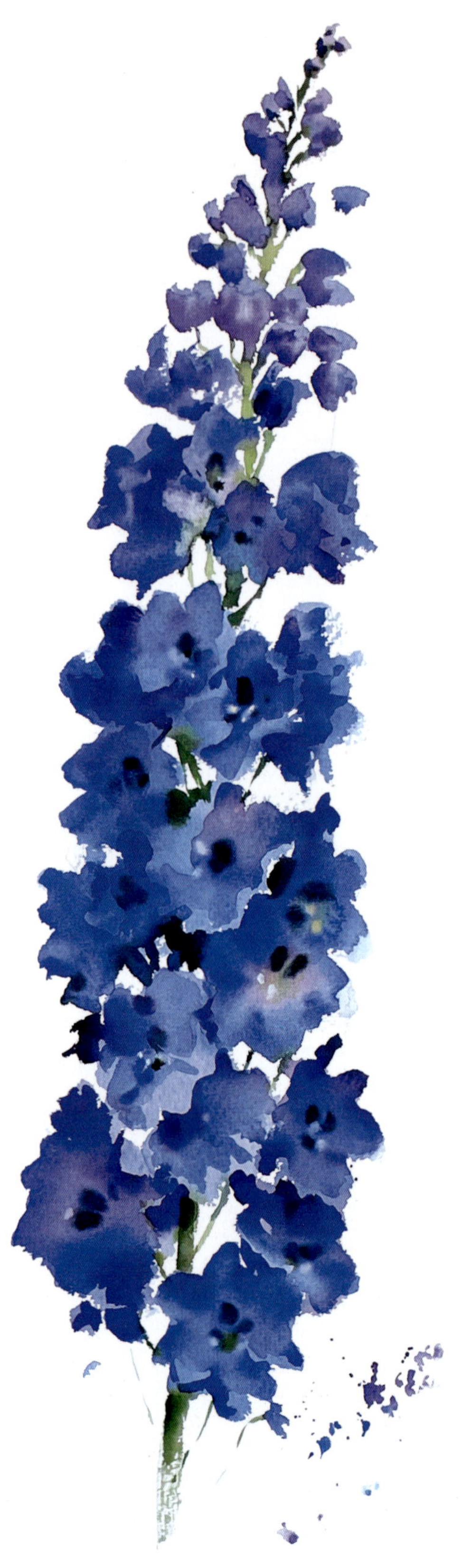

Transparency and Opacity

The exciting thing about watercolour is that many of the pigments are made of substances that are transparent in themselves, meaning that light can reflect back not only from the paper but pass through the particles of paint like stained glass. A few pigments even refract (deflect) the light. The many colours available are derived from a number of different pigments that vary in their transparency. Some are less transparent than others, allowing less light through them, and some are made from opaque substances, limiting the bounce back of light to the spaces of paper between each particle.

Good-quality manufacturers offer a whole range: transparent, semi-transparent, semi-opaque and opaque. The different properties are physical and affect not only the translucency but the flow rates, radiance and brightness of the colours. Knowing a pigment's degree of transparency or opacity is therefore a crucial component in watercolour painting, and allows the artist to control the overall appearance of the painting and the end result. It means concentrated colour can still be transparent, and light and brightness can be introduced.

◄ **Blue Delphinium,**
51 x 15cm (20 x 6in)
The transparent nature of the pigment used to make Ultramarine Finest allows the colour to maintain transparency even when painted in rich, concentrated hues.

▶ The comparison between transparency and opacity in similar hues is easier to recognize in some colours. Here, the transparent nature of the organic pigment Quinacridone Red and the opacity of the metal pigment Cadmium Red are clearly visible, whereas the difference between the opacity of Cadmium Yellow and the transparency of Indian Yellow is harder to ascertain. Hence, it is important to know the property of the colour.

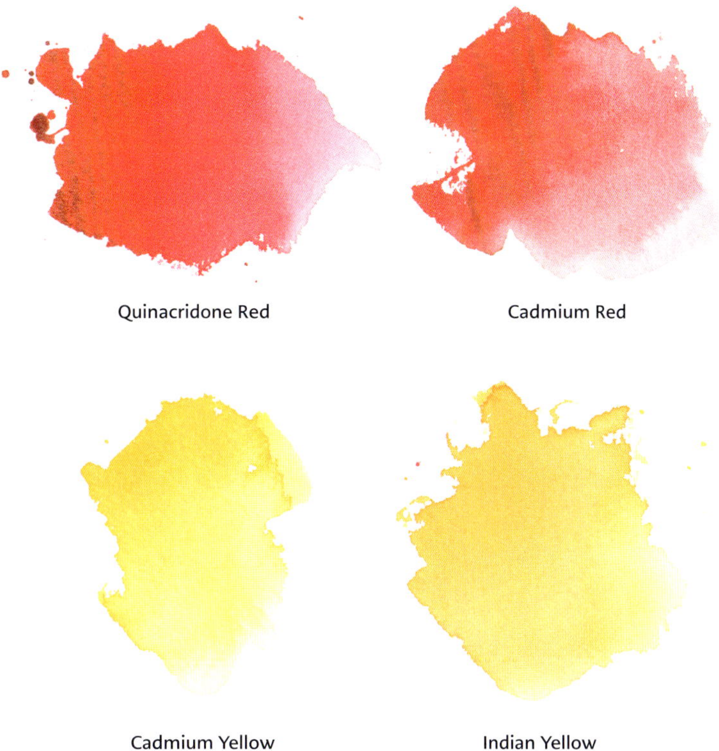

Information Symbol

Manufacturers know how vital this information is to the artist, and usually mark it clearly on the tubes. The information is presented in the form of a small square symbol: fully blocked for opacity; empty for transparency; a diagonal line dropping from left to right for semi-transparent, and the square half-filled diagonally to show semi-opaque.

The information about individual colours is available in the manufacturers' catalogues, and levels of transparency vary by brand. However, over the page I offer some pointers as to the level of transparency. These generalities may not always hold true nowadays, as some traditional colours have been replaced with more lightfast, non-toxic alternatives and might not fully replicate the previous colour's property.

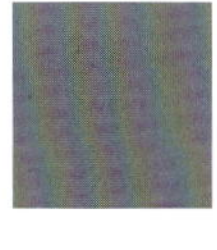
Opaque

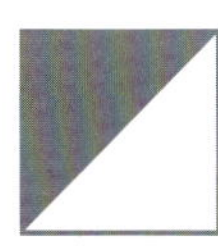
Semi-opaque

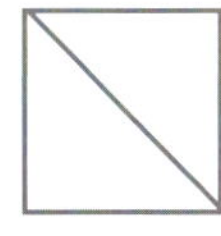
Semi-transparent

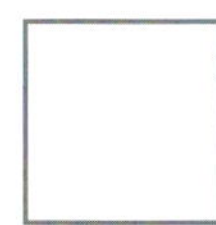
Transparent

What's in a Name?

The name of the colour offers useful information as to the level of transparency. For example, many modern pigments are made from carbon, an organic pigment with transparent attributes. These colours tend to be given long chemical-sounding prefix names, such as Quinacridone, Perylene, Dioxazine or Phthalo. This informs you that they are most likely transparent or semi-transparent colours.

Additionally, a colour prefixed with 'Transparent' is, of course, transparent, and colours labelled 'Permanent' are usually transparent or semi-transparent.

On the other hand, pigments with metal prefixes, such as Cadmium, Cobalt or Titanium, are inorganic and derived from metals. They are likely to be at least partially if not fully opaque because metal is a denser material.

The earth colours, such as Ochre, Sienna and Umber, are traditionally derived from iron oxide. These inorganic mineral pigments range from the browny yellows of Yellow Raw Ochre, Raw Sienna and Raw Umber to the red brown of Burnt Sienna, and the greener brown of Burnt Umber. The lighter hues tend towards transparency, becoming semi-opaque in Burnt Umber, more opaque with Light Red, and fully opaque in colours such as Indian Red or Venetian Red.

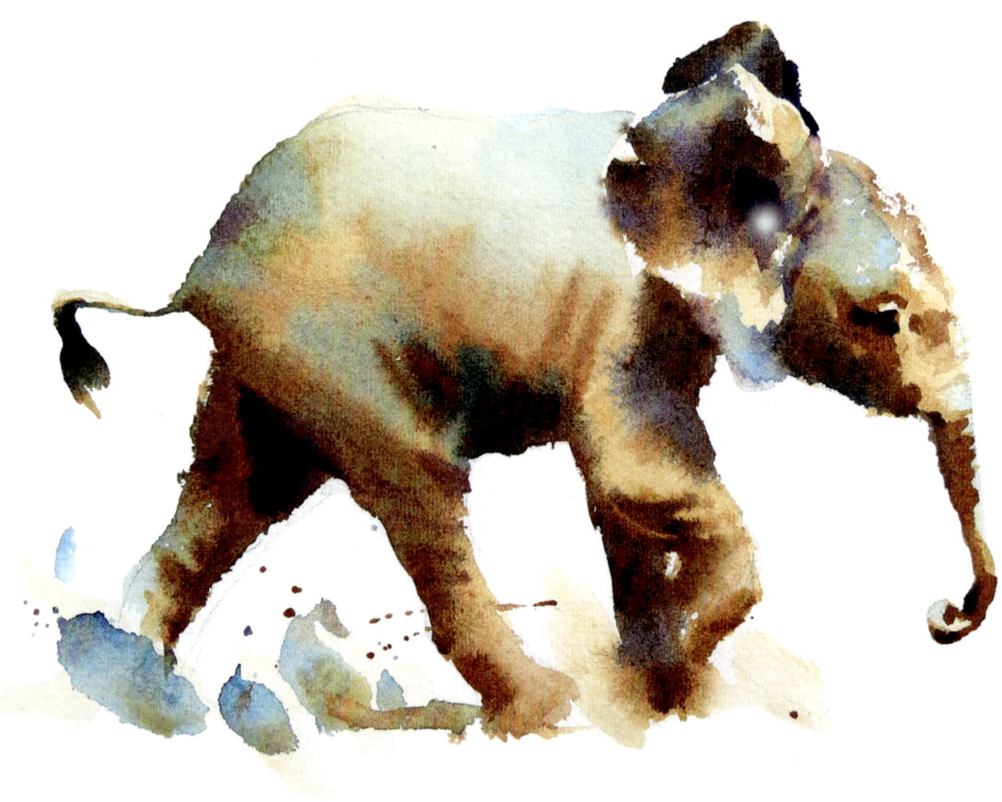

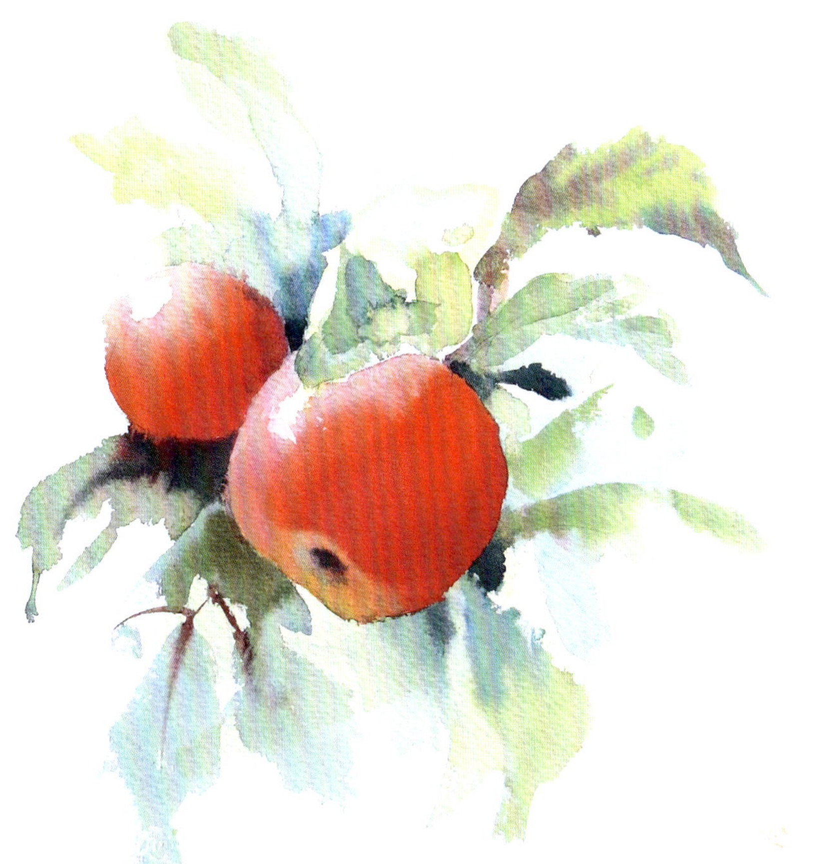

◀ **Gravetye Apples,**
15 x 15cm (6 x 6in)

Cadmium Red is a brilliant primary red. Being derived from metal, it is highly opaque. Here, it is dropped neat into a pale wet tint to deliver its richness in a single layer. Subsequently, Cadmium Yellow's opacity is employed to introduce a reflected light on the underside of the apple.

◀ **Too Young to Know,**
20 x 25.5cm (8 x 10in)

Four earth colours are used here to incrementally deepen the tonal values: Yellow Raw Ochre is followed by Raw Umber for the body colour, with Burnt Sienna used for the darker creases; finally, Burnt Umber is mixed with Schmincke Violet and Prussian Blue for the deepest shadows.

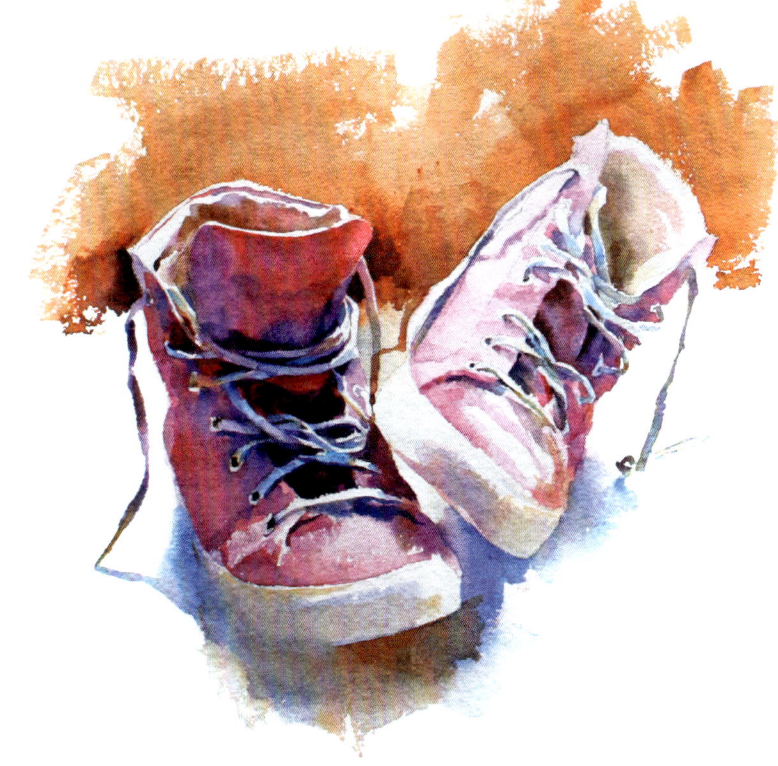

▶ **Shoes with Attitude,**
51 x 51cm (20 x 20in)

Quinacridone is a highly transparent pigment derived from carbon. It ranges in colour from yellow to purple but is used predominantly for pinks and reds. Ruby Red (Quinacridone/Permanent Rose) is the cool pink used to paint these shoes.

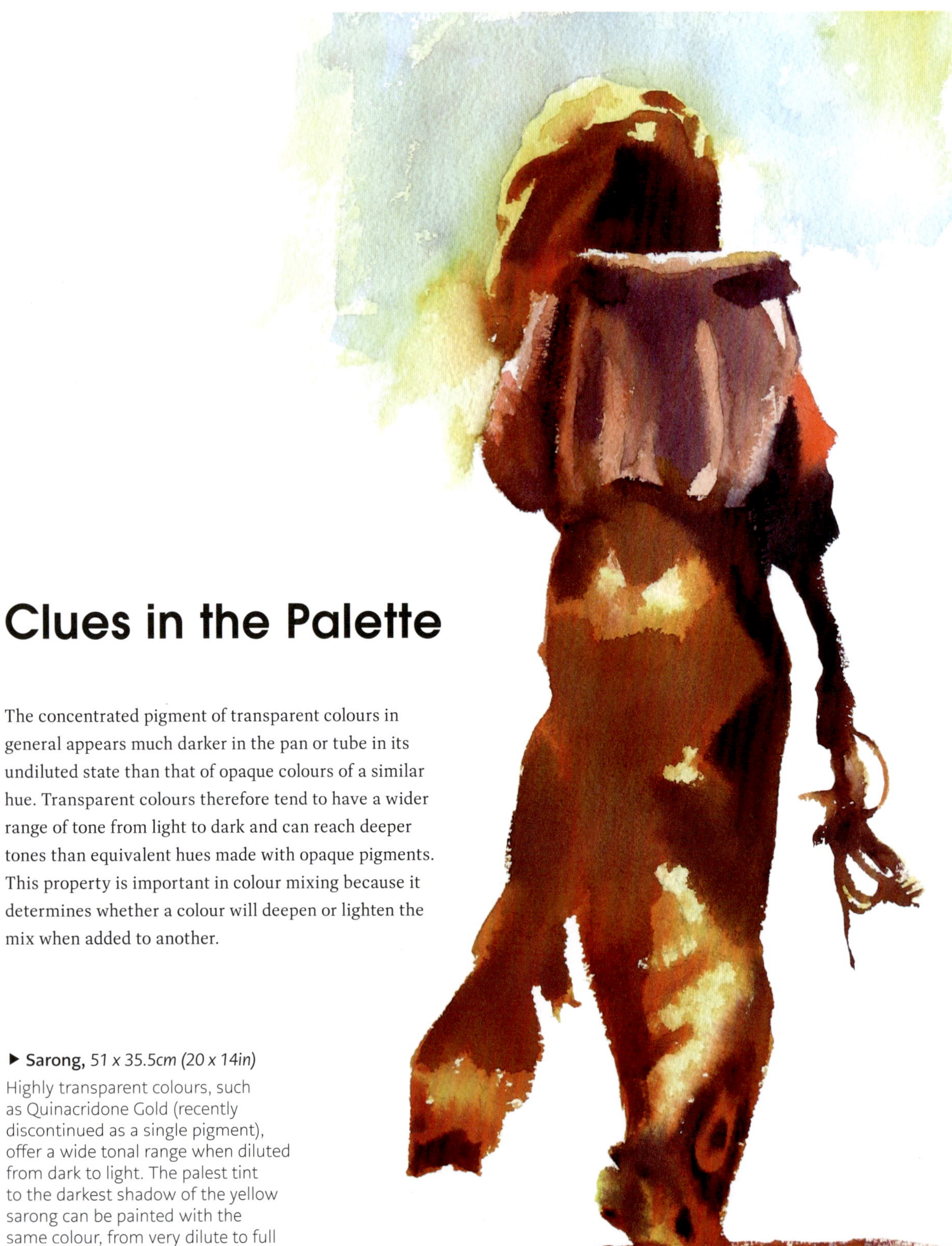

Clues in the Palette

The concentrated pigment of transparent colours in general appears much darker in the pan or tube in its undiluted state than that of opaque colours of a similar hue. Transparent colours therefore tend to have a wider range of tone from light to dark and can reach deeper tones than equivalent hues made with opaque pigments. This property is important in colour mixing because it determines whether a colour will deepen or lighten the mix when added to another.

▸ **Sarong,** *51 x 35.5cm (20 x 14in)*
Highly transparent colours, such as Quinacridone Gold (recently discontinued as a single pigment), offer a wide tonal range when diluted from dark to light. The palest tint to the darkest shadow of the yellow sarong can be painted with the same colour, from very dilute to full concentration.

▸ Rinsed from the brush, the opacity of the Cadmium Yellow pigment turns the water cloudy, while Quinacridone Red leaves a transparent tint.

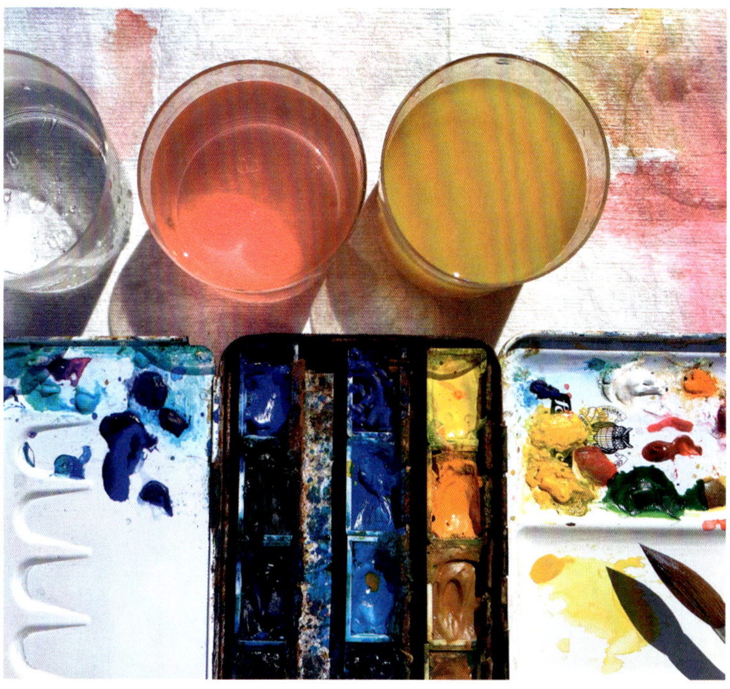

Revelation in the Rinsing Pot

One of the best ways to discover whether a colour is transparent or opaque is to pick up some colour on a brush and rinse it off in a clear water pot. Transparent colours tint the water, whereas opaque colours turn it cloudy. Place both pots over a white cloth with a black line underneath: the line is obscured by the opaque colour but visible through the transparent colour.

▸ This sunset is painted with three opaque primaries each derived from a metal pigment: Cerulean Blue (Cobalt), Cadmium Red and Cadmium Yellow (Cadmium). Mixed for the dark horizon, they cannot make a deep black due to their opaque light bright hues. The pigment particles creep slowly upward into the wet red paint to create lovely meandering threads by capillary action.

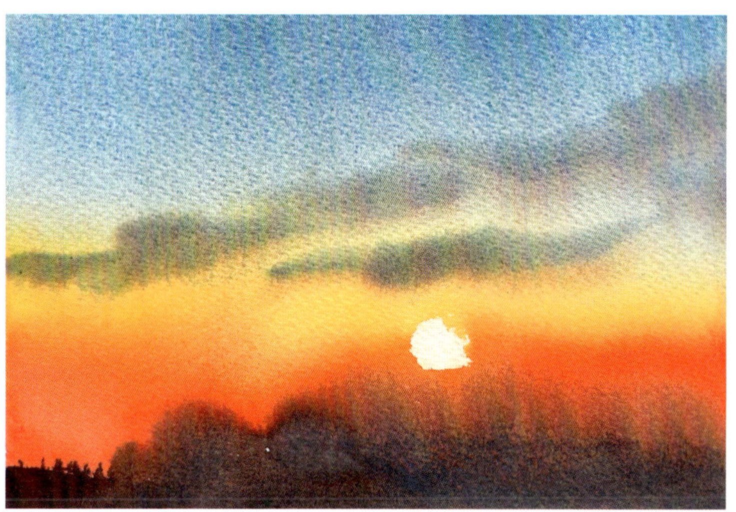

Practice, Practice, Practice

Get Wise to Opacity

A colour should not be chosen for its hue alone just to match a subject. Colours should be chosen in combination to make the whole painting, ideally with the smallest number of pigments possible. Traditionally, many readymade watercolour sets come with the opaque Cadmium Yellow as their main warm yellow. Beginners assume they can mix this freely with other hues (blue and red) to make green and orange, for example. But even though the yellow is bright, it is fully opaque and as such may well dull the mix.

Say we mix Cadmium Yellow with Cadmium Red to paint a bright orange on a branch. Both colours are bright in themselves and both opaque, so if we lay too many layers, the light returning through them from the white paper will be blocked. If an opaque yellow is used with Cobalt Blue (semi-opaque) to make the green for leaves, and then laid in multiple layers, the painting could end up rather dull.

This does not mean you should shy away from using the opaque colours: in single layers they offer brilliant hues and bright, rich colouring, but you do need to know the risk they present in mixing and layering. If the greens in a landscape are mixed predominantly with opaque yellows, for example, and with much over-layering, the opacity will blot out transparency. Additionally, if the pigment is pushed around too much on the paper, a muddy result will ensue.

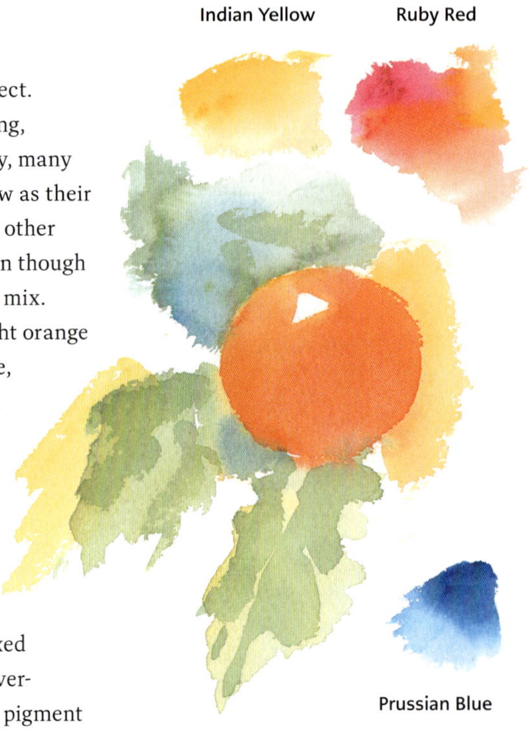

Indian Yellow

Ruby Red

Prussian Blue

▲ Three transparent colours are used here – Indian Yellow, Ruby Red and Prussian Blue – so they can be layered several times and still allow light through.

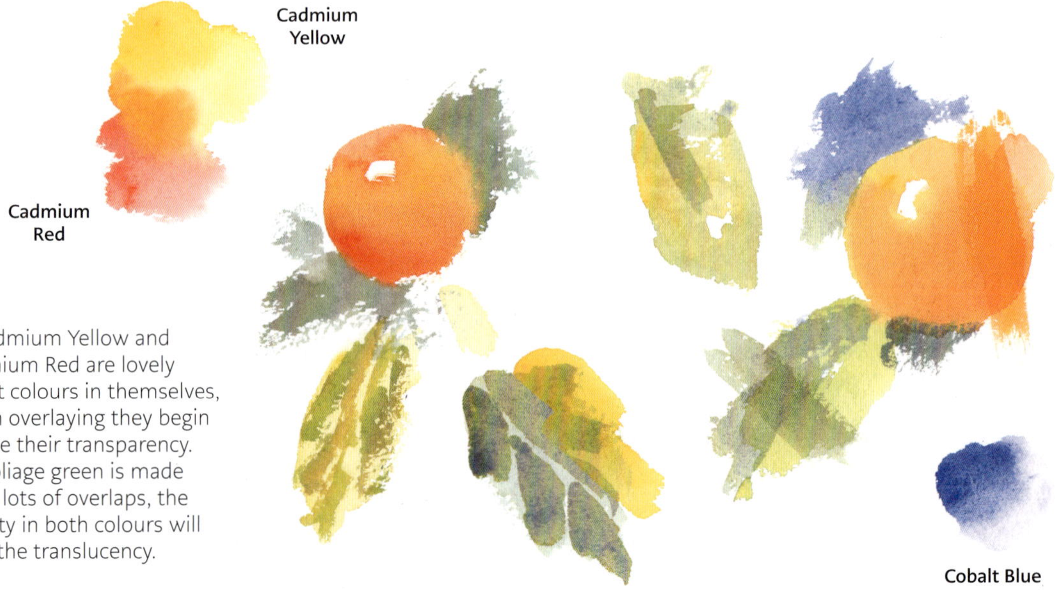

Cadmium Yellow

Cadmium Red

Cobalt Blue

▶ Cadmium Yellow and Cadmium Red are lovely bright colours in themselves, but in overlaying they begin to lose their transparency. If a foliage green is made up of lots of overlaps, the opacity in both colours will limit the translucency.

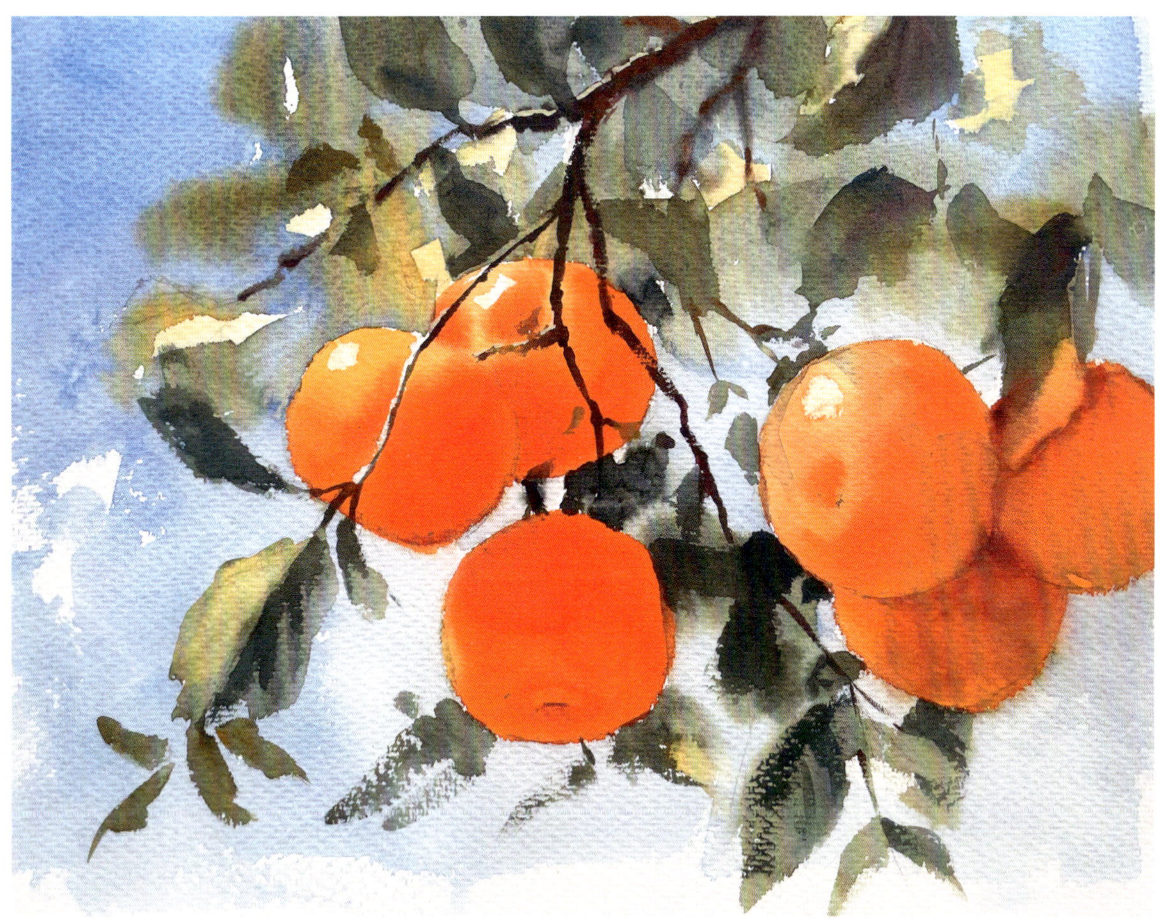

▲ The same three transparent colours are used here: Indian Yellow, Ruby Red and Prussian Blue. By using the same transparent yellow in the orange for the fruit as in the green for the leaves, transparency and harmony is ensured.

Colours:

Indian Yellow

Ruby Red

Prussian Blue

Brushes:

19mm flat brush

Size 8 round brush

Size 10 round brush

If in doubt, apply opaque colours in the minimum number of layers, or err on the side of mixing and layering with the more transparent colours until you become familiar with the properties of your colour set. There are many transparent yellows, reds and blues from which to choose nowadays.

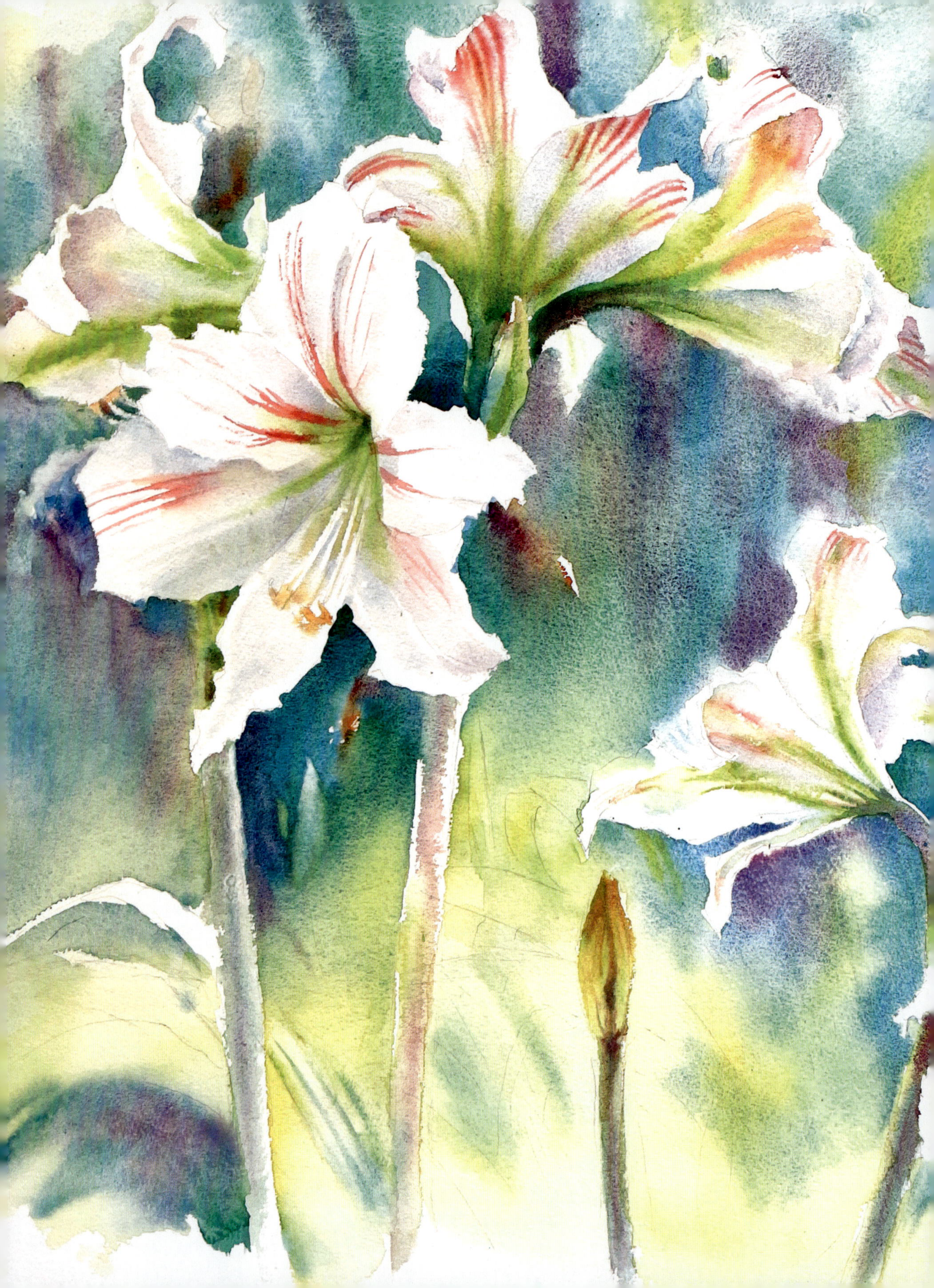

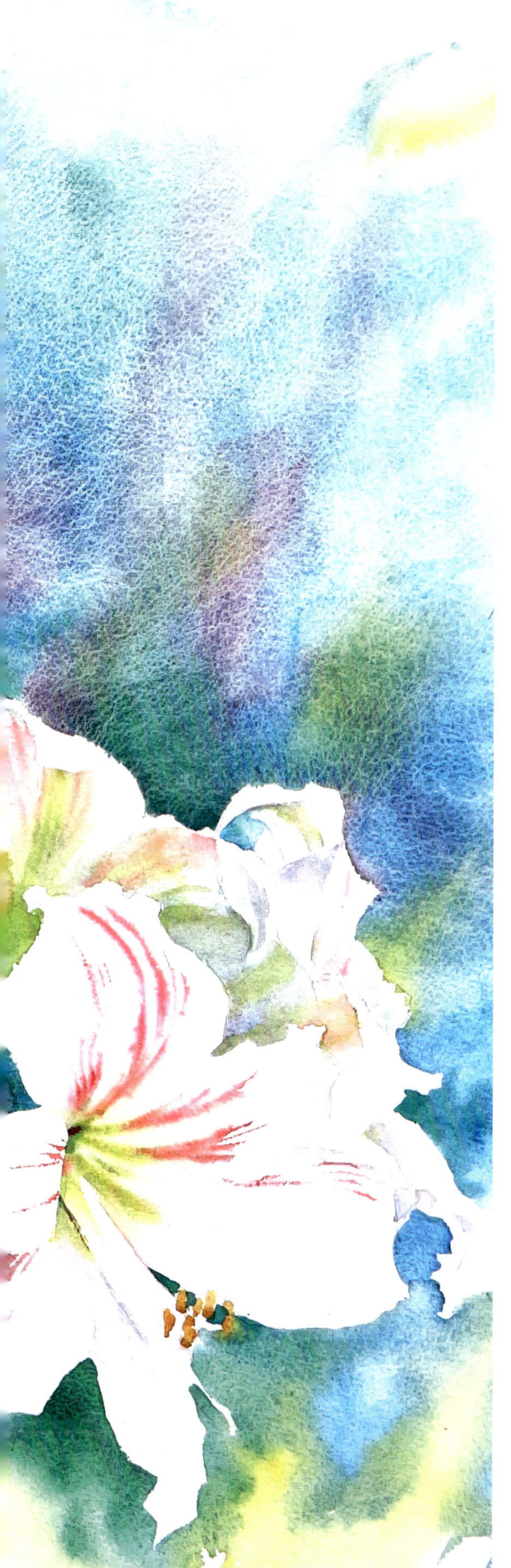

CHAPTER 3

The Staining Medium

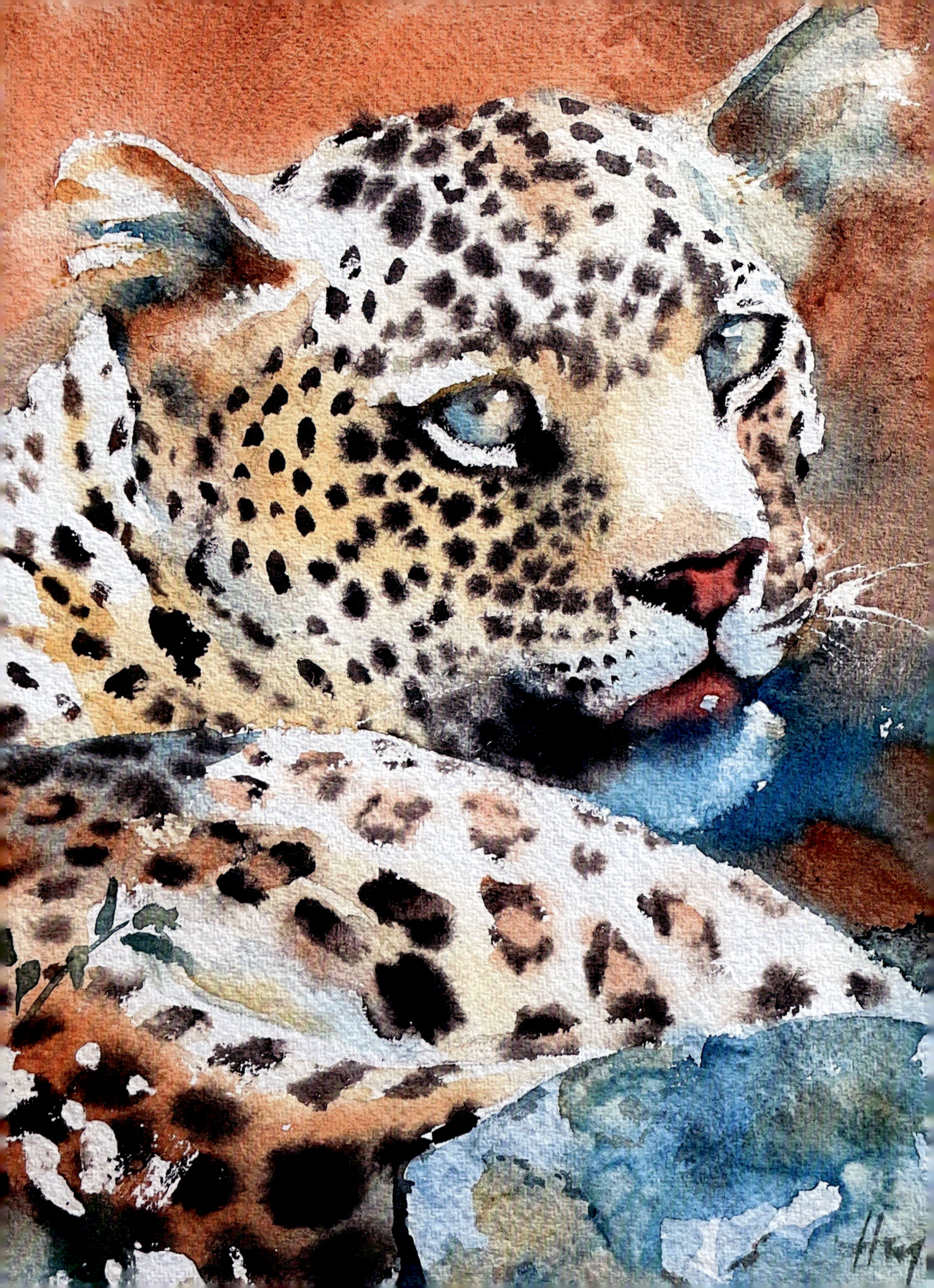

An Unforgiving Medium?

Watercolour is essentially a staining medium. Because mistakes made with staining colours are difficult and sometimes impossible to eradicate, it is principally for this reason that watercolour has earned its reputation as an unforgiving medium.

The staining quality of the colours depends on the chemical and physical properties of the pigment, but not all colours stain the paper to the same degree. This attribute refers to how deeply the pigment adheres to, or enters, the fibres of the paper and affects its ability to be lifted or manipulated after drying. Watercolours are therefore categorized as staining, semi-staining, or non-staining. Not all colours are super-stainers, and the non-staining colours can be very forgiving. Knowing the difference can save you a lot of worry!

◀ **Silent Gaze,**
30.5 x 23cm (12 x 9in)
Prussian Blue, a super-staining colour, is used in this painting. Once laid, it stains the paper and its trace cannot be removed. Sepia, which is used for the spots, is semi-staining; though its depth of tone can be lightened, it too will always leave a staining trace.

▶ **Basilica San Lorenzo,**
25.5 x 25.5cm (10 x 10in)
Here, the non-staining colours Raw Umber, Light Red, Burnt Umber and Ultramarine Blue were chosen. When faced with complicated architectural detail, I often choose non-staining colours so that I can get straight into the painting, knowing I can correct drawing errors later by lifting the colour.

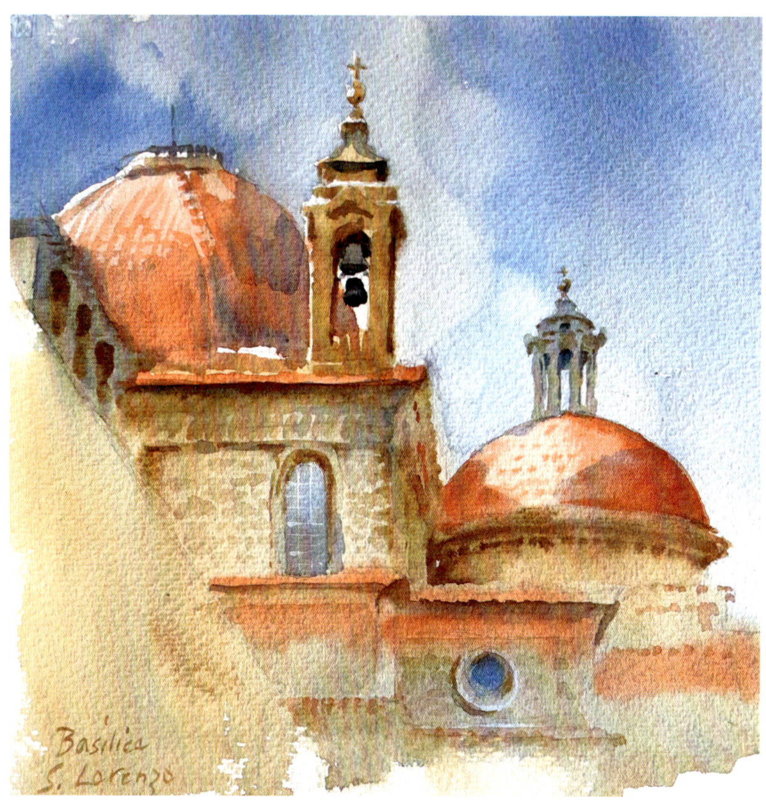

Staining Properties

The degree to which a pigment stains the paper ranges between highly staining and barely staining. Those that stain highly tend to be the fine, lightweight particles, as they are able to seep into and between the fibres of the paper – more so if the paper is made from cotton. The staining effect is a property of the pigment and very useful for the stasis of a watercolour. Staining colours penetrate deep into the paper and are difficult to lift or remove, especially once dry. They are therefore excellent for layering and glazing because they stay put, but mistakes are hard to correct. This does not mean that a rich concentrated patch of a staining colour cannot be lightened by lifting off to some extent, but the more dilute traces of the pigment always remain as a stain.

Examples of traditionally staining colours in my palette include Prussian Blue, Alizarin Crimson, Brown Madder and Schmincke Violet. Many of the more modern organic colours made from carbon are staining or moderately staining pigments, as carbon is such a fine lightweight material and can seep into the paper fibres more readily than a dense, heavier metal or mineral pigment.

Non-staining pigments sit more on the surface of the paper, making them easier to lift or scrub away even after drying. They are ideal if you want to be able to lighten tones or make corrections. Non-staining pigments are also termed 'lifting' colours.

Semi-staining pigments fall between the two extremes, allowing for some lifting and correction while maintaining a degree of permanence. The majority of colours fall into this category.

▶ Paint manufacturers use a triangular symbol to show the staining property of a colour. The triangle is blocked in if the pigment is highly staining; half-filled in if semi-staining; and clear if the colour is non-staining.

Highly staining

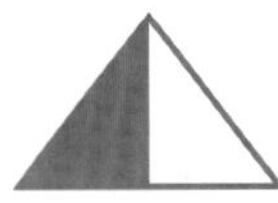

Semi-staining

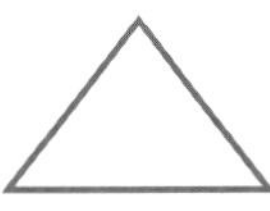

Non-staining

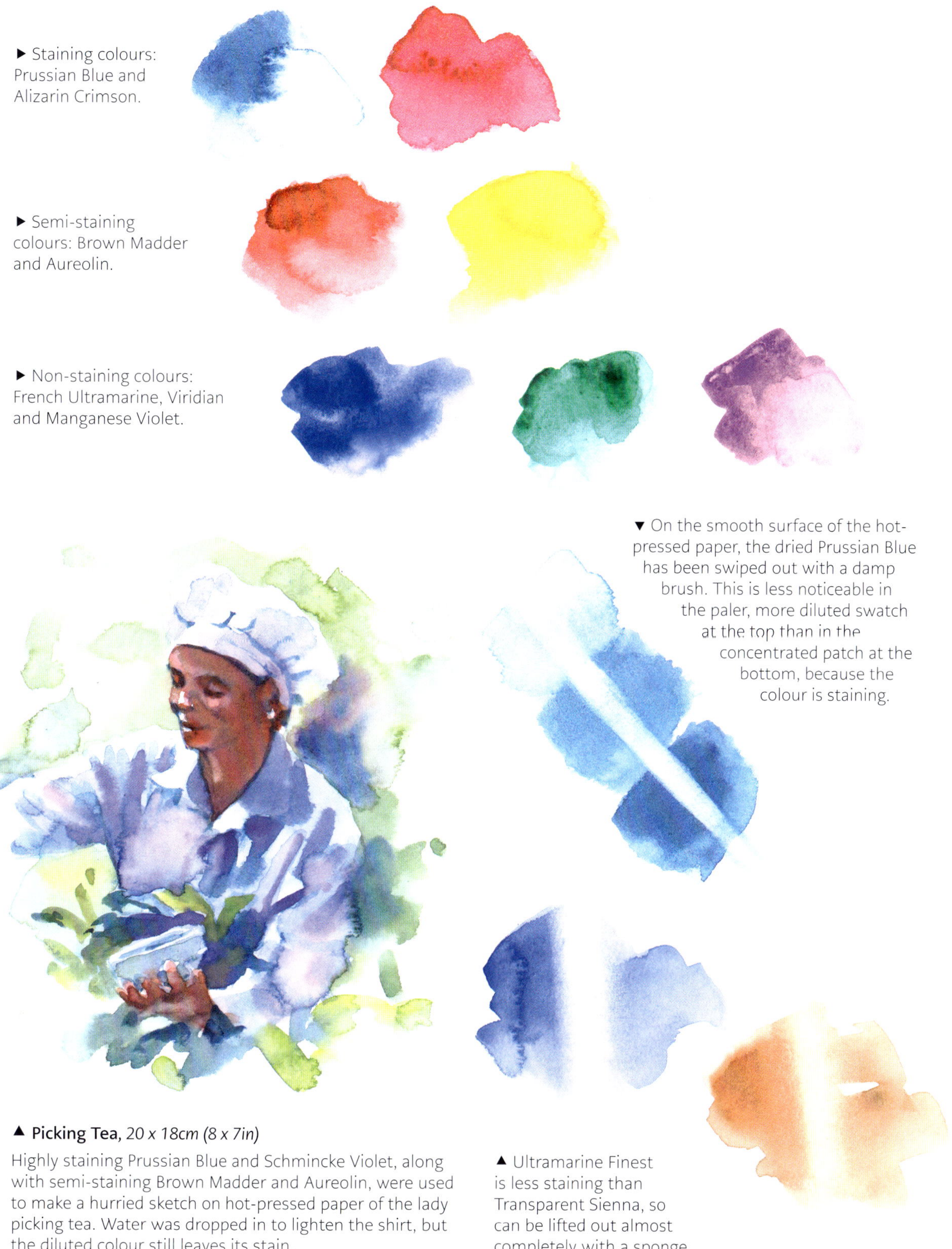

▶ Staining colours: Prussian Blue and Alizarin Crimson.

▶ Semi-staining colours: Brown Madder and Aureolin.

▶ Non-staining colours: French Ultramarine, Viridian and Manganese Violet.

▼ On the smooth surface of the hot-pressed paper, the dried Prussian Blue has been swiped out with a damp brush. This is less noticeable in the paler, more diluted swatch at the top than in the concentrated patch at the bottom, because the colour is staining.

▲ **Picking Tea,** *20 x 18cm (8 x 7in)*

Highly staining Prussian Blue and Schmincke Violet, along with semi-staining Brown Madder and Aureolin, were used to make a hurried sketch on hot-pressed paper of the lady picking tea. Water was dropped in to lighten the shirt, but the diluted colour still leaves its stain.

▲ Ultramarine Finest is less staining than Transparent Sienna, so can be lifted out almost completely with a sponge.

Super Stainers and Semi-stainers

Staining colours, depending on whether they are semi-staining or fully staining, are hard or impossible to shift once laid, and are often the cause of uneven washes, seams and unintended hard edges. Their staining property, however, makes them very stable in layering and maintaining transparency. This makes staining colours ideal for painting the overlapping layers of architectural detail with its hard-edged structures and three-dimensional tonal values, or the overlapping layering in landscapes, portraits and still life.

Unwanted edges can easily occur with staining colours once the edge of a wash or brushstroke dries, as it cannot be removed or softened. But many semi-staining colours can be lifted to some degree, so knowing which colours have this property contributes hugely both to fixing mistakes or avoiding them. See Chapter 6 on edges (page 116) for more detail on this issue.

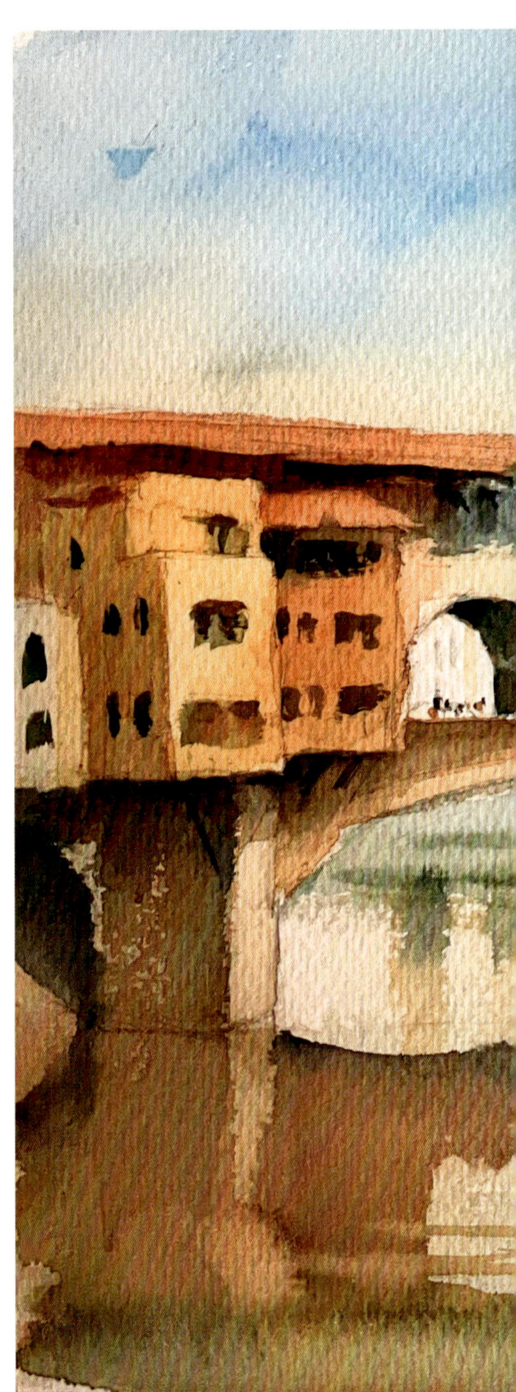

▼ To avoid an unwanted seam from a staining colour within a shape like this silhouette, rather than starting in the middle with the tower, start at one side and paint towards the other. In this way, you can create a seamless wash as there is only one edge to keep wet rather than two.

▼ Ponte Vecchio, *28 x 38cm (11 x 15in)*

To delineate the cuboid house structures on the Ponte Vecchio in Florence, I chose Prussian Blue, a staining blue, which helped me to keep the shadows clean and crisp.

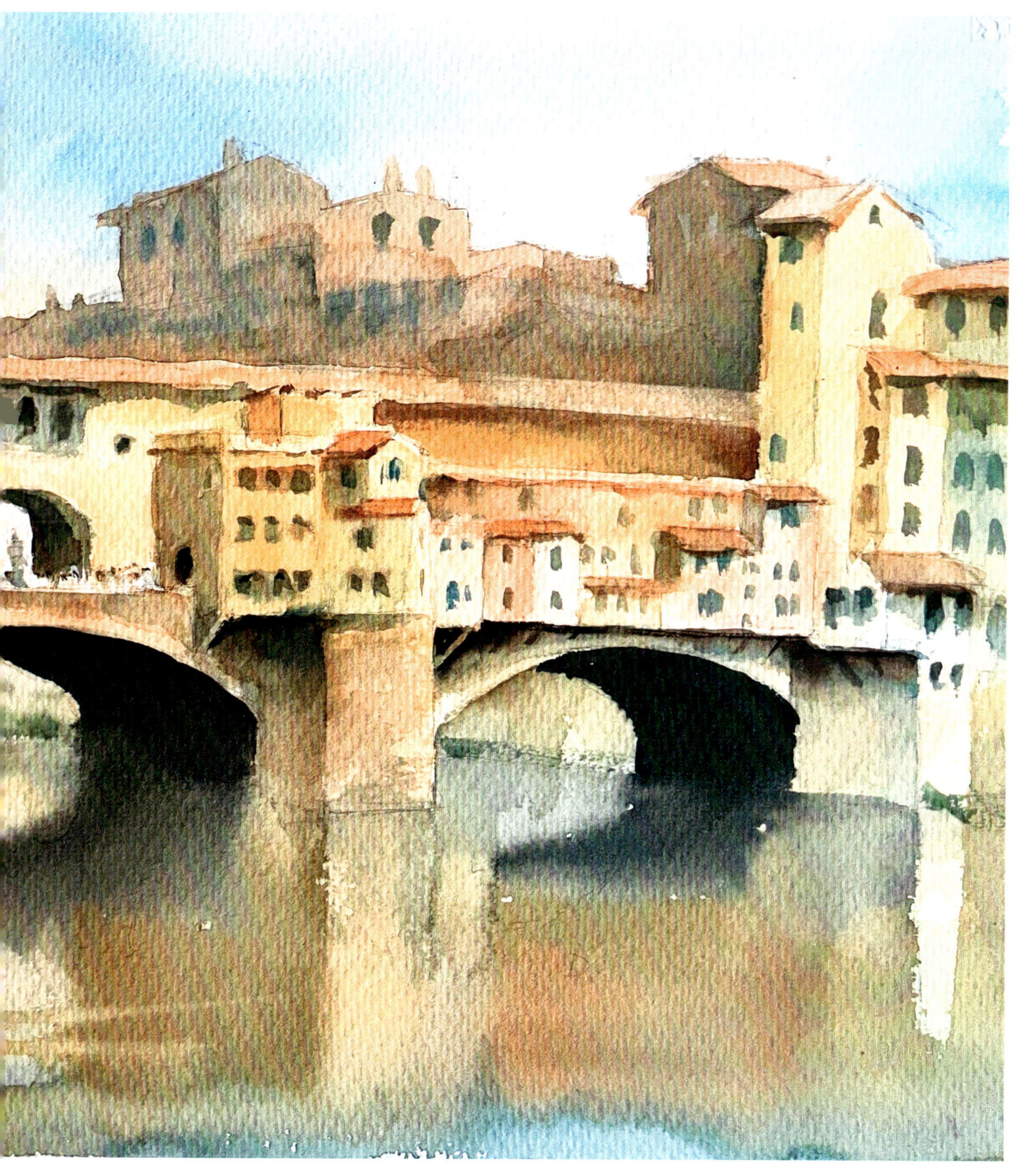

Non-staining and Lifting Colours

Since watercolour is in essence a staining medium, only a few colours are fully non-staining. The colours that stain less or hardly stain can be lifted off the surface of the paper to differing degrees, with a brush or a sponge, either when wet or dry, and some leave little trace. Using pigments that have this property means you can more easily remove seams and soften edges, fix mistakes, eliminate accidental cauliflowers and regularize uneven washes. The lifting colours are sometimes accompanied by a granulating or sedimentary characteristic in which the pigment settles on the paper to form an attractive mottled texture.

Because non-staining colours lift, they can also be shifted accidentally when subsequent wet layers are painted over the top. This is often the cause of, or contributes towards, muddy or dull colouring: particles of pigment are loosened and reactivated by water, and mix unintentionally with added colours to make duller mixes and are sometimes pushed into unattractive clumps. To avoid this happening, subsequent brushstrokes should be laid gently. Caress the paper with the brush, rather than dragging or rubbing with the brush, being mindful not to disturb the under-washes.

Because non-staining colours can lift, they are deemed more forgiving, allowing the watercolourist to paint more confidently in the knowledge that dark tones can be lightened, seams softened, and cauliflower blooms disguised if things go awry.

▶ In my palette, Ultramarine and Burnt Sienna are very useful non-staining pigments. I call the lifting colours 'kind', because they allow so much modification. I use them frequently when painting portraits so I feel safe to adjust the positions of features as I search for the likeness of the subject.

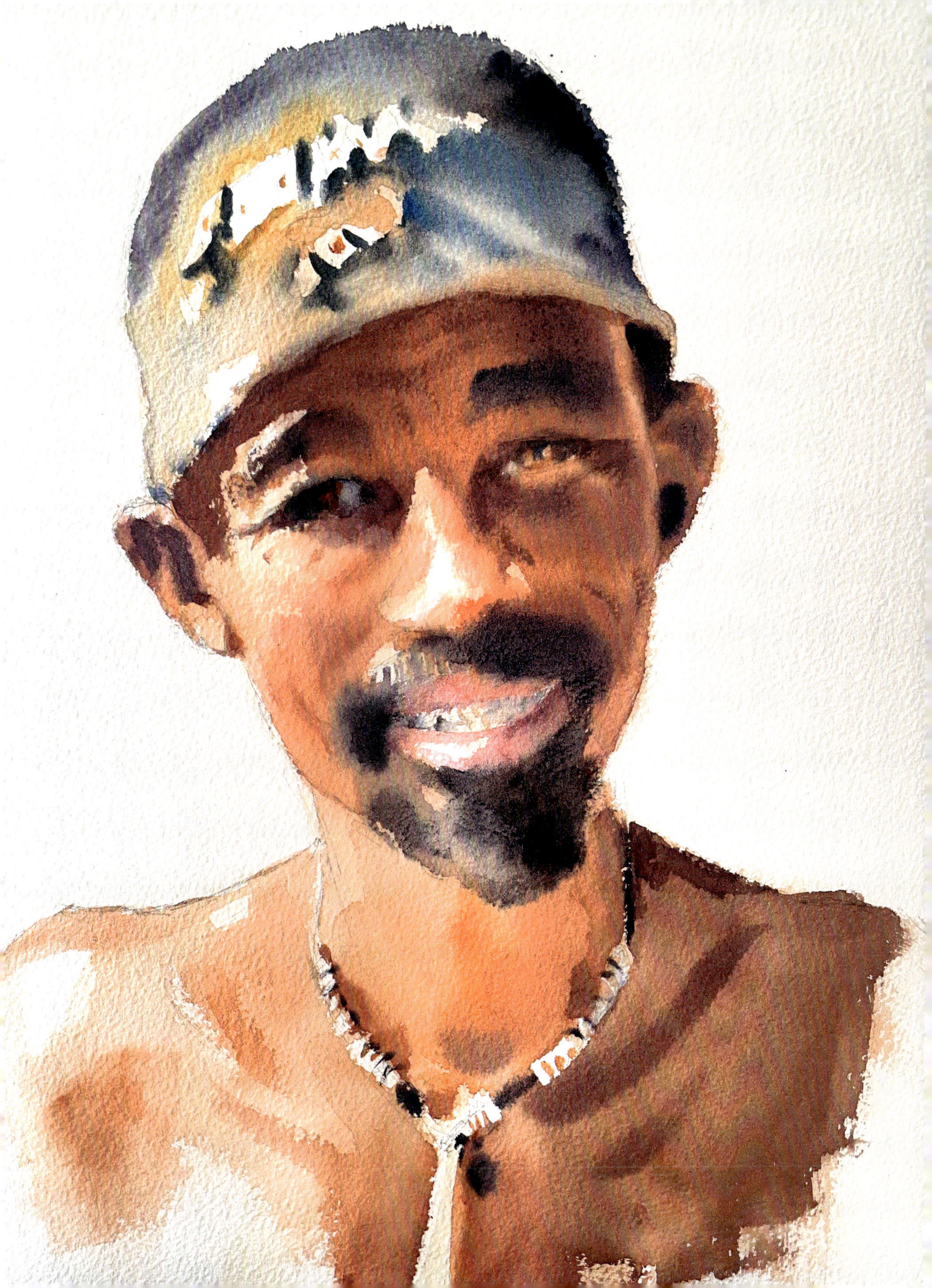

Practice, Practice, Practice

Lifting in Action

To lift excess or erroneous colour from the paper, use a clean, damp brush for small and precise areas and a sponge for large areas. Rub gently to agitate and loosen the pigment as you re-dissolve the gum arabic. Too much friction will harm the surface of the paper, so be mindful of your action. If it becomes too wet, let it dry before continuing. Always use a clean brush or sponge, and repeatedly clean off the lifted colour after each agitation so you are not adding pigment back onto and into the paper.

As well as being a remedy, lifting off is a creative technique for re-introducing light back into paintings, as the two paintings on these pages show.

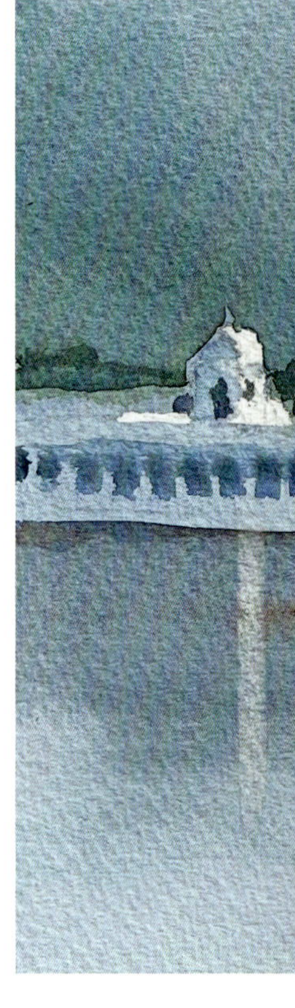

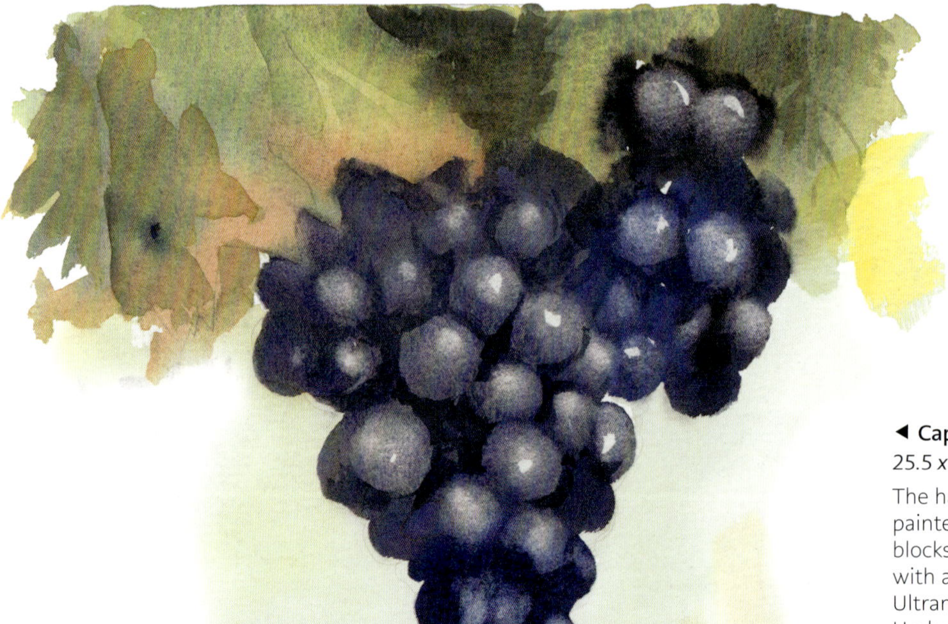

◀ **Cape Grapes,**
25.5 x 28cm (10 x 11in)

The hanging grapes are painted as two triangular blocks of deep, dark colour with a mix of French Ultramarine and Burnt Umber, both of which are lifting colours. With a small, damp brush, the bloom and highlight on individual grapes is lifted out from the darkness to create the bunch of grapes.

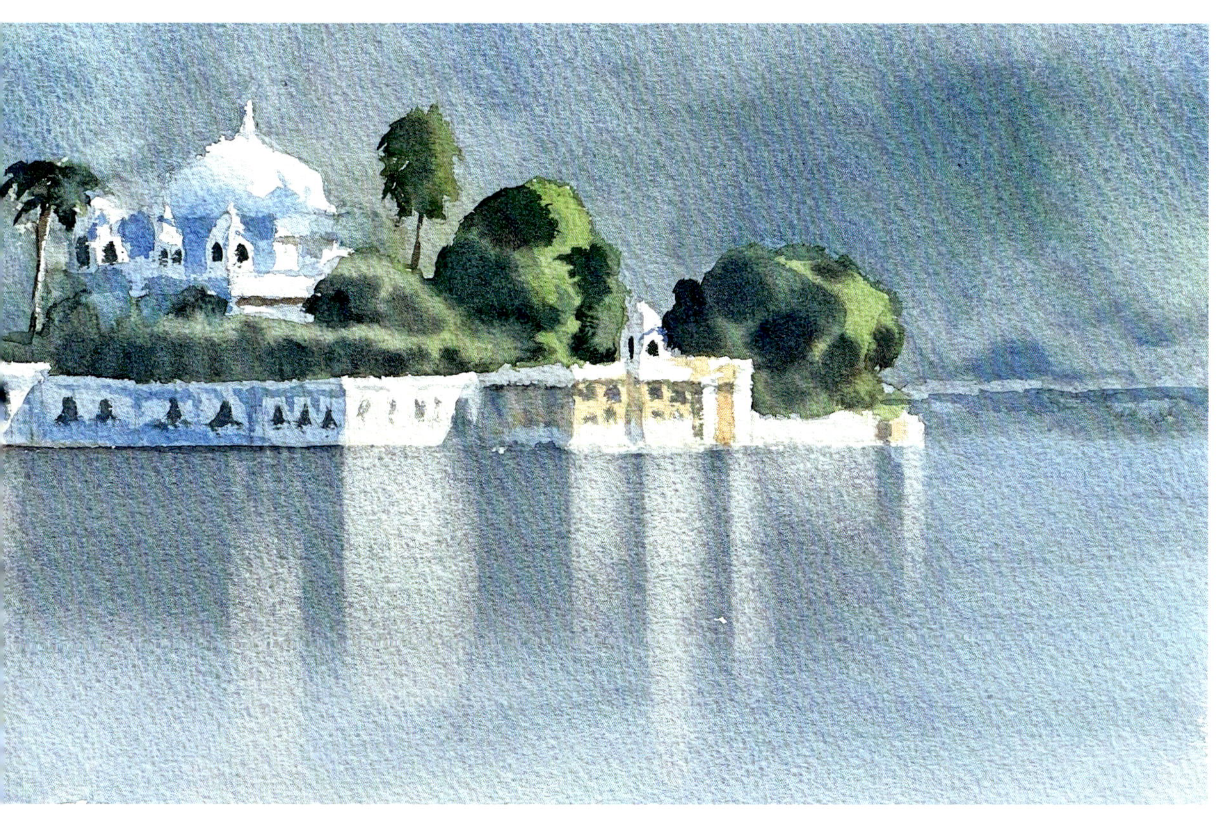

▲ **Lake Pichola, Udaipur,**
12.5 x 28cm (5 x 11in)
A dilute grey wash, mixed with Transparent Sienna and Ultramarine Finest, is painted below the palace. Using two pieces of card as straight-edged stencils, the paint below the highlighted white walls is swiped away in one swift movement with a clean sponge, instantly creating the lighter reflections in the water.

Colours:

French Ultramarine

Ultramarine Finest/Blue

Burnt Umber

Transparent/Burnt Sienna

Indian Yellow/Aureolin

Brushes:

19mm flat brush

Size 6 round brush

Size 8 round brush

Size 10 round brush

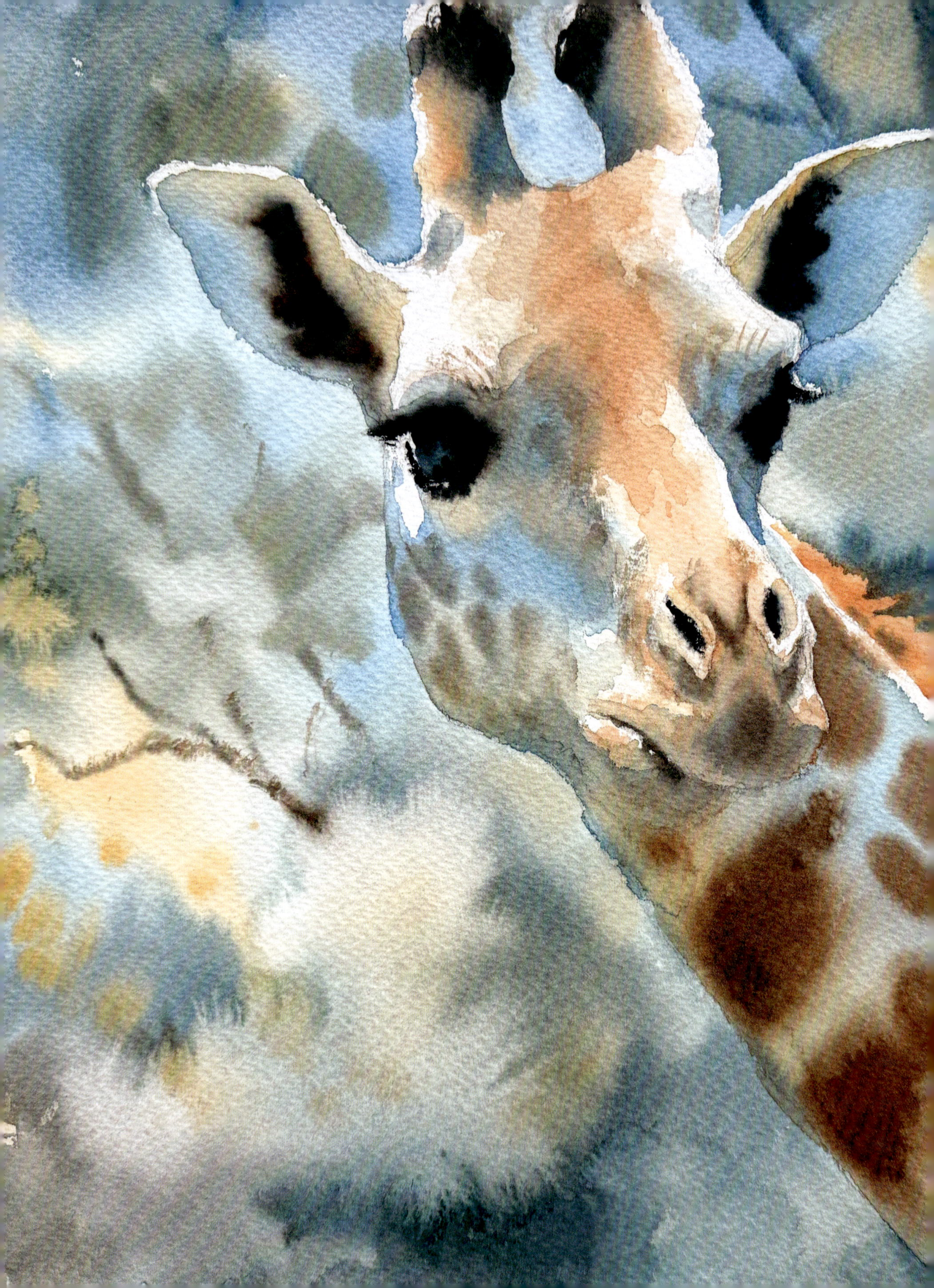

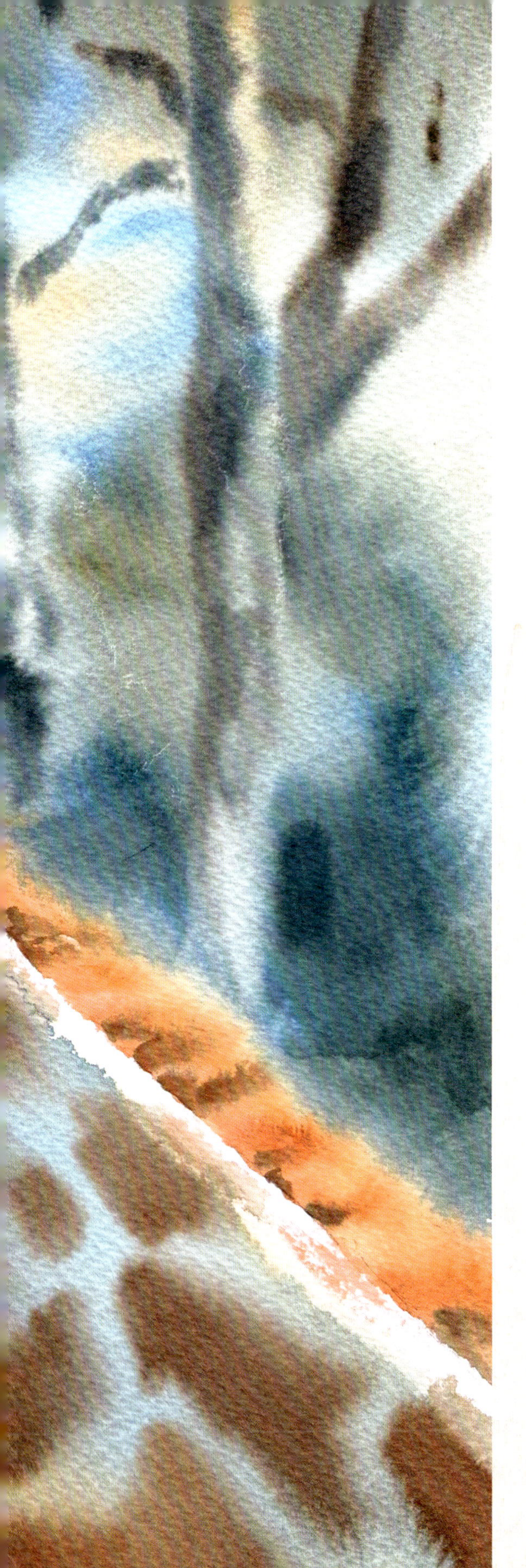

CHAPTER 4

Mud Happens

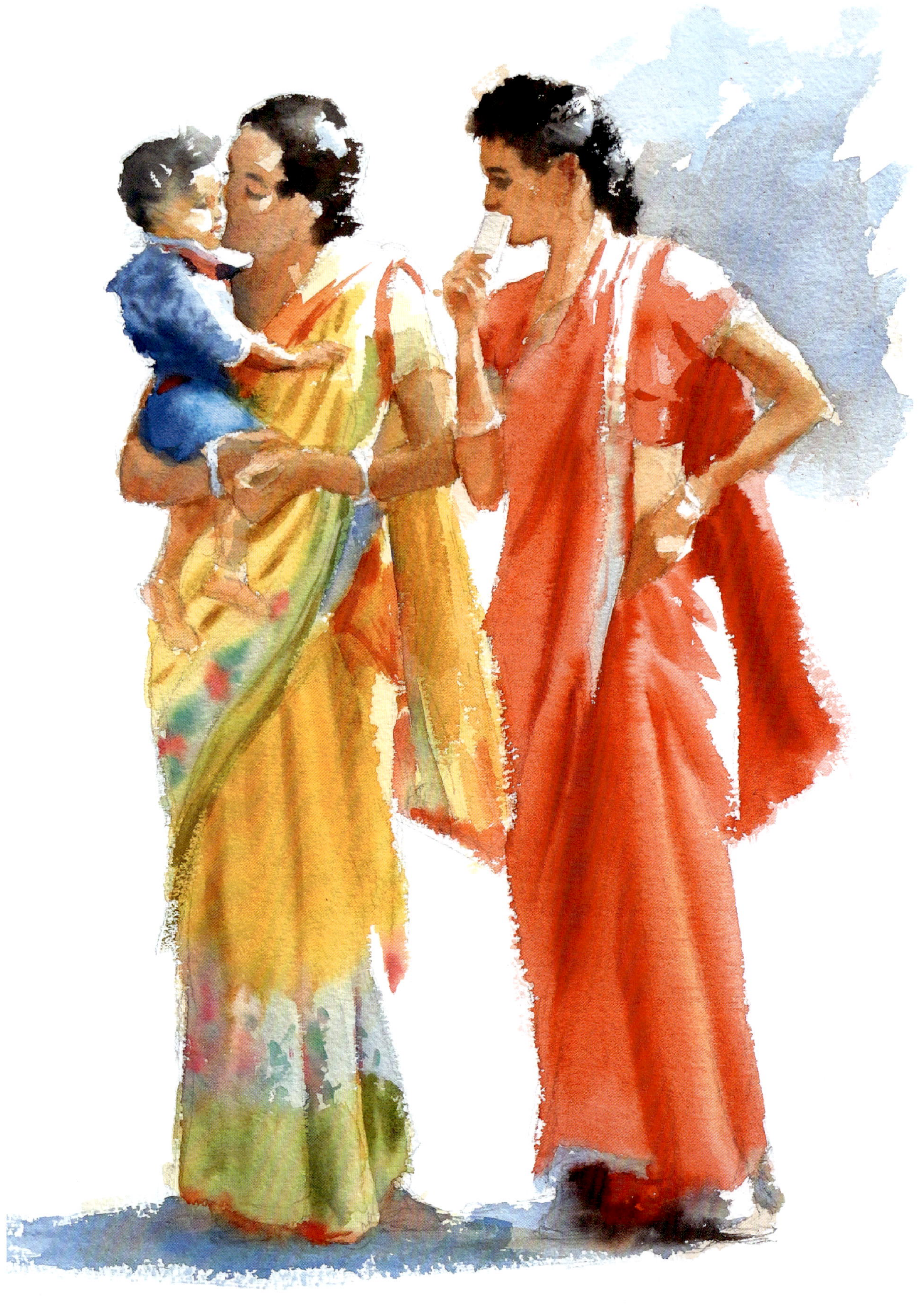

Dull and Muddy Watercolour

Muddy watercolour is a frequent complaint of many an aspiring watercolourist. It manifests when a painting becomes dull or takes on a dull, muddy appearance, leaving the painter wondering why. I alluded to this occurrence in the previous chapter while mentioning multiple layering and the misuse of opaque colours or pushing paint around unnecessarily. A lack of knowledge of the opaque or staining properties of the colours engaged is therefore the main culprit. As you have seen from the previous two chapters, the differing properties of the watercolour pigments affect how watercolour adheres to the paper, presenting both challenges and opportunities.

◀ **Conversation in Red and Yellow,** *51 x 35.5cm (20 x 14in)*

The opacity of Cadmium Red and Yellow Ochre, used here to darken the folds in the saris, could have dulled the colours if layering had been used. Instead, I touched the deeper colour into the wet paint, allowing it to grade the folds within the first layer of paint and thus maintain maximum transparency.

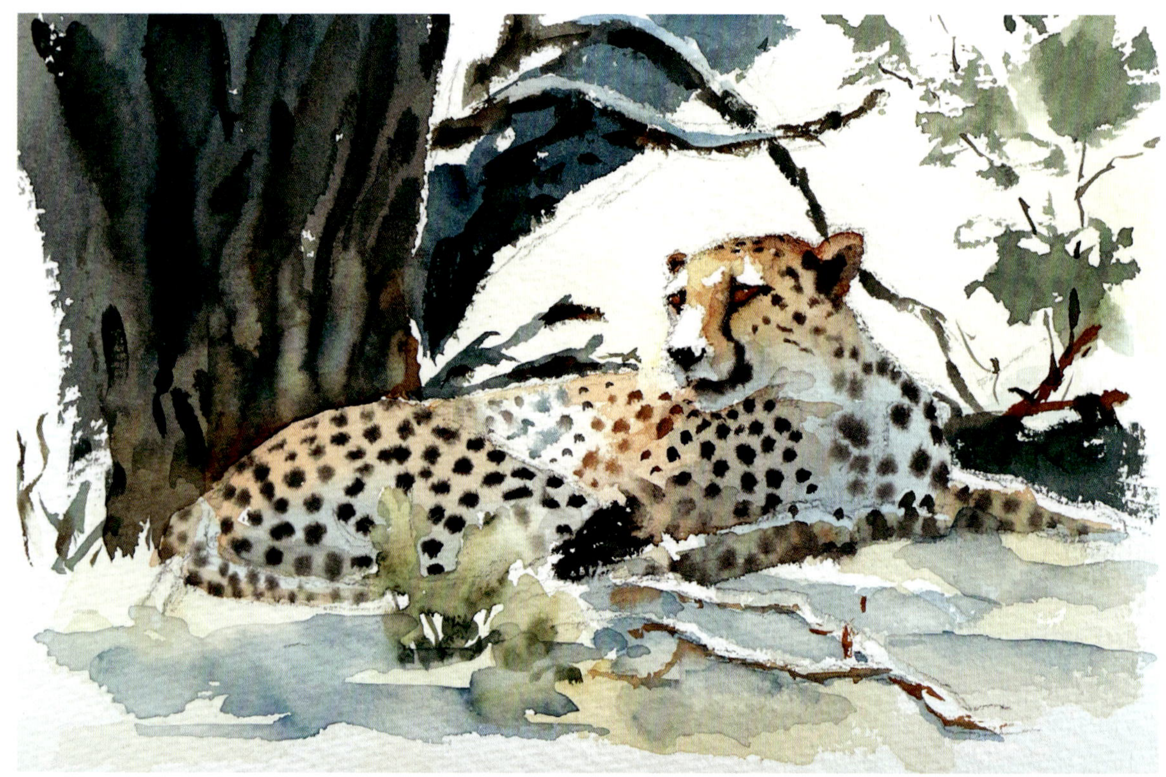

Why Mud Happens

There are several reasons why watercolours take on a muddy appearance. Many relate to colour mixing and using dirty and casual mixes. Other causes are overworking, adding too many brushstrokes or brushmarks, using brushes that are too small, pushing paint around, losing transparency under too many layers, layering opaque colours, or deadening colour by hesitant increments.

Sometimes, muddiness is caused by accidentally shifting non-staining colours when laying subsequent brushstrokes or washes and inadvertently pushing loosened paint into clumps. If working from photographic reference, it may be the failure to see the colour within the shadows by painting them as greys or blacks instead of lively colour-rich shades. Dark mixes, like the bark of the tree above, can easily turn muddy if they are not laid directly and boldly in a minimum of layers. Needless to say, the causes of muddy watercolours are often intertwined.

◀ **In the Shadows,**
18 x 28cm (7 x 11in)
Burnt Umber and Prussian Blue are blended on the palette in a concentrated mix and brushed straight onto the paper with a big brush to paint the trunk of the tree. Not only does this apply the dark colour in a single transparent layer but also allows an attractive irregular edge to the left side of the trunk. Bark texture is added with neater colour before the wash dries, maintaining a single film of paint.

◀ Neutral Grey is an attractive readymade grey, lovely for monochrome, but I would not use it in mixing because it is made from three pigments already (red, yellow and blue), so using it would mean adding too many pigments to a mix. Greys can always be made from the yellow, red and blue already in use in the painting, thus ensuring harmony and vibrant colour by limiting the number of pigments.

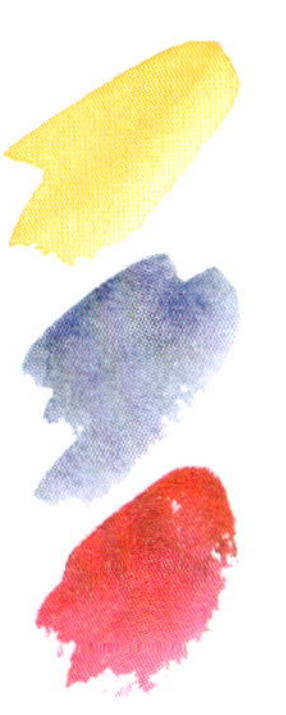

◀ The mixed grey here is a combination of Prussian Blue, Ruby Red and Indian Yellow.

Colour Mixing

Let's begin with colour mixing. The nature of pigment mixing is additive. This means that as you mix or add physical colours together they tend towards darker colouring, as witnessed when all three primary colours, red, yellow and blue, are mixed/added together and make browns, greys and blacks.

For the highest clarity, it is wise to limit your mixes to not more than three pigments: this is always possible, since all the colours can be made from various combinations of yellow, red and blue. Adding more colours/pigments tends to dull the mix.

Manufacturers of watercolour paints try to make as many colours as possible from single pigments so that when artists blend colours together on the palette they are using the minimum number of pigments possible to maintain vibrant mixes.

Some colours, however, have to be made with two or even three pigments combined. This is done to make the particular hue, or to improve permanence or lightfastness; to replicate a traditional colour with a non-toxic replacement; to make readymade secondaries, darks and neutral colours, or simply to introduce interesting colours to the range.

No colour is a problem in itself – there is no such thing as a 'bad' colour – but when it comes to mixing with other colours, or overlapping layers, the multiple pigments and the subsequent tendency towards darkness increases the risk of dulling the mix. Even though a mix may look fine sitting alone in the palette, when it is overlaid or over-layering another colour the risk of dulling the colouring is heightened.

Lay it and Leave it

Watercolour likes to be laid and left to dry without interference or interruption. The pigment particles settle happily on the paper if floated on in a direct fashion, without unnecessary excess brushing or dragging to and fro. Uninterrupted, they will settle in an orderly but random pattern that maximizes their translucency and the attractiveness of their appearance.

For this reason, my main aim in watercolour painting is to keep my pigment happy. This may sound quirky, but it's absolutely true! The pigment does not like to be pushed around or dragged back and forth, and will not reward me for doing so. It is a lively substance that is willing to please if left to do its own thing. It really does know best. The trouble is, we painters enjoy the action of painting: we love wielding the brush, mixing the colours and brushing the paint across the paper - but watercolour is a fluid medium of minimum fuss, where less is usually more. The lowest number of brushstrokes, the fewest colours, minimum layers and the least manipulation makes for a happy watercolour.

▶ **The Price of Gold,**
38 x 28cm (15 x 11in)
Wet into wet blending on the paper enables a variety of tonal values to exist within one layer of paint. Here, the violet sarong, orange coconuts and the black of the bike are all laid in direct mixes, with the darkest tones added wet into wet with no layering.

▼ The advent of carbon colours in the mid-twentieth century was a huge boon in making transparent secondary colours out of single pigments: Transparent Orange (pyrrol), Phthalo Green (phthalocyanine), and Schmincke Violet (dioxazine).

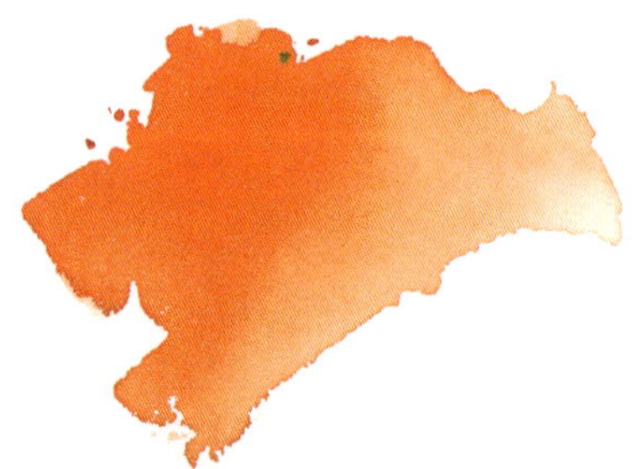

Transparent Orange

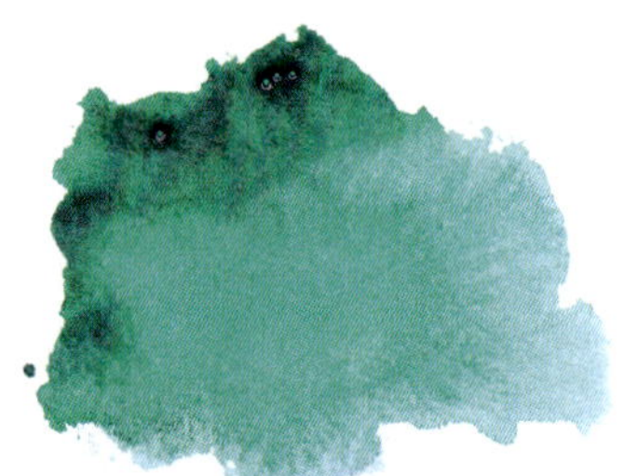

Phthalo Green

Schmincke Violet

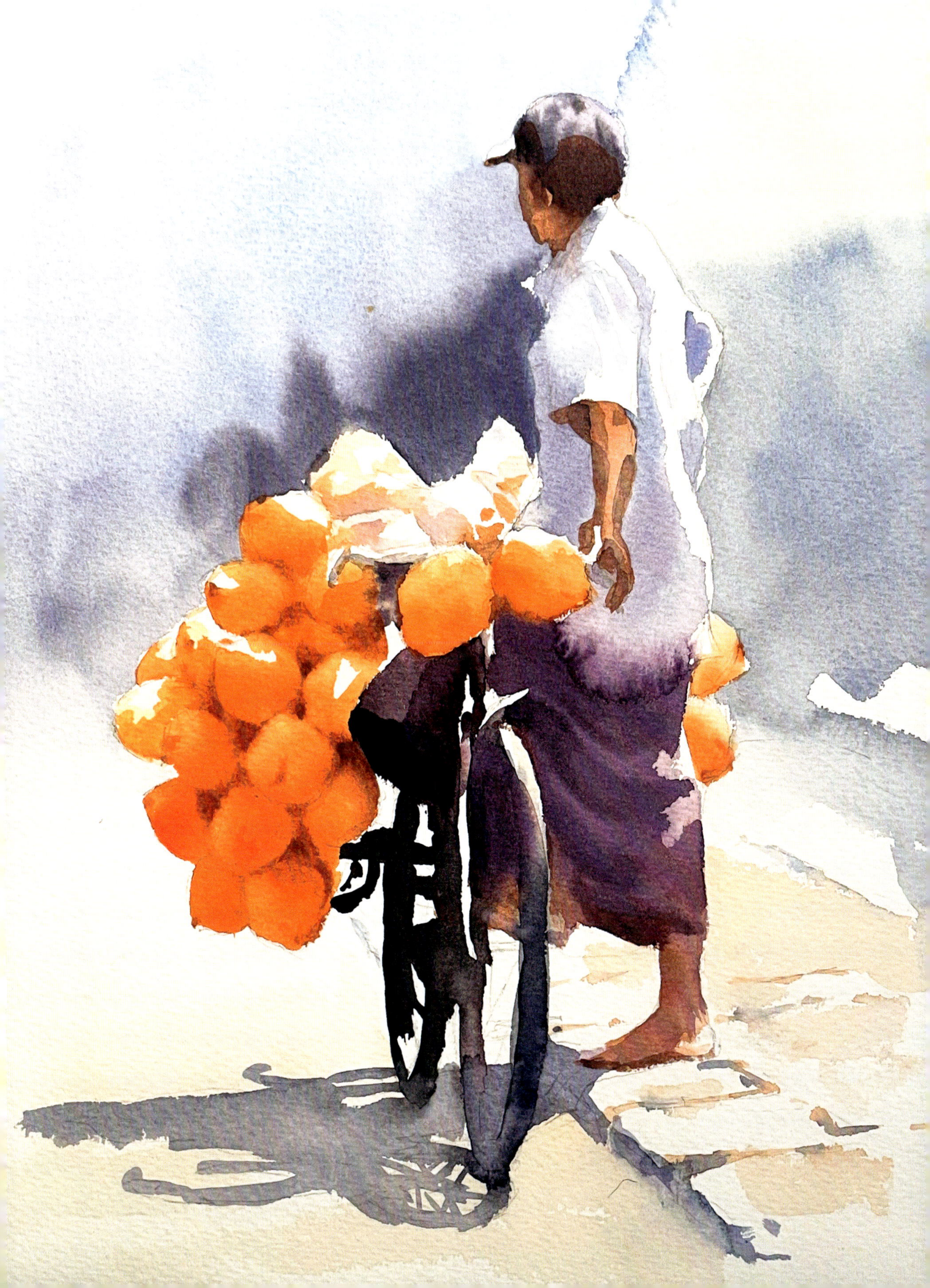

Bigger Brushes

Pigment likes to be laid and left to settle without interference. Muddy and dull colouring is often caused by using too small a brush and delivering the paint with too many small, joined-up or overlapping brushstrokes. It is better to grasp a bigger brush and lay the paint more boldly. My advice is to use the biggest brush possible for the area to be covered. One large brushstroke is, by default, more efficient than several smaller brushstrokes joined together or laid side by side. Not only is it quicker to lay paint with a bigger brush, but it will lay a more even and therefore more attractive stroke or wash. The particles of pigment are delivered in a single load, settling uninterrupted on the paper. They are happy!

The flame-like shape of the round brush and the pointed tip means that any small brushstrokes of the same colour can also be made with the bigger brush.

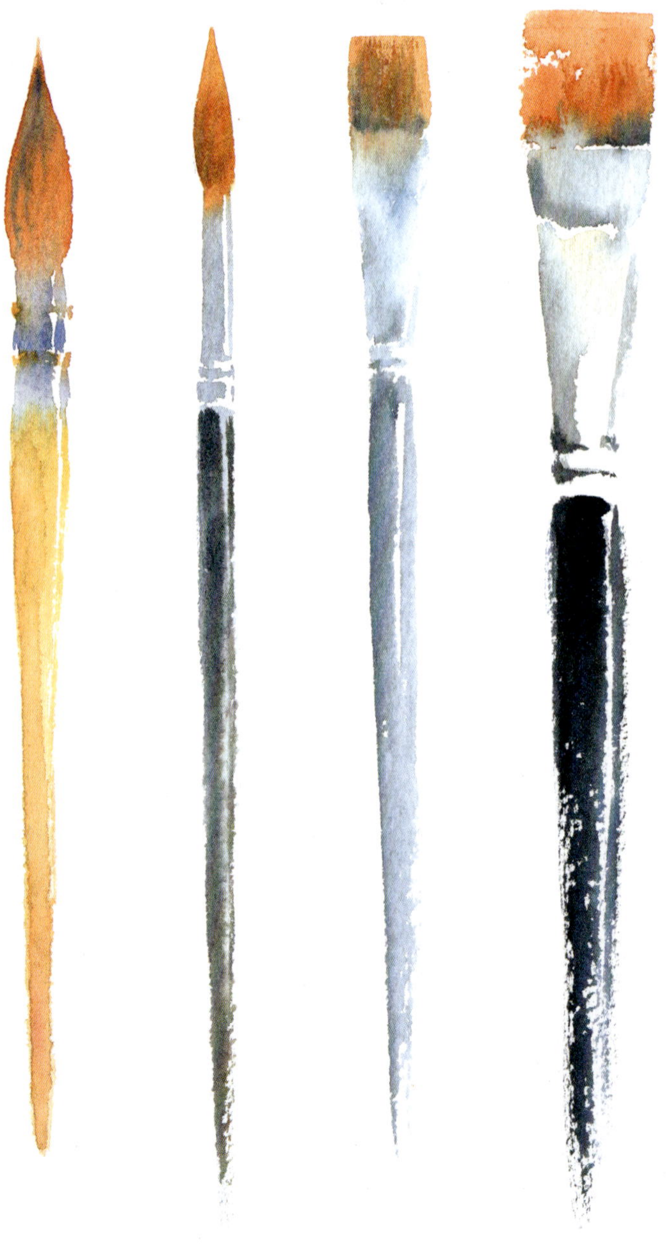

Flat Brushes

A flat brush is an excellent instrument for laying initial washes, as it makes broad, even strokes and prevents the artist from being 'picky' in the early stages. To load a flat brush, push it down to its ferrule to fill the hairs with paint. If the area to be painted is large, and you want to pre-dampen the paper to aid blending, a flat brush also lays a more even film of water than can be delivered with a round brush (unless it is laid on its side to emulate the broad, even stroke of the flat brush).

Handling the Brush

Hold the brush at the widest point of the handle above the ferrule. Lightly grip it between thumb and forefinger, resting it on the index finger, so it can roll loosely within the grip and be angled in any direction on the paper.

Practise loading your brush fully in the palette. Roll and twirl the whole head in the paint mix, angling it sideways to ensure the entire brush-head is filled with paint. There is little point in using a big brush to lessen the frequency of brushstrokes if it is not fully loaded (although there are times when a big brush needs only a small load).

I prefer brushes that are made with natural hair, as they release their load in response to pressure from the hand. They are therefore easier to control when held at any angle than brushes made with smooth nylon filaments down which the watery mix must flow in obedience to gravity. The fine barbs along the strands of natural hair act to hold paint within the brush, releasing it only when the artist exerts pressure. Conversely, they retain paint when pressure is released. This puts the painter firmly in control of delivering the shape of the brushstroke desired and releasing the right amount of paint.

◂ Watercolour brushes are designed to be highly versatile. A round brush or mop, of various sizes from 6 to 14, and a flat brush are all you need.

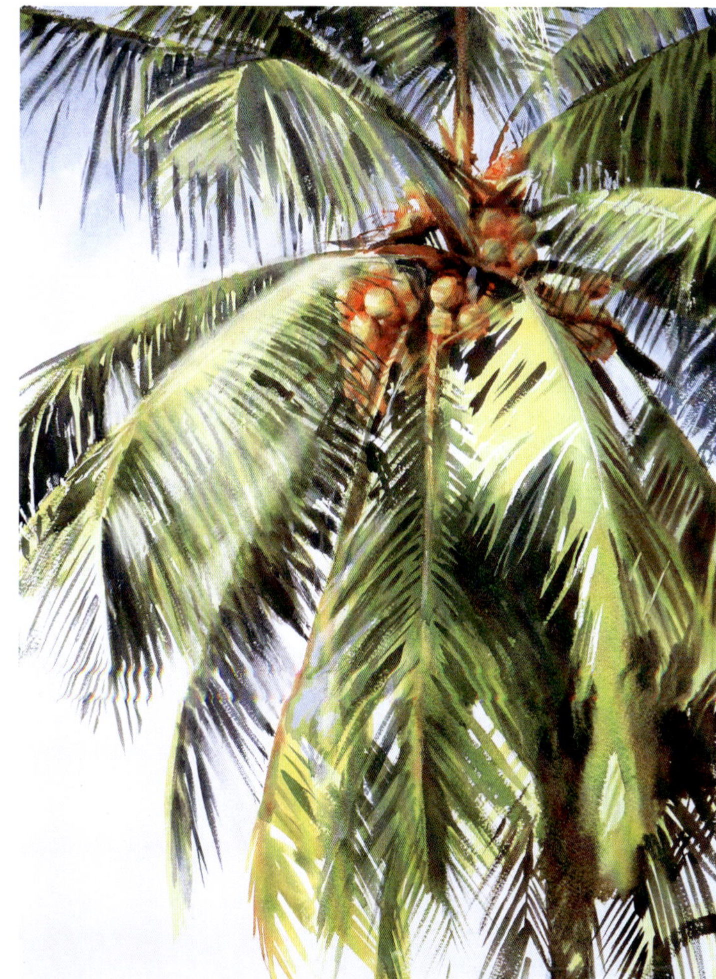

▸ **Palm Tree Homage to Winslow Homer,** *76 x 56cm (30 x 22in)*

The palm fronds are painted with a 19mm flat brush and size 12 and 14 round brushes, using the pointed tips to paint individual fronds or to paint the shaded spaces between them.

Back and Forth

Uneven washes and unwanted lines are often caused by dragging a brushstroke back and forth across the paper. Avoid the temptation to take your loaded brushstroke back and forth multiple times across a painted area. If you can lay the paint in one stroke, use one stroke. If you have missed out patches on the paper, then it's fine to take the brush gently back across to fill in missing parts, but be aware that you risk disturbing the initial lie of the pigment particles settling naturally

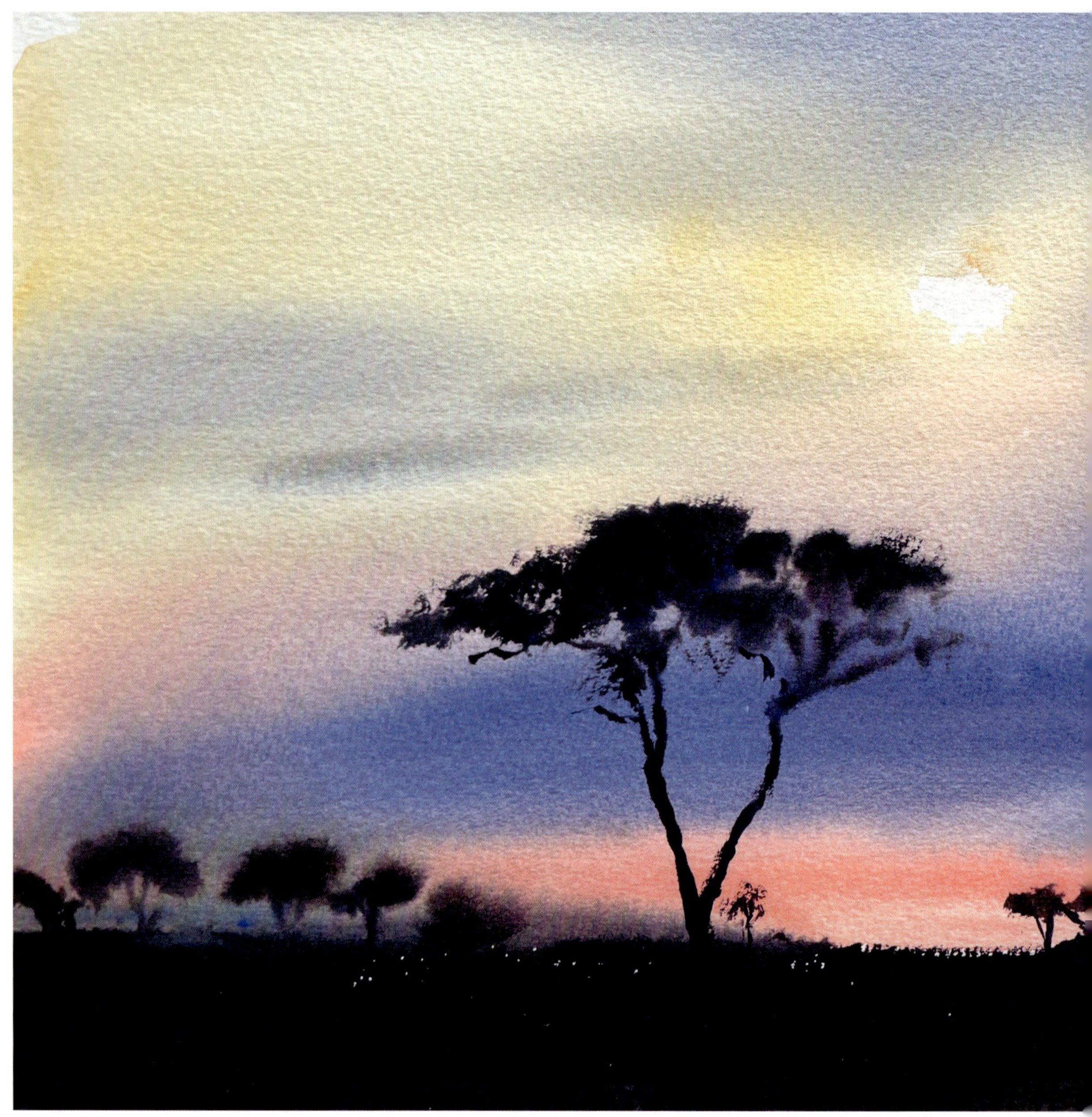

(and happily) upon the paper. If the desired area of cover is laid with the first couple of strokes, leave it well alone, lift your brush off the paper and return to the palette.

To even out a wash it may be necessary to take a brushstroke back across the same area twice, or more. If possible, aim to return the stroke in the same direction to avoid dragging the paint back and forth. Think of the pigment particles being floated across the paper, wanting to settle in an orderly yet random fashion with the least interference. This way you will lay your wash mindfully and can trust the brush to deliver.

Occasionally, repeated and even vigorous brushing is necessary. It is not wrong to coax and manipulate paint into position when required, but if the paint has been laid satisfactorily at first pass, leave it well alone. The pigment is happy! You will not improve the appearance by dragging the brush back across the area. Paint does not like being pushed around; even less so once it is drying.

◀ **The Sum of all Colours,**
28 x 38cm (11 x 15in)

The colours for the sky – Indian Yellow, Alizarin Crimson and Ultramarine Finest – have been brushed in with a minimum of strokes and allowed to blend and settle without interference. Likewise, the silhouettes have been applied with a concentrated mix of all three colours and applied in a single layer.

▶ **Hidden Depths, Ararat, Augrabies Falls, South Africa,**
25.5 x 40.5cm (10 x 16in)

One of the reasons I like painting in hot, arid landscapes is because paint dries quickly. The depths of this canyon are built with overlapping washes. Each must dry before a subsequent wash is laid, especially to retain crisp, clean edges to the cast shadows.

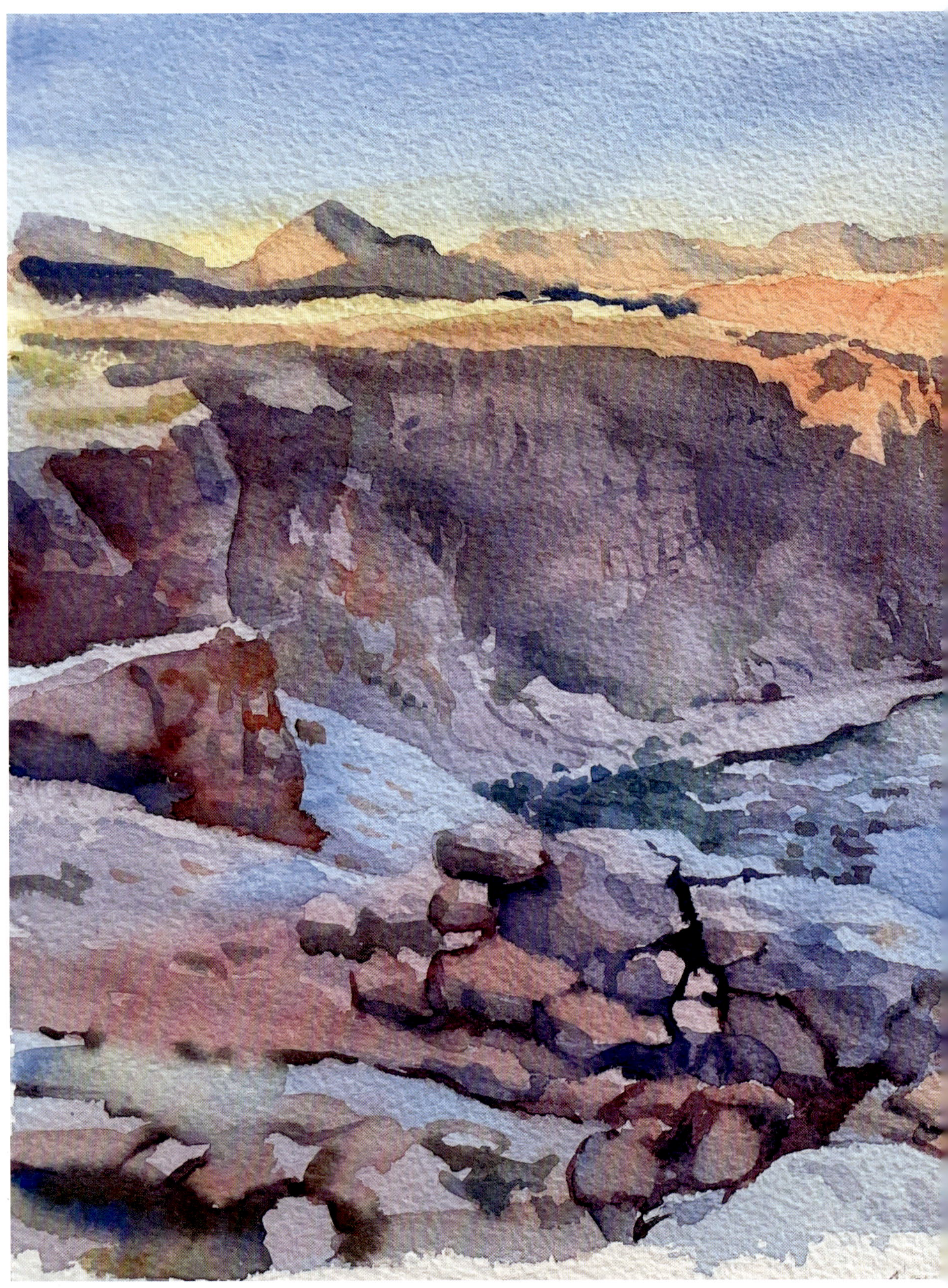

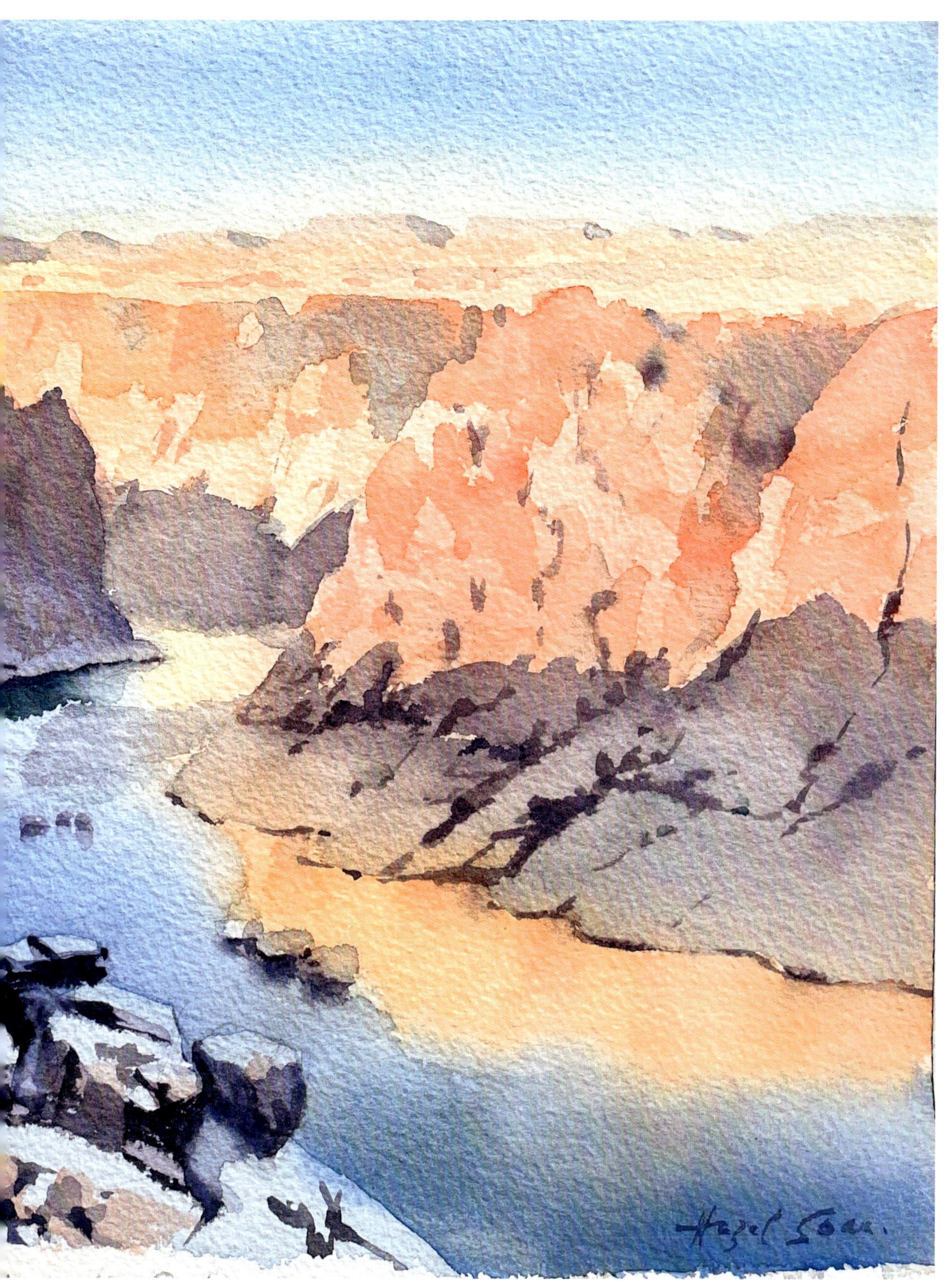
Hazel Soan.

Wait, Let Paint Dry

Interfering with a drying wash and touching it before it is completely dry is the cause of countless ruined watercolours. As soon as you introduce a damp brush, the water content will redistribute the particles of pigment, pushing them outward in an uneven bloom. Unless you are deliberately intending to create a bloom or intentionally adding more concentrated paint, avoid touching a drying wash. Resist the temptation to apply a subsequent layer before the first layer has thoroughly dried. You will inevitably disturb the adherence of the gum arabic while it sets the particles in place.

Evaporation varies constantly, but there are indicators to help assess when the watercolour is fully dry. For example, a very wet wash may cause some buckling or warping of the paper, which flattens out once the paint is dry. Damp paint presents a sheen when held to the light, which disappears when the paint has dried. Even then, one should wait.

I view the paper surface from the side to assess when it has returned to flatness, but even then it may only be surface dry, so I wait a bit longer to be absolutely sure. To disturb a drying wash, or even an almost dry wash, disturbs the attractive natural lie of the pigment particles and damages the lovely appearance. This cannot be undone, so my motto is always wait, then wait some more, and 'if in doubt, chicken out'!

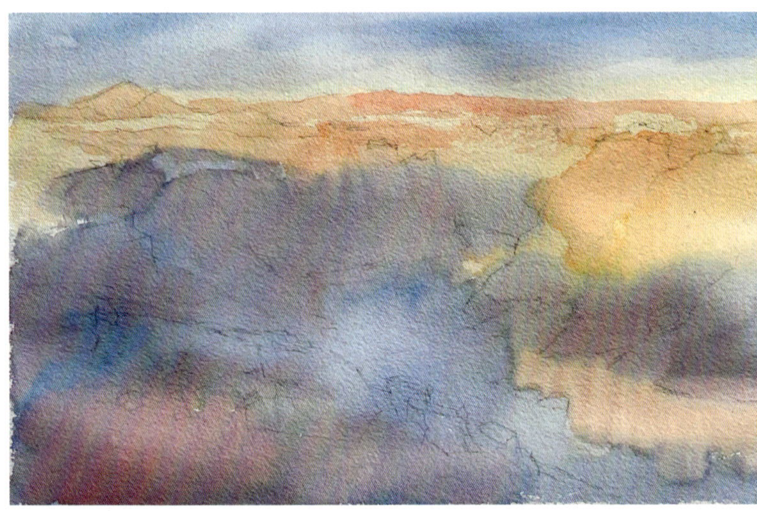

◂ This is the under-wash for the previous painting, showing the buckling of the paper on the sketch block before it had dried. Until it was absolutely flat and bone dry I dared not proceed with painting any more layers to build up the canyon landscape.

◂ Touching a drying sky with a damp brush unsettles the smooth lie of the wash. The particles of blue pigment spread outward to gather at the edge of the bloom. It is better to leave even an unsatisfactory wash alone than to try to fix it while the paint is drying.

Watching Paint Dry

Attending to one's watercolour and watching paint dry is an integral and intriguing part of watercolour painting. You can learn a lot from watching paint move and the resulting effects as water evaporates. In dark or very wet mixes, for example, the paint dries lighter in colour than it appears when wet. By watching it dry and lighten in tone, you will become more confident at mixing a deeper value in the future.

Waiting for paint to dry fully before overpainting is so crucial I cannot emphasize it enough! I know how hard it is to wait. I too am tempted and sometimes succumb, always to my regret. Consequently, I keep my brush occupied by bringing more than one sketchbook while painting *en plein air*. When I cannot resist wielding the brush, I paint a 'secondary' painting on the other pad while I wait for the first painting to dry. Sometimes the second actually turns out better as I learn from the first and am less anxious.

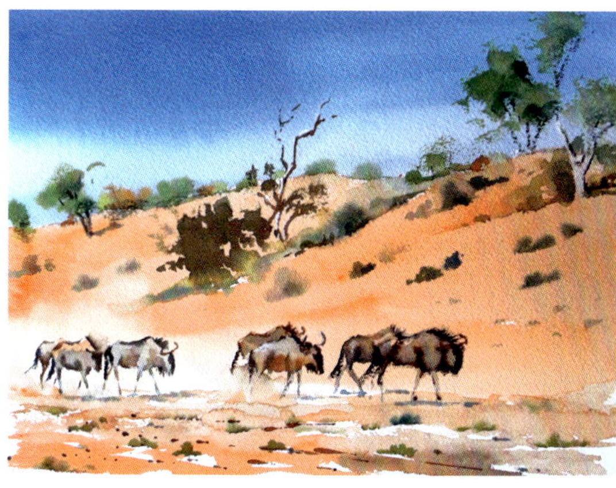

▲ **Lines in the Sand,**
28 x 38cm (11 x 15in)

In this first painting I used Ultramarine Finest, Light Red and Indian Yellow, a combination I have used often to paint the fascinating lines of wildebeest as they head to a waterhole, backed by red dunes punctuated with dull green shrubs.

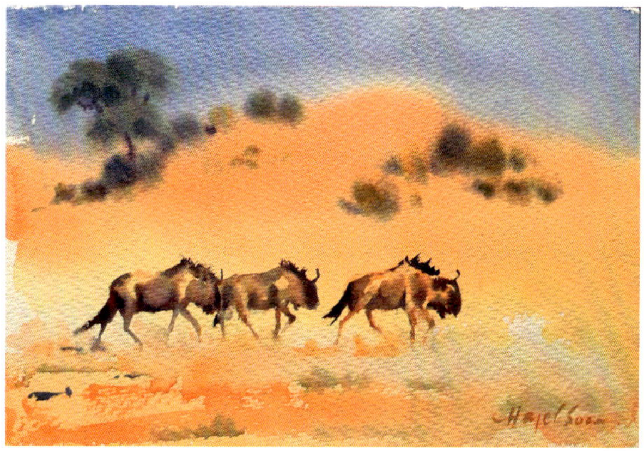

▲ Painting a second study of the same scene emboldened me to experiment with a combination of opaque colours I would not normally mix for the Kalahari dunes: Cobalt Blue, Cadmium Yellow and Cadmium Red. All three mixed together to make pleasing browns and blacks for the passing wildebeest.

Painting Wet into Wet

The need for patience with drying holds true for layering and overlap, but colours can be blended on the paper while they are still wet. The colours disperse attractively on the paper as the pigment particles mingle and a gentle grading of tonal values occurs. With wet into wet techniques, speed and readiness are necessary. Painting moving subjects, like the wildlife on these pages, allows little time for drying, so the wet into wet technique is ideal. It enables a lot of information to be included within a single layer, and transparency is optimized at the same time.

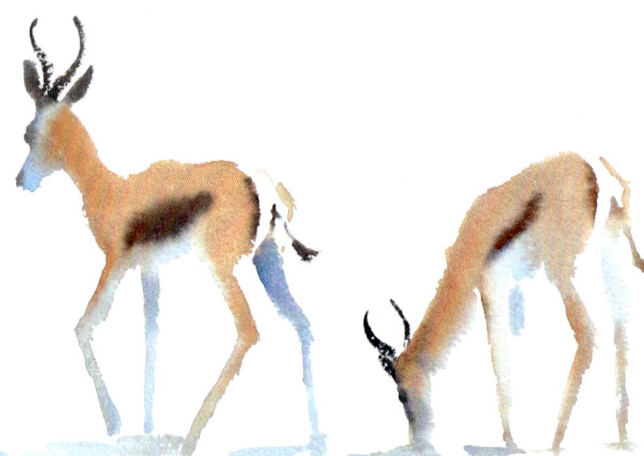

◄ The overall shapes of the springbok are painted with a dilute wash of Ultramarine into which Burnt Sienna is touched wet into wet. The stripe is added with drier colour and bleeds slightly into the wet paint.

▲ The crisp-edged highlights on the jackal have to be left out of the wet into wet blend as there is no time for even a pale under-wash to dry.

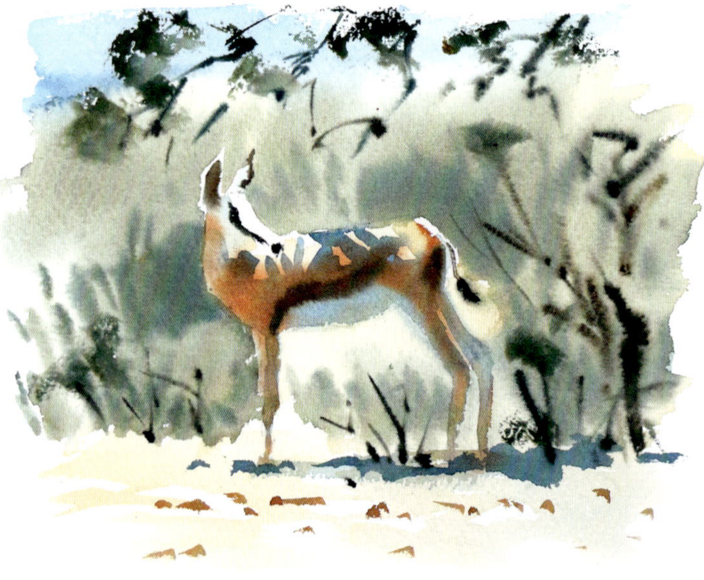

◄ Including a background setting requires the painted contours of the springbok to be dry, but the grasses and foliage can be added wet into wet with a rigger and almost dry paint.

Maintaining Transparency

Watercolour relies on light bouncing back from the paper, so the fewer layers the more translucent the watercolour will remain. One of the surest ways to avoid muddy colouring is to lay the required tint, tone or shade of a colour as early as possible. The establishing first layer is often dilute, presenting little compromise to transparency. However, every layer, stroke and mark matters from then on, so the more directly you can lay the required values for the mid- and dark tones, the fewer layers you will need and the fresher your watercolour will appear.

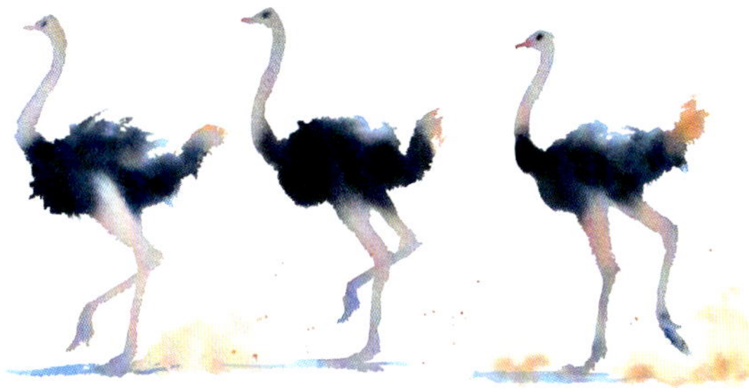

▲ The shape of each ostrich is painted with a pale wash in the colour of the neck and legs and the black of the feathers dropped in while this is still wet to maximize translucency through this dark colour.

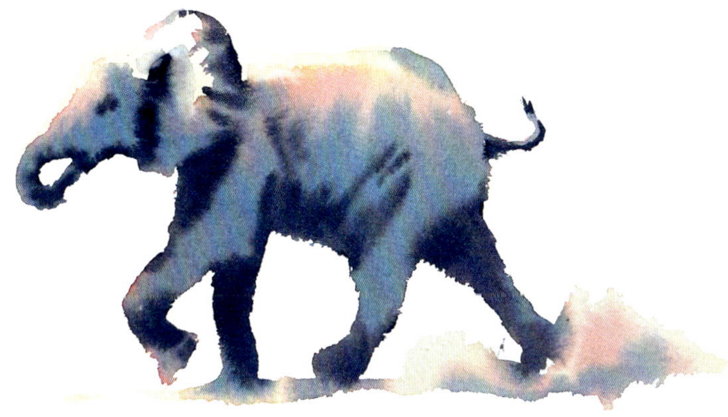

▶ A vibrant grey is the result of blending Yellow Ochre, Alizarin Crimson and Prussian Blue wet into wet on the paper, perfect for this baby elephant.

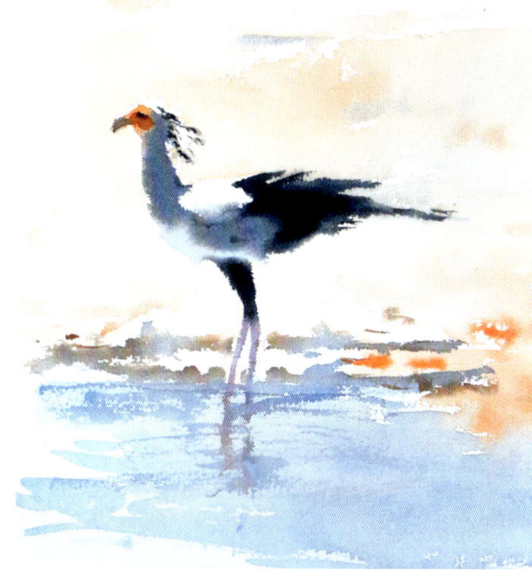

▲ There is no problem with the background sand colour being added before the black of the feathers had fully dried, as the resulting bleed contributes to the feathery texture.

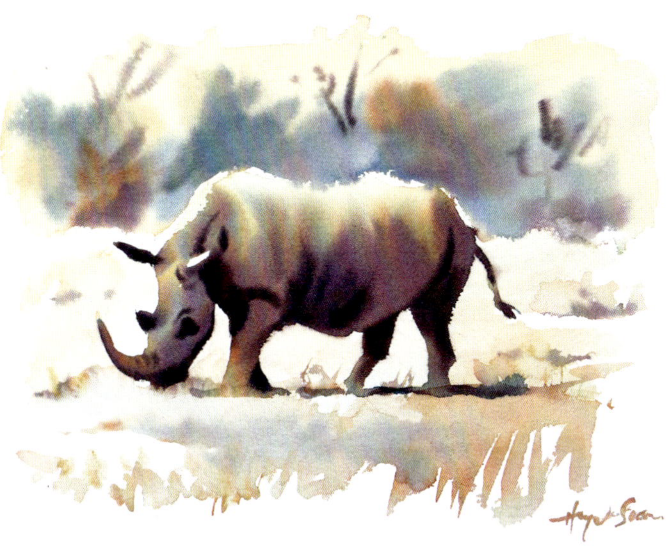

▶ Leaving a sliver of white paper for a highlight along the back of the rhino enables the background to be painted without having to wait for the colour on the rhino to dry.

Unintended Bleed

Wet into wet techniques bring their own challenges. Brushing colours in before other patches are dry comes with the chance of unintended bleeds or an uncontrolled spread. Trying to mitigate this can be another cause of dulling watercolour.

The temptation is to dab the unwanted spread with a rag or kitchen towel, which may work on very light tints but on mid- and darker tones usually creates a dull, unattractive mark and dulled appearance to the remaining paint because excess pigment particles have been lifted in an unnatural way. It is better practice to use a brush to move or remove paint. The brush should be slightly damp – enough to make a point but with no water in the hairs. Lift the stray colour with the tip or side of the brush or even push it gently back to where it came from. This might take several turns, but the appearance is more sympathetic to the natural lie of the pigment particles. If the colour is non-staining (see page 44), the excess bleed can also be lifted off when the paint is dry.

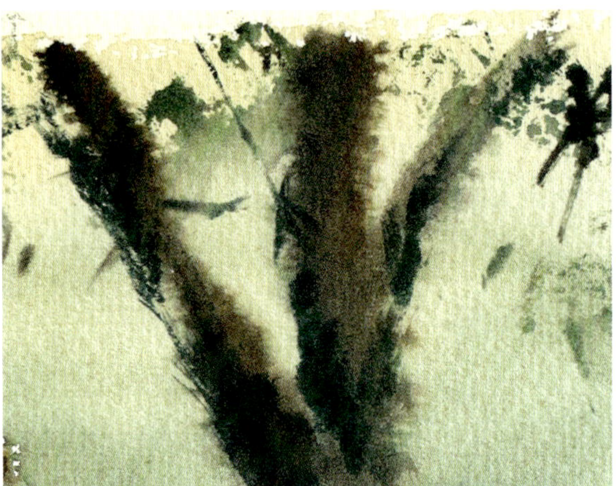

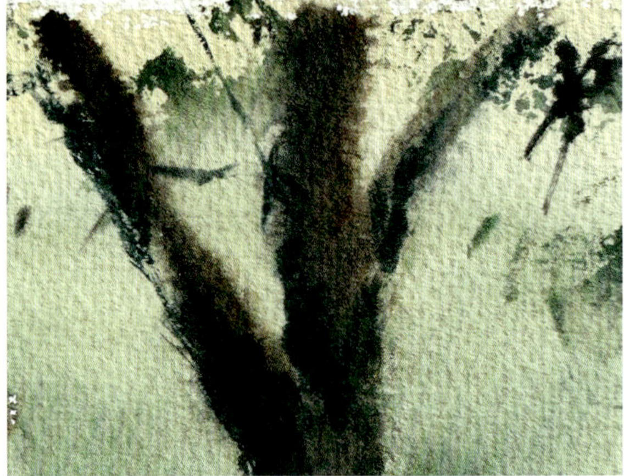

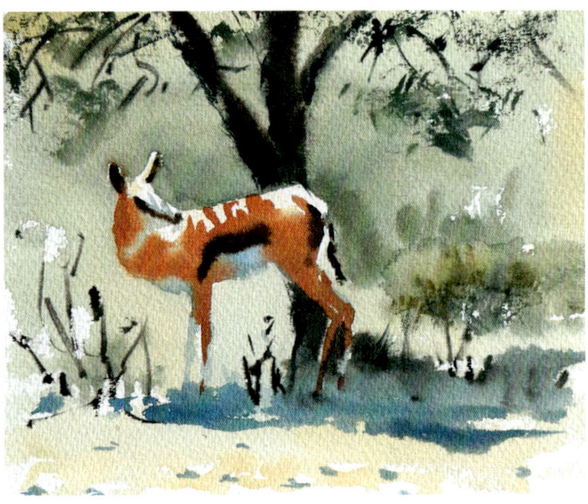

▲ These tree branches were added into the background before it was dry enough. This caused a slight bleed of the dark colour into the pale green wash, which lost the crisp edge I was seeking. Because Ultramarine and Burnt Umber are non-staining, I was able to lift the pigment with the tip of a clean damp brush when the painting was dry.

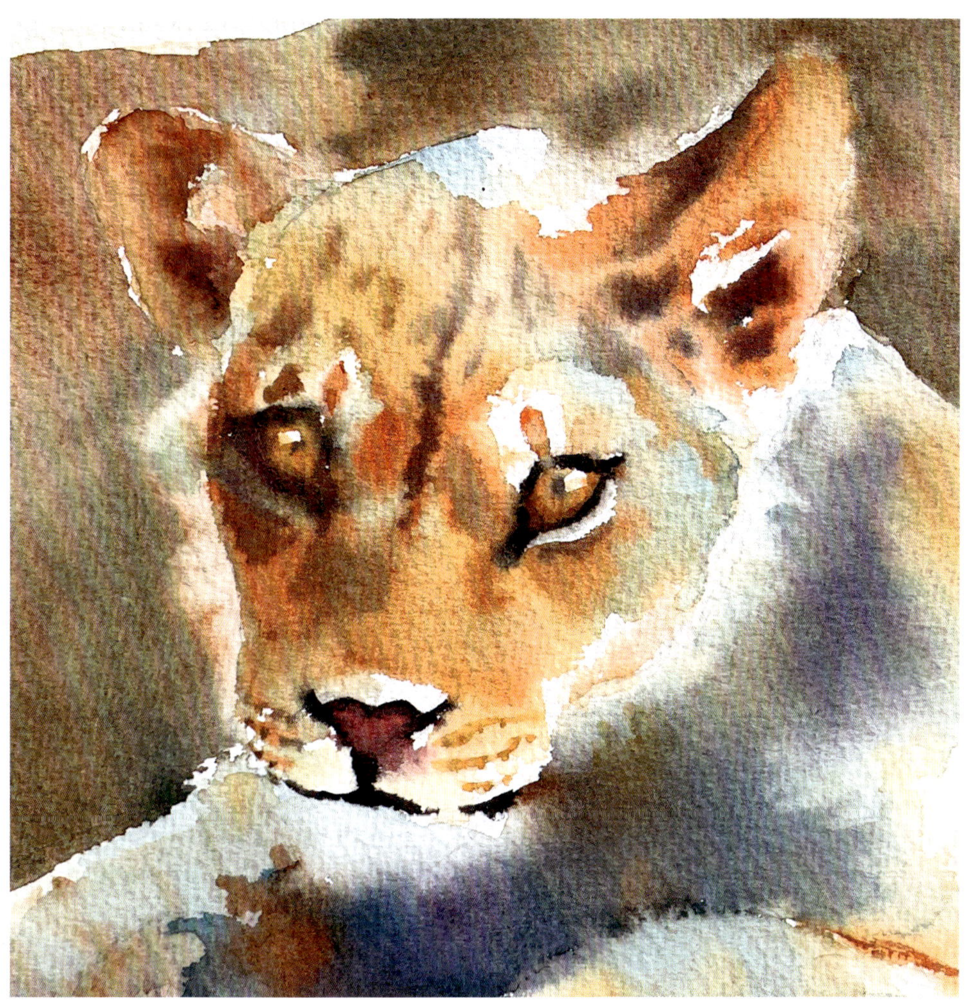

Push Back

Since added colour always spreads outward when it is touched into a damp area, a touch or drop of clear water from a brush can also be used to encourage unwanted pigment to reverse direction and return it to where it came from. If it does not go exactly as planned first off, use the water in a push-me-pull-you effect from either side, letting the flow do the work of moving the pigment particles back and forth until they are repositioned where you want them. The resulting appearance looks more natural than if you pat the area to remove the wayward paint.

▲ A small amount of clean water has been touched in with a size 8 brush around either side of the face and below the mouth. This 'pushes' the paint back to lighten the halo effect created by the soft down on the young lion cub's cheeks and chin.

Grubby Palette?

Muddy colouring may be caused by mixing colours on a dirty palette or mixing casually, carelessly adding colours into unknown blends already in the well. It is vital to clean the mixing area of the palette regularly as residual dried paint can mix unintentionally into fresh colours and compromise the clarity of the mix.

Vibrant watercolour requires clean water and a clean and controlled palette. I am a stickler for cleaning my palette and am also careful to mix new colours on a clean area of the palette, or into a known mix, so that I know exactly what pigment blend I am about to lay on the paper. I do not need a huge amount of palette space, even to make quite large watercolours, and with quality paint it is rarely necessary to squeeze out vast amounts of colour or prepare huge pools in a well. In a regular working palette the pans will yield their colours quickly once activated with water, making colour lift a quick and efficient process when a mix needs replenishing.

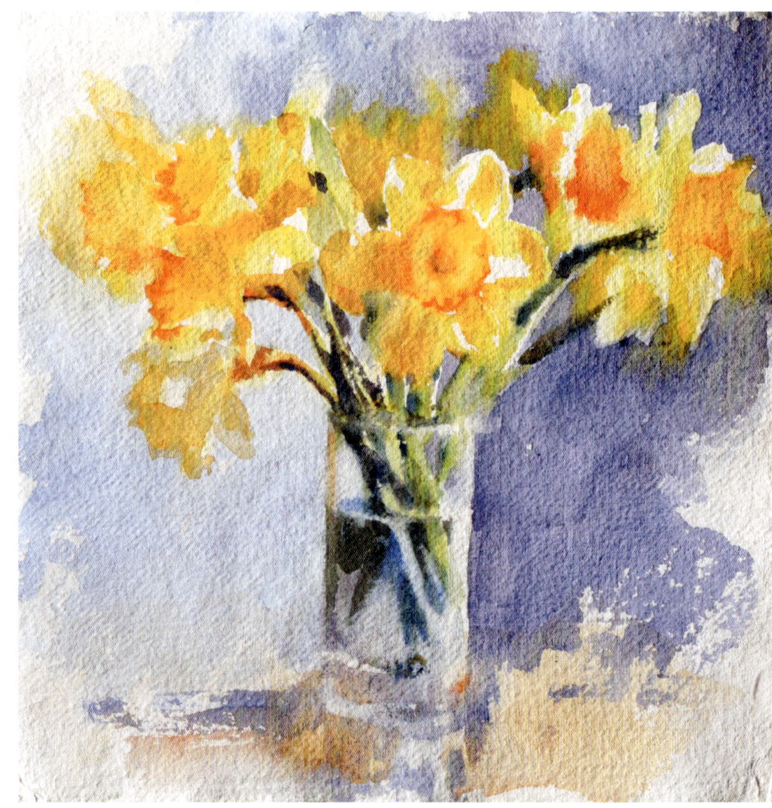

▸ The daffodil yellows started in very light tones of cool Aureolin and warm Indian Yellow, gradually deepening into Yellow Ochre and Orange. There was no need to rinse out the pale yellow tints from my brush, but it was necessary to clean the brush before applying the Yellow Ochre.

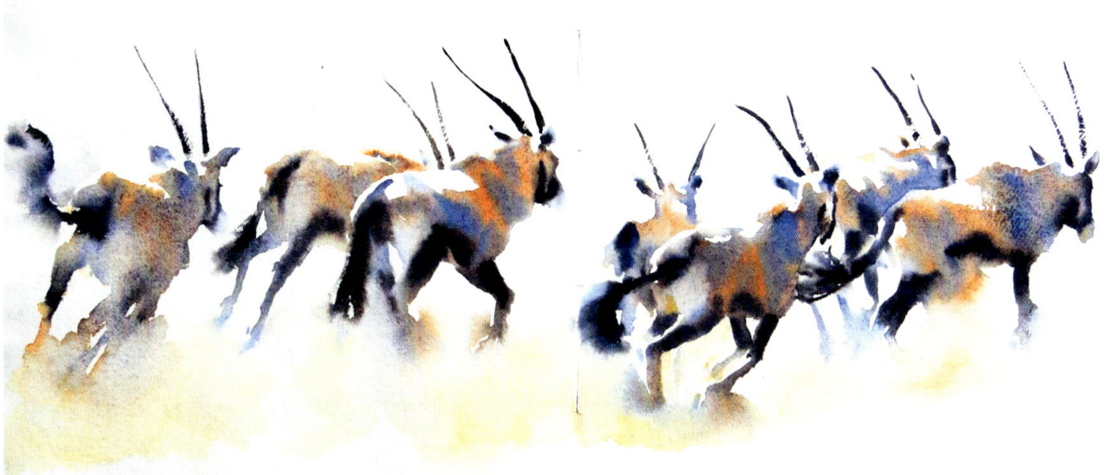

Clean Tools

Rinse brushes thoroughly – dirty brushes carry leftover pigments that contaminate clean colours. If traces of a complementary colour remain in the brush, even the tiniest amount will dull its opposite. Indiscriminate rinsing can also bring problems, so only rinse the brush when the contents within it will compromise the next colour. If a colour can safely be added to the subsequent mix there may be no need to rinse out (or waste) the pigment from the previous brushstroke. Unnecessary rinsing risks loading too much water into the brush and may make the next stroke too wet. For example, if I am painting with a procession of earth colours, as they are all made with the same pigment, I may not rinse the brush out before I load the next earth colour.

▲ **Thunder of Hooves,**
30.5 x 73.5cm (12 x 29in)
Most watercolours are built from light to dark: here, the light and mid tones of the antelopes' bodies are painted first and the black markings added last, so the rinsing pot only got really grubby at the end.

Dirty Water

Dull watercolour can also be due to using dirty rinsing water, although I know of brilliant professional watercolourists who manage to use quite dirty water to paint shimmering watercolours, or mix on what looks like a dirty palette, and still produce magical results. This does not work for me. I recommend three clear water pots (so you can see the state of the water clearly), small in size if managing a limited supply. Aim to keep one pot completely clean throughout the painting, and refresh it if it becomes contaminated. This ensures there is always the means to apply a clean clear glaze or tint right up to the end of the painting. Of the other pots, one is used for full rinsing, and becomes dark and dirty, especially with opaque colours and dark tones, so the brush is rinsed again in the second pot.

Too Many Layers

Brushing wet paint in an overlapping layer over thoroughly dry paint allows for clear distinct layers and avoids the muddy or dull watercolour that occurs if the under-layers are disturbed before they are completely dry. However, sometimes, even though all layering has been painted onto fully dried paint, dullness still develops. This can be caused by applying too many layers, or layers that do not make a significant enough difference to justify being added.

Watercolour is a transparent medium, and the overall colouring is achieved from both the mixed colours and the overlap of the layers that creates new colours. If too many layers, however dilute, are applied, the effect is to compromise the ability of light to pass back to the viewer from the white paper and to darken colouring through the mixing of pigments. If some of the many layers include opaque colours (see page 32–33), the light is restricted further.

Given this propensity, it is safer to use transparent colours for glazing and to build depth, and to limit the number of layers and colours. This is not to suggest you avoid the opaque colours, as they are needed for their brilliance, covering power and immediate punch, but they are best avoided when building depth and form through layering as they will quickly obscure light.

▶ **Tilting at Windmills, Santorini,**
38 x 28cm (15 x 11in)

This demonstration was built up with overlapping panels of blues, greys and dark greens. By keeping the number of colours to three (Phthalo Blue, Indian Yellow and Transparent Sienna), and each mix clean, the risk of dull greys has been averted.

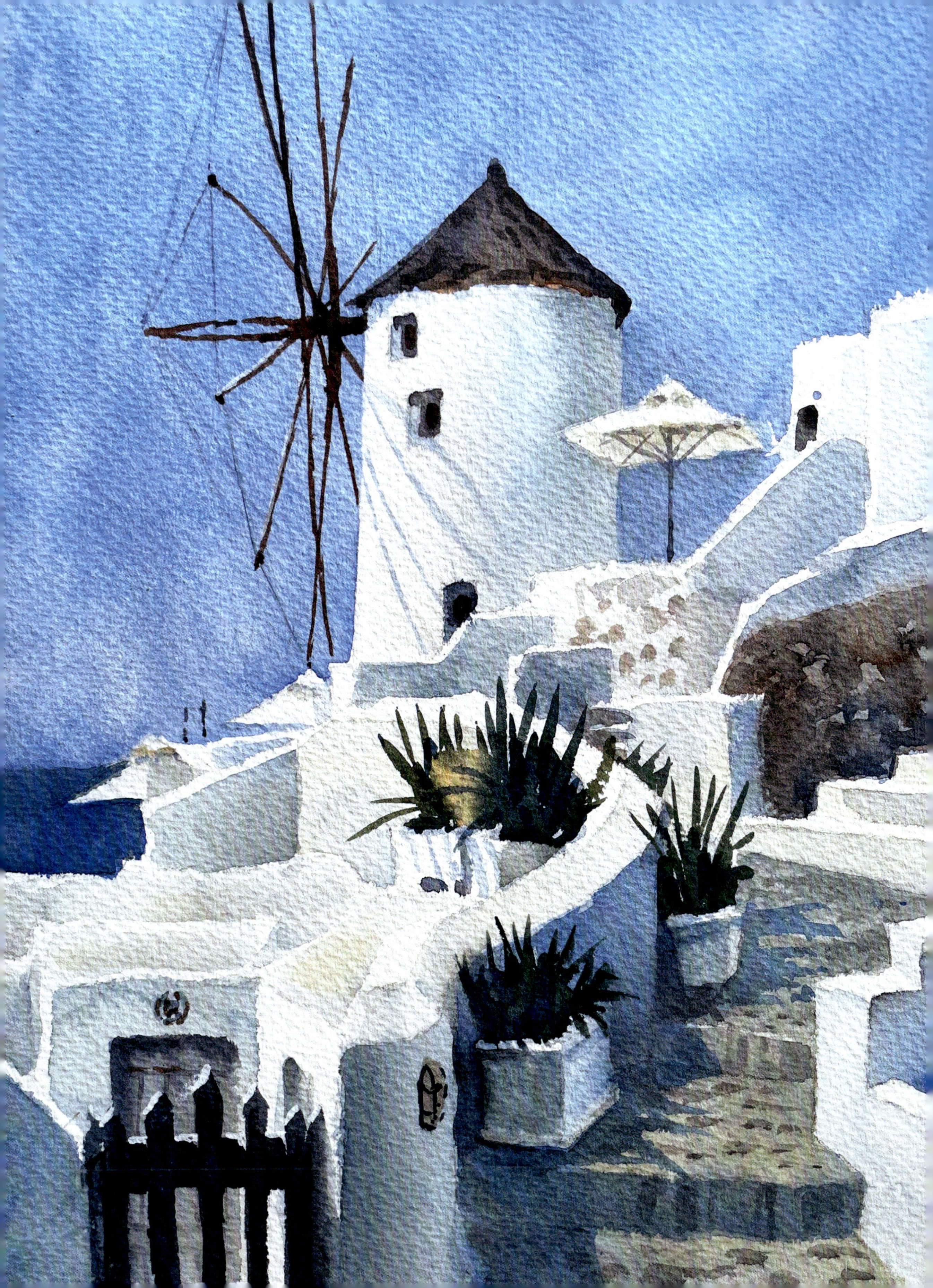

Afraid of the Dark?

Watercolours love contrast, whether blatant or subtle; contrast excites the eye and adds dynamism to the composition. Rich, dark colours and shades can make watercolours look really strong and vibrant. However, dark tones can be scary to apply and can cause consternation. The consequent hesitation results in an attempt to deepen the dark colour incrementally, making a dull, lifeless dark tone that lacks transparency from too many layers being applied, and lacks verve because it is laboured.

Instead, be brazen, be bold! Mix and lay strong darks with more immediacy, straight off the mark. Let them dry before judging their depth of tone. Then, if you do decide they look too dark, you can always lift off some of the pigment to gently lighten the tone. Strong concentrated colour on the paper behaves like paint in dry pans: the top level of pigment particles can be lifted off to a greater or lesser extent with a clean damp brush, sponge or cloth. Apply gentle pressure. Adding the water breaks down the dried gum arabic, releasing the pigment particles exactly as it does from the paint in the palette. Even staining colours give up their darkest hue when painted neat on paper, as the rich concentrated paint sits on top of the underlying stain.

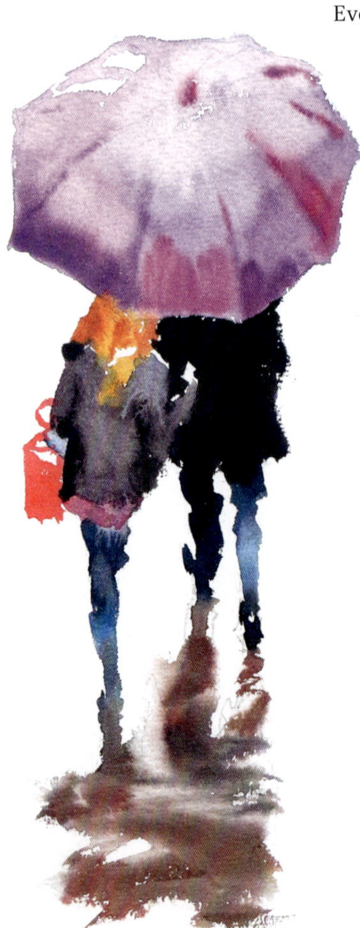

◄ **Duo (Figures in the Rain),**
28 x 15cm (11 x 6in)

The man's body beneath the umbrella is painted first with a pale guiding shape of Indigo. Then the deep black of the coat and left leg is added immediately with neat Indigo, wet into wet, to ensure a clean, vibrant black.

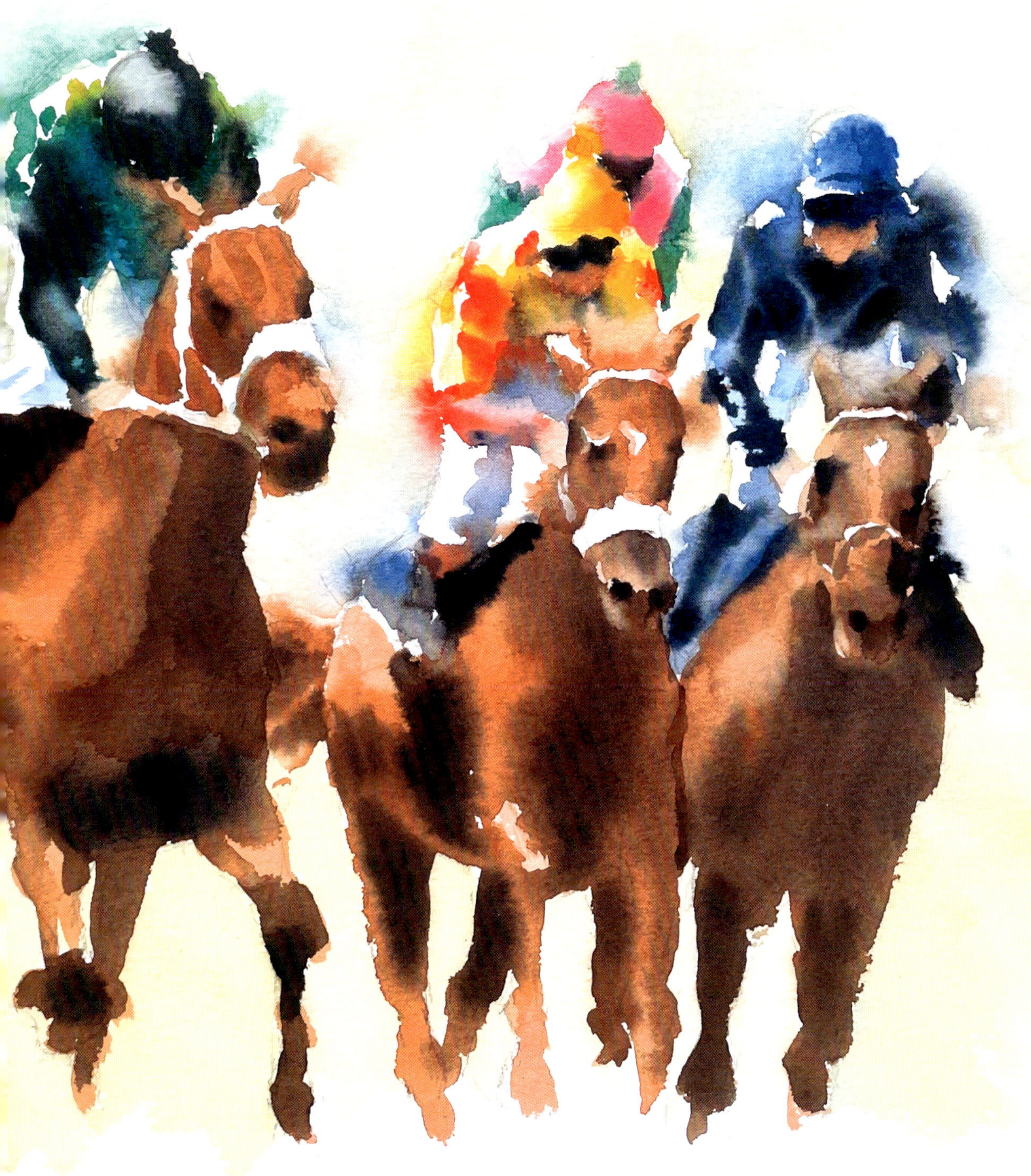

▲ **Racing Colours,** *35.5 x 35.5cm (14 x 14in)*

Ultramarine Blue and Transparent Sienna are combined to make the rich deep brown for the horses' chests. Added into the local hue of lighter brown (pure Transparent Sienna) painted over the horses' hides, the deep brown blends in a single wet layer, maximizing the liveliness of contrasting tones.

Overworking

When watercolourists talk about 'overworking', they usually mean they have 'worsened' a painting that looked better earlier or dulled a painting that was initially more vibrant. Instead of improving the watercolour as they hoped, by adding more brushmarks, extra detail or more layers, they have sacrificed some of the freshness previously present without any beneficial effect. A sense of regret is the usual result.

Watercolours tend to be painted up close, and few of us can see our own paintings with a fresh eye to know what our painting really looks like to others, so we find it hard to judge when to stop.

The solution is to pause as soon as you have covered the paper with sufficient information to represent your subject and as soon as you find yourself in any doubt as to how to proceed. There is little point pausing before this, as you need overall cover of the white paper to be able to judge effectively.

Use the hiatus as a breather. Step back and look at your painting from a short distance, between six and ten feet. I often use my gut as the judge. If you 'feel' something works, even if it is not finished as you intended, it may be better to leave that part alone. Note what pleases you and avoid messing with it.

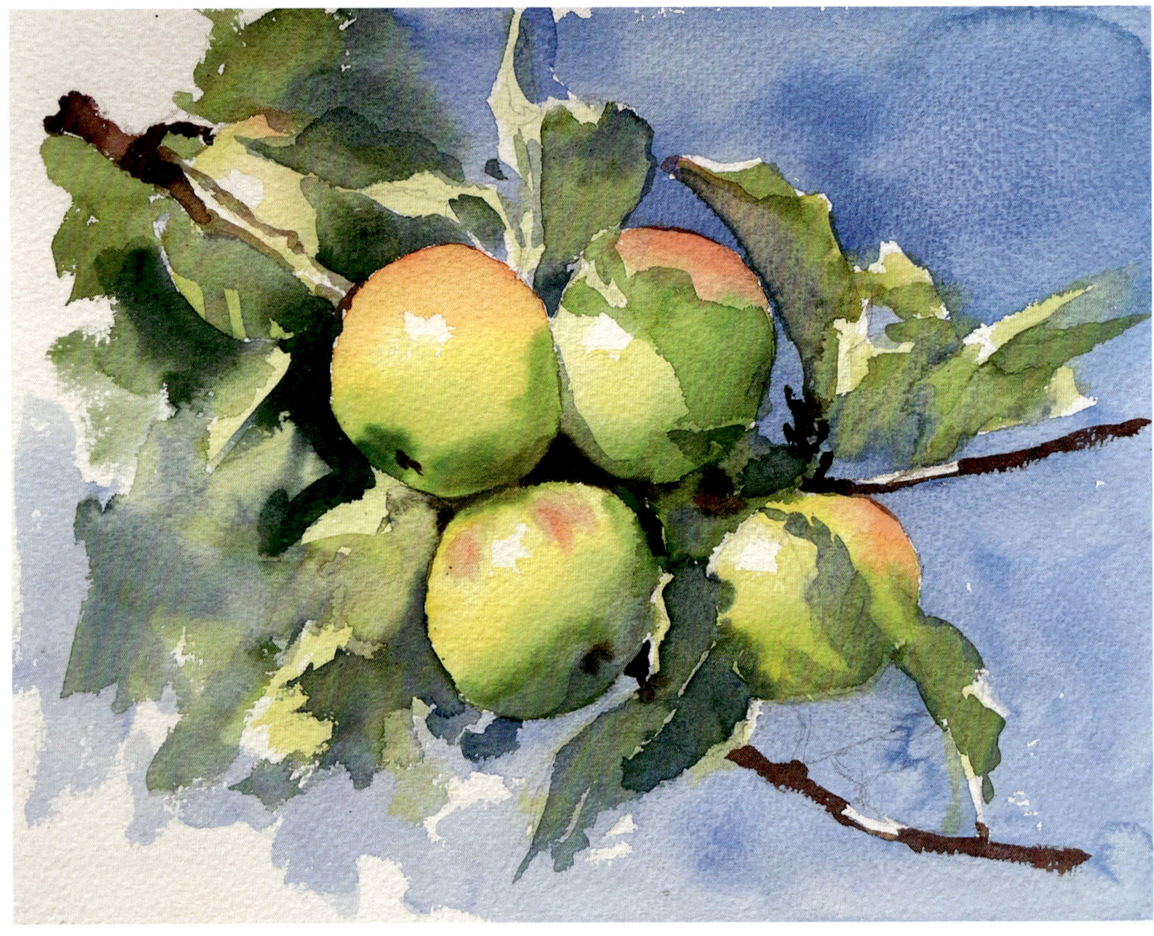

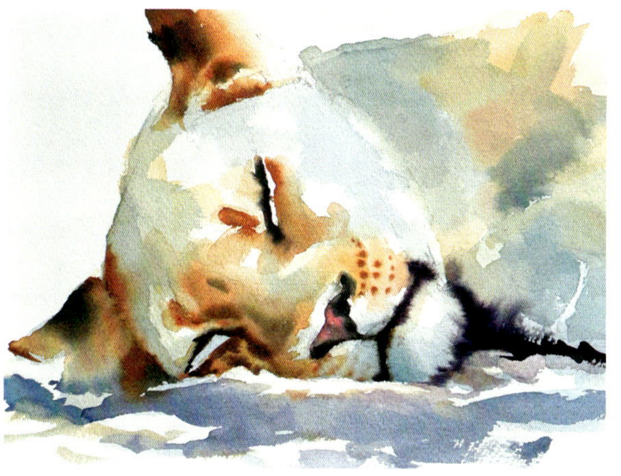

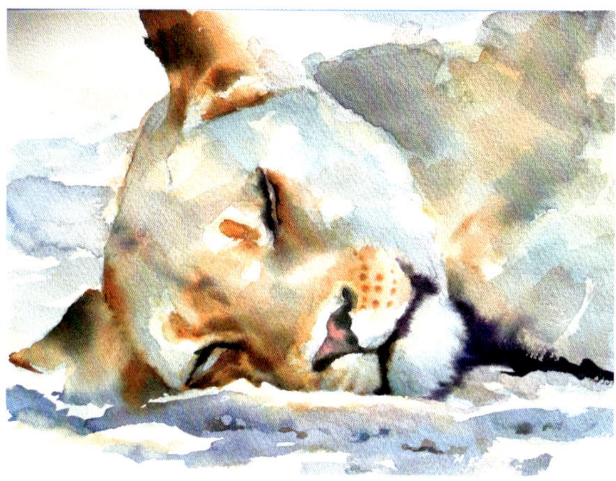

Stop before the painting looks overdone – adding layer after layer can cause the paper to saturate with pigment, dulling vibrancy and blocking light.

A Fresh Eye

Tonal and compositional imbalance stand out more clearly from a distance. You can also use a smartphone, photographing the painting and viewing it in the small format. Turning the image into black and white will immediately offer you a fresh eye: the pattern of tonal values is easier to assess when viewed in monochrome.

If you have a mirror to hand, show the picture to the mirror and view it in reverse: this enables you to see the painting afresh for a couple of minutes before recognition creeps back in and impairs judgement.

None of these aids will guarantee success, but by moving away from proximity to your painting you do two things: you break the temptation to keep on adding brushstrokes in the hope they will 'work the magic', and you create the opportunity to judge your painting as if seen for the first time. Be prepared to like your own painting!

◂ These apples were painted for an online workshop demonstration of wet into wet technique. Not only did lack of time prevent me taking them any further, but I could see on the screen that they looked round, fresh and appetizing, so I was happy to stop!

▴ Such is the nature of this exquisite medium that watercolours can be called finished at any time. Even though I went on to add deeper tones and more form to this painting of a sleeping lioness, I would have been just as happy to leave it in the less finished state shown on the left. I am still not sure which version I prefer!

Unintended Shift

Some of the most frequently used colours in landscape painting are Ultramarine Blue, French Ultramarine, Burnt Sienna, Raw Sienna, Raw Umber, Burnt Umber, Cobalt Blue and Cerulean Blue. These colours are all relatively non-staining and can be lifted off the paper to differing degrees. Some of them are also granulating. This is very useful for manipulation in grading and adjusting tonal values, but if subsequent layers of paint are laid too wet or with too vigorous a brushstroke, the gum arabic may be reactivated inadvertently and settled colour is loosened and shifted by mistake. The loosened pigment is then picked up in the hairs of the brush and dragged to a new position, or mixes with the new colour being applied. This is the perfect recipe for making mud. Not only have the particles of pigment been lifted and the wash disturbed, they now intermingle with other pigment particles they were not intended to meet. Landing where the brush has dragged them or excess water has forced them to gather, they dry in the wrong place and settle in unnatural clumps. This is indeed unhappy pigment!

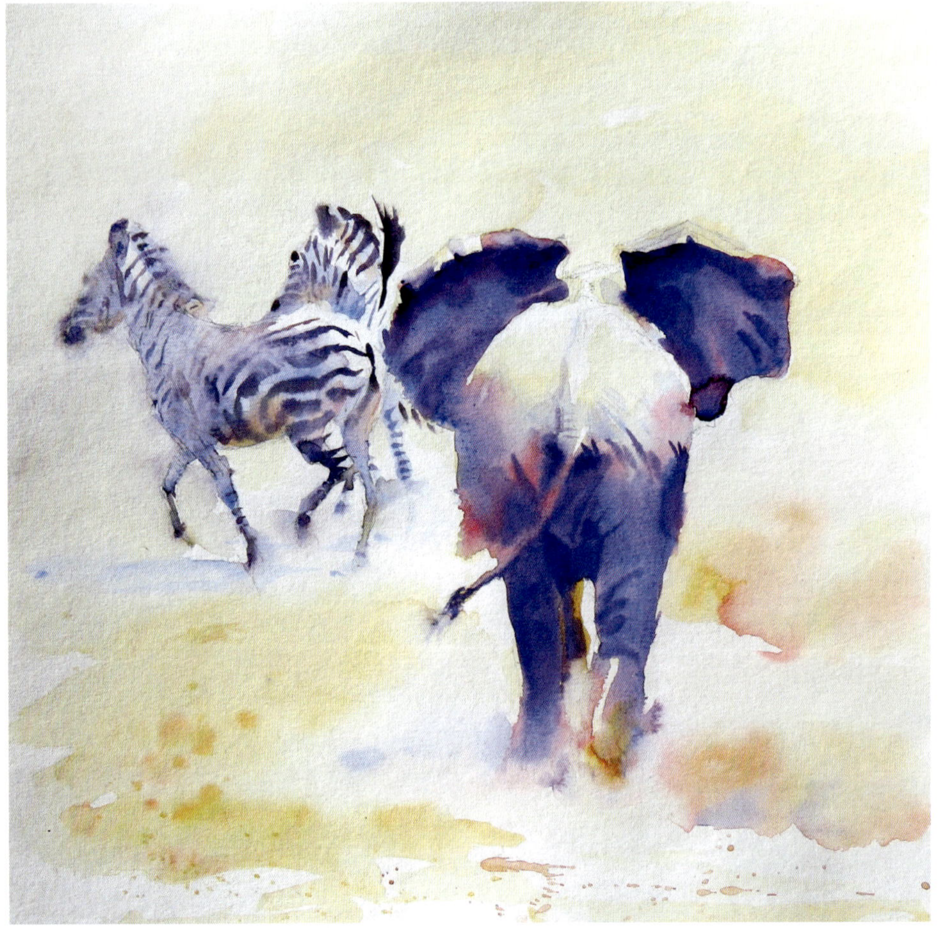

◄ **Skittish,**
38 x 39cm (15 x 15in)
Here, Cobalt Blue, a non-staining colour, has been re-wetted to cause a smudging of the zebra's legs and stripes to suggest the blur of movement. In this case, the effect created was deliberate, but it shows how readily lifting pigment can be shifted from its dried position.

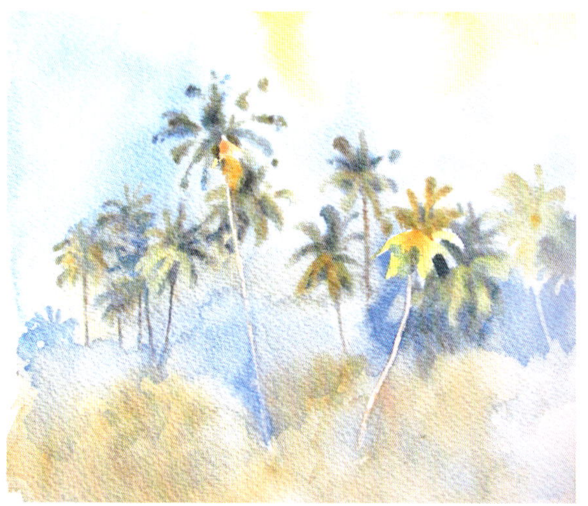

◀ **Palm Trees from the Balcony, Sri Lanka,** *25.5 x 28cm (10 x 11in)*

Using two non-staining colours, Cobalt Blue and Raw Sienna, in tandem in this quick sketch meant I could manoeuvre the fronds of the palm trees around on the paper. The risk is to dull the greens. When I saw this happening, I stopped.

Do Not Disturb

Non-staining and granulating colours can of course be overpainted. The gum arabic is designed to set and hold them in place, but the overlaying brushstrokes should be gentle – caress the paper rather than rub or scrub – and the water content not excessive. It helps to use bigger brushes and flatter brushstrokes so that the sweeping action of the brush is not centred in the tip. Think of the pressure exerted by the downward force of the brush like that of a person standing on thin ice: by flattening out the body, the load is spread and prevents the ice from cracking. So too, by taking the pressure off the point of the brush, the pressure of the stroke is spread more evenly over a wider area, protecting the previous layer of paint from being disturbed.

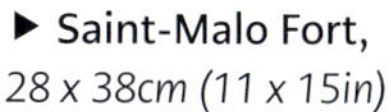

▶ **Saint-Malo Fort,**
28 x 38cm (11 x 15in)

Burnt Umber is used for the dark shadows between the corbels supporting the turret because its non-staining, granulating nature makes it easy to shift the tones from dark to light. However, as it is so easy to disturb these details, I waited until the walls were painted before adding them.

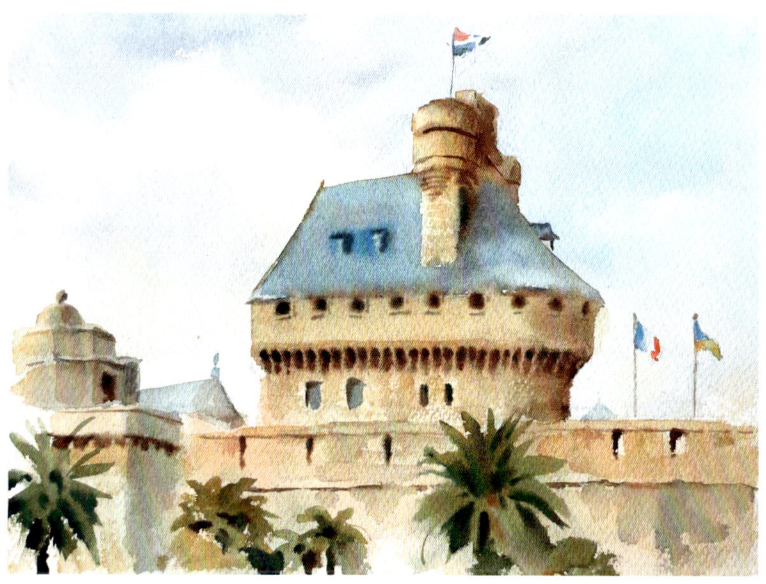

Pigment Clumping

If you see clumping developing, it may be safe to blot immediately - but not indiscriminately - to carefully lift the excess paint. However, often it is better to wait to fix the problem after paint has dried, as scuffing damp paper can make the matter worse and increase the dull appearance.

If pigment clumping has occurred, it may be possible to lift the loosened pigment from the painting. Take a clean damp brush (or sponge if the area is large) and gently agitate the clumped pigment before lifting it off in the brush, or pat it gently with a rag or kitchen towel. Clean the pigment from the brush or rag with each lift so you do not reintroduce pigment residue back onto the paper. Having removed the clumped particles, the agitated area may take on a slightly leathery or scuffed appearance where the paper surface has been disturbed. If so, wait for the area to dry completely, then apply a tinted glaze of a fresh, clean, transparent colour. This can re-invigorate the appearance.

▶ **Santorini Palace,** *25.5 x 28cm (10 x 11in)*
The blooms on the right are the result of not waiting for the paint to dry, causing a backrun and subsequent pigment clumping. Compare this area with the clarity of the rest.

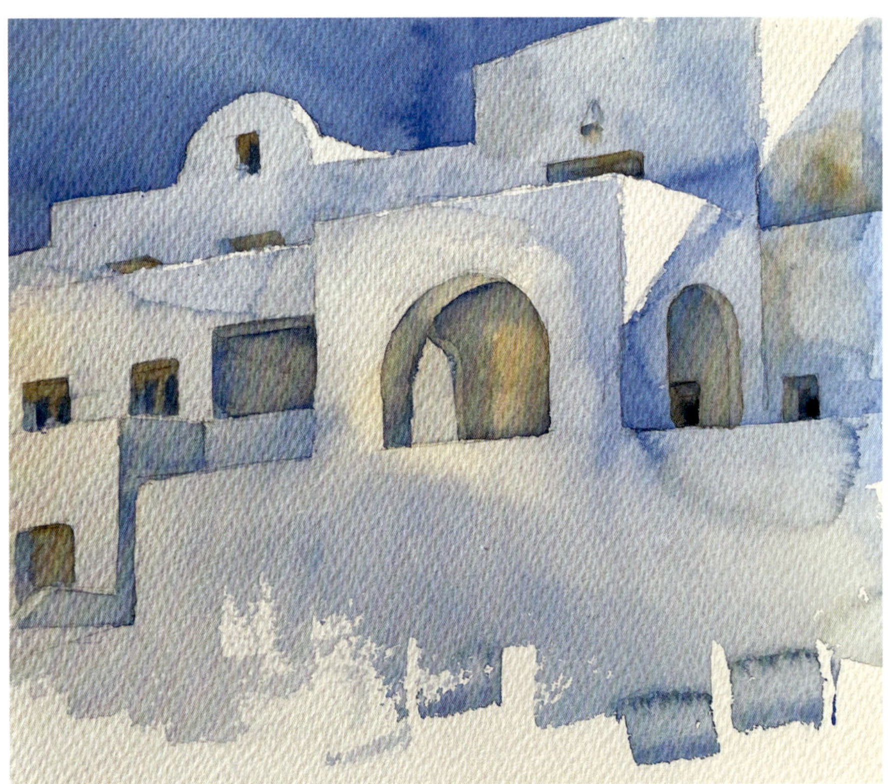

Dull Shadows

Beware dull shadows, especially if painting from photographic reference, where shadows often look blacker and darker than they would in real life. Mix your greys and darks from colours already used in the painting. Get into the habit of choosing all your colours before you start the painting and limit the combination to as few as you think possible to achieve the outcome you seek. Since pigment mixing tends to darkness, there will be two or three in your set that will likely be perfect to mix together for making the greys, browns and blacks needed in the shadows. It is therefore unlikely you will need readymade shades of grey to deepen the shadow colours.

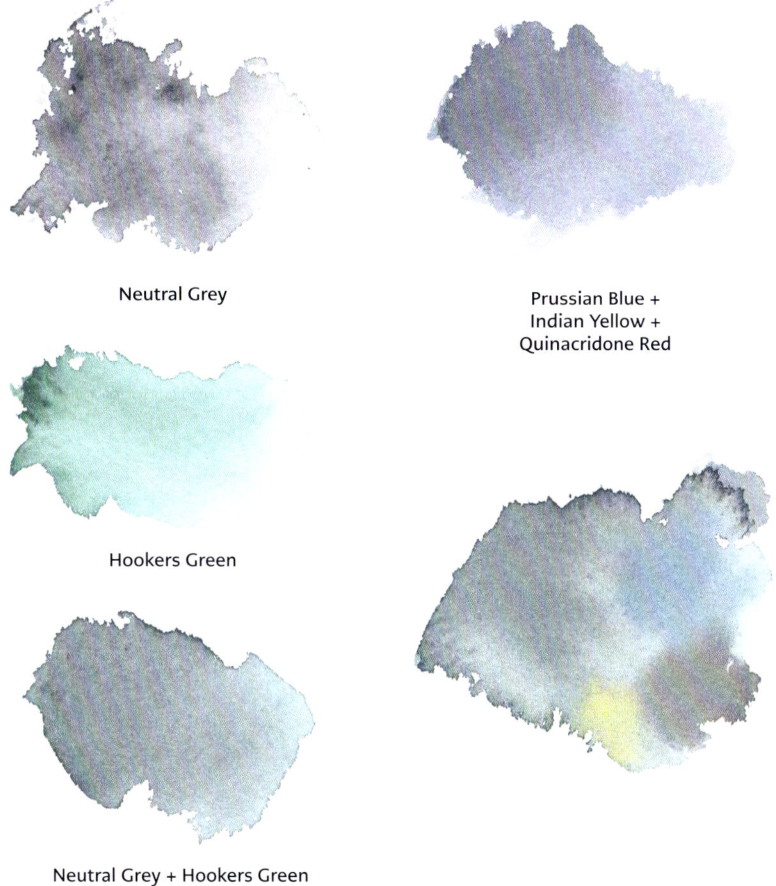

▲ Readymade greys like Neutral Grey (shown above left) include multiple pigments and, though they can be used to make attractive greys, as shown with Hookers Green here, they run the risk of dullness. This is caused by mixing too many pigments as part of the painting process, hence it is preferable to mix your greys from colours already in the painting, as demonstrated by the swatches on the right mixed from red, yellow and blue.

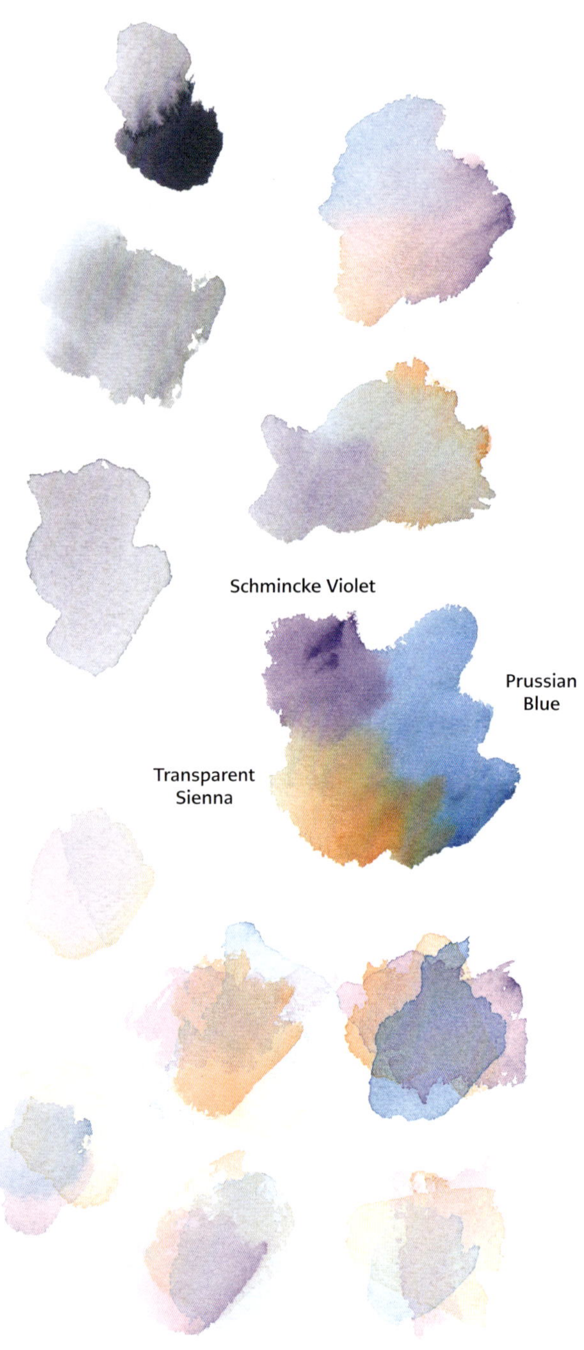

▲ ▶ **Tender Touch,** *38 x 35.5cm (15 x 14in)*

Transparent colours mix to make vibrant blacks and greys. Here, Prussian Blue, Transparent Sienna and Schmincke Violet make a fine black. Compare the mixed grey with the more lively greys created by blending and overlapping the three colours wet into wet and wet on dry on the paper as I have done on the elephants – a much fresher and more lively set of greys develop.

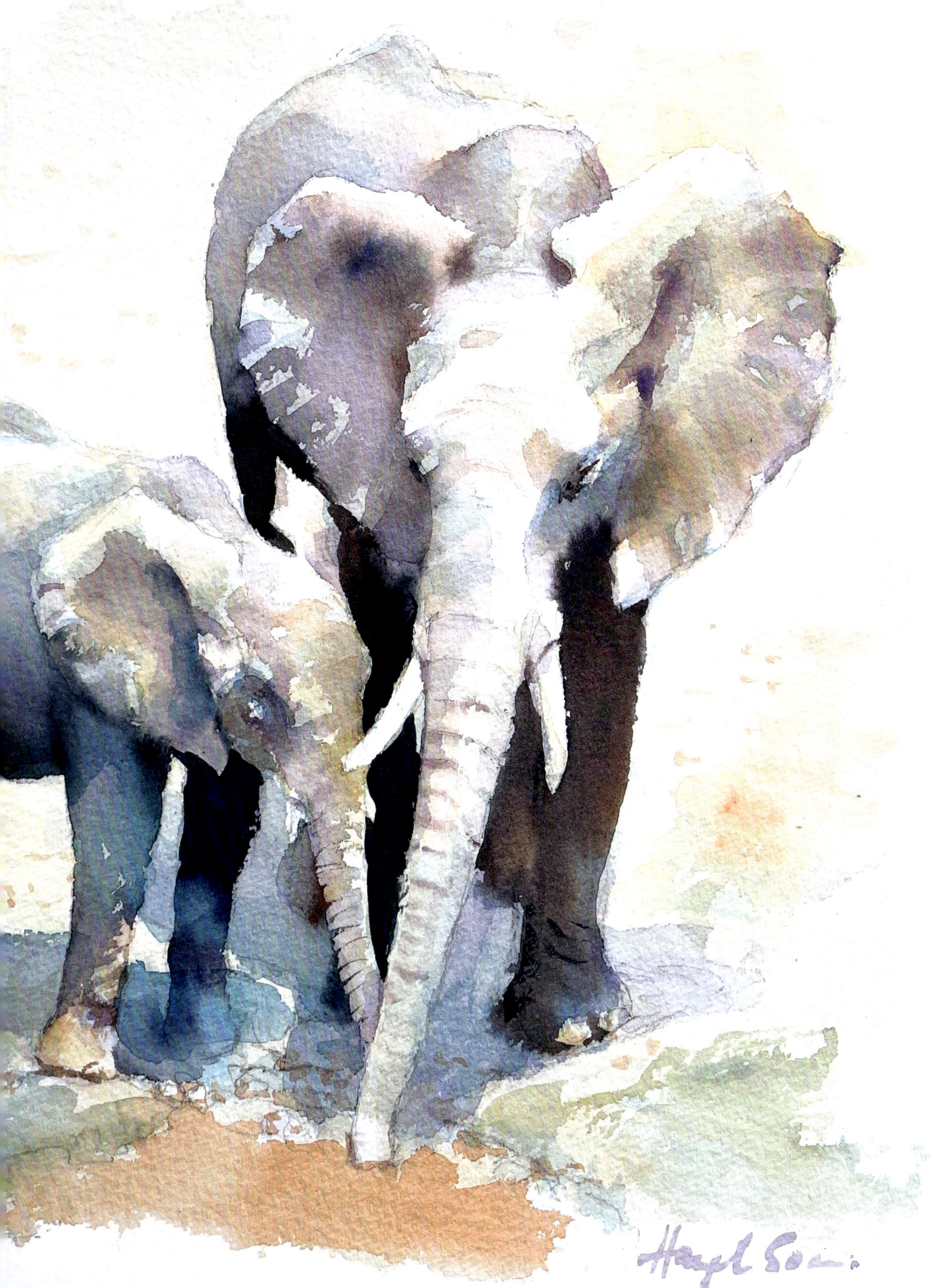

Practice, Practice, Practice

The Lion's Mane

This Kalahari male has a magnificent black mane we can use to practise laying the colour directly to maintain freshness and avoid muddy colouring. Mix with purpose, and avoid mixing more than two or three colours at a time.

Plan your colours and stick to a limited palette to reduce the risk of overtaxing. I have chosen Yellow Ochre, Transparent Sienna, Prussian Blue and Schmincke Violet, but I am going to use Sepia for the facial features, as it allows me to reach a rich dark more quickly. However, being opaque, it risks muddying the colouring, so I will not use it anywhere else.

You also need to focus on colour placement. Keep dark colours separate from light - allow light bright colours to breathe by not dragging dark pigments into them accidentally. Work from light to dark - build darker tones as directly as possible while leaving the lights intact.

Colours:

Yellow Raw Ochre

Transparent/Burnt Sienna

Prussian Blue

Schmincke Violet

Sepia

Brushes:

19mm flat brush

Size 6, 8, 10 and 12 round brushes

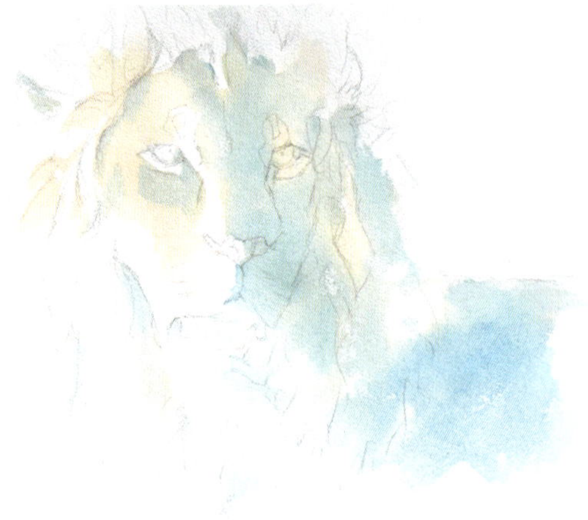

1 With pale washes of Yellow Ochre and Prussian Blue, I mapped in the warm and cool under-layers while leaving white paper untouched for the light.

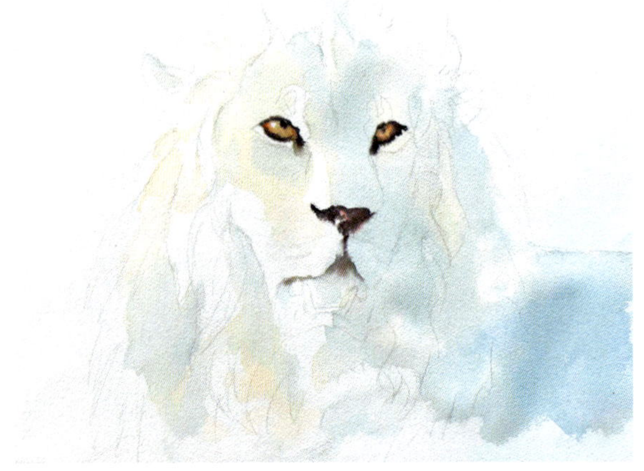

2 I outlined the facial features next, with Sepia. I dampened the paper a little around them to soften the brushstroke and went in as dark as I could so that they would not need retouching later.

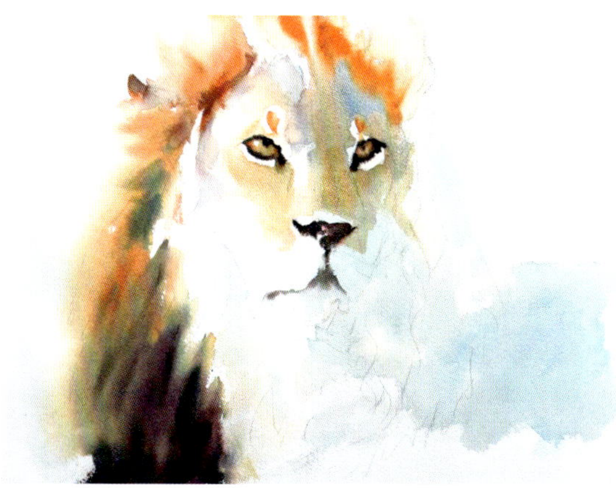

3 I built up the mane and face colours wet into wet, from light to dark, using Yellow Ochre, then Prussian Blue, Burnt Sienna and Schmincke Violet, starting on the lighter side and moving across to the shadier side.

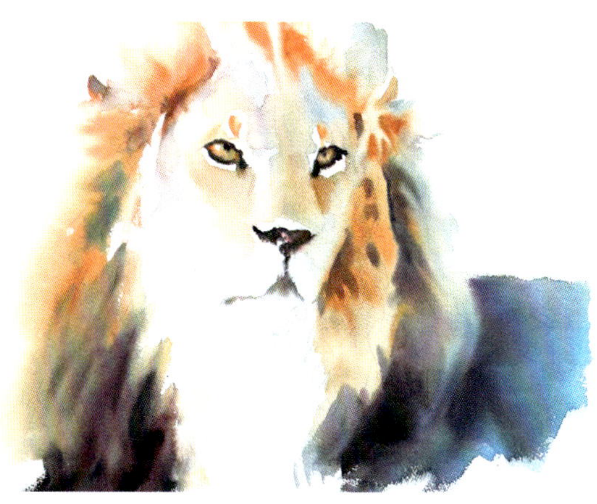

4 The deep colours were mixed on the palette and laid in a rich, concentrated, single wet wash to maximize a vibrant transparency within the dark colour.

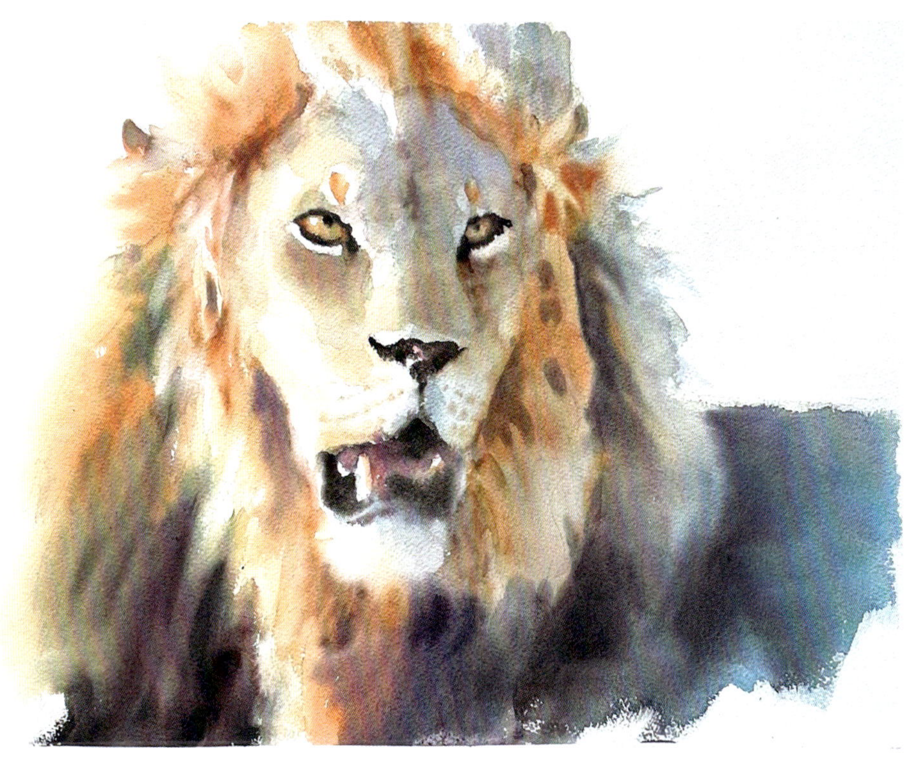

5 Finally, I tackled the open mouth and then the beard, using clean water to push the colour outward to form the chin.

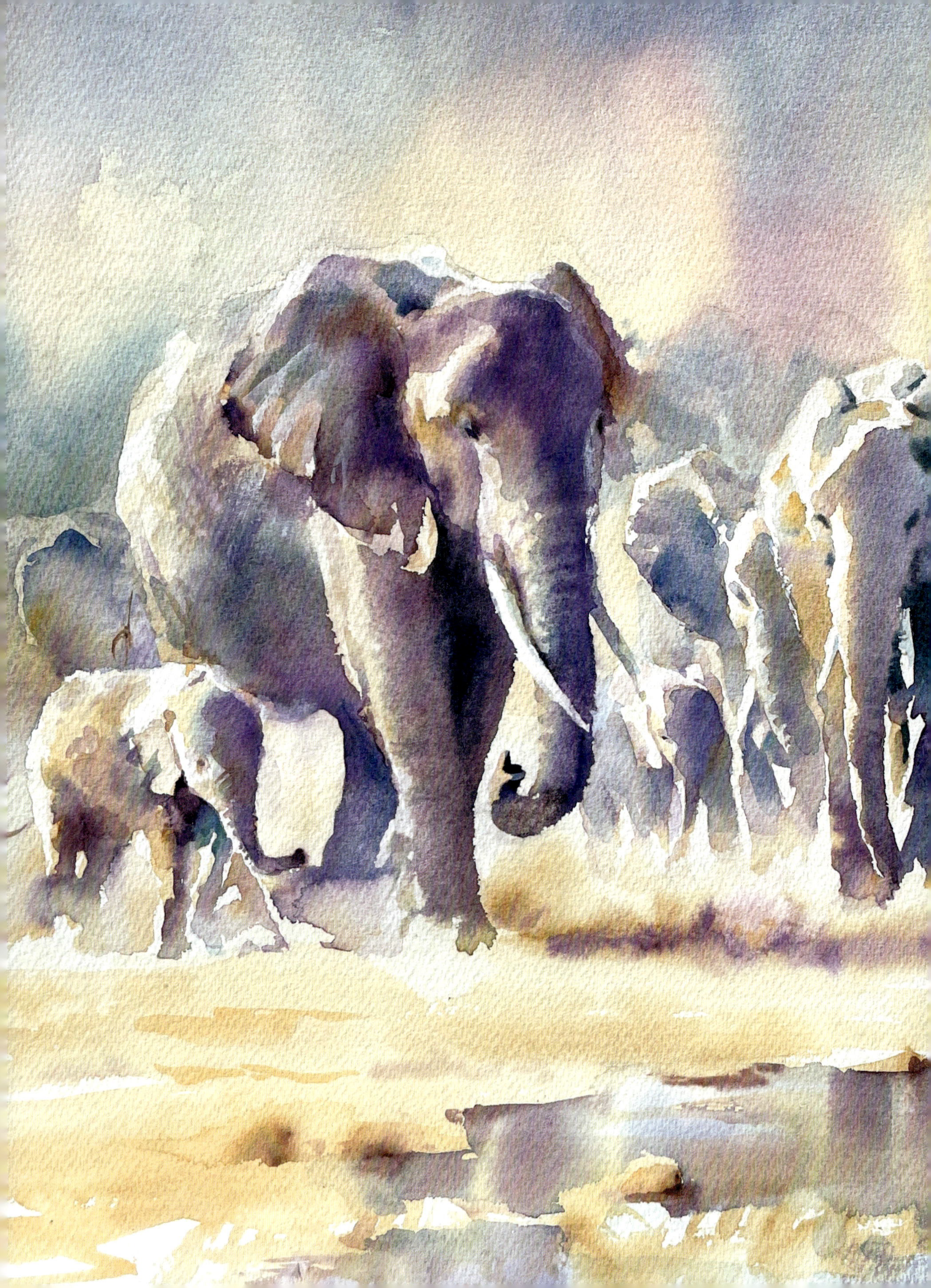

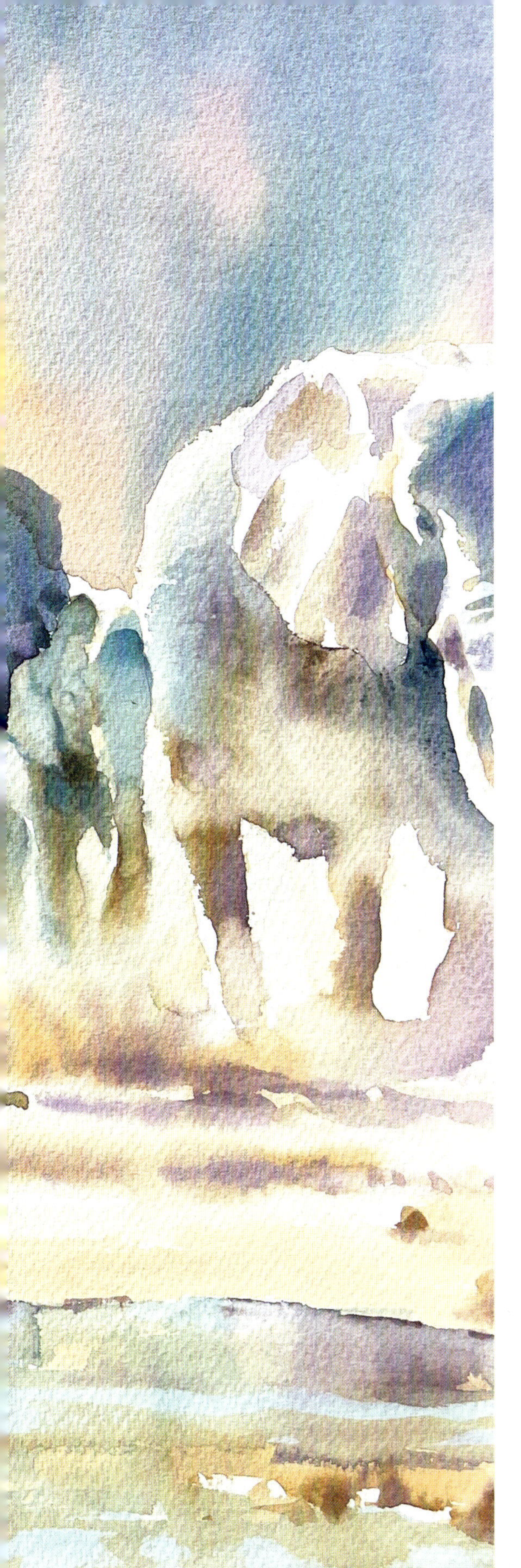

CHAPTER 5

Controlling the Water

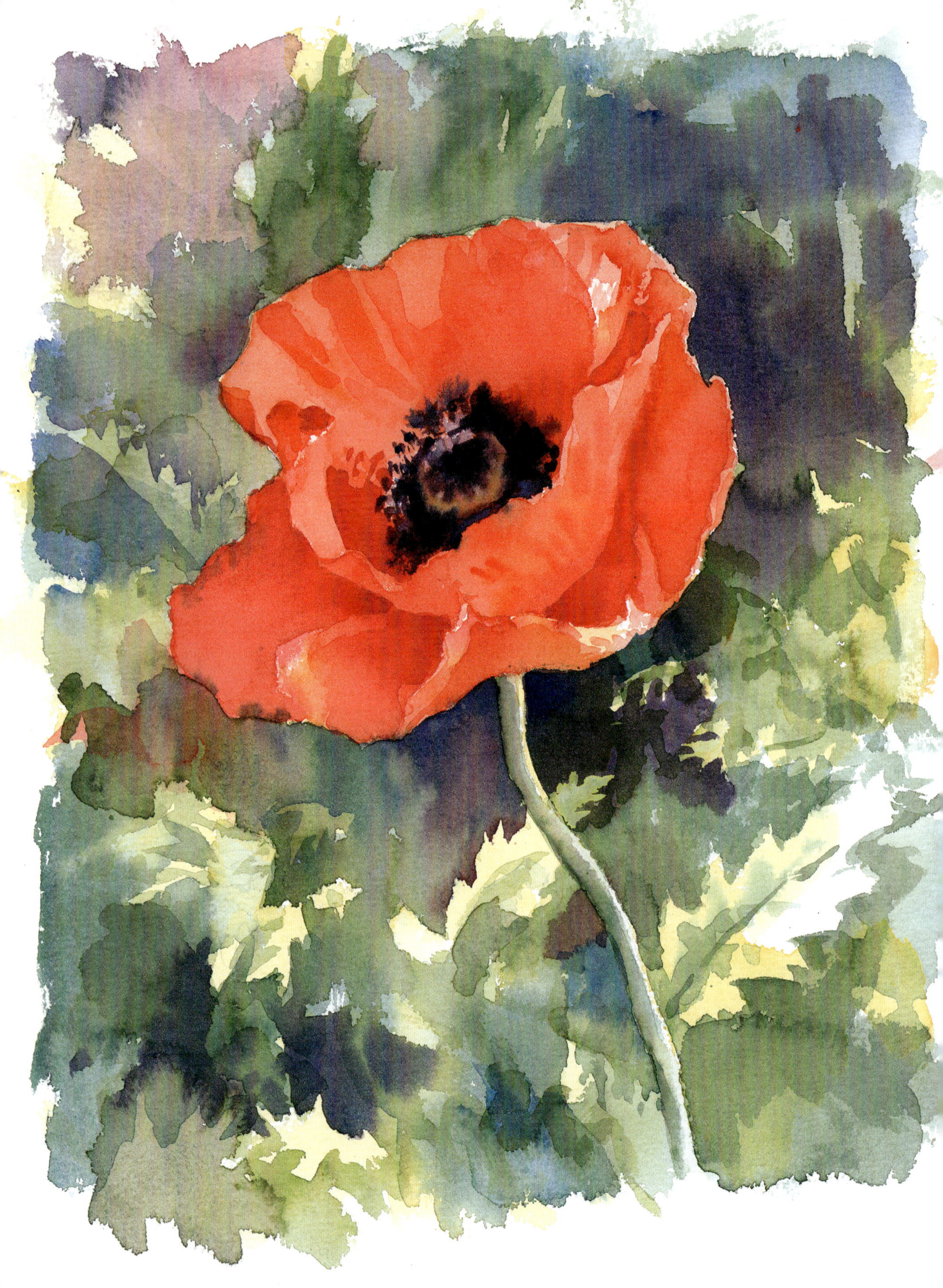

Just Add Water

The previous chapters have addressed issues relating to the pigments that provide the wonderful range of colours in watercolour painting, but sometimes it is lack of control of the water that is actually causing the problems.

Since watercolour paint is diluted with generally accessible water, it is an extremely practical medium and has become one of the most popular painting media for use in any location, inside or out. In this regard it often appears easy to use, even though it is actually quite technical. Ironically, it is often the very fluidity and movement of the water itself, as it mixes in the palette or floats the paint across the paper, that causes consternation in watercolour painting, because it fosters the notion of unpredictability and being out of control. Misuse and miscalculation of the ratio of water to pigment in mixes is the cause of many of the problems that beset budding watercolourists. However, the movement of water and its physical tendencies can be understood and harnessed to advantage, as we shall discover in this chapter.

▶ The movement of water causes attractive effects to occur as the pigment particles are carried in the flow of the water.

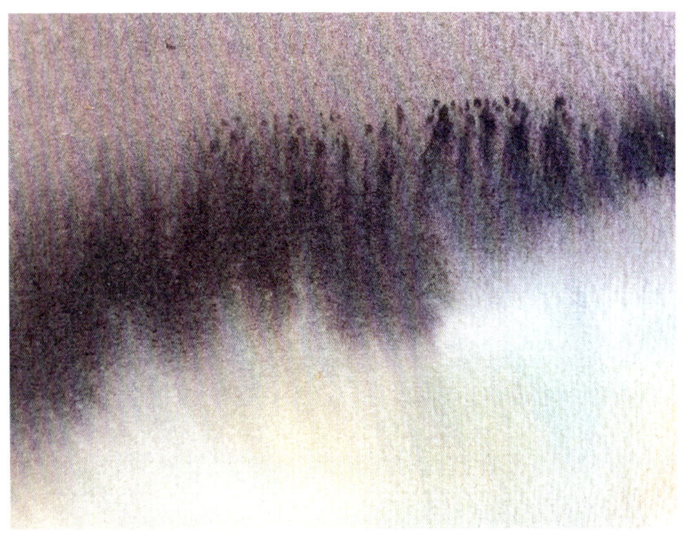

◀ **Dancing in Red,**
35.5 x 28cm (14 x 11in)
Adroit management of the water content, in both the laid wash and the colour about to be applied, enables the centre of the poppy to exhibit both soft and crisp edges around the ovary, suggesting the stamens fluttering in a gentle breeze.

Go with the Flow: The Physics of Watercolour

How is it that such an attractive medium can ever appear dull in a painting? Modern watercolour has been honed to perfection over two centuries and is arguably an exquisitely beautiful medium in and of itself. The colours are wonderful, both in concentration and dilution, and blend flawlessly with others. Even the dried watercolour pools in the palette look fresh and inviting. Surely if we just put more trust in the watercolour medium to deliver its appealing outcome we have the key to retaining watercolour's innate freshness?

To do this means letting go to some extent and allowing the action of water to obey its natural tendencies, even if it means feeling slightly less in control. Perhaps 'control' is the wrong word to use in the first place; it is better to think of harnessing the water and developing a more intuitive feel for exploiting its physical properties. Watercolourists do not need to be experts in physics to understand the medium, but a little knowledge will help resolve some of the frustration because the actions of watercolour come down to physics. The main physical influences on watercolour painting are gravity, surface tension, capillary action and diffusion.

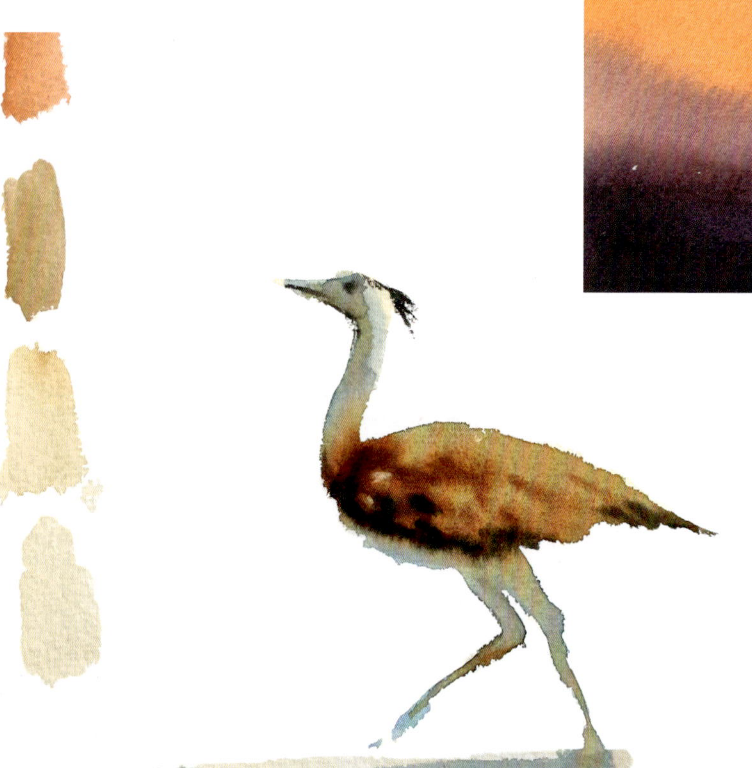

▲ The exquisitely perfected colours of watercolour blend attractively on the paper.

◄ Even this simple sketch of a kori bustard and the swatches testing the colours have charm in the watercolour medium.

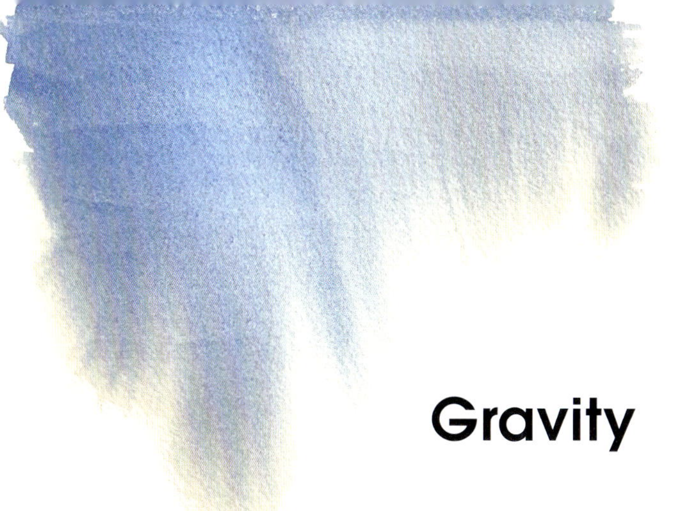

◂ By re-wetting the paper and tilting it at an almost upright angle, gravity forces the paint to flow downward, creating a feathery drift.

Gravity

The force of gravity is well understood, and ignored at one's peril in watercolour. Gravity acts to direct a downward flow on the wet paint. If the paper is tilted at an angle and the paint applied very wet, it may cause it to run down or drip across the painting. Gravity's force should always be taken into account, especially when holding paper on your lap or knees in case you accidentally direct paint to flow in an unintended direction. However, gravity should be seen as an ally, as we can use this force to guide the flow of the pigment on the paper and from the brush, and to assess the consistency of wet mixtures on the palette.

Watercolourists incline their work at an angle to take advantage of the downward pull gravity exerts or keep the paper laid flat when they want to avoid its grasp. Using the downward flow on the sloping leaf of a palette is also a great help in judging the right consistency of the paint before loading the brush. We'll talk more about that later.

▾ **Sparring Partners,**
20 x 25.5cm (8 x 10in)
There has to be trust in the medium to deliver when dealing with the flow of paint. I tilted the paper to direct the darker Burnt Umber into the lighter wash, but the result was not predictable. Hence, I positioned the springbok only once the wash had dried, to ensure the best contrast against the lighter background.

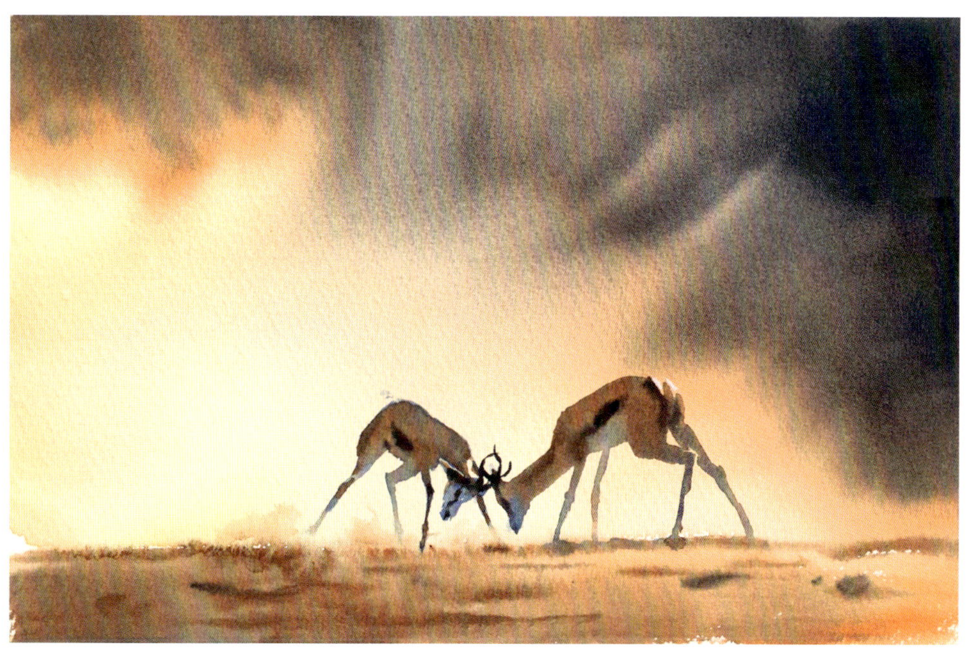

Surface Tension

Paper by nature has a high surface energy that attracts liquids and would normally absorb wet paint quickly (like blotting paper). Watercolour papers, however, are specially prepared with a glue size to make the surface less absorbent, and the rough fibrous surface is filled with air pockets, both of which lower the surface energy. This enables liquid paint to sit in droplets or puddles on the paper surface and surface tension enables the wet paint to 'hold itself together' on the paper even when it is subject to the gravitational pull of being held at a slight angle. Due to gravity, more pigment settles at the bottom of a tilted wash but this beading effect prevents the water running down and off the paper. As a result, many pleasing effects can be created, including the slightly darker edges visible at the contours of a wash where excess pigment has gathered. Wetting the paper creates a more cohesive surface, raising the surface energy and allowing the paint to flow and spread out. This is the action harnessed by the wet into wet technique.

Surface tension also affects mixing in the palette. Plastic palettes have a smooth, hydrophobic surface that resists and repels water, so the paint forms in pools, making it hard to judge the exact consistency and colour of a mix. Metal and china palettes, on the other hand, have a higher surface energy than plastic, and encourage the spreading out of wet paint, making it easier to judge the consistency and colour of a mix. Surface tension also causes the water to cling together as a meniscus on the slope, which becomes a reliable gauge for assessing the amount of water in a mix.

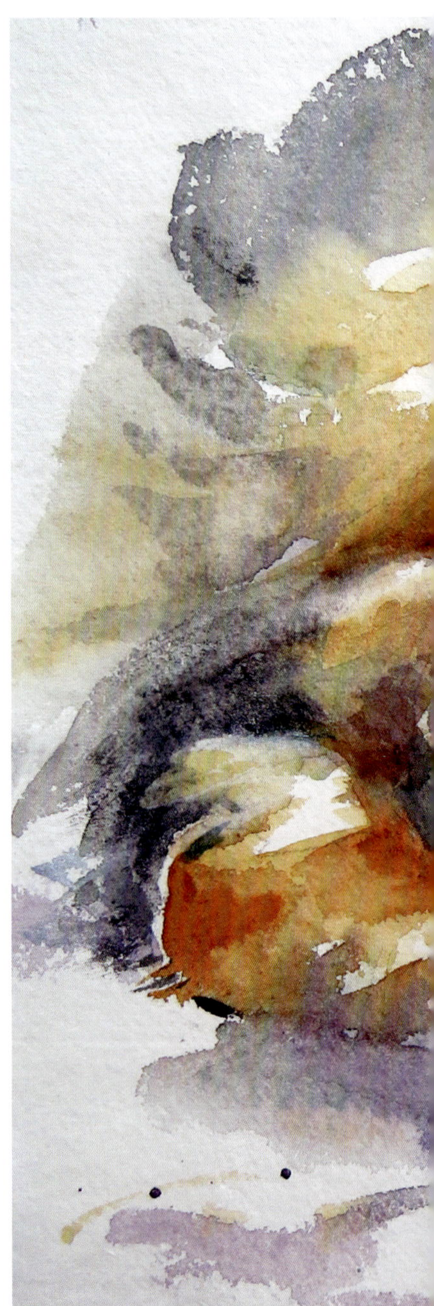

▶ **The Watchful Gaze,**
40.5 x 51cm (16 x 20in)

In the wet into wet technique, the paint is encouraged to spread rather than bead up by wetting the surface before the paint is applied, as in the blonde mane, or by adding the colour into a previous and still wet wash, as on the forehead and cheeks.

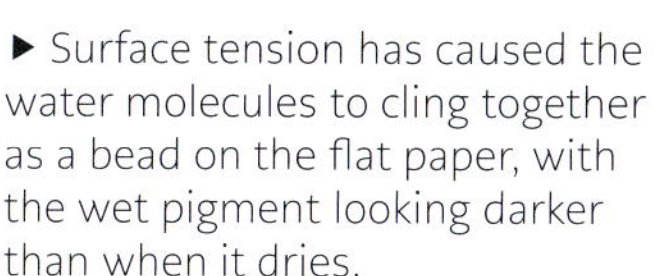
▶ Surface tension has caused the water molecules to cling together as a bead on the flat paper, with the wet pigment looking darker than when it dries.

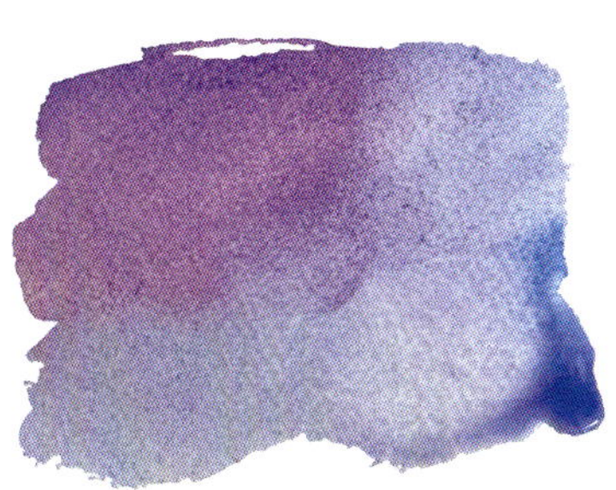

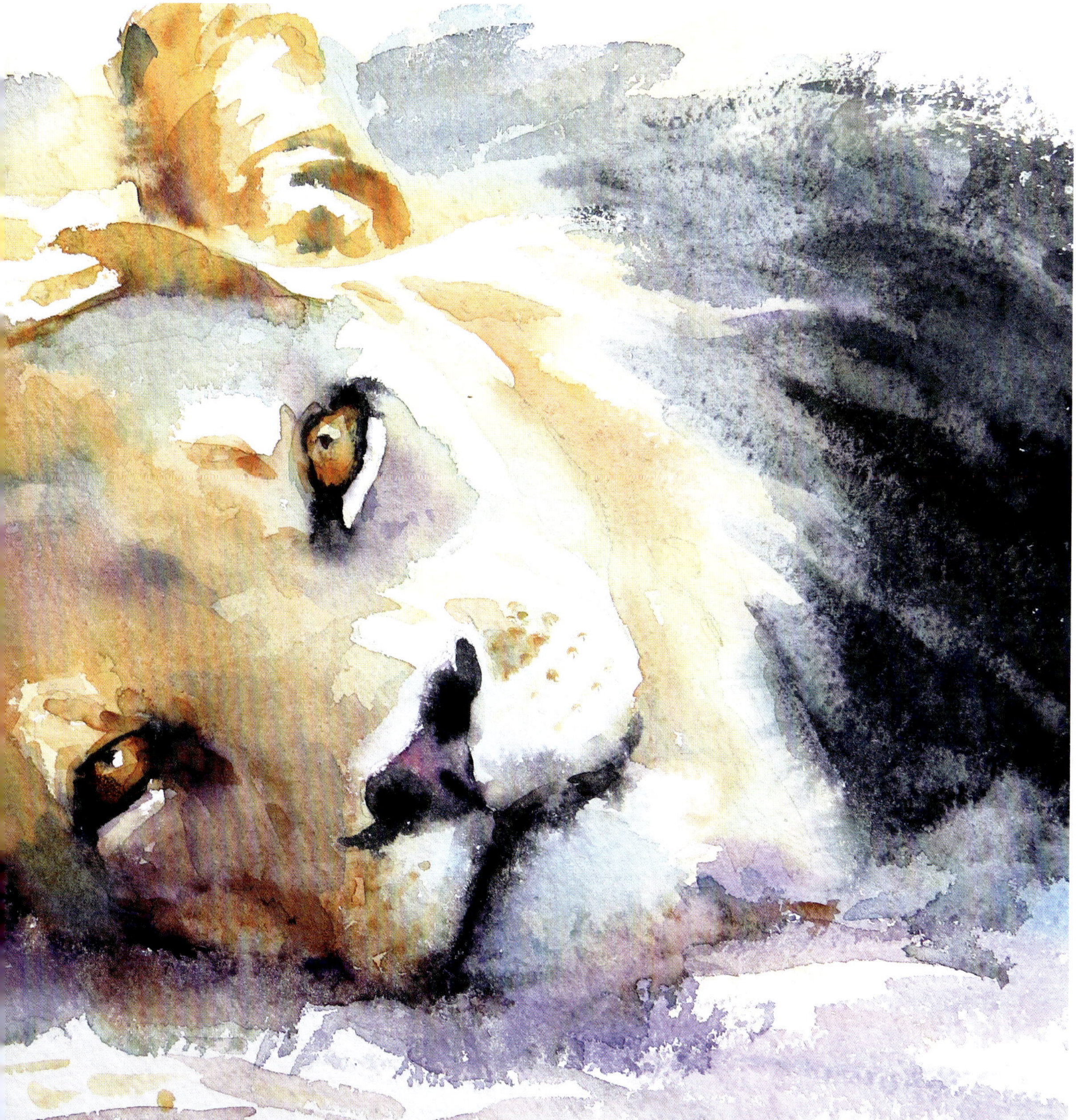

Capillary Action

Capillary action refers to how water moves through paper and pigment, using adhesion and surface tension to draw it along, sometimes against the pull of gravity. The fibres of the paper create tiny capillaries that draw in the liquid when water is applied and help the pigment to spread and blend on the paper. More absorbent paper pulls water faster, creating soft blended edges; less absorbent paper, such as hot-pressed paper, slows capillary action, leading to sharper edges. If water is already on the paper, paint will flow outward into it, in smooth transitions. Likewise, if water is applied to dry or damp paint, it will pull the pigment out towards the wetter region.

Capillary action is responsible for the feathery strands and threads and the blooming effects known as backruns or cauliflowers created when wet paint or water runs back into a drier area of a wash. Although these effects are often unintentional and sometimes unwanted, they can also be very beautiful and can be engineered by harnessing the capillary action of the water.

It is also capillary action that allows the brush to lift up and hold water from the water pot and to enable a brush or corner of kitchen towel to soak up and retain the moisture from an unwanted pool of water on the paper or palette.

▼ The upward flow of the paint along the skyline is created by the capillary action that draws the pigment upward into the preceding wash. The effect nicely represents the soft African grasses against the dusky sky.

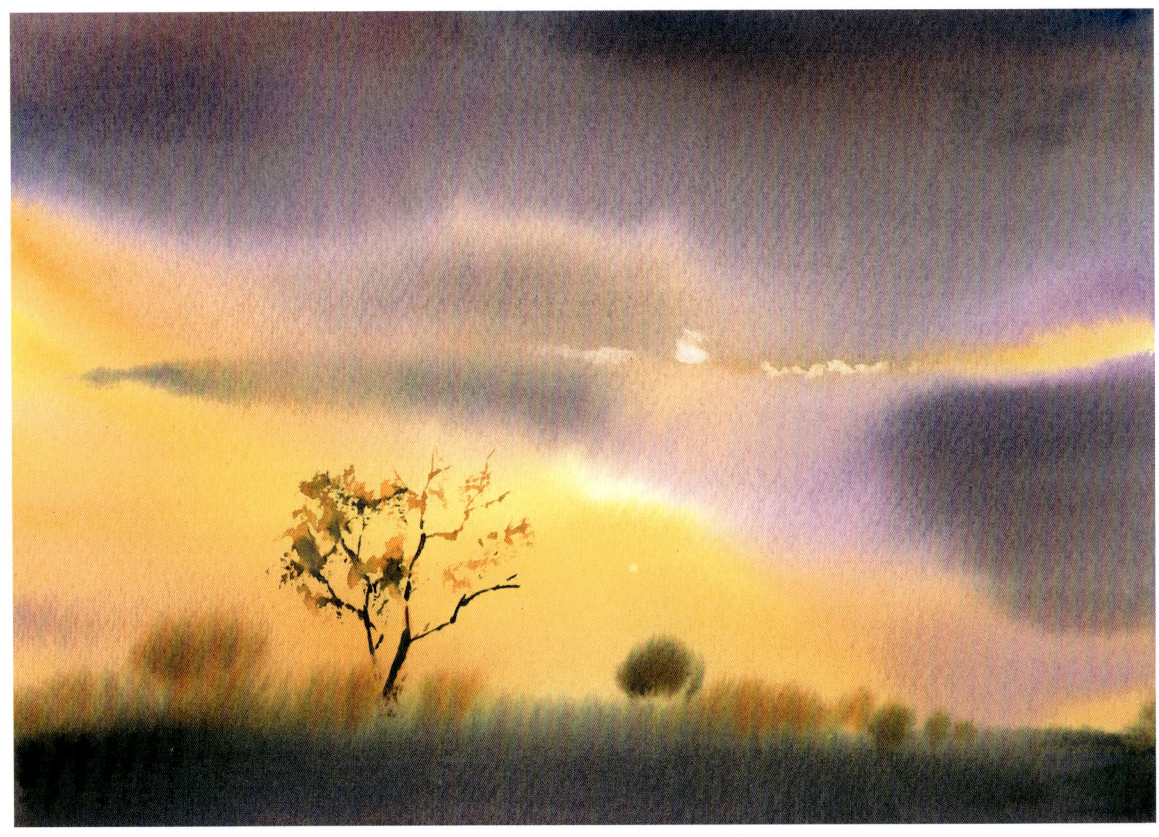

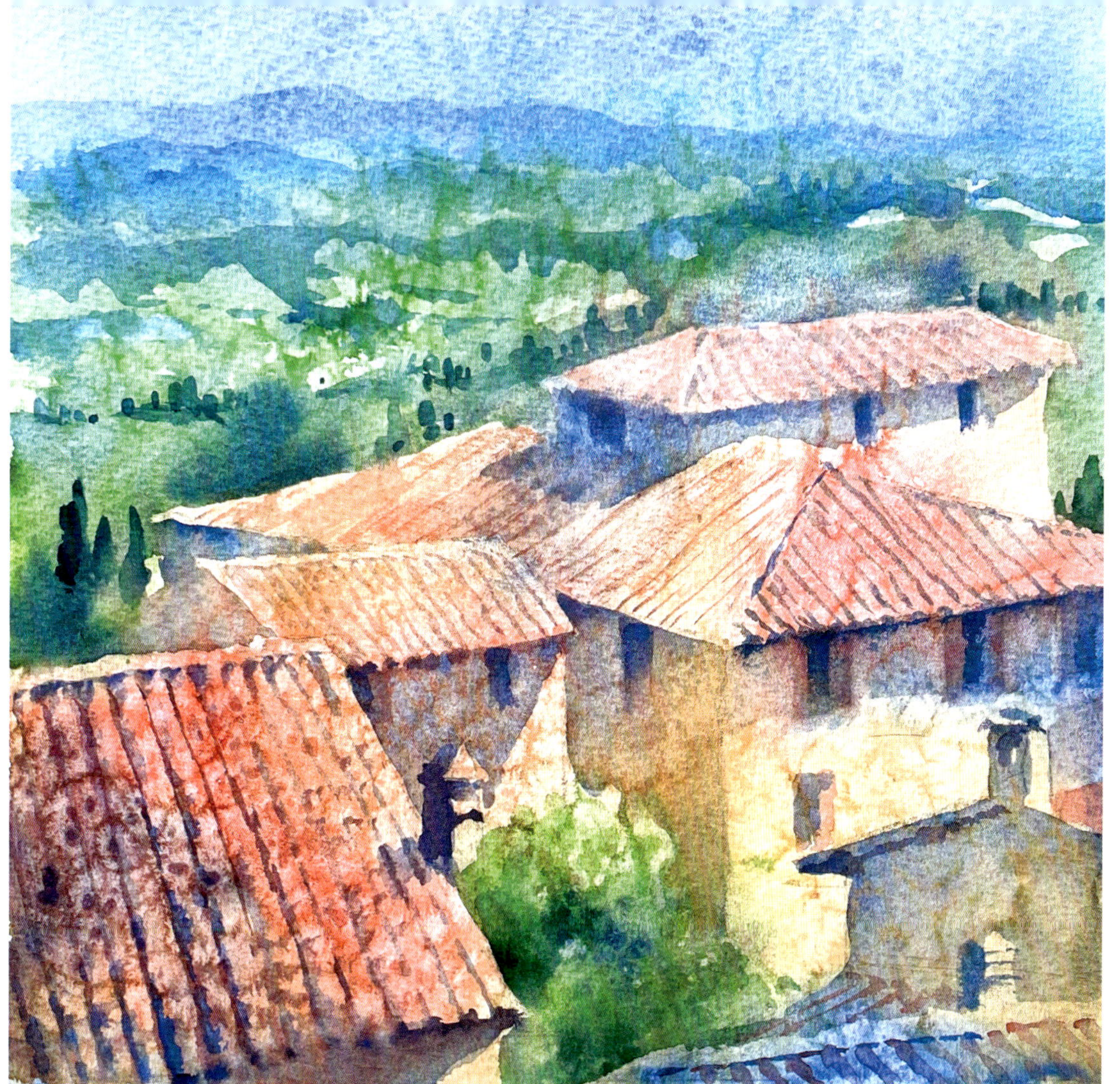

Diffusion

▲ **From the Eye of the Bird,**
28 x 28cm (11 x 11in)

When you sprinkle salt into wet watercolour, the salt absorbs water by osmosis, disrupting the normal diffusion and capillary action and creating starburst-like patterns where pigment dries around the grains. The result is an attractive texture ideal for the Italian pantile roofs and stone walls in this painting.

Watercolour pigments spread and disperse in water by means of diffusion. This works alongside capillary action to create soft gradients and organic textures. However, diffusion occurs because of differences in concentration rather than the structure of the paper. It is diffusion that causes the pigment particles to spread out in a random fashion across the paper. In physics, this movement is known as Brownian motion; this refers to the random and irregular movement displayed by small particles suspended in fluids. In watercolour, the displacement is caused by countless collisions between the pigment particles and the water molecules as they float across the paper. Wet into wet techniques exploit diffusion to encourage the pigment particles to disperse and mingle to create the attractive blends characteristic of the watercolour medium.

Granulation and Separation

Granulation is one of the physical characteristics of the watercolour medium that harnesses gravity to great effect but can also cause muddiness. Granulation creates a mottled effect when pigment particles settle in the dips on a rough paper surface. It is sometimes referred to as sedimentation. Many of the earth and metal colours have this characteristic since they are made up of relatively heavy pigment particles. Once they settle, the pigment particles can easily be shifted by excess water.

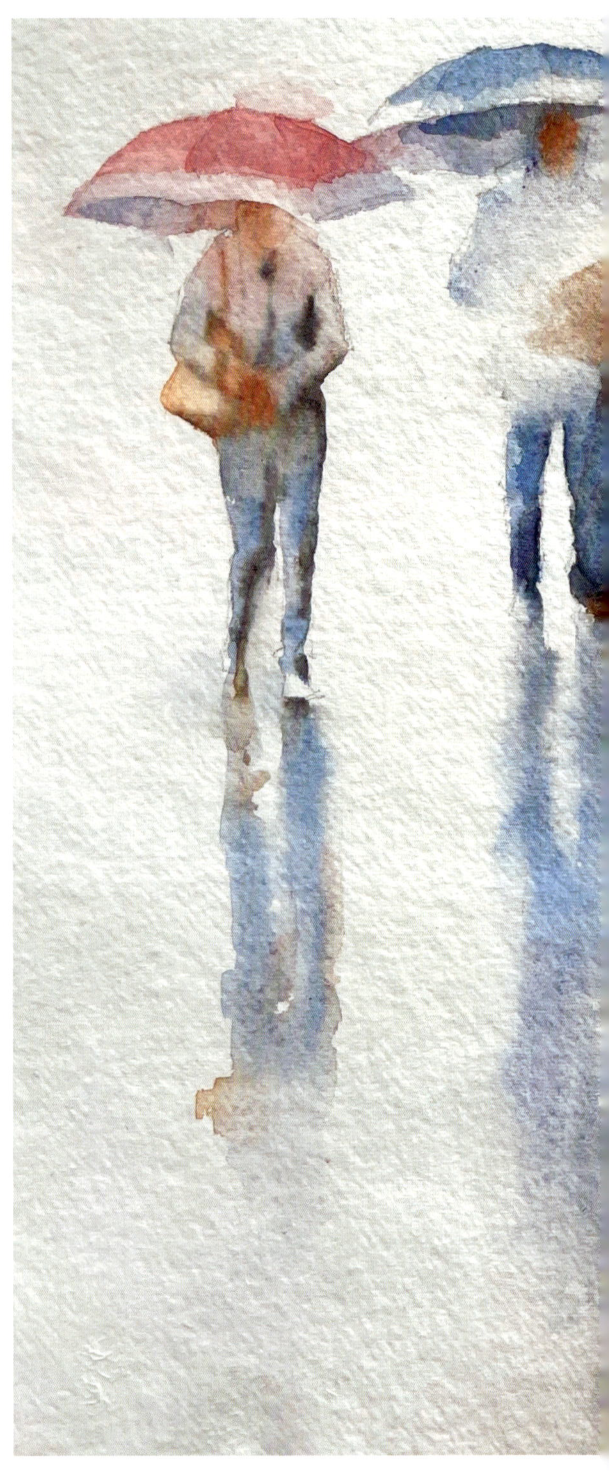

Managing the Water

Even though physics controls the actions of the water and pigment, there is no known formula that can calculate how much water to pigment a particular mix requires. Mixing the right paint consistency can only be learned through experience. Adding the right amount of water to pigment and laying paint at the right time is quintessential to the success of watercolour painting, but on no two days is evaporation the same, and environmental factors always come into play. Whether it be humidity, sunshine, cloud or wind, the amount of water required for any mix is unpredictable until you actually start painting, and then has to be continuously re-evaluated throughout the day. Experience naturally enhances judgement, so be kind to yourself, especially as a beginner, and accept that it takes time and practice to master this aspect.

▶ **Umbrella Company,** *35.5 x 51cm (14 x 20in)*

In this painting, water is used literally, to make the subject look wet! The blurred figures were washed out only after the paint had dried, thanks to the lifting attributes of Ultramarine and Burnt Sienna. To amplify the effect of granulation, a rough paper has been used and held at a flat angle.

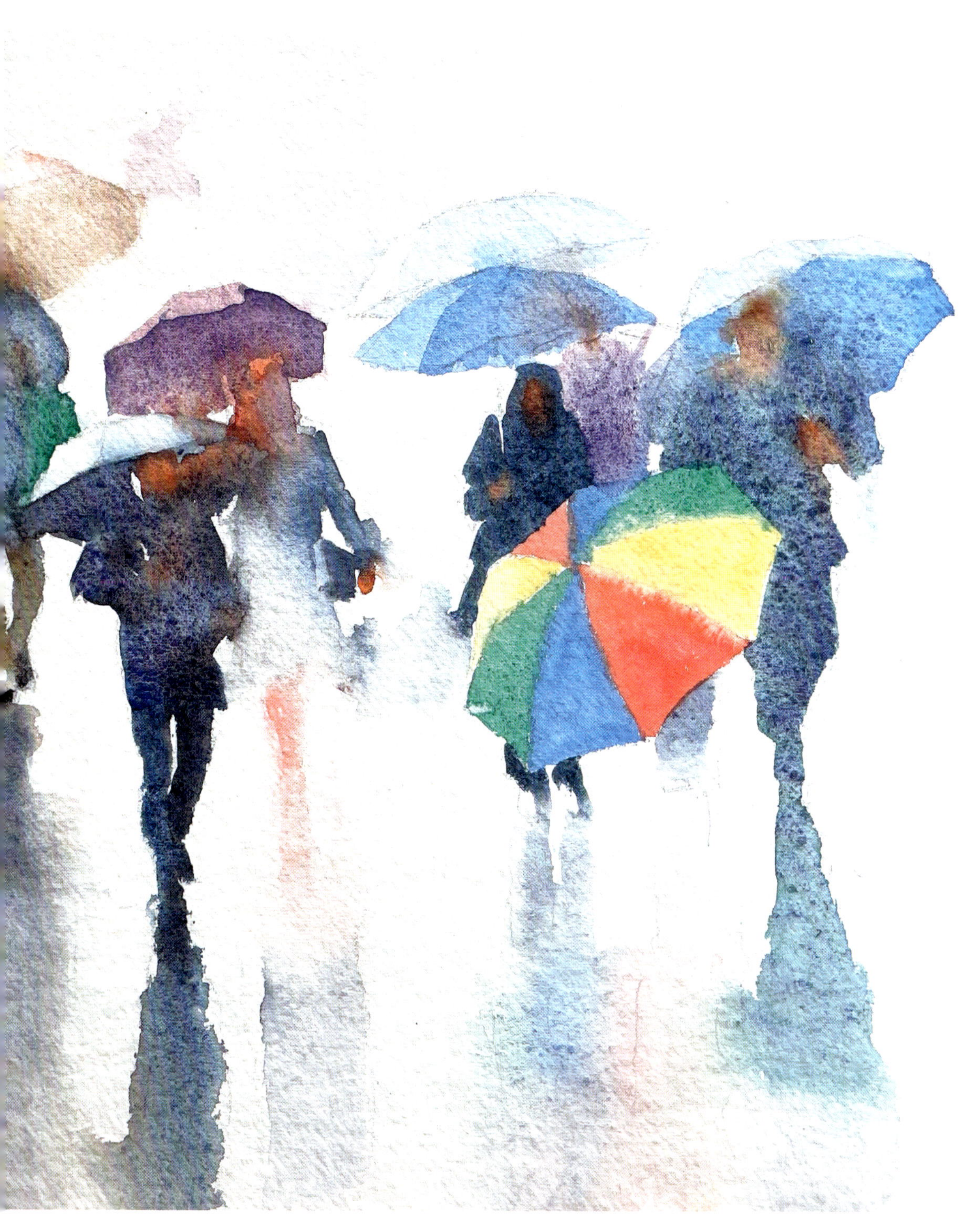

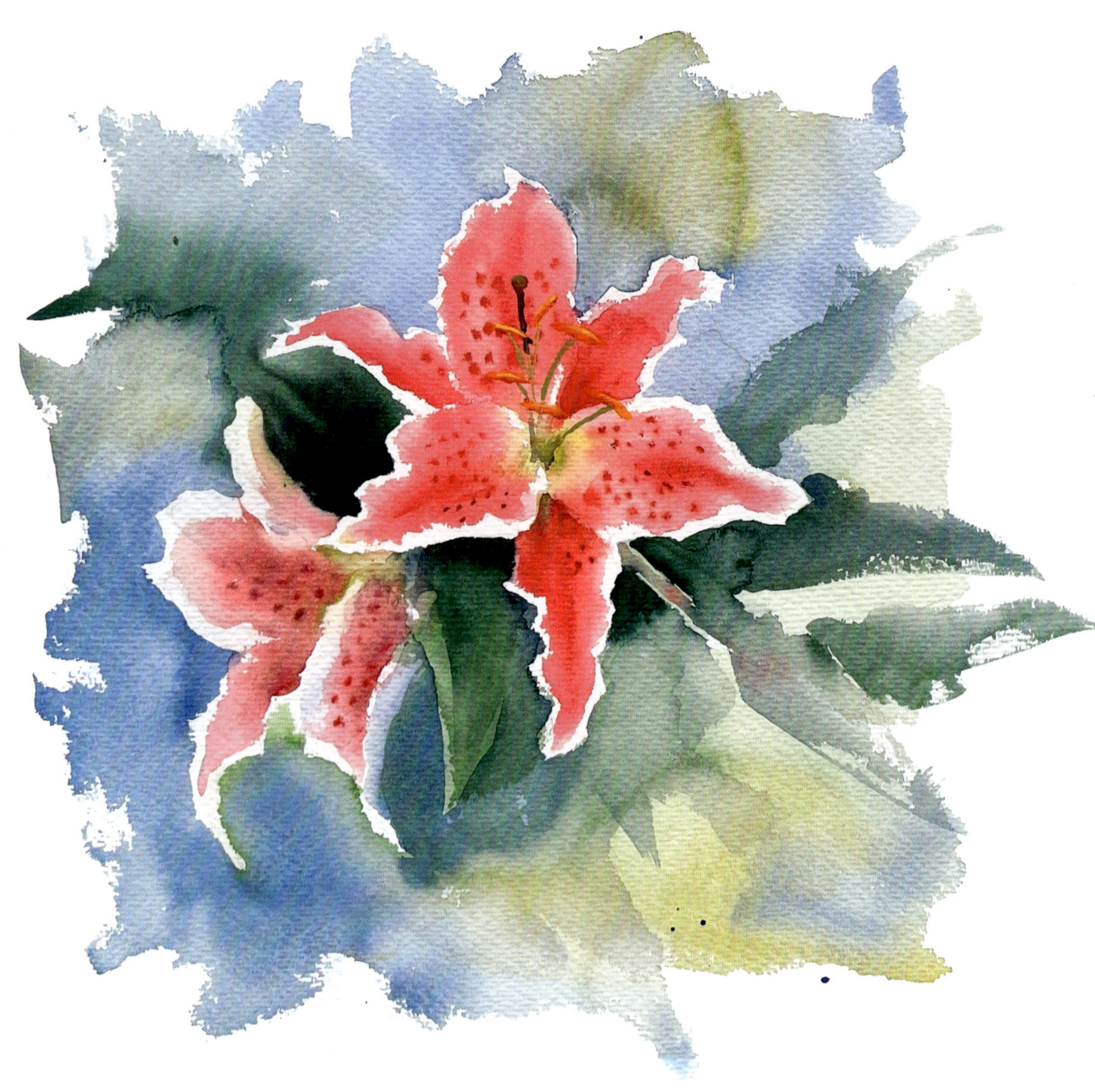

▲ **Stargazer Lilies, Broadway,**
30.5 x 33cm (12 x 13in)

Flowers are the perfect subject for evaluating the differing amounts of water required in paint mixes: a very wet but not overly dilute wash for the background foliage, less wet for the pink of the petals, slightly drier for the dark leaves, quite dry concentrated paint for the crimson spots, and almost dry paint for the stamens.

▶ Fine-tune the water content of mixes by practising the wet into wet technique. Painting from life forces quick decision-making, while the wet into wet technique fosters good water management as drier colour has to be added into wetter areas at the right moment to limit or expand the extent of the pigment spread.

Over-wetting

Since more water to pigment is required for lighter tints, and less for dark or concentrated tones, the water content in the brush and on the palette has to be adjusted for each and every colour and mix. There is rarely a need to use excessive amounts of water. Most problems in watercolour are caused by involving too much water, rather than too little.

Mixing takes place on the palette, but the wells should not be swimming in tinted water. Too much water leads to weak, washy colour, which results in washed-out pigment, dull colouring, uncontrollable blooms and very buckled paper. Wet paint looks darker, and dries much lighter on the paper than it appears in the palette, so you cannot tell the true colour of your paint in the palette if it is too wet. Rather than adding more pigment to a very wet mix, mop out the excess water from the palette with kitchen towel or rag and restart the mixing process, otherwise you will waste a lot of valuable pigment trying to enrich a mix with too much water in the first place. Determining the right amount of water to pigment is learned with practice, but gravity and surface tension play an important and useful role in helping us assess the appropriate amount.

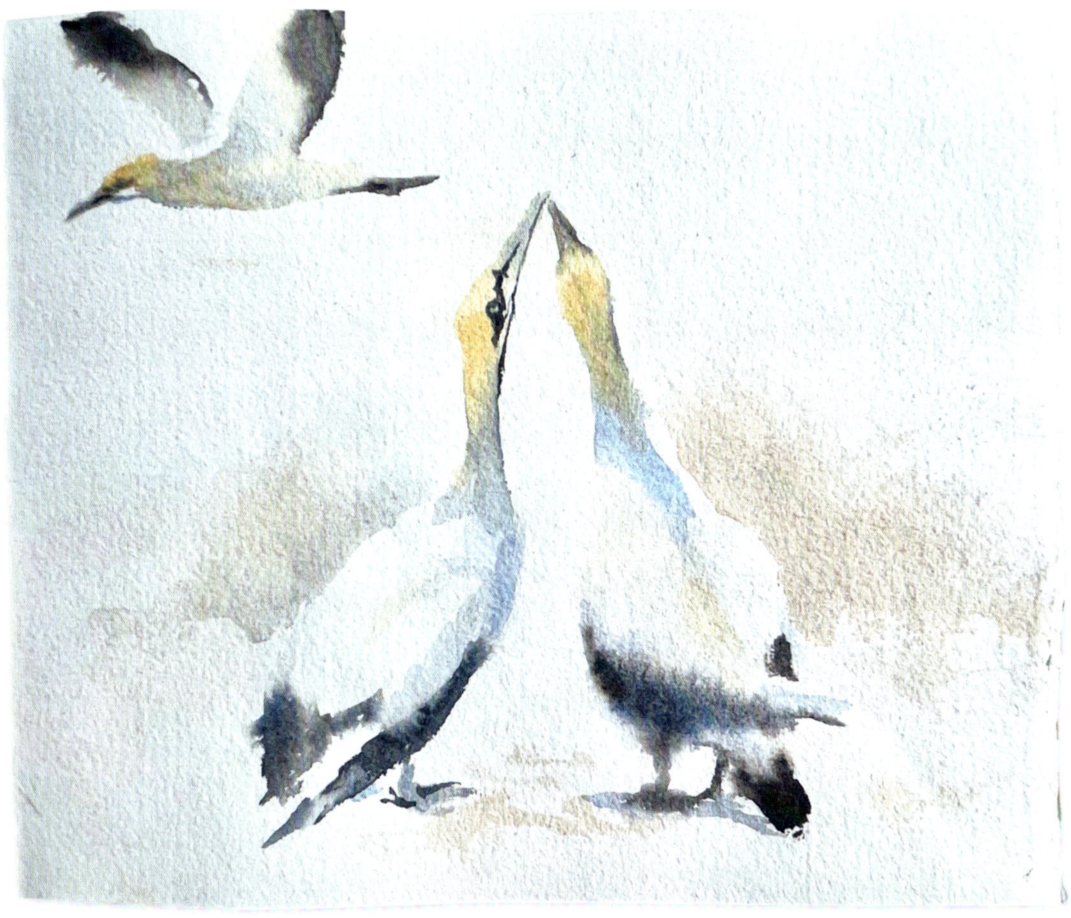

The Slope of the Palette

Watercolour is diluted and mixed on the palette before being applied to the paper because the binder, usually gum arabic, has to be dissolved before the paint is taken by the brush to the painting. One of the main problems beginners face is in judging how much water to mix with their paint, especially since wet watercolour looks darker on the palette than it is in reality.

A good field palette is designed with at least one sloping side so the artist can use gravity to help assess how wet to make the mix, simply by watching its flow down the palette slope. The water content runs downward, pooling on the slope in a bead, leaving the true colour of the mix at the top. On the slope, the meniscus provides me with an ideal gauge for the fluidity of the liquid mix. If too much water is added it will break and the paint will run downward, into the gutter and even off the palette, but if the water molecules cling together and hold the colour on the slope I have control. Thus, by harnessing the effects of gravity and surface tension, I have a good guide as to when to stop adding water to a mix.

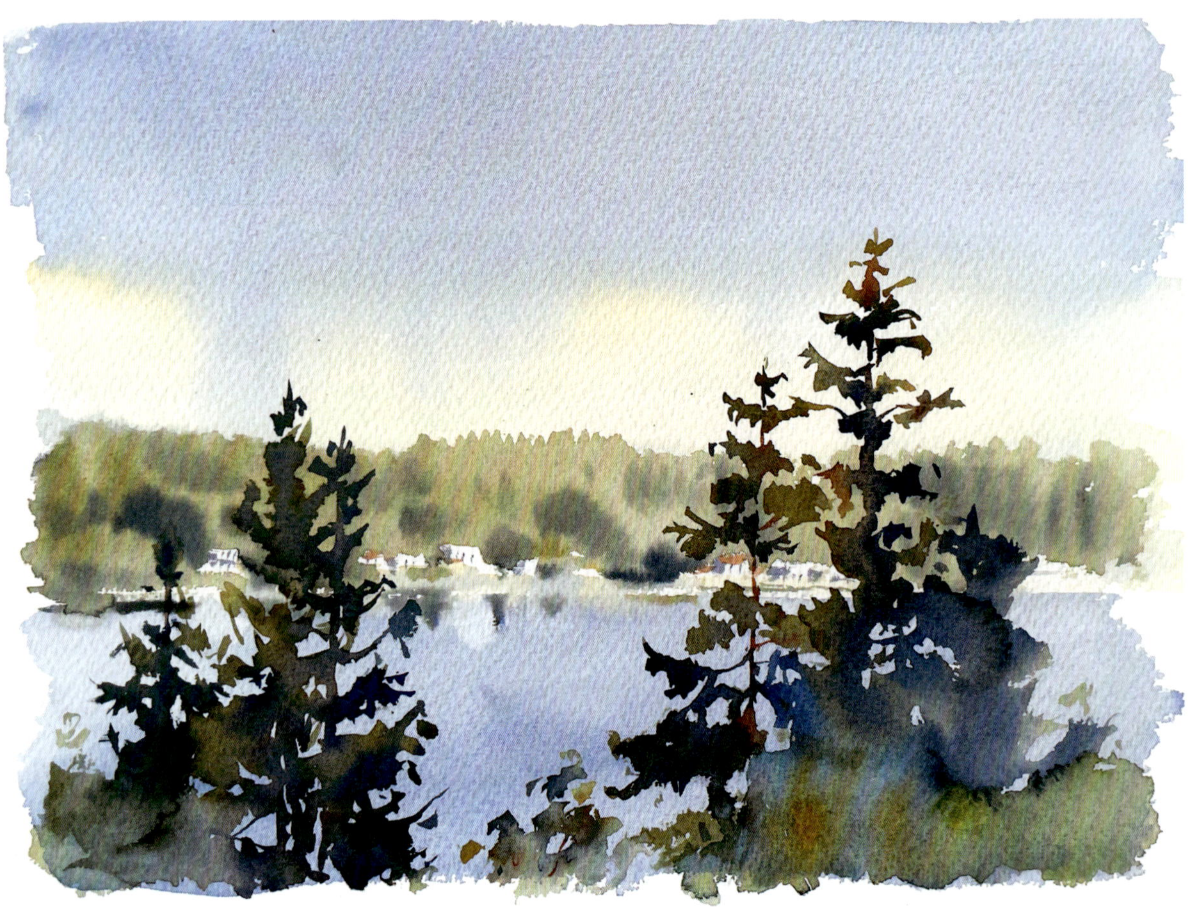

Very dilute tints and large amounts of paint are better mixed in the flat wells, otherwise the paint will run down the slope uncontrollably. A good palette is usually designed with both flat and sloping wells. In a flat well it can be hard to assess the true colour of a wet pool of paint, as it looks darker than it really is. I tend not to mix too much pigment at a time, then I can push the colour to one side in the well with the brush to see the real strength and not be fooled by the darker pool in the middle.

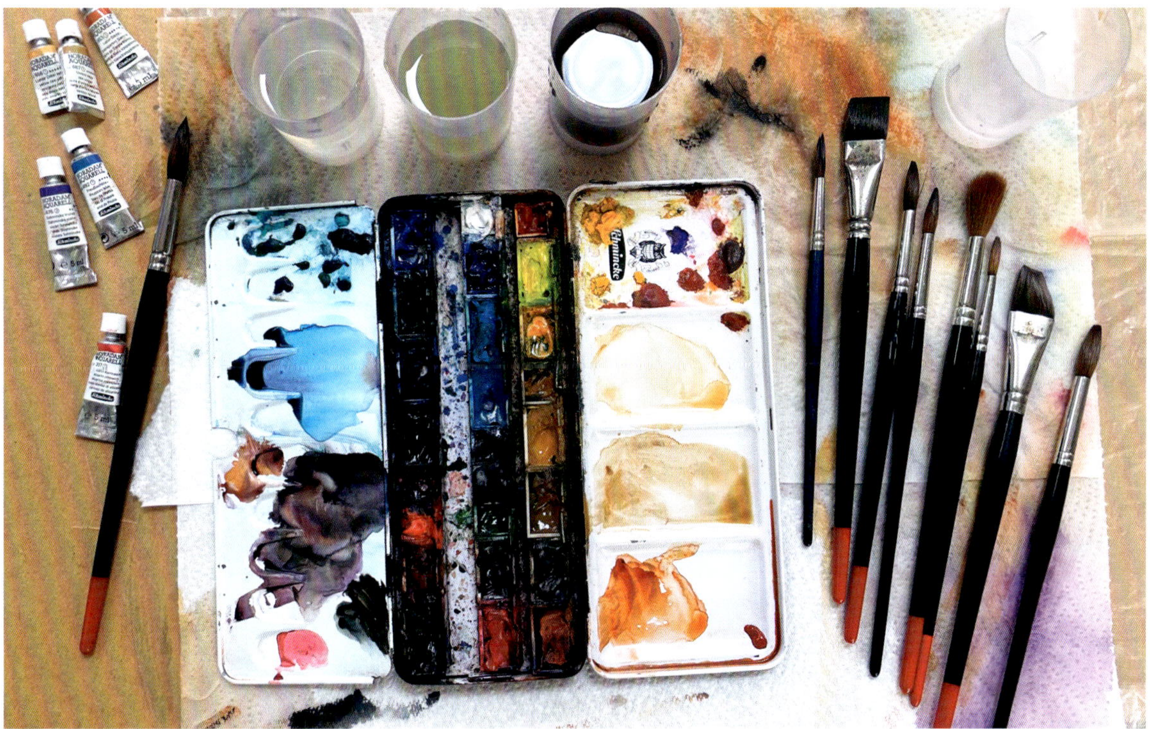

◀ **Lake Sammamish,**
28 x 38cm (11 x 15in)
The sky wash used both leaves of the palette: the pale Aureolin was mixed in the flat well of the palette, and the Ultramarine Blue on the sloping side. The drier greens for the foreground trees were mixed with the same two colours on the sloping side so that any excess water would seep out down the slope.

▲ An enamel field palette has fold-out leaves, which helps greatly with water control. The palette, when open, has a sloping leaf (on the left), which leans away from the palette, and a flat leaf (on the right) with several wells. By watching the water from a mix bead, or run down the sloping side, the amount of water to pigment can be readily assessed.

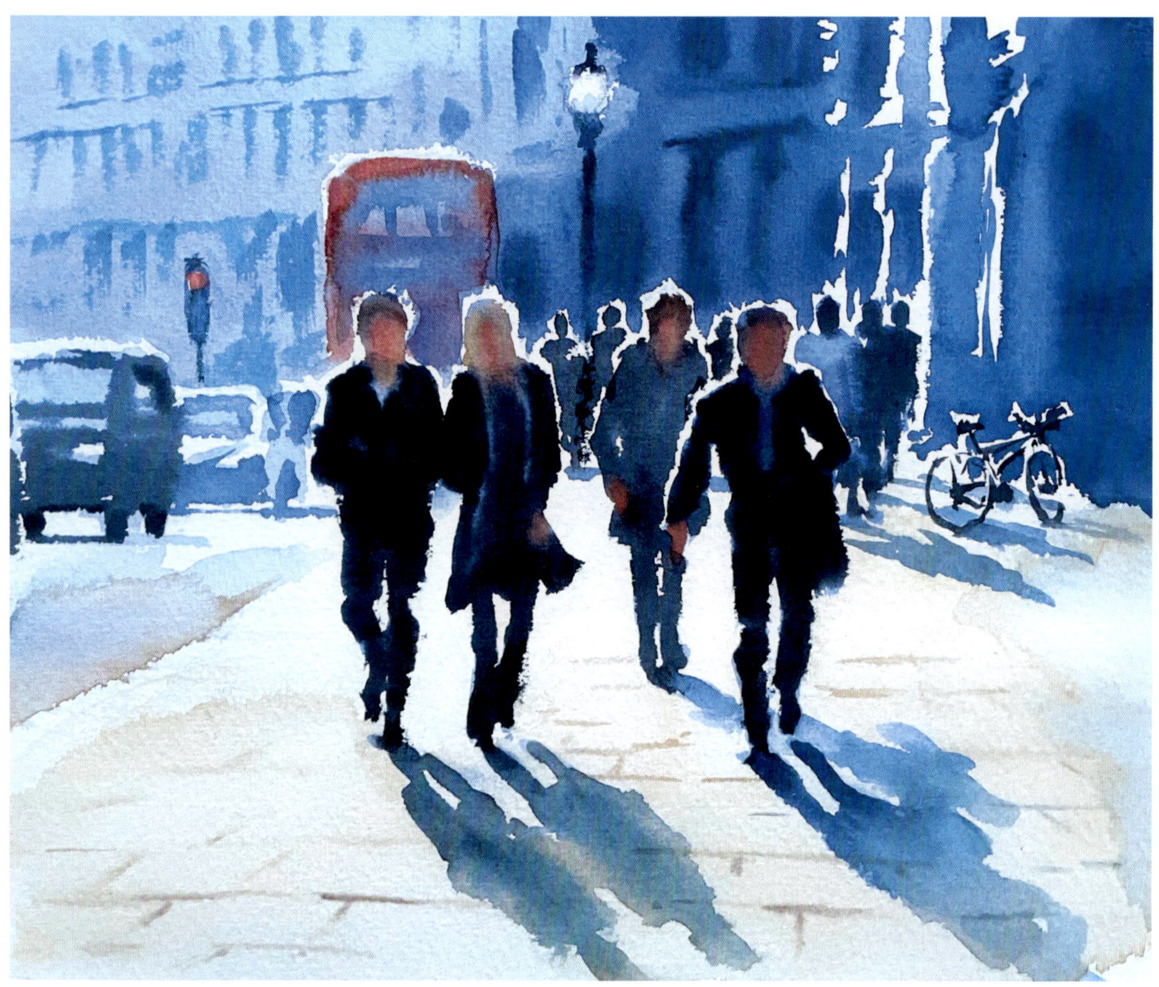

The Water in the Brush

To avoid making over-wet mixes, when you bring the brush to the water pot, aim to draw into the brush only the amount of water estimated for the current wash, stroke or mix. If you submerge the brush in the water each time you mix, you will draw out a full load each time and you will lose the pigment already on the brush. The excess water will dilute the paint far too much and force you to add more and more pigment. Instead, dip just the tip or half the body of the brush into the water to control the amount held within the hairs. Tap the brush on the side of the pot to release excess water, or dab the heel on some rag or kitchen towel.

Again, this comes with practice, but gradually you will find yourself automatically tapping off excess water or dabbing the kitchen towel to adjust the amount of water in the brush. I place a couple of sheets of kitchen towel under my palette and find it is often saturated with water and paint stains by the end of a painting from continuous dabbing to adjust the water content in the brush.

◀ **Regent Street Lights,**
25.5 x 30.5cm (10 x 12in)

Even though the background washes required far more water than the dark silhouettes, a size 10 brush was used to paint all the painting. The amount of water held in the brush was adjusted for each element of the composition, with the tip alone used to shape the figures' limbs.

You Have Control

Of course, when the brush is being rinsed out to clean off unwanted pigment, it should be completely submerged in the water pot and swished around to release the paint from between the hairs, but during mixing, aim to lift only the amount of water needed for the mix and no more.

While I normally advocate for bigger brushes, in high humidity, where evaporation rates are very slow, it may be wise to control the water on the paper by painting with flat or smaller brushes. A size 8 round brush laid on its side can make quite a broad stroke and lessen the amount of water on the paper.

▶ **Mont-Saint-Michel,**
20 x 18cm (8 x 7in)

It had only just stopped raining when I painted these ramparts. I had to adjust the wetness of the washes for a very slow evaporation rate and add very dry colour for the small, dark window details. I painted small in size and used a size 8 brush to lay the washes for the walls.

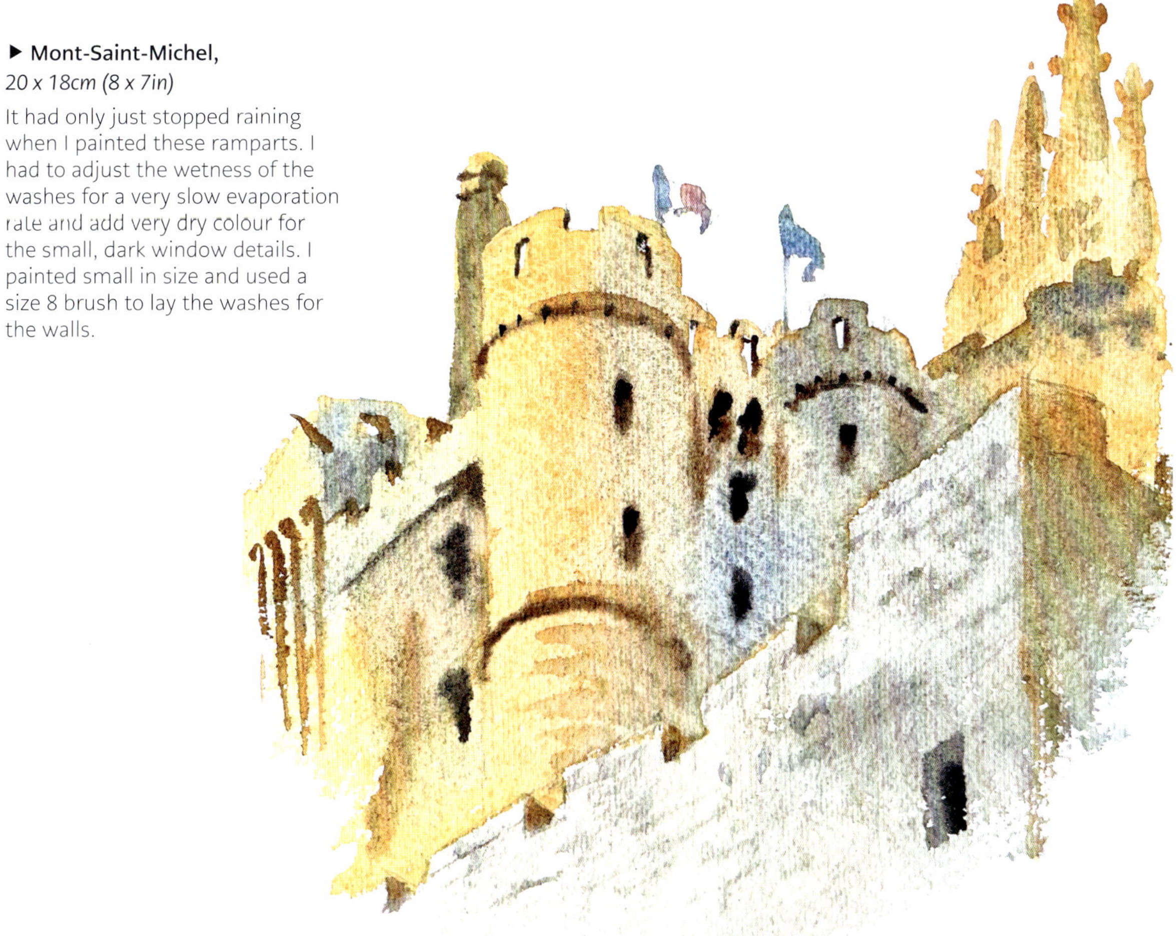

Backruns

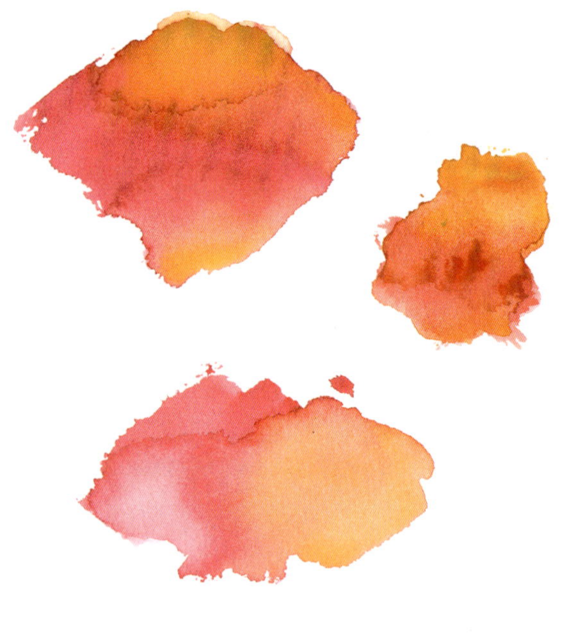

There is nothing wrong with backruns – they are a lovely feature of fluid watercolour – but if they happen where you don't want them, they can be very annoying! They occur when wet paint runs back into drier paint, causing the flow of pigment to stall, gather and settle. If a wash is equally wet all over, adding wet paint or more water will usually blend smoothly, wet into wet, only causing a run back if a section of the wash dries unevenly, trapping a still-wet area from spreading smoothly.

Dilute paint should rarely be applied to paper in such a wet state as to form puddles or pools unless a backrun or pooling is desired. Not only will the paper buckle uncontrollably, but the excess water will dry unevenly or run back into drier paint to cause a bloom (also known as a cauliflower).

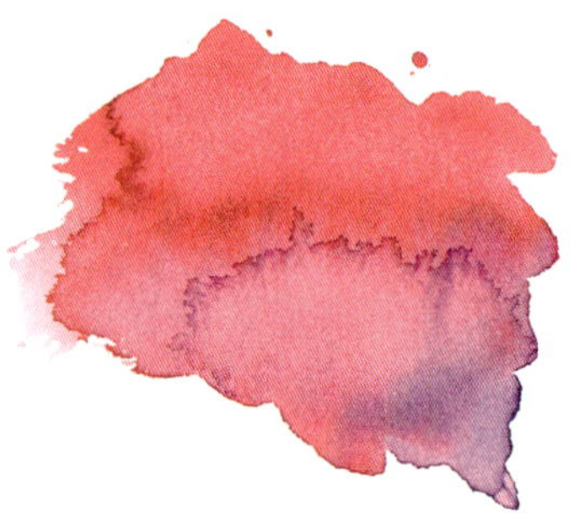

▲Here, wet Alizarin Crimson and Cadmium Yellow are forced into making backruns by adding excess water from the sides. The frontline of the backrun shows the pattern caused by capillary action as the outward-moving pigment is drawn into the drying, settling paint.

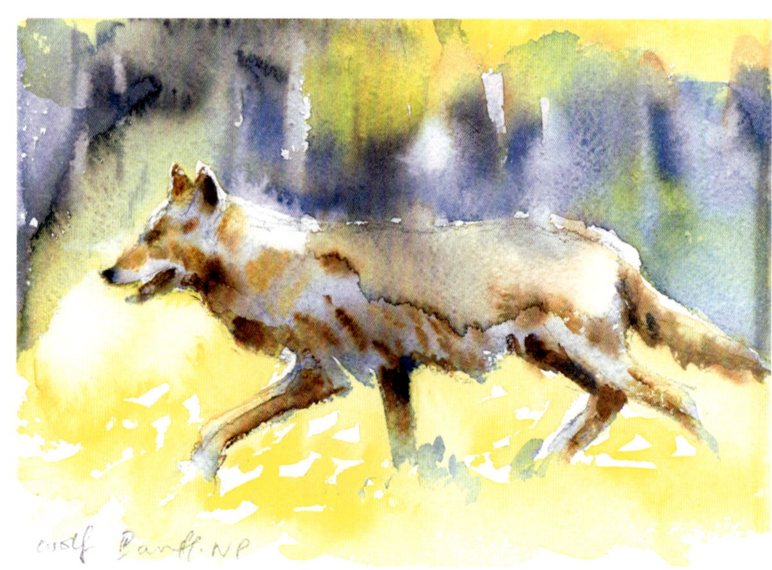

▶ **Lone Wolf,** *28 x 18cm (11 x 7in)*

A fortuitous backrun indicates the moulting coat of a lone wolf near Jasper in Canada.

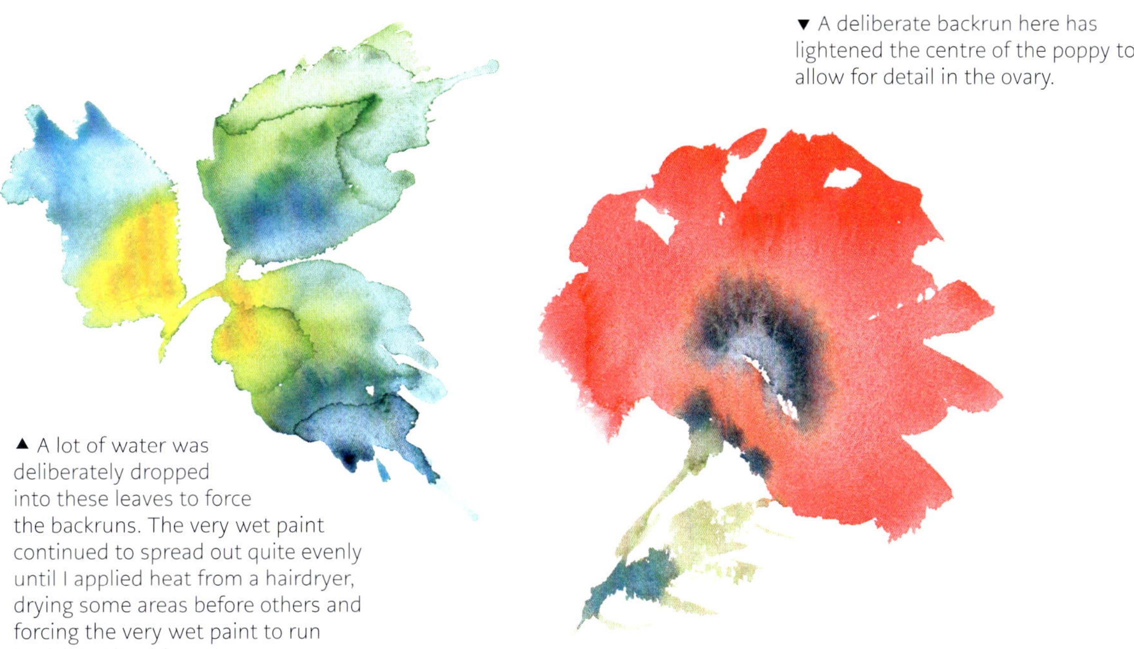

▼ A deliberate backrun here has lightened the centre of the poppy to allow for detail in the ovary.

▲ A lot of water was deliberately dropped into these leaves to force the backruns. The very wet paint continued to spread out quite evenly until I applied heat from a hairdryer, drying some areas before others and forcing the very wet paint to run back into the drier areas.

Pooled and Gathered Pigment

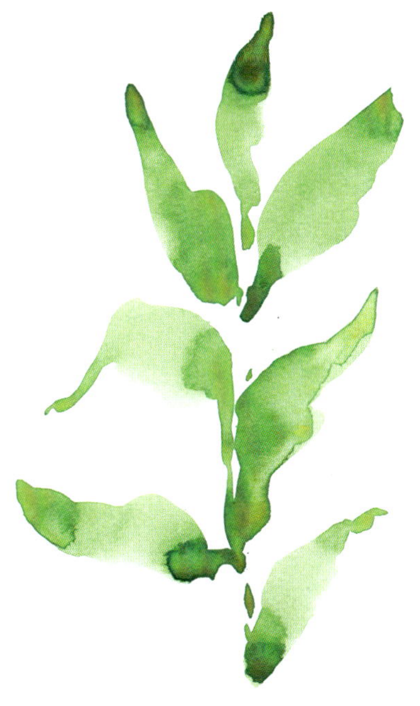

▲ On hot-pressed paper, pooling water can make attractive tonal exchanges within single brushmarks, as shown by these leaves painted in individual strokes of a size 10 brush.

Pooling water is active, as water is unlikely to sit still, spreading outward by diffusion or capillary action and carrying pigment particles in the flow. As it seeps backward and outward in a wave or ripple direction centred by the source of the water, it meets areas that are already drying and is forced to stall, leaving pigment to gather and settle in an irregular arc as the water evaporates (or an irregular circle if water is dropped directly from above) – this is a backrun. If planned or intended, these patterns are lovely, but if unintended, the bloom of clumped pigment is difficult to remove or disguise and impossible to shift if the colour is a staining pigment.

Pooling pigment may look dark in colour on the paper, but is actually very dilute, and, in the backrun, lightens the area behind the frilly front line of gathering pigment. On the smoother surface of hot-pressed paper, wet paint can pool and gather without running back and will dry in an attractive variation of tone where the pigment runs into the remaining wet area, as seen in the leaves to the left.

If you work upright or at a slope, gravity will carry the water downward; if it runs off the paper, it is immediately obvious that the mix is too wet. But if you work flat, excess water sits in pools or flows along the slopes of buckled paper, making it hard to create an even wash, even by tipping the paper. Hence, using too much water then causes problems.

Buckled Paper

Paper is a fabric, so when wet paint is applied, the fibres absorb the water and swell. If water is applied unevenly or in excess, some areas expand more than others. As the wet paper dries, the fibres contract. The areas with more water take longer to dry, creating tension between the wet and dry parts. These tensions cause the paper to buckle or warp, as the structure of the paper is unable to maintain its flatness under the strain.

Thin papers tend to warp easily, so use a thicker paper, of 300gsm or higher, to minimize buckling. As thicker paper is more expensive, you may prefer to 'stretch' thinner paper instead.

◀ ▶ **Saint-Malo Fort,** *28 x 38cm (11 x 15in)*

In the damp weather, the dilute under-washes for sky and sand have caused the paper to buckle in two horizontal waves, as shown by the shadows they have cast. I waited until the paper had flattened before adding the fort, rocks and beach.

Stretching Paper and Sketchblocks

Some artists pre-stretch their paper by soaking it with clean water before painting and taping it down to a rigid surface with gummed tape. This way, the shrinkage occurs evenly as it dries because the fibres are pulled equally in all directions. The downside is that your supply has to be pre-planned.

Unless I am using a very heavy paper (such as 600gsm), I tend to tape the dry paper onto a rigid board with strong masking tape just before I start painting, making sure it is taped evenly all around. This also enables it to contract equally in all directions as the fibres dry. I tend to avoid going too close to the edges with wet paint so that water cannot seep under the tape and dissolve the glue. If any portion of the tape lifts during painting it has to be re-secured immediately to prevent uneven tension developing.

Buckling is also minimized by controlling the amount of water in the brush to avoid over-wetting, and by allowing the paper to dry fully before applying more wetness to reduce over-saturation of the paper.

Nowadays, watercolour paper is sold in handy sketchblocks, which contain several sheets of paper glued around their edges to form a block, backed by a rigid board. This makes an effective stretching mechanism and ensures each sheet flattens evenly as it dries. A small unglued slit is left on one side to make it easy to separate the painting from the rest of the block once dry, but I sometimes even tape over this small slit if I am painting very wet in wet.

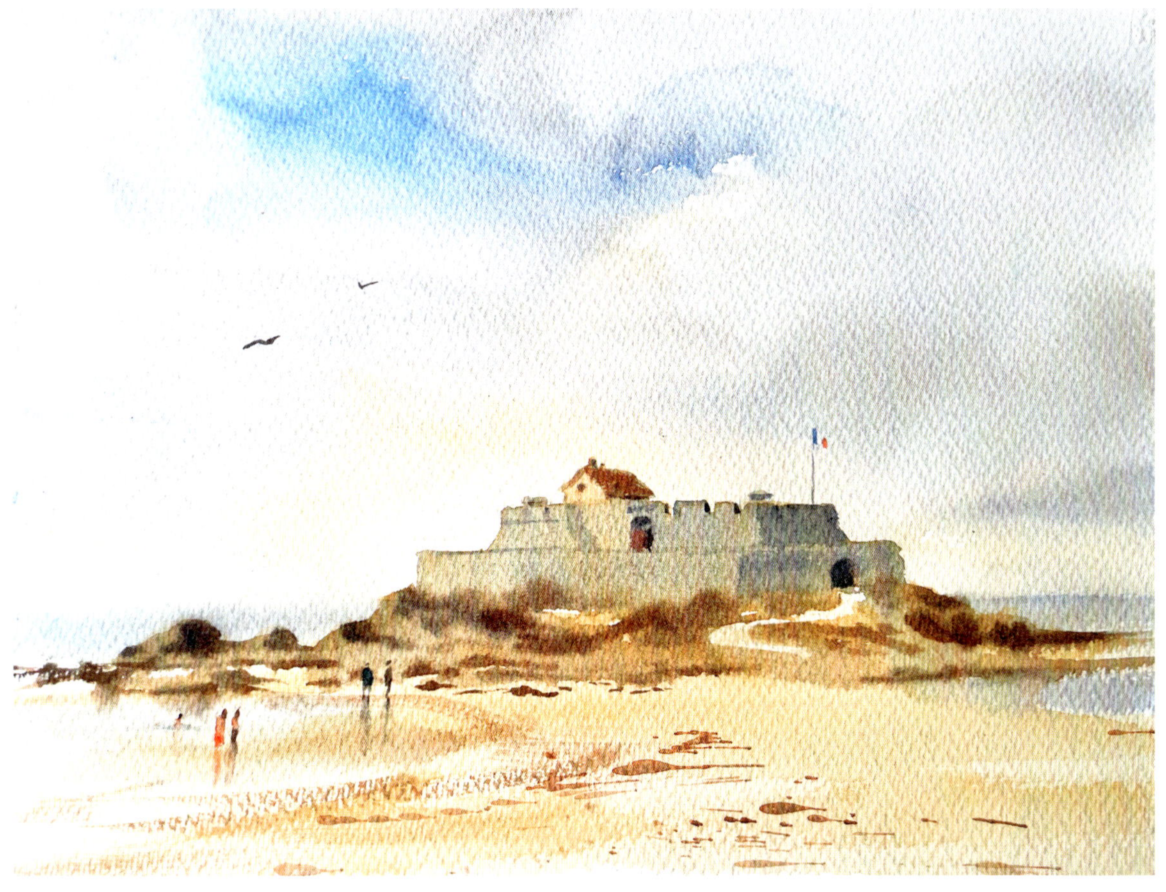

Too Little Water

Water management is the Goldilocks zone of watercolour painting: too much is a problem, but so is too little! If the paint is too dry for the area to be covered, or the brush is too small, this results in streaky paint and uneven washes because the pigment cannot float 'en masse' across the paper. Instead, the drier pigment has to be physically dragged or pushed into position using several strokes of the brush. The brushmarks remain visible in the passage of watercolour and usually present as unattractive streaks. This issue can be averted by increasing the size of the brush, because a larger brush holds a greater amount of water than a small brush and automatically offers a broader wash with each stroke (unless you only use the tip, which would result in similar streaks). Alternatively, if you only have a small brush, use the side of the brush and the whole of the brush, rather than just the tip, to lay your strokes.

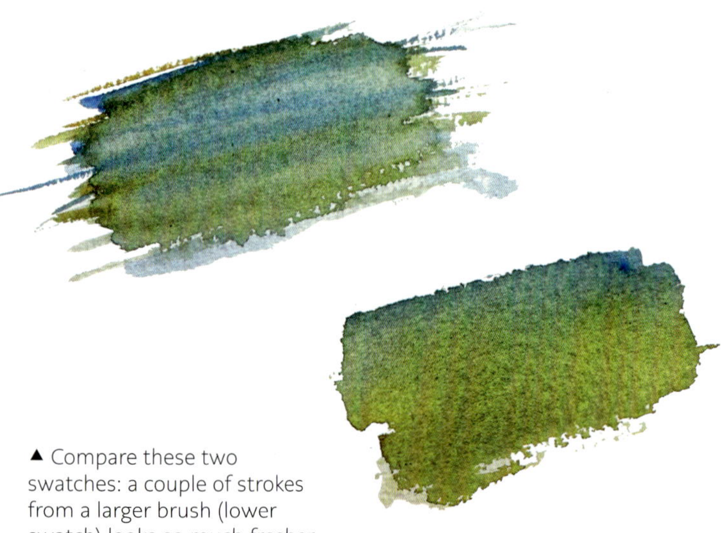

▲ Compare these two swatches: a couple of strokes from a larger brush (lower swatch) looks so much fresher and more attractive than the patch made by 'joining together' smaller, repetitive strokes with a small brush (upper swatch).

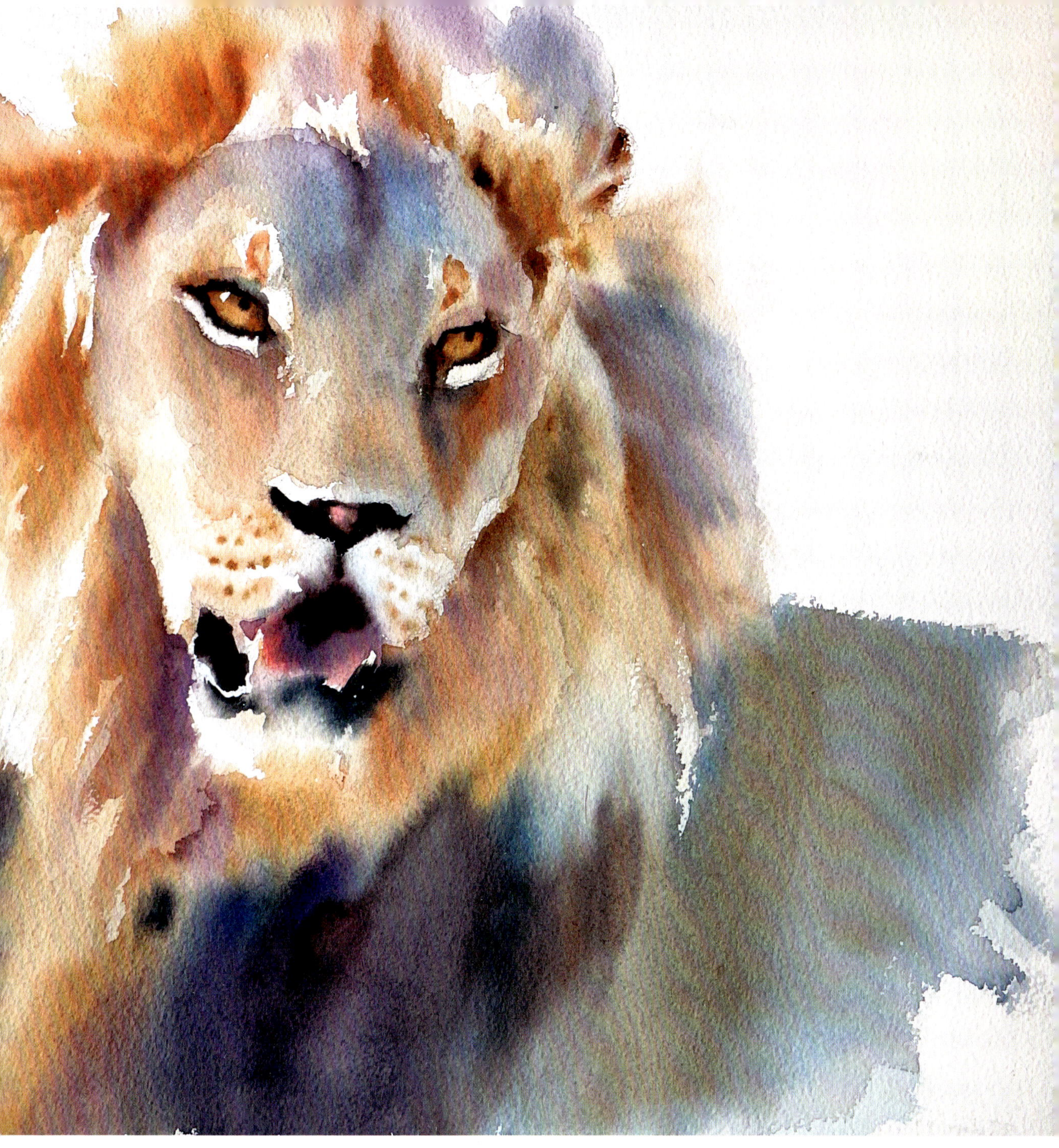

▲ **Kalahari King,**
38 x 56cm (15 x 22in)

The hair on this lion's mane has been painted with large brushes, first with a 19mm flat and then a size 12 round and a 10 round. The black around the eyes is painted with the smallest brush, a size 6.

Brush Size

Since round watercolour brushes have fine tips, small brushes are rarely needed for laying passages of paint and are intended for describing fine detail and fine lines. Small brushes should be avoided when laying washes and in the initial stages of a watercolour. Many aspiring watercolourists find it scary to use a big brush and feel more comfortable with a small brush, but this fear is based on a false security: they should actually worry more about using the small brush.

Of course, the fear comes from the copious amount of water that a big brush can hold, but as we have seen, there is no need to dip the brush fully into the water: the aim is to load the brush with as much or as little water as needed by dipping carefully and discriminately, and dabbing excess water judiciously out of the brush on a towel. Why join up several smaller strokes when a bigger brush can lay the same area with just one stroke? Why limit the flow of this quintessentially liquid medium? My advice is to always err on using a bigger brush if you want to lay clean washes and even patches of colour. Keep your small brushes for the fine detail.

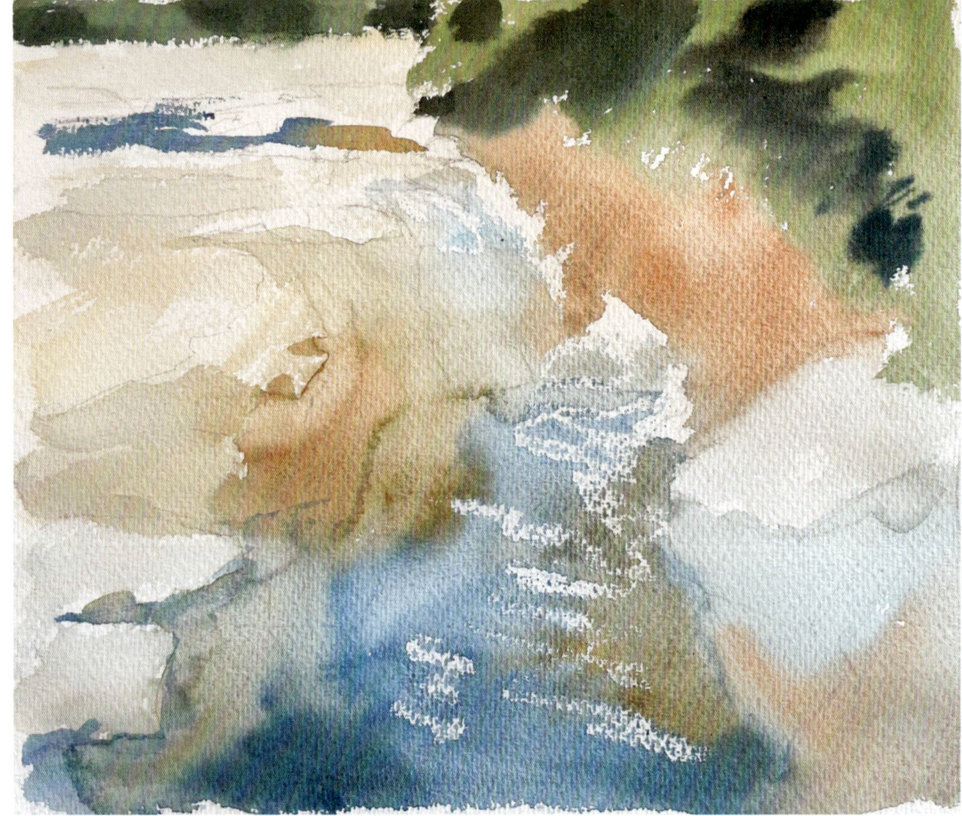

▸ The initial washes of this landscape were brushed in with a large, fully loaded round brush. The brush was dipped completely in the water pot and then drawn and tapped against the side of the pot to eject excess water before going to the palette.

Unfortunately, brush sizes are no longer standard, so suggesting actual sizes may be of little help, but I find I rarely use a small (size 6) round brush. Depending on the subject and paper size, I most often start with a 19mm flat brush or size 10/12 round brush, often swept on its side, only reducing to a size 8 as the passages of paint become smaller and more finalized. I also use a narrow rigger brush for fine linear marks, and occasionally a reservoir brush to randomize foliage marks.

When the tips of my brushes become worn, I press the tip on its side in the palette, to make a wedge, so that I can still paint a fine line if needed. Brushes last for many years and the only brushes I replace often (i.e. every few years) are the size 8 or 10.

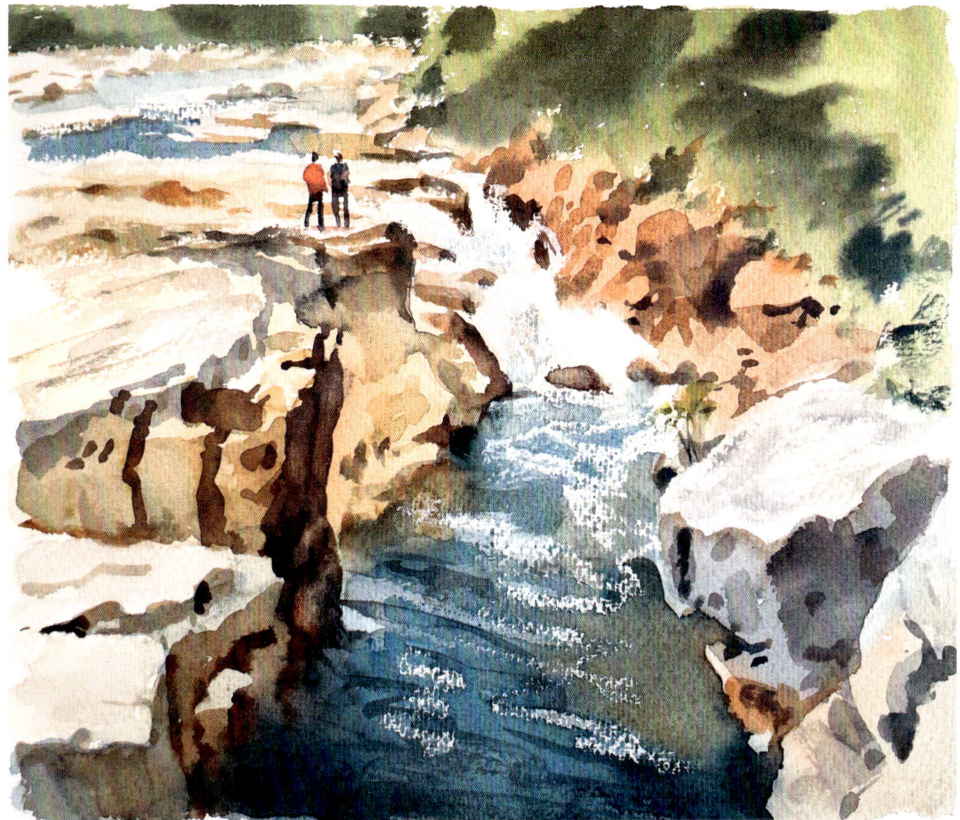

◀ **Adirondacks Waterfall,** *30.5 x 33cm (12 x 13in)*

The rest of the painting was painted with the same large brush, but only the top section (near the tip) was loaded for the rock fissures. I used the tip of a smaller brush for the figures.

Practice, Practice, Practice

Controlling the Water

Skies demand control of the water content over a large area. Our subject for this practice session is a cloudy sky above rocks on a beach. Use as large a sheet of paper as you can manage – the smaller the easier, but this should be a challenge as we are aiming to make a seamless but interesting variegated wash for the sky. My sheet is 35.5 x 51cm (14 x 20in). We will use non-staining/lifting colours so that our sky has more chance of blending in a seamless fashion and we may also be able to correct small aberrations in the sky.

Colours:

Ultramarine Finest/Blue

Yellow Raw Ochre

Transparent/Burnt Sienna

Brushes:

19mm flat brush

Size 8 round brush

Size 10 round brush

1 I outlined the tops of the rocks and the horizon line, to tell me where the sky wash should end, then prepared dilute Yellow Ochre and Ultramarine Blue Finest in the palette before wetting the sky area with clean water from a flat brush. I brushed in the Yellow Ochre to warm the tops of the clouds, followed immediately by the blue for the clear sky and underside of the clouds.

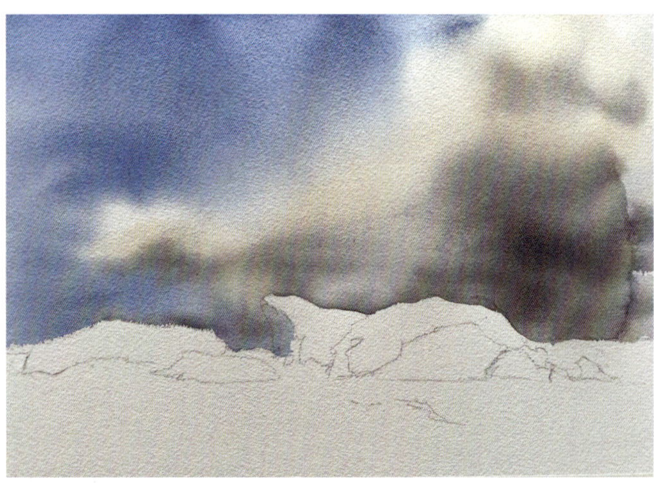

2 I quickly added some Burnt Sienna to the blue to turn it to a neutral grey and immediately brushed in the dark underside of the cloud while the wash was still wet, so that the paint would blend seamlessly. A large backrun developed on the right-hand side, but as the image could be easily cropped I decided it was safer not to fiddle with it.

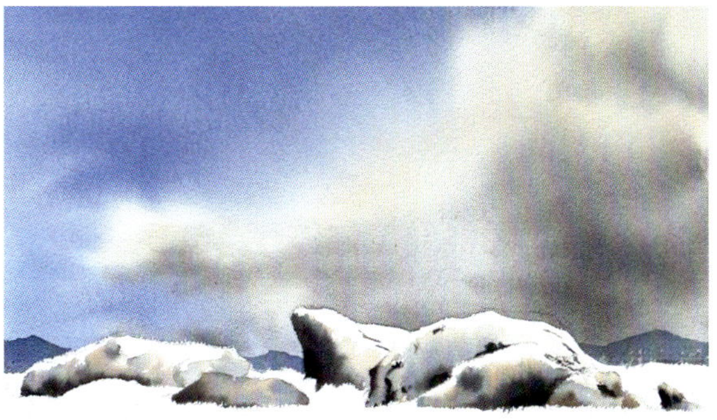

3 The rocks were painted from left to right, wet into wet, first with dilute Yellow Ochre and then by adding less wet Burnt Sienna, then a slightly drier mix of the blue/brown grey, before finally adding the deep shadows with a dry black mixed from concentrated Burnt Sienna and Ultramarine.

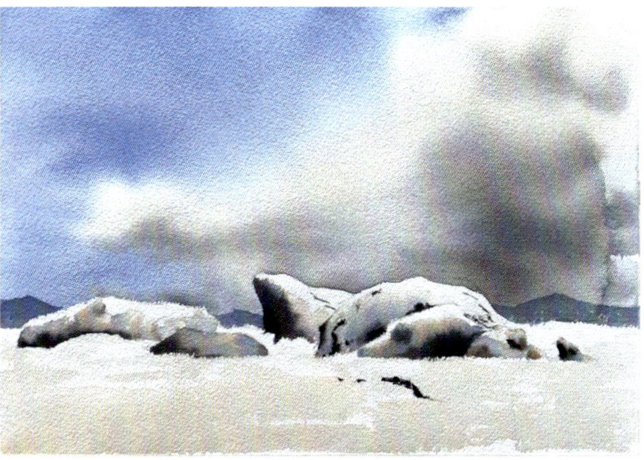

4 A pale wet mix of Yellow Ochre and Burnt Sienna was brushed horizontally across dry paper for the foreground area, leaving a few gaps of untouched paper between the brushstrokes to animate the undulating sand. Once dry, a slither of dark seaweed was added with the concentrated black mix.

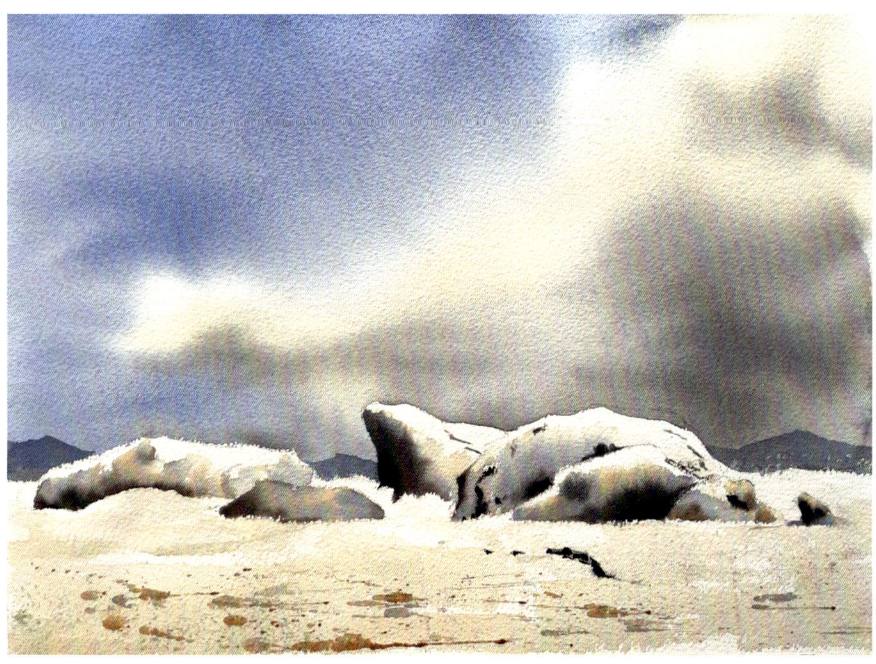

5 Dilute mid-tone Burnt Sienna was loaded onto a size 8 brush and flicked horizontally across the foreground to suggest footprints in the sand. A sheet of paper was placed over the rest of the painting to protect it from aberrant flicks! As you have seen, the watercolour process requires constant adjustments in the amount of water to pigment for each and every mix.

As water is also used as a method to re-introduce light in a watercolour and can lighten colours after they have dried, it is a reliable recovery aid. Just knowing that a dark colour can be made lighter post-painting should enable you to be bolder when applying dark and strong colours.

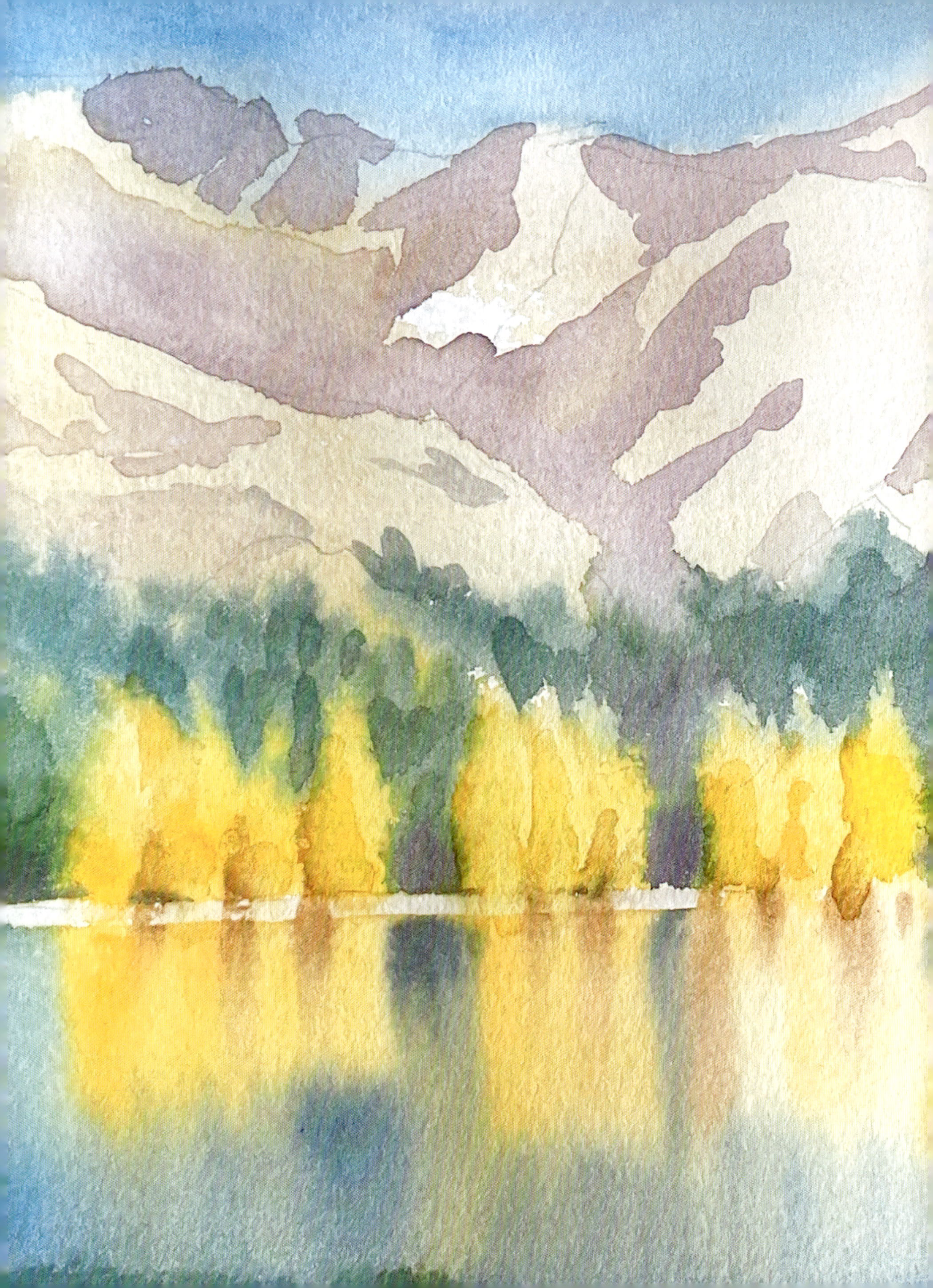

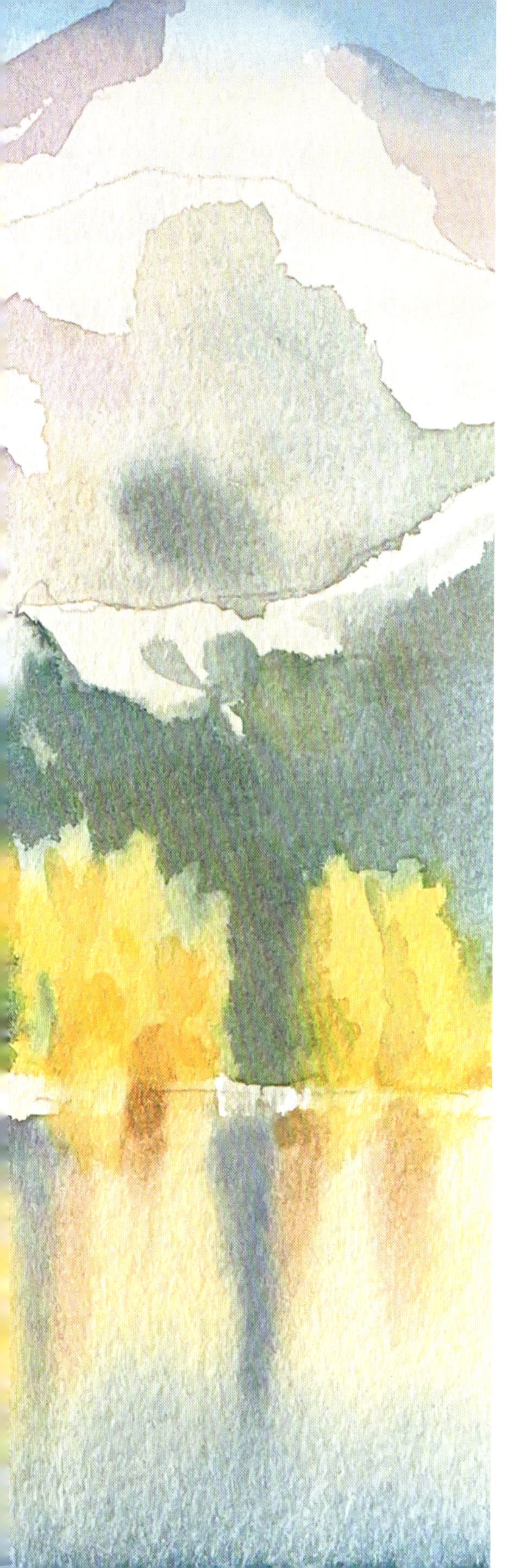

CHAPTER 6

On the Edge

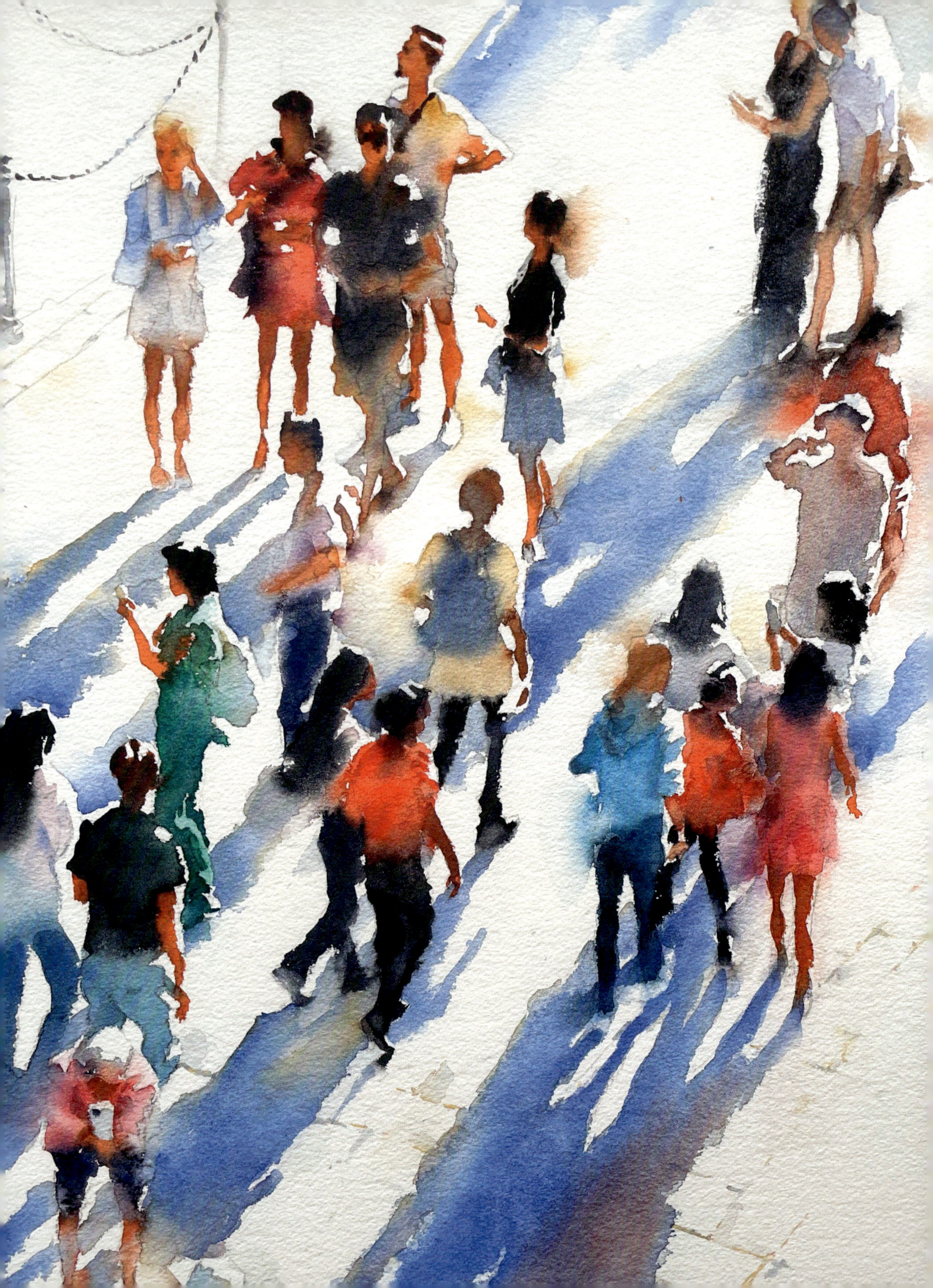

Contours and Edges

In all painting, the attributes of the visible brushstroke count towards the success of the artwork, and watercolour is no exception. The unique characteristic of the contour of a wash or the interesting edge to a brushstroke can be determining factors in a painting. However, these elements are often not given enough attention while painting, especially by inexperienced painters, and can therefore cause problems. The edge to a wash, brushmark or brushstroke can be beautifully descriptive and meaningful or it can be dull, ordinary and even irritating.

Watercolour is a transparent medium in more ways than one: if brushstrokes are laid carelessly, lazily or in presumptuous or repetitious fashion, they will let the viewer know!

◀ **To the Movies,**
56 x 38cm (22 x 15in)
By taking pressure off the heel of the brush as it paints the limbs, a broken, irregular edge is made to the brushstroke, creating interest to the lit side of the figures. In their long shadows, where Ultramarine Blue blends into Yellow Ochre, the contours show an attractive play between the warm and the cool colours.

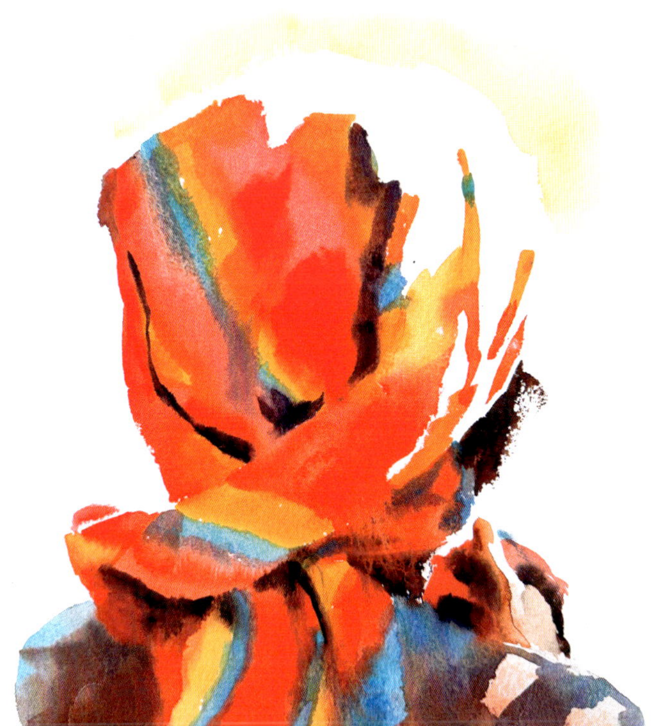

▶ The spontaneous, unlaboured edges of the watercolour brushstroke shown across this detail display an attractive appearance in themselves.

The Key to a Good Edge

For a watercolour wash or brushstroke to retain an attractive edge it is best laid directly in one movement or stroke, avoiding the temptation to go back over it again once laid. When the brush is asked to meet the same contour twice it may compromise the natural lay, and a repeated or doubled edge rarely looks as fresh as a single laid edge.

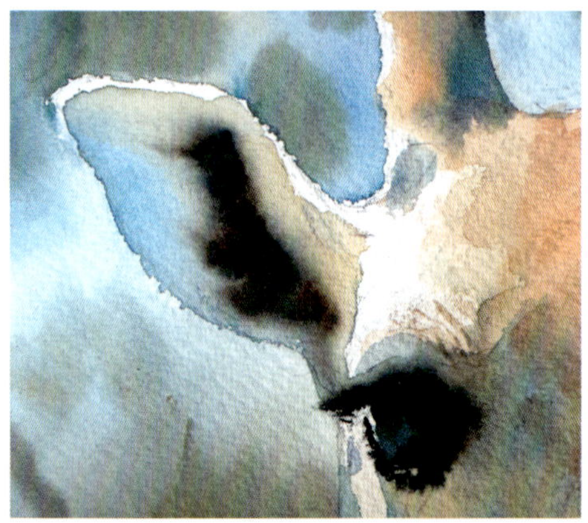

◄ ▲ The settling of the wet paint as it is brushed across the textured surface of the watercolour paper with the caress of the brush creates an attractive deckle to the edge of the wash.

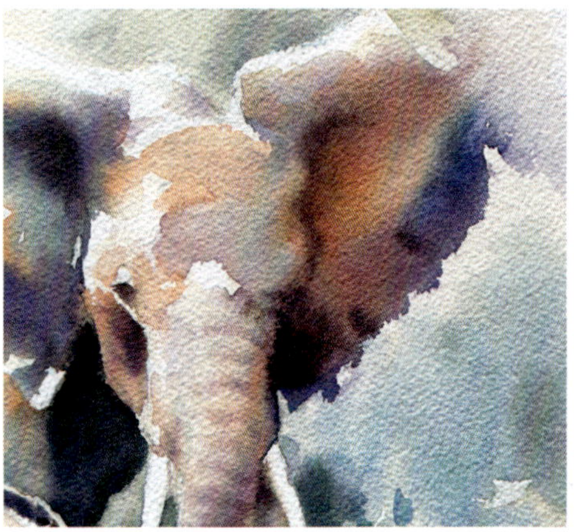

◄ Laying the passage of paint that creates the edge of the ears with the deep, rich, final colour at the outset has ensured an undisturbed and spontaneous 'raggedy' edge, ideal for the elephant's ear and appealing to the eye.

► When the pigment is very dilute and allowed to pool, the pigment particles may gather at the outer edges of the brushmark to deliver an attractive, slightly darker, outline to the wash.

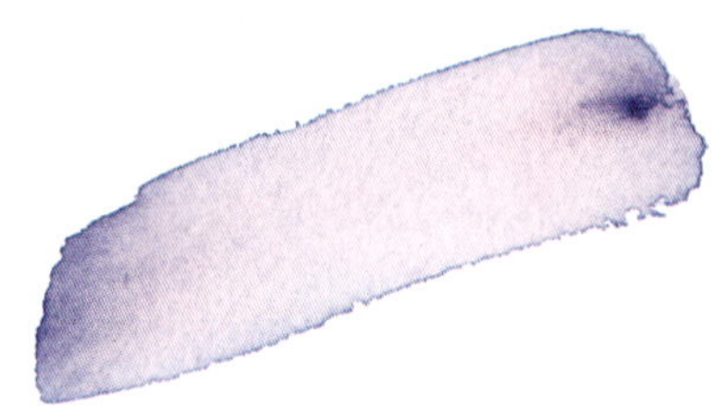

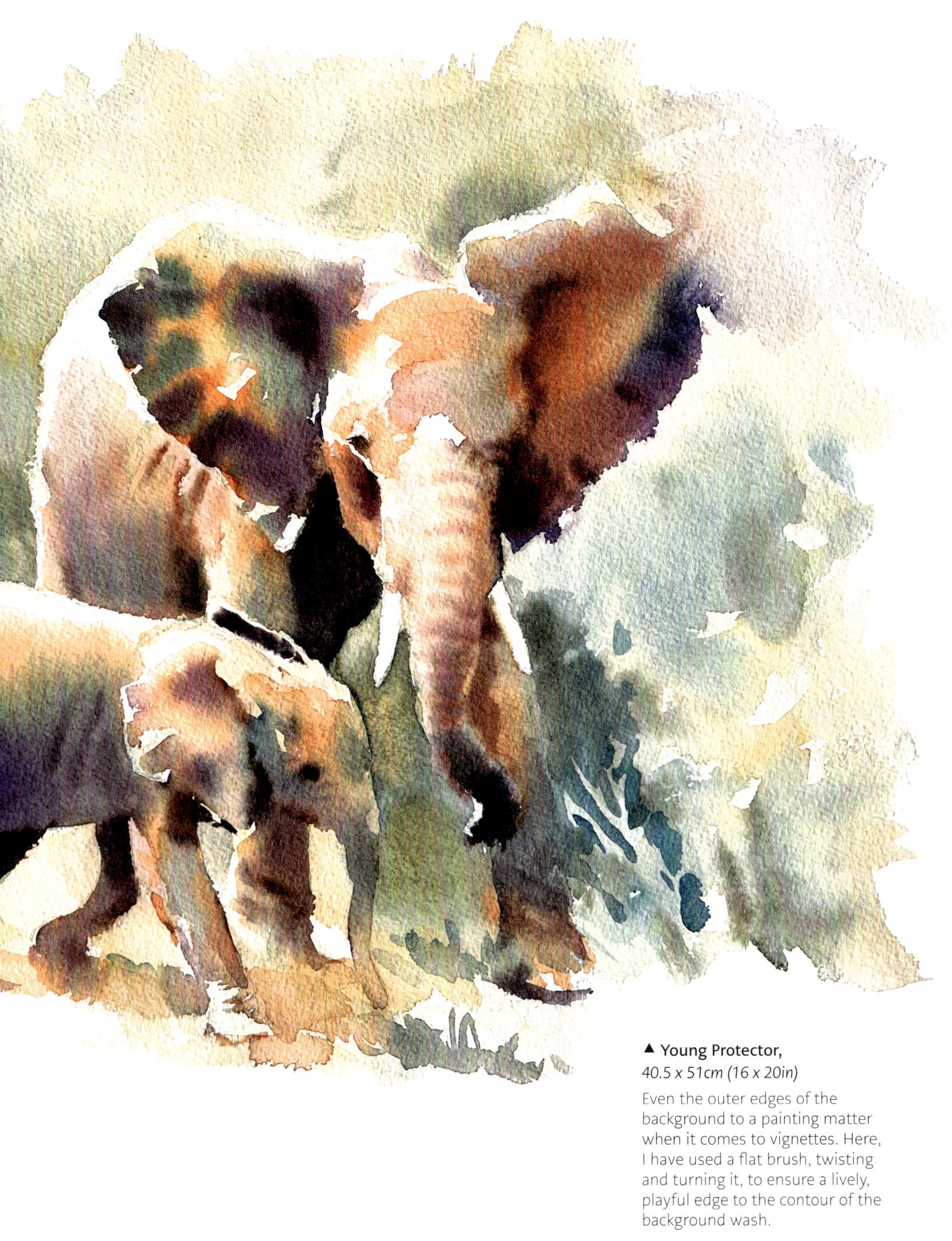

▲ **Young Protector,**
40.5 x 51cm (16 x 20in)

Even the outer edges of the background to a painting matter when it comes to vignettes. Here, I have used a flat brush, twisting and turning it, to ensure a lively, playful edge to the contour of the background wash.

Unwanted Seams

When paint is brushed onto dry paper, a hard edge will form around the edge of the stroke, mark or wash as and when the paint dries. This is the principal attribute of one of the two main techniques in watercolour painting, known as wet on dry. In large washes and passages of colour, when we wish to prevent a hard edge from forming between the brushstrokes, we can dampen the paper first, either with water or from a previous wash – as in the method behind the other main watercolour technique, wet into wet.

A large size wash requires a series of joined-up brushstrokes. In order to prevent unwanted seams from forming between the strokes, the paper must either be pre-dampened or paint laid swiftly before the edge of any previous stroke has time to dry. Sometimes though, even with good planning, the drying time catches us out and the paint dries unexpectedly, creating a hard edge within the body of the wash. The seam this creates may interfere with the beauty of the passage of colour or compromise the even appearance of a wash.

▶ **Rotorua,** *18 x 28cm (7 x 11in)*

To make sure there were no seams in the rising white steam, I dampened the area first but forgot about the dark trees in the background to the right. I had to darken that area afterward to disguise the annoying seams I had created.

▶ I started with the tower and carried on the silhouette on the buildings first to the left, but the seam to my right dried before I was able to rejoin it, causing an unattractive seam.

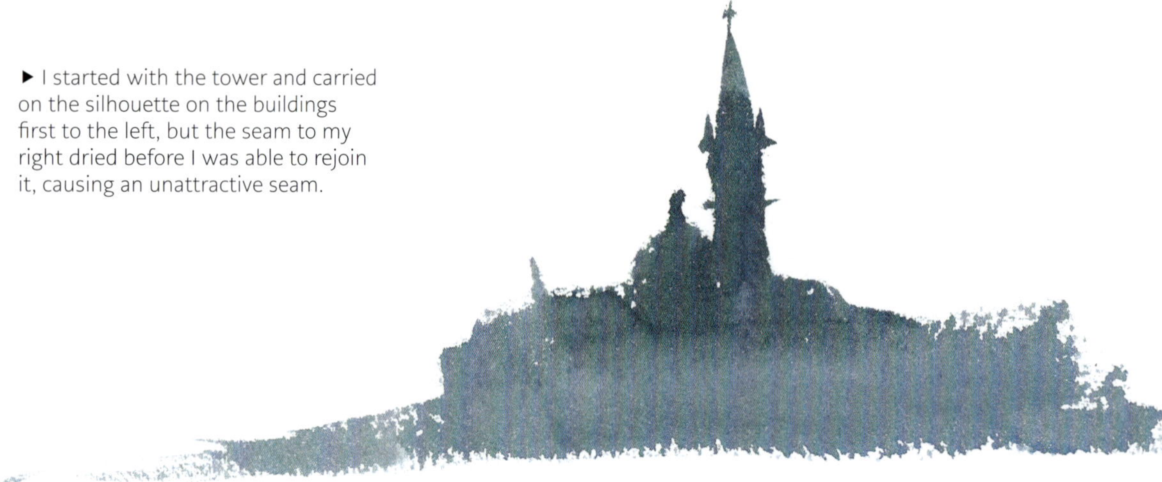

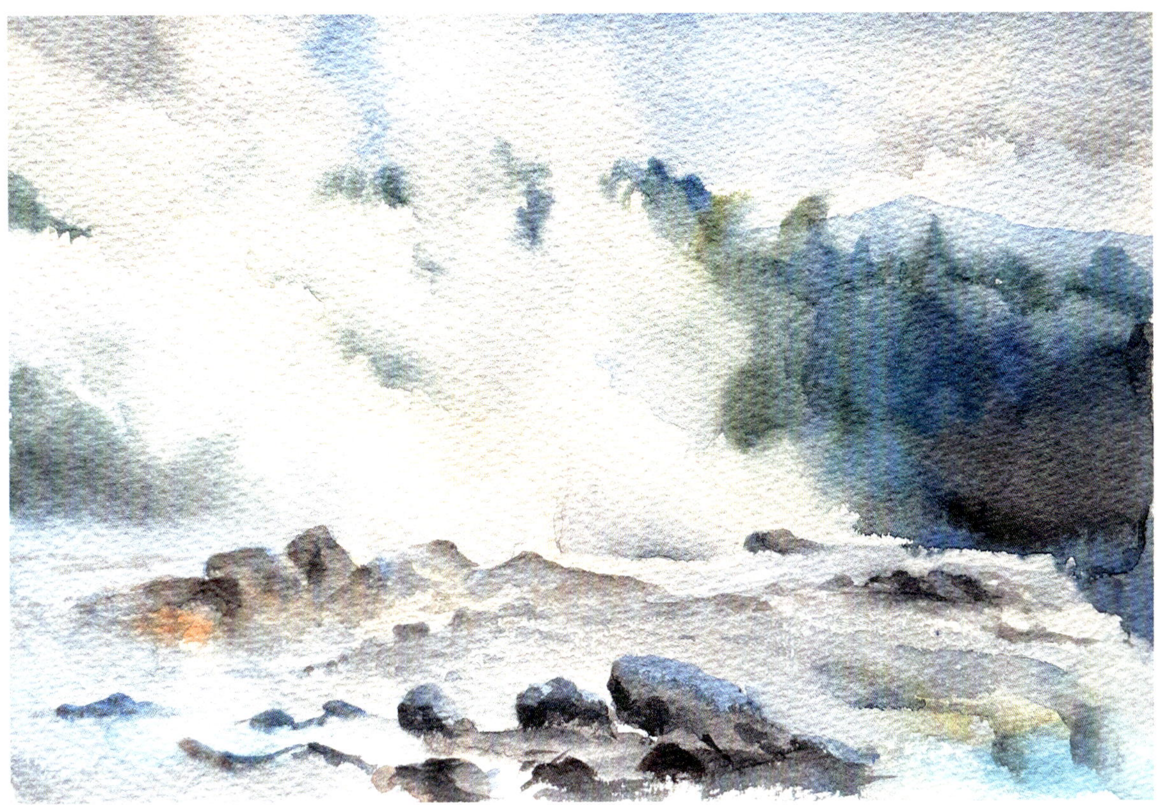

Preventing Seams

To avoid seams, plan and be prepared. For example, when painting a large background area around a feature, work either from the left-hand side to the right-hand side or vice versa, rather than from the centre outward, so that you only have one edge to the wash to worry about rather than two.

Have clean water and a clean brush ready at all times to dampen the paper ahead of the edge of the wash, in case you have to leave it to mix more paint.

Always attend to your washes while they are drying. For example, buckling may cause paint to run into a dip, or excess paint in the corner may run back into the wash. Be ready to tilt the board and solicit gravity to even the wash out, and have the corner of a tissue at hand to draw out excess water gathered in a corner.

If there is any safe 'breathing space' within the area of the wash where you can pause, such as the position of a tree branch, a building, or even a flagpole, use it. Take advantage of the chance to pause mid-wash, reload your paint and brush, or re-dampen your paper.

Above all, make sure you know the staining and lifting properties of your colours and take advantage of them. Staining colours provide immovable edges, whereas the edges of non-staining colour strokes can be lifted or partially lifted to soften, reduce or eradicate seams. It is often possible to soften a hard edge made with non-staining, lifting colour, such as Cobalt Blue or French Ultramarine, but never possible to soften the edge of a staining colour such as Prussian Blue or Phthalo Blue.

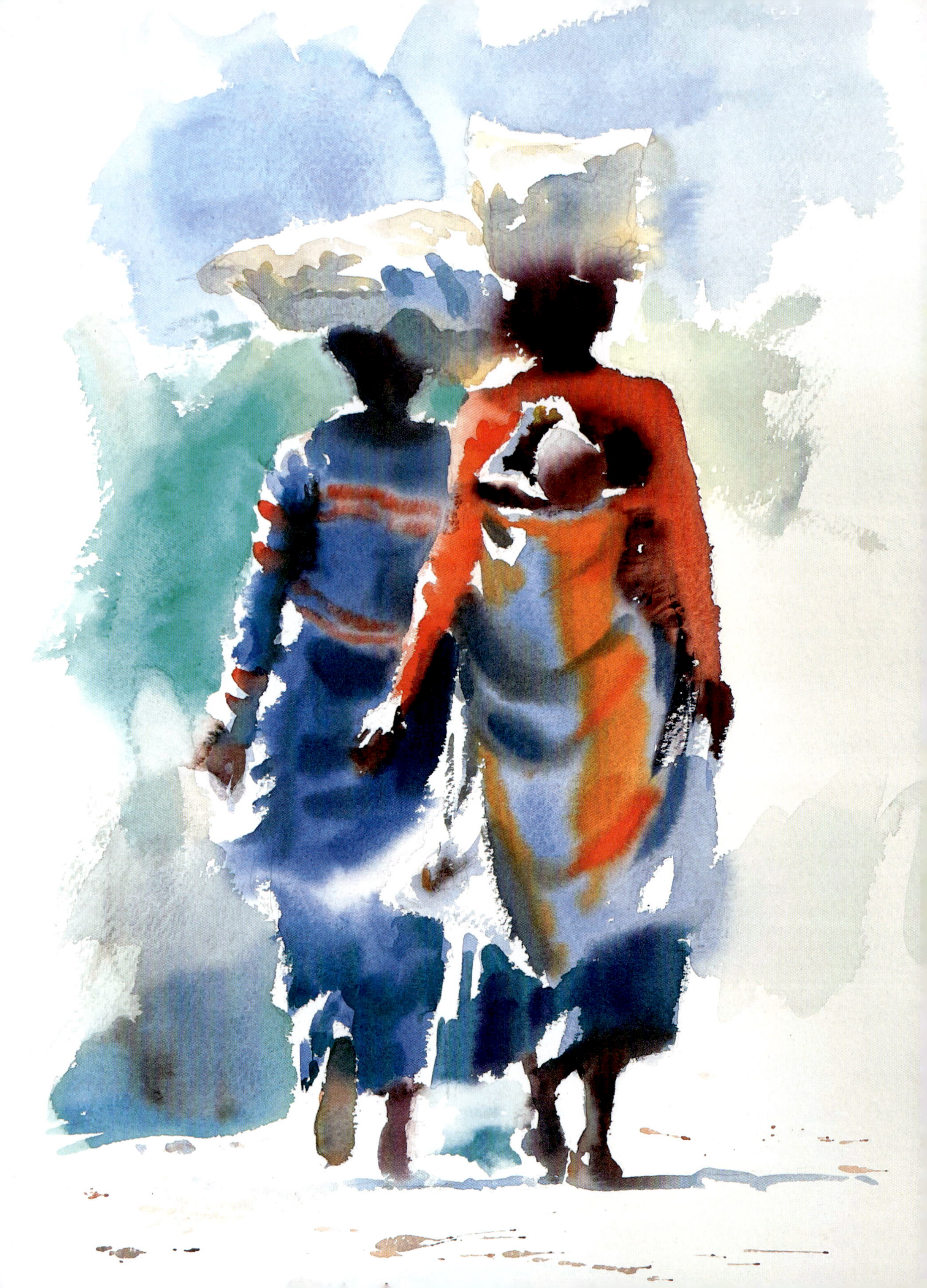

It May Not Be a Problem

Hot weather and poor planning may lead to unwanted hard edges, seams and loss of light areas, but it may not always matter. Sometimes an unwanted seam is not the problem you suppose. For example, a sky wash is often painted in the initial stages of a watercolour. Unwanted edges may appear in the wash and immediately prompt the desire to correct them or even to abandon the painting and start anew. However, I would suggest patience and tolerance: at the start the sky seems a dominant feature against the white paper, but once the other layers are in place and the deepest darks applied, the sky is likely to be one of the lightest parts of the painting; as such, any aberration in the wash probably won't matter.

In the painting opposite, for example, I was annoyed by the seam that developed in the sky above the left-hand lady's head and was tempted to soften the blue edge. Even though it would have been possible as the blue is painted with the lifting colour Ultramarine Finest, in doing so I would risk drawing more attention to it rather than leaving it well alone. Watercolours do not have to be perfect to work!

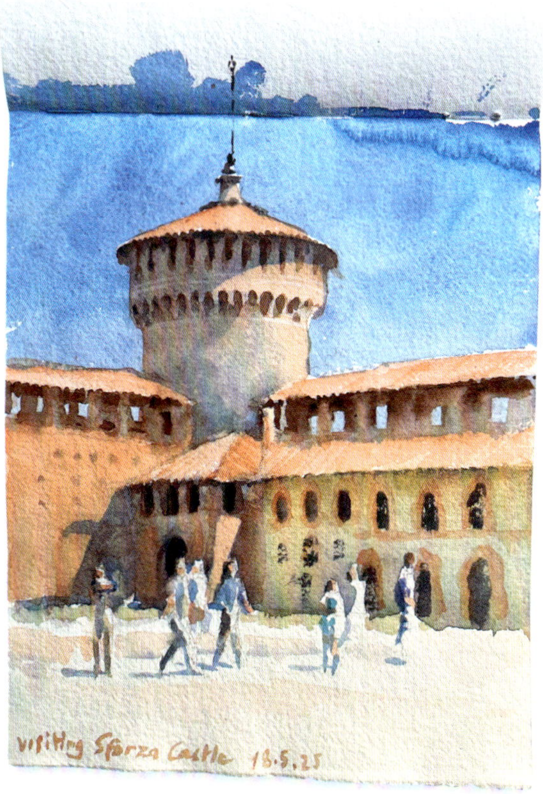

◀ **African Synchrony,**
56 x 38cm (22 x 15in)

The seam in the sky wash above the woman on the left bothered me. However, if I had not drawn it to your attention I doubt you would have noticed it in a negative way, as the liveliness of the lady's movement overtakes the 'aberration' in the wash.

▶The frilly seam caused by the backrun top right doesn't harm the painting in the sketchbook, but if it were to be framed it might benefit from being softened or trimmed. It is Cobalt Blue so should lift easily.

Dabbing and Blobbing

One of the common habits that beginners fall foul of is what I call 'dabbing and blobbing', especially when it comes to painting foliage or flowers. This is the habit of making multiple dabs with a small brush in the hope that the blobs of paint might collectively represent leaves on a tree or blossoms on a shrub.

Figurative watercolour painting is not about 'recreating' the real world; it is about representing something interesting about the real world on a flat piece of paper in a meaningful and artful way. Painting is an art that must entertain the eye before it can touch the heart or reach the soul, so all the marks you make should be exciting, descriptive and above all meaningful. Trees might be covered in a multitude of leaves, but when you come to paint them you have to look at the foliage masses, not the individual leaves; you have to represent the form with the play of light and shadow. Take advantage of any leaves that escape the outer contour, as they can be painted with the dance of the brush in attractive random brushstrokes.

▼ Even in a quick sketch like this one of hills in New Zealand, simply by varying the foliage forms between soft-edged shapes in the shadows (wet into wet) and hard-edged forms in the light (wet on dry), the eye is entertained.

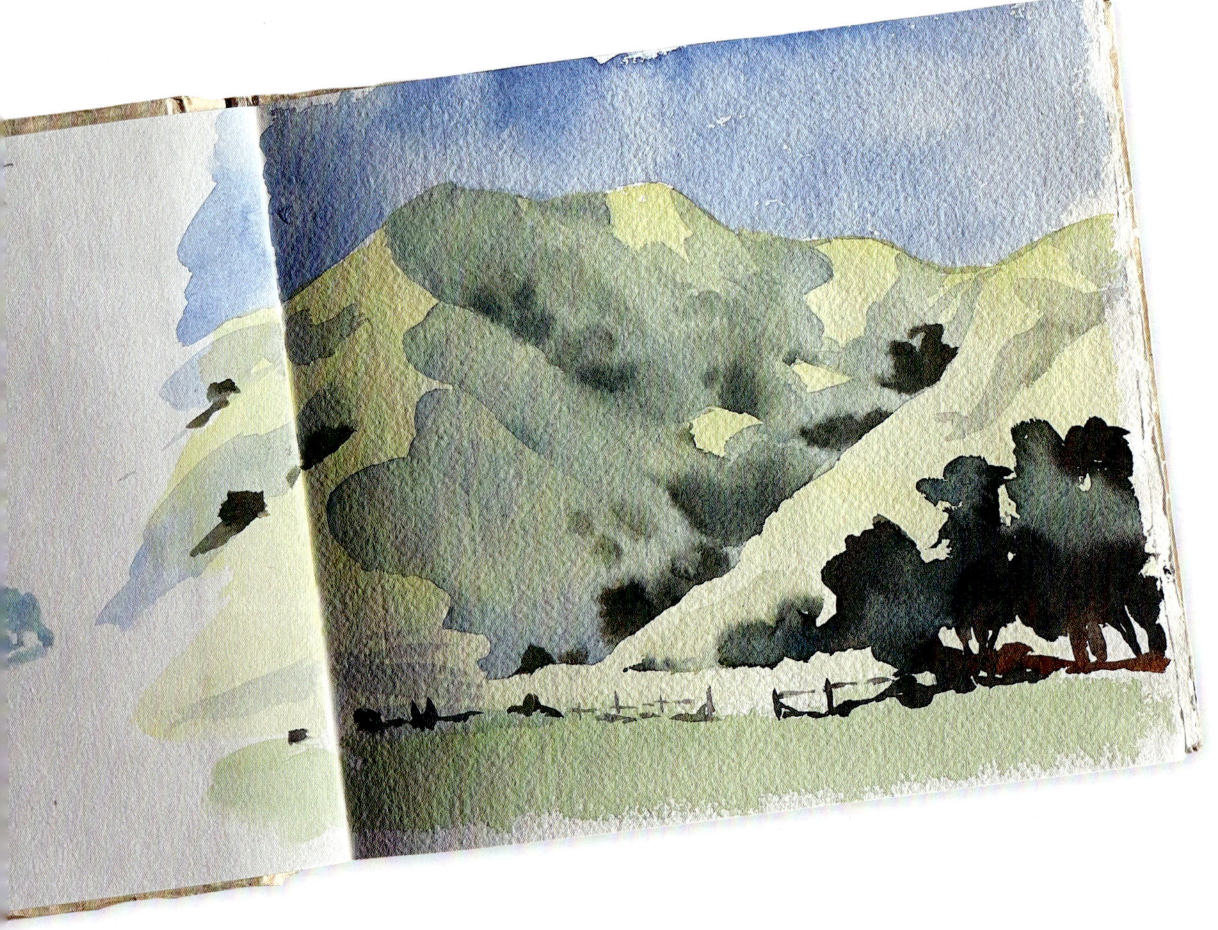

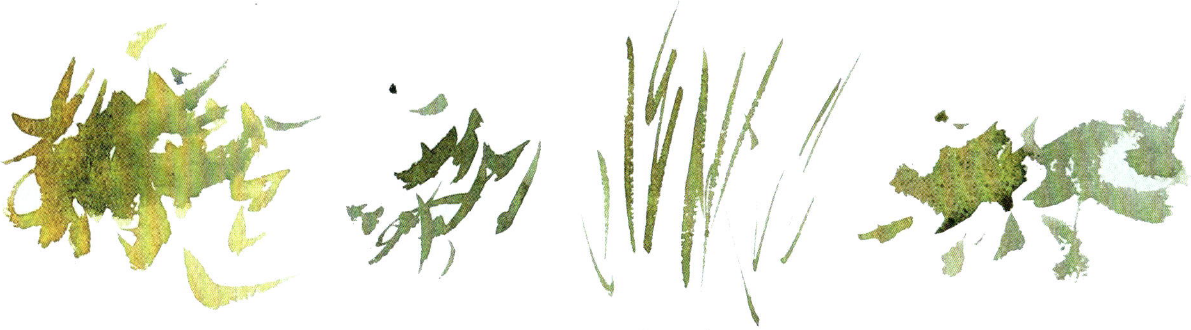

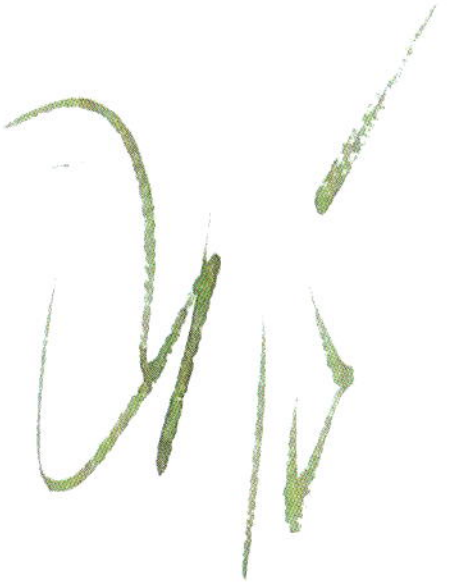

▲ You are not obliged to show every leaf or blade of grass! A cluster of green brushmarks will read as foliage. Group irregular brushmarks rather than trying to paint actual leaf shapes. Do not overcrowd, use a few strokes to represent many, and allow the brush to dance on the paper, twisting and turning it in a loose grip.

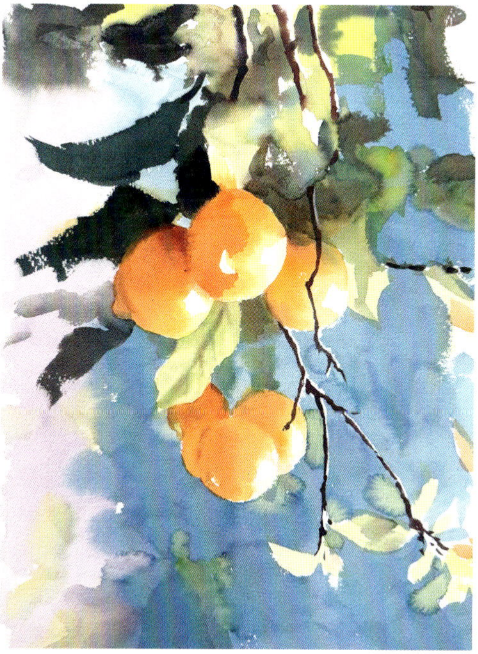

▶ **Liquid Sunshine,**
51 x 35.5cm (20 x 14in)

By describing just a few leaves as specific leaf shapes and encouraging wet into wet blending and loose, large brushstrokes among the rest, a dynamic rendition of the lemon tree foliage is achieved in a lively fashion.

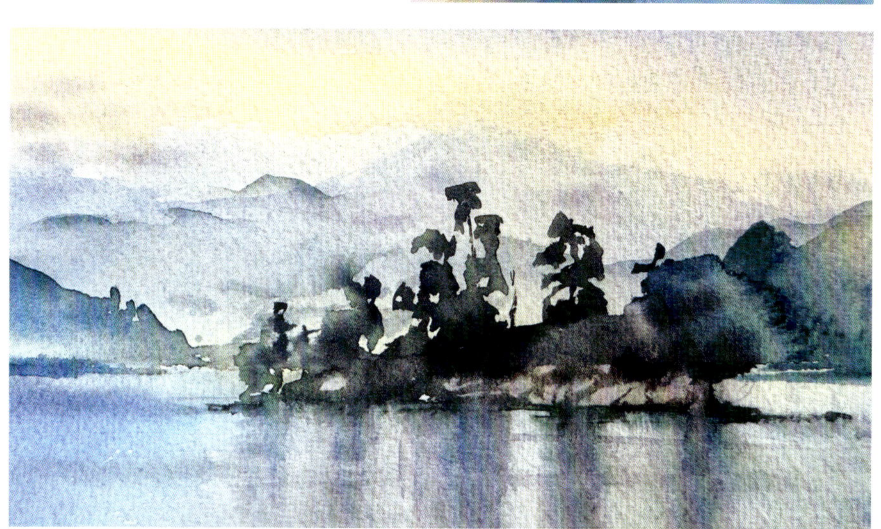

▶ **Lowering Cloud, Port Levy, Banks Peninsula,**
38 x 28cm (15 x 11in)

In this detail, you can see that the foliage of the pine trees is made up of loosely painted positive brush marks combined with more carefully allocated negative spaces between them, creating a convincing shape to each pine tree and the overall shape of the stand.

Make Edges Attractive

Making attractive edges to a brushstroke is a matter of brushwork, trusting the brush to deliver the watercolour with a sweep or a delicate dancing touch.

To create a fragmented edge, for example, favour a rough surface to the paper, so that the hills and valleys in the tooth of the paper help to break up the hard edge. The tip of the brush delivers a crisp edge, whereas the heel of the brush can offer a more fragmented stroke, especially as you release pressure on that side of the brush.

Caress the paper with your brush, rather than drag it across the paper. Use the wet on dry technique for hard edges and definition and add colour wet into wet to create soft edges, blends and flow. Encourage a lost and found technique to your edges: ambiguity in the shadows, definition in the light.

If you find it hard to let go, try painting bigger. Size matters as bigger can in fact be easier: it enables you to use bigger brushes and allows more room for error, while moving your whole arm brings more sweep, energy and dance into your brushstroke. If you normally sit to paint, try standing.

▶ **Tall Story,** *56 x 38cm (22 x 15in)*

Look closely at all the edges here, first around the contours of the giraffe, which are mostly created with wet paint on dry paper, and then the markings within the body, mostly soft-edged, which are painted wet into wet. Note how the paint has been encouraged to flow to give the impression of soft hair on the neck and mane.

▼ Hot-pressed paper has a smooth surface. This gives the dried pool of diluted watercolour a sharp edge and can offer tonal exchange within the brushmark.

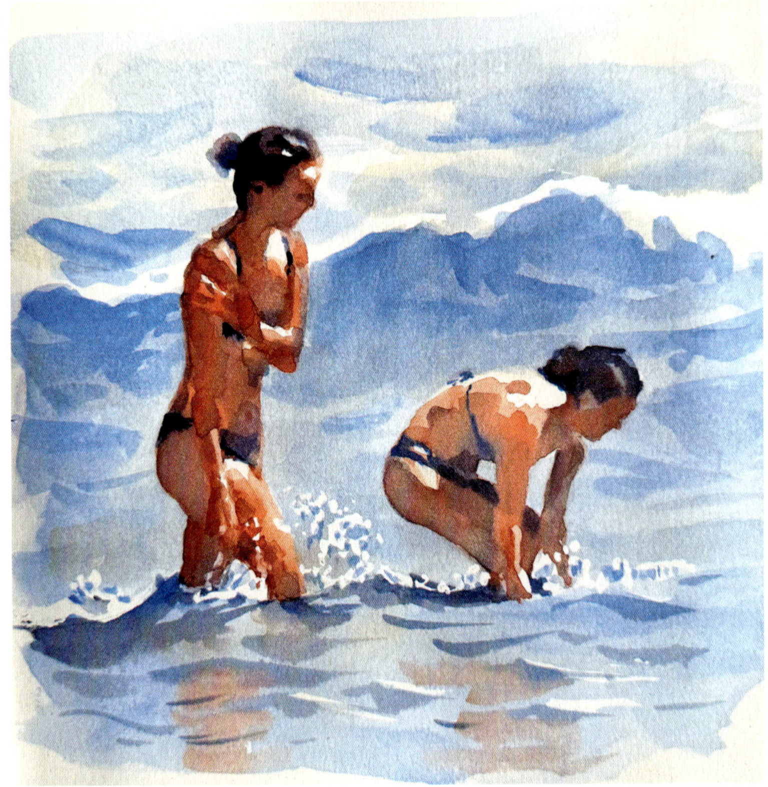

◀ **Beach Girls,**
25.5 x 25.5cm (10 x 10in)

The smoothness of hot-pressed paper does not allow the same level of blending as cold-pressed or rough papers, but the more staccato appearance is equally beautiful and particularly good for detail and for botanical paintings.

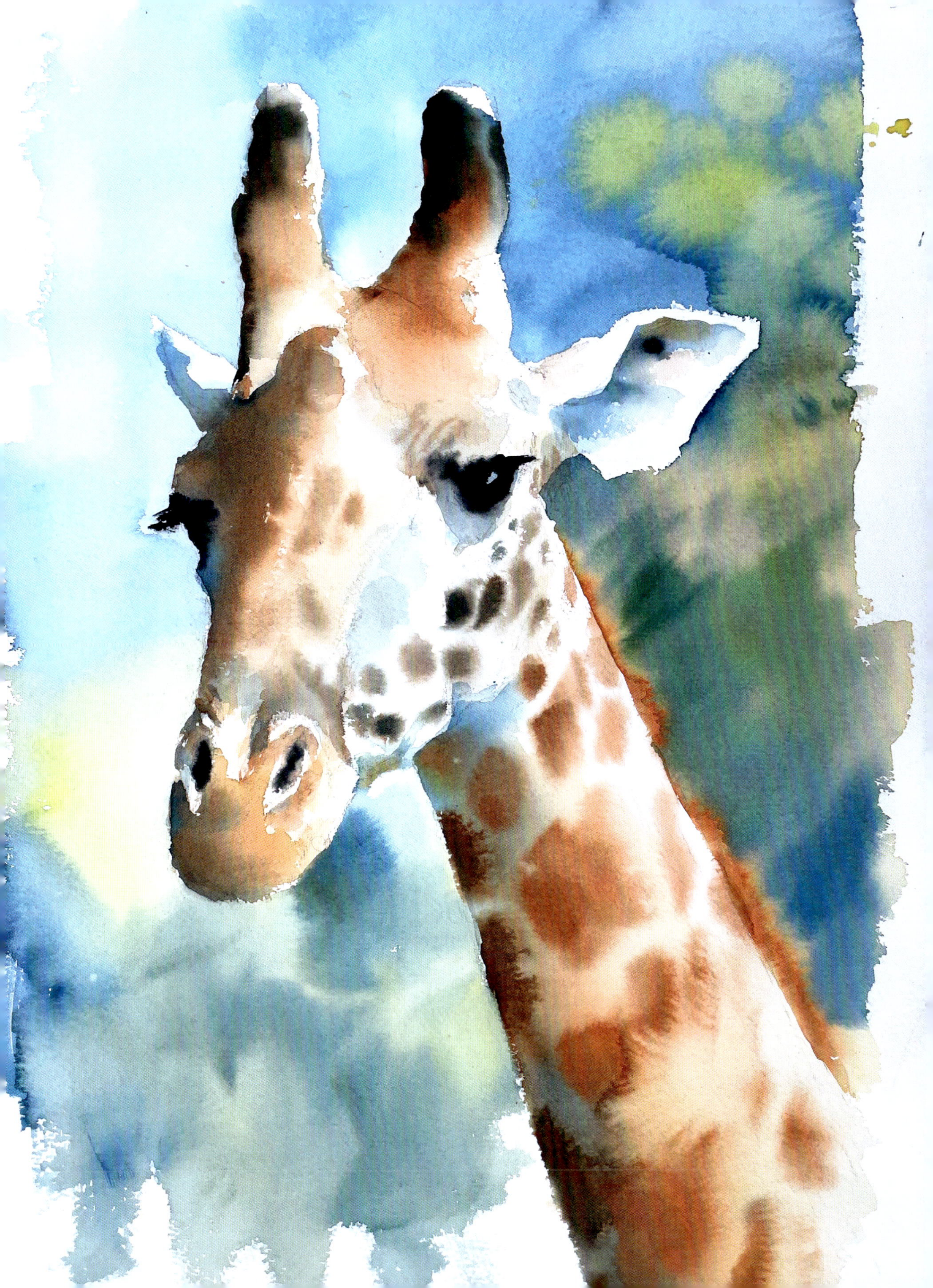

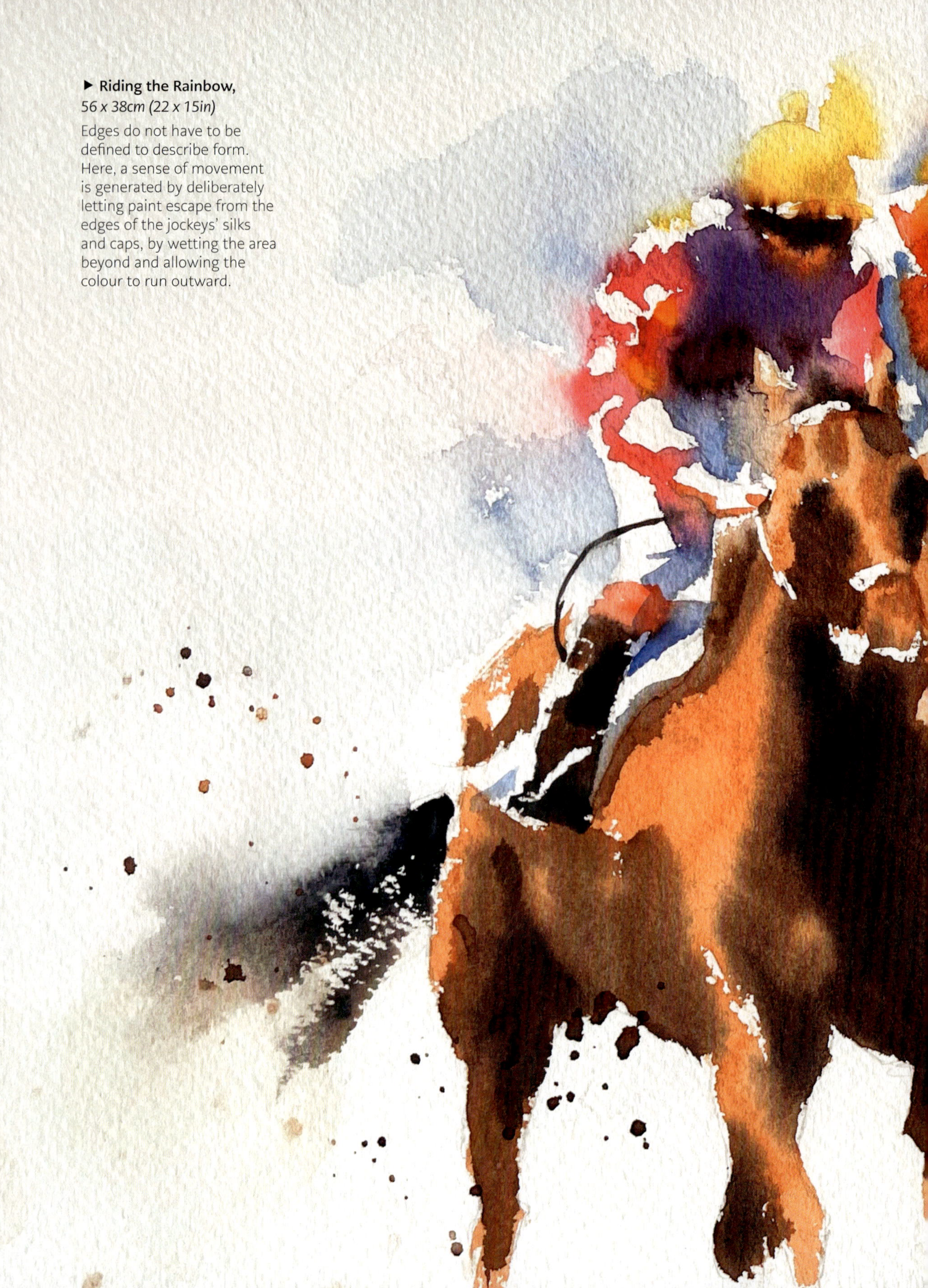

► **Riding the Rainbow,**
56 x 38cm (22 x 15in)
Edges do not have to be defined to describe form. Here, a sense of movement is generated by deliberately letting paint escape from the edges of the jockeys' silks and caps, by wetting the area beyond and allowing the colour to run outward.

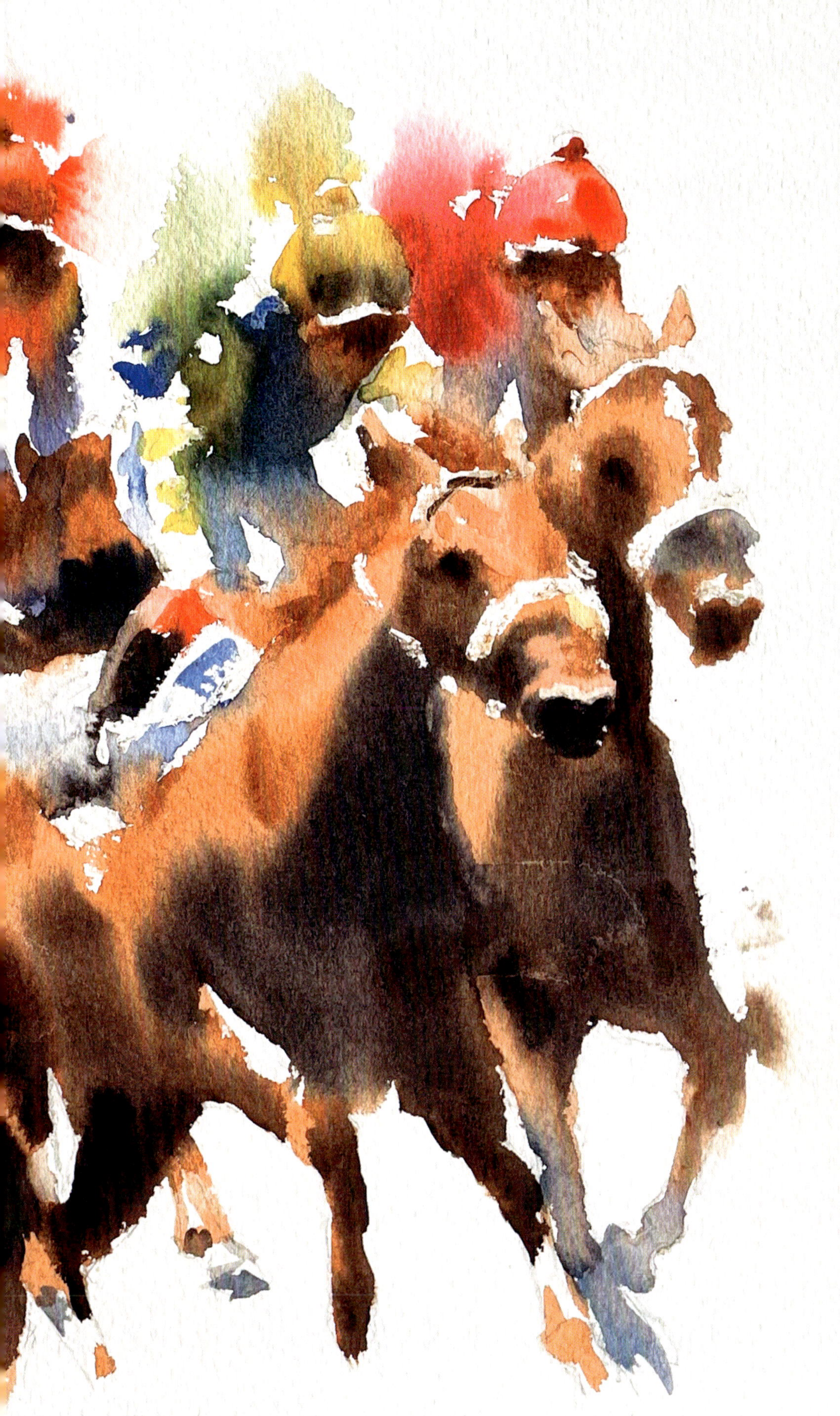

Practice, Practice, Practice

Breathing Spaces

The Duomo in Milan is a very beautiful but complicated building to paint, and with only an hour and a half, I needed a plan. I look for breathing spaces within a composition that allow me to pause between washes, either to reload my palette and brush or sometimes just to catch my breath or gather courage for the next section. Lit or highlighted areas often provide good breathing space, as a crisp edge is likely to be appropriate, but holding points can also be found within areas of shadow due to be darkened further.

The Duomo was lit from the side with its main face in shadow, so I divided the facade into five sections between the main columns to create breathing space in the wash and enable me to touch in window and cornice details while each section was still damp.

Colours:

Ultramarine Finest/Blue

Raw Umber

Burnt Umber

Yellow Raw Ochre

Brushes:

19mm flat brush

Size 8 round brush

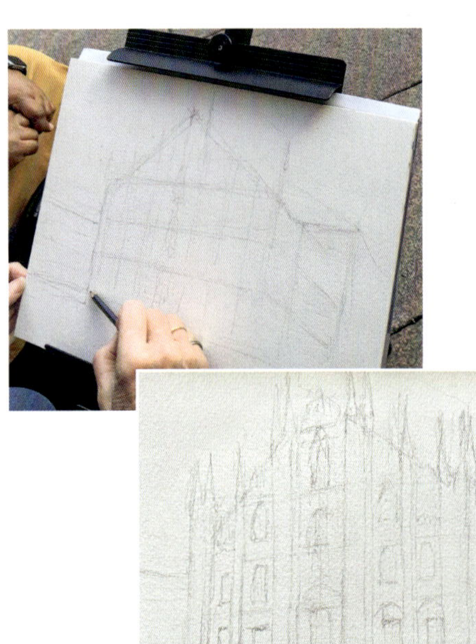

1 I drew the main triangular shape of the cathedral and divided the front facade into the six columns with the window sections in between. This immediately made the complexity of the facade easier to grasp.

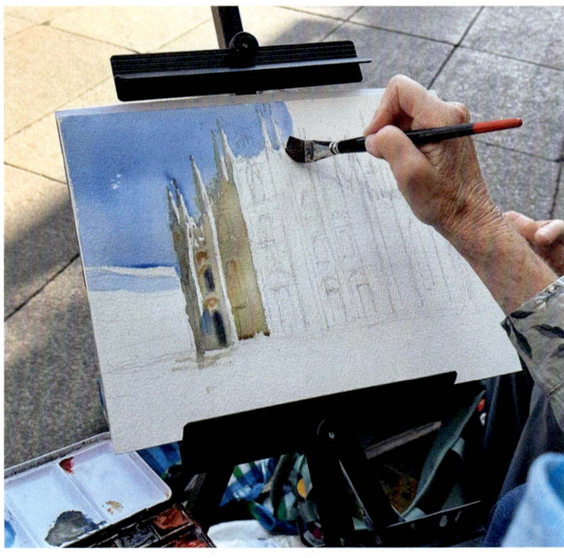

2 Had the day been warmer I would have tinted the whole front of the cathedral with Yellow Ochre at the start, but it was quite damp. To speed things up, I began with a darker mix of Raw Umber and then realized it would be better to paint the sky first, in Ultramarine Blue, leaving out the lit side of the spires as I went around the top of the structure.

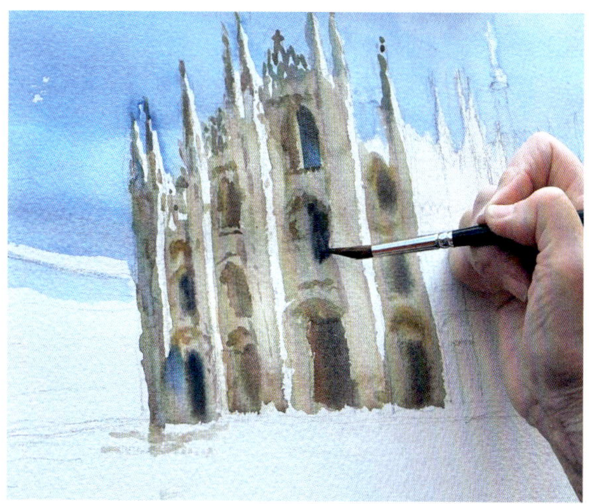

3 I continued section by section, adding the architectural features around the windows in neat Raw Umber with a dark mix of Burnt Umber and Ultramarine for the windows themselves.

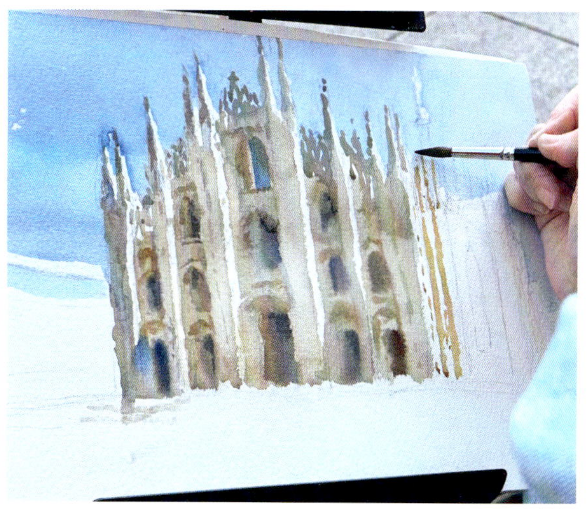

4 I implied the remarkable sculptures on top of the spires above the columns with a series of Raw Umber squiggles.

5 I tinted the facade with Yellow Ochre to link the structure together while retaining the three-dimensional form of the columns. Where the sun began to highlight the spires, I left the white paper untouched. To create a sense of scale, I added some figures in front of the enormity of the cathedral.

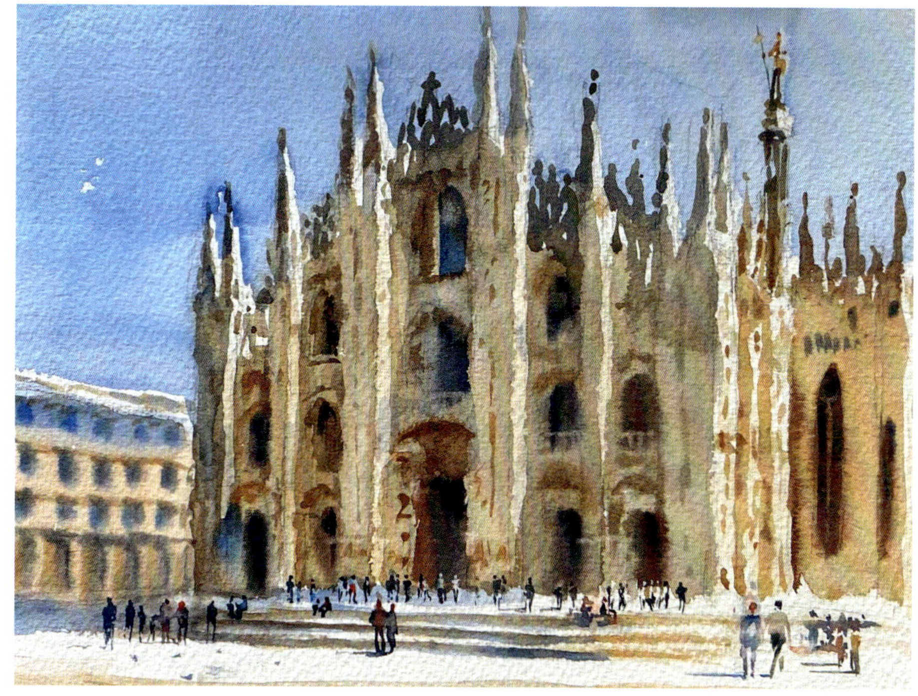

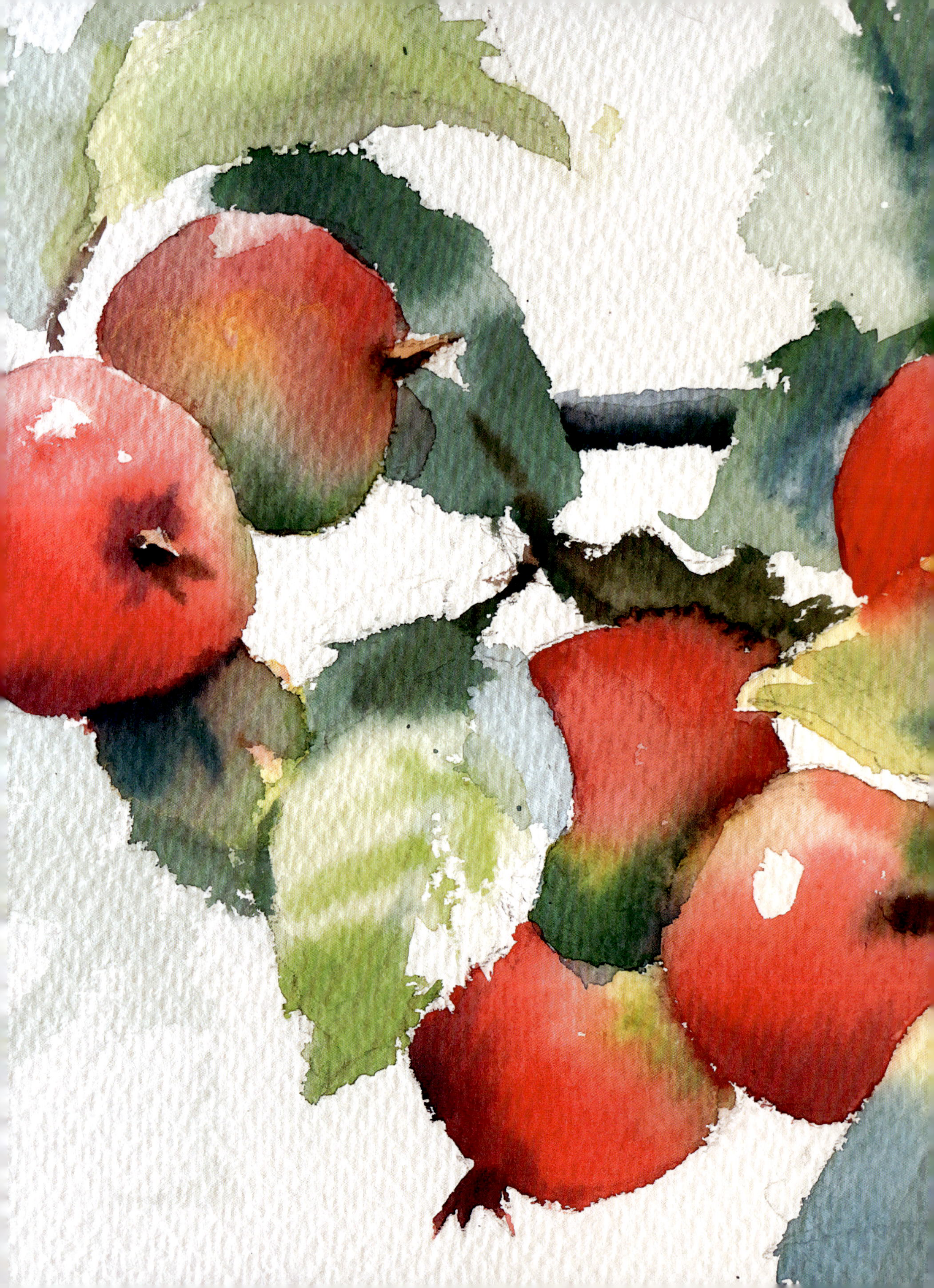

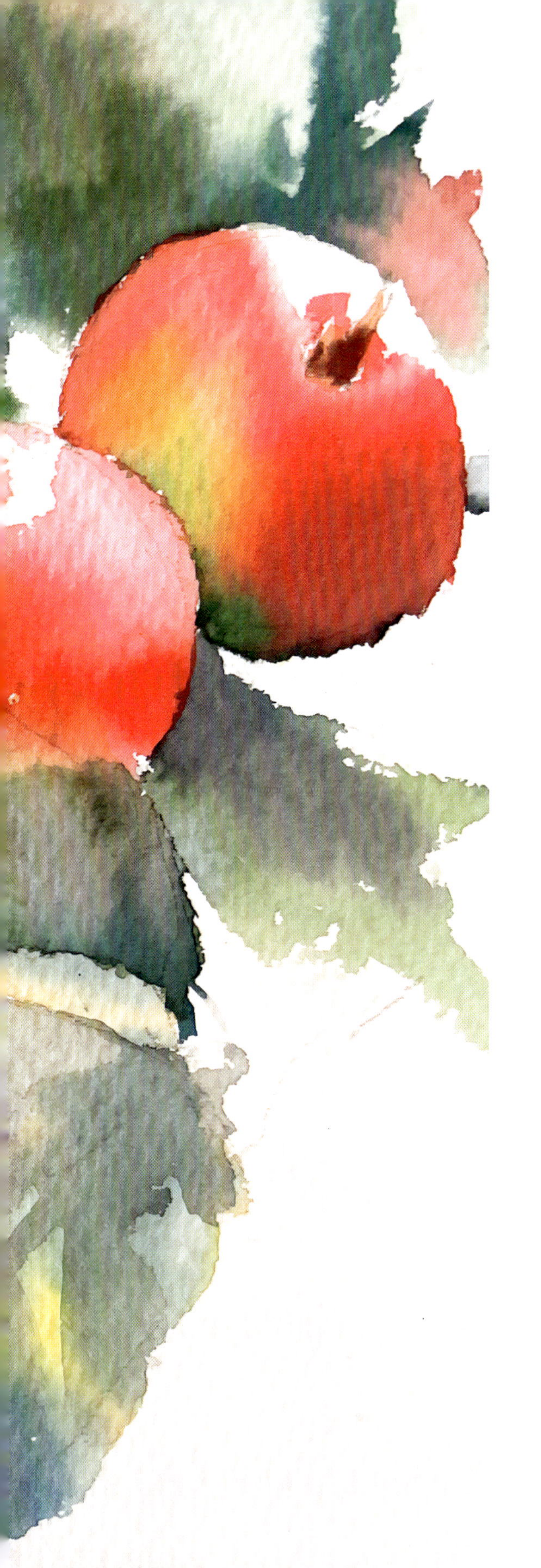

CHAPTER 7

Lost Highlights

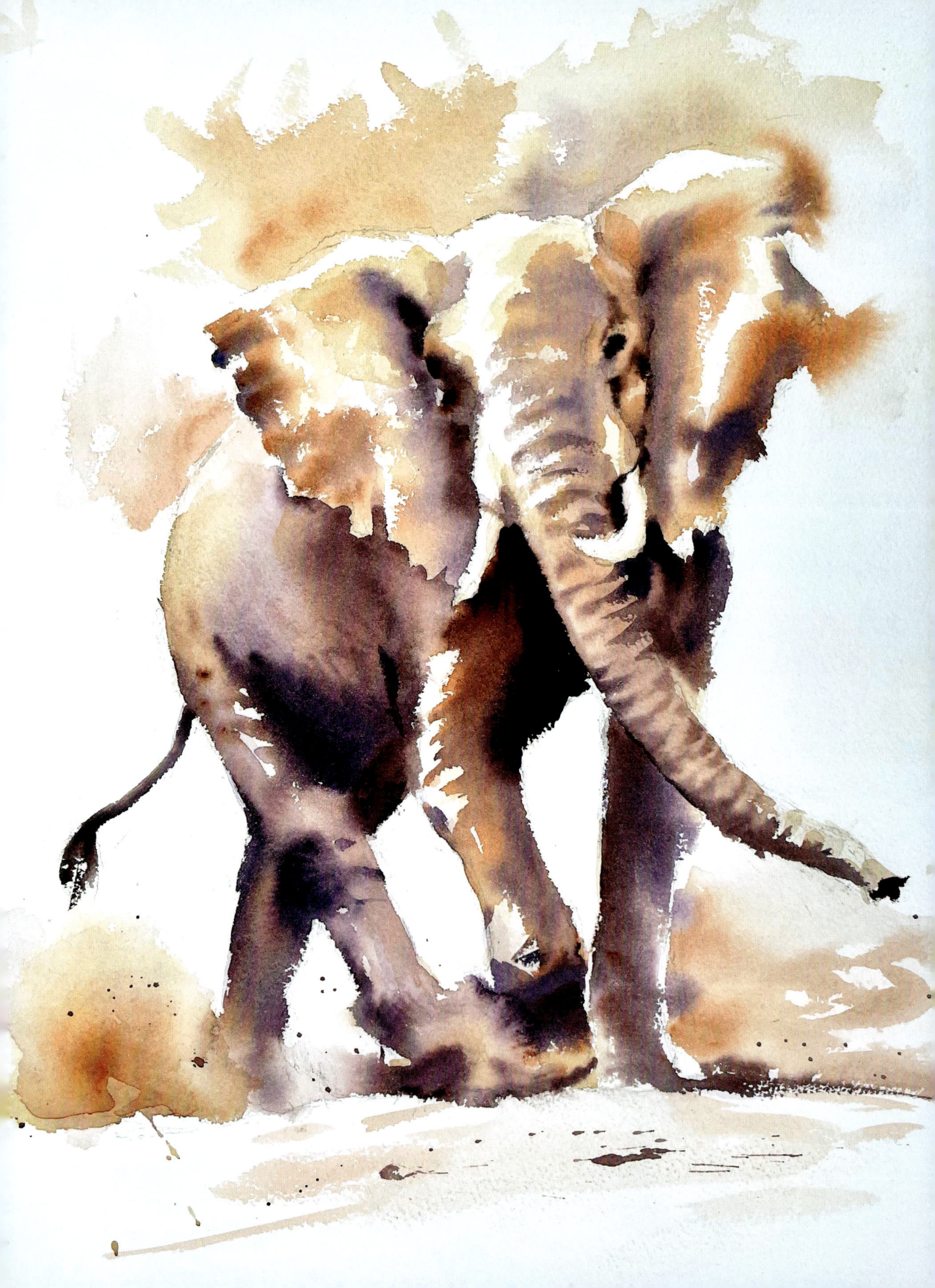

Losing the Light

In watercolour, the brightest light is represented by the white paper, even if it is actually a creamy colour, and failure to preserve white space can lead to a flat-looking watercolour with the lost light difficult to bring back. There are, thankfully, techniques that can be applied to help retrieve small areas of lost light, such as white paint, scratching off, and lifting and sponging (which can also be used on large areas).

As the aim is to leave highlights as untouched white paper, there are also aids to help preserve the white paper, such as masking fluid and wax resist. Masking is the main contender, and an ideal solution for tricky-to-retain highlights. However, most watercolourists want to be able to create the main highlights simply by leaving white paper spaces and gaps between brushstrokes and within washes. The organic negative shapes left by surrounding brushwork have a fresh, natural-looking appearance and a punchy appeal that is hard to replicate with masking fluid.

◀ **Mock Charge (I hope!),**
56 x 38cm (22 x 15in)

The gaps and spaces left between brushstrokes and washes create fresh, organically-shaped highlights on the ears and between the creases on the thighs and knee of the elephant.

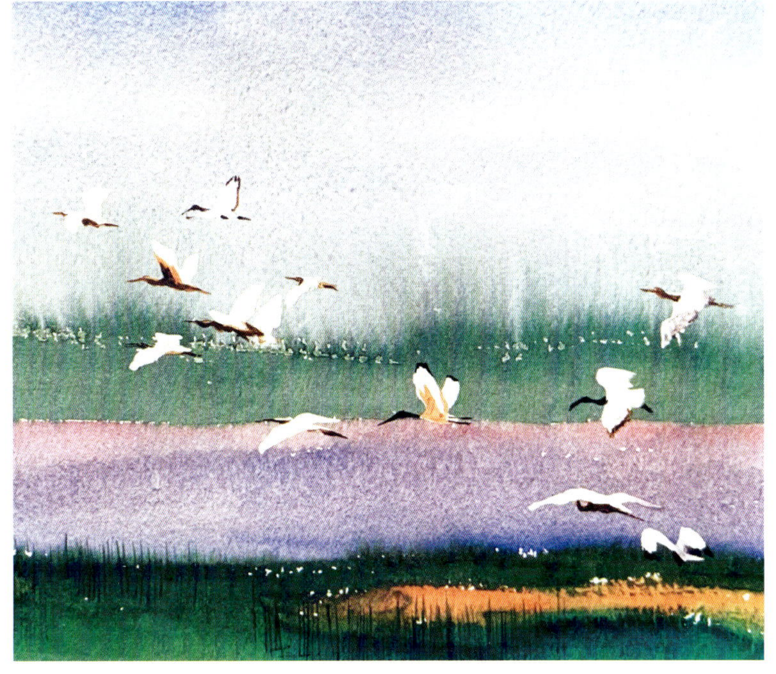

▶ **The Sound of Wings,**
28 x 28cm (11 x 11in)

Here, masking fluid has been used carefully to preserve the specific shapes of the white birds in flight, enabling the background washes to be painted freely and uninterrupted across the paper.

Preserving the Light

Before we look at ways to retrieve lost light, let's look at ways to make it easier to retain in the first place. Ideally you should aim to retain the light between brushmarks, without any aids, so that you get used to leaving negative space. Leaving out a space for a highlight is not easy: watercolour is challenging precisely because we cannot paint the light and we find that not painting something is much harder than actually painting something. But it comes with practice, especially when you realize the shape of the highlight may not be important so long as it correlates to the lit side of the feature it is describing.

This means you need to be aware of the direction and angle of light. If you are painting from life this will change throughout the day, swapping sides as the sun passes through its zenith at noon, so make sure you keep to a consistent direction of the light. I often place an arrow in the top corner of the paper to remind myself from the start.

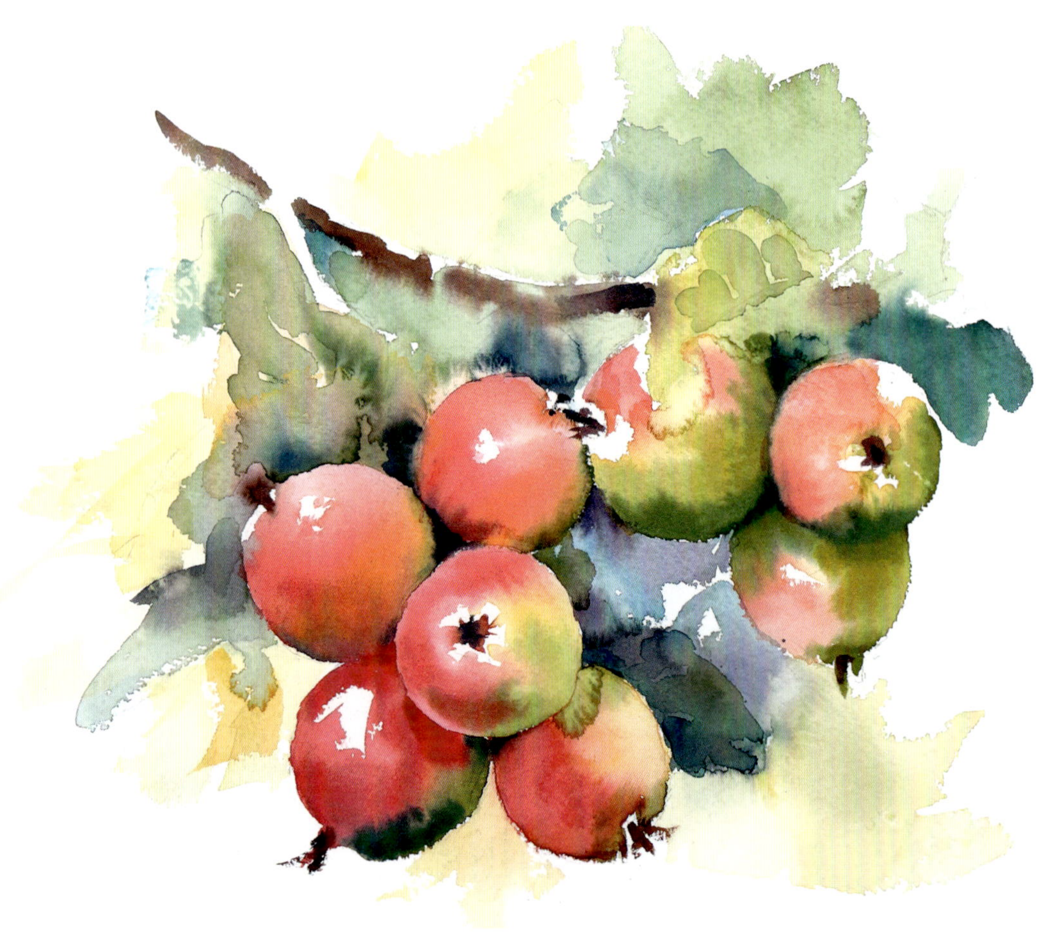

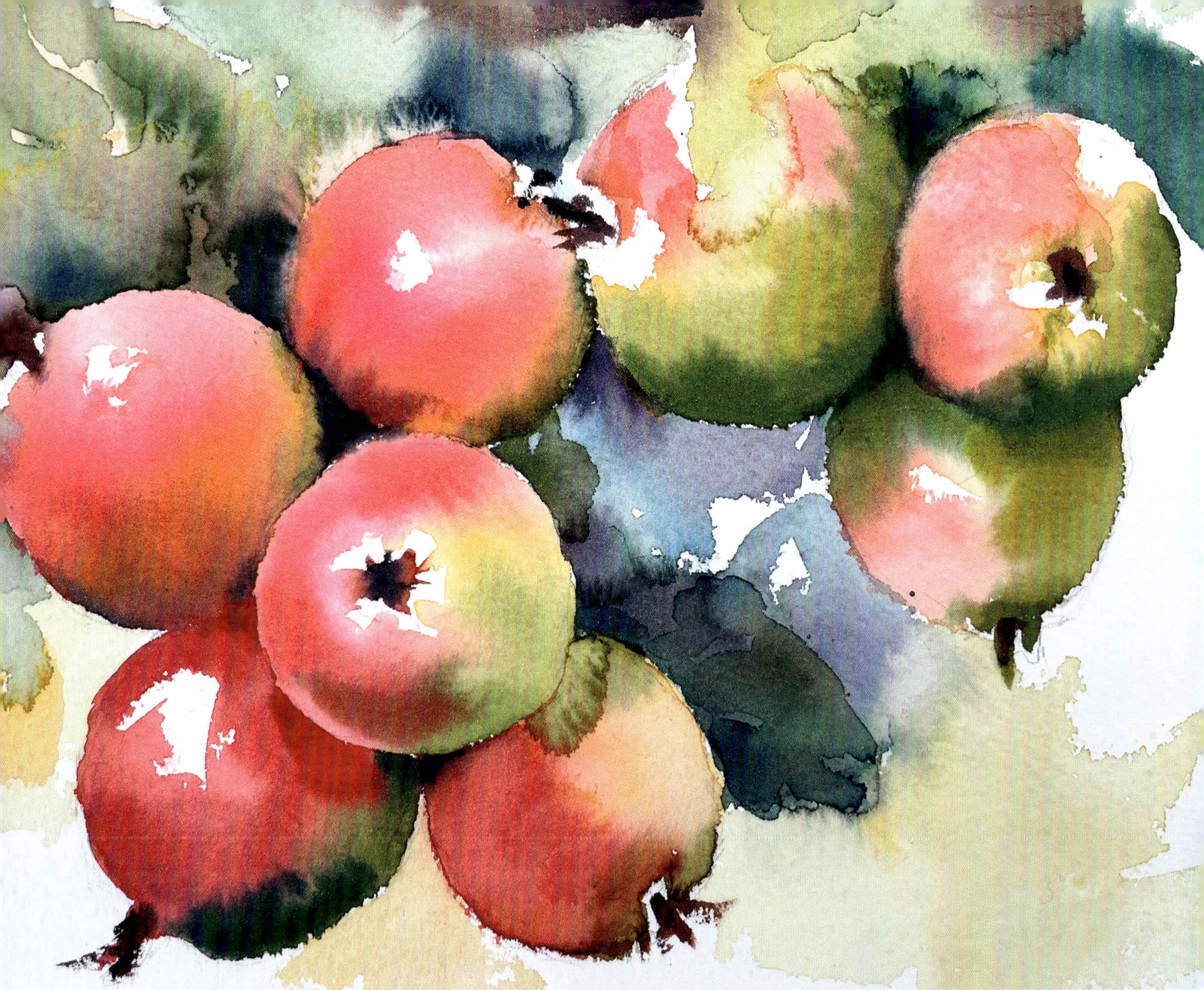

◄ ▲ **Royal Crop,**
35.5 x 51cm (14 x 20in)
When I painted the apples, the light was flat but their sheen told me the main source of light was from above and front, so I knew where to leave out the highlights.

Make sure all your highlights are on the same side of all the objects represented in the composition, so that your painting will read correctly in terms of light and shade. Under sunlight, light comes mainly from above, even if it comes from an angle. You can safely leave highlights on top of features that are below your eye level, so long as they are not in shadow. In other words, apply logic: once you know where the light is coming from, the sides of objects facing the source of light will display the lightest tone, those facing away, the darkest tone, and those in between, a mid-tone. Any reflected light on the shaded side is never as light as the lit side.

Leaving White Paper

In watercolour, the pencil sketch acts as the guide for the brush: it tells the brush both where it can go and where it cannot go. The drawing for a watercolour need only contain enough information for the initial stages: if more drawing is needed, it can be easily added later over dried watercolour. The main information needed, in order to lay a confident first wash, is where to leave out any highlights, i.e. where the brush must avoid so you can leave out patches of untouched white paper. The brush is a versatile instrument and can be manoeuvred around any shape to create interesting and arresting negative shapes and spaces. Get used to trusting the brush, and try not to over-control: hold the brush at the widest part of the handle with a loose grip. Err on the side of leaving excess white space, i.e. broader patches, as these areas can be tinted later if too much light remains.

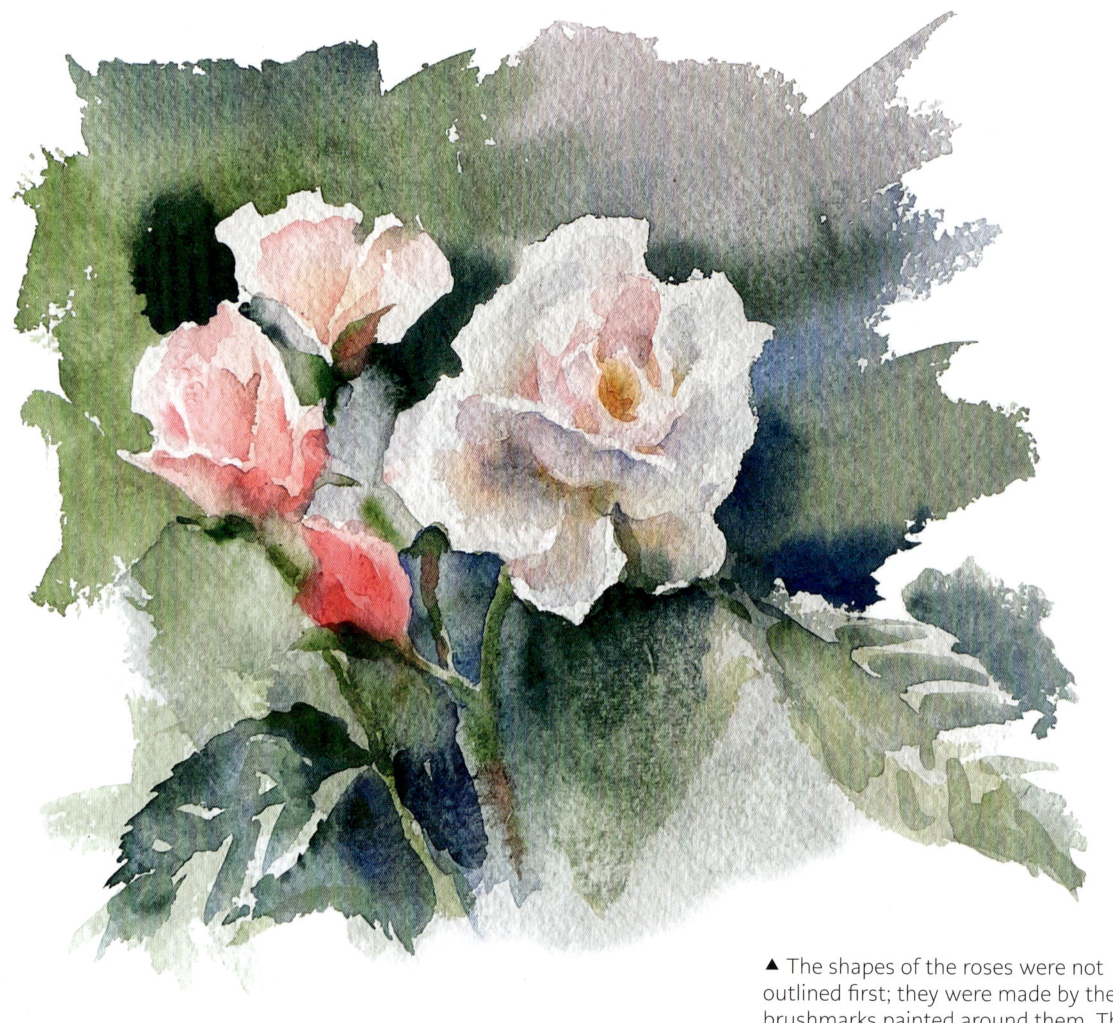

▲ The shapes of the roses were not outlined first; they were made by the brushmarks painted around them. This has given them an interesting contour.

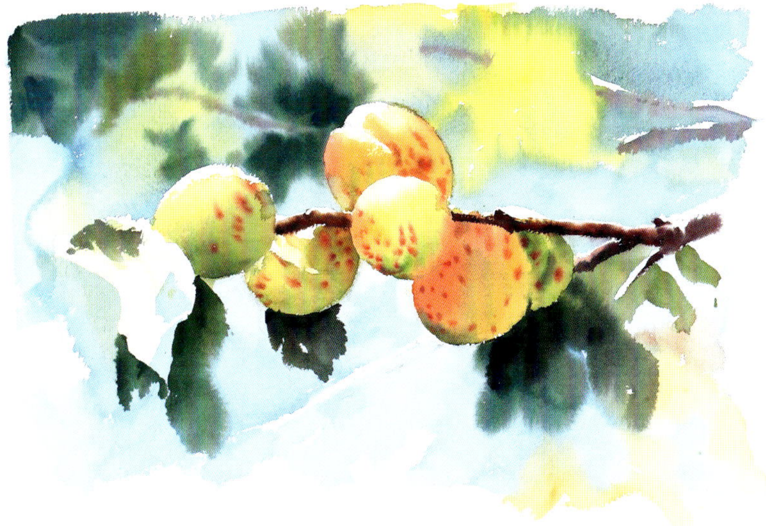

◂ The apricots were painted before the background, leaving ample white paper for the lit branches and any leaves that fell in front.

▾ To alternate the values, the portion of leaf in front of the fruit on the left-hand side is painted a darker tone against the lighter part of the apricot, and a lighter tone against the darker, shaded side of the fruit.

If you know roughly where the untouched paper highlights need to be, it is not necessary to outline the shapes with a pencil before painting. Instead, try to shape the space with brushwork by painting around it, as the contours created are more likely to excite the eye than when the brush slavishly follows a line. When you do give yourself a pencil guide, try not to follow it too exactly; let the brush have some leeway either side of the line.

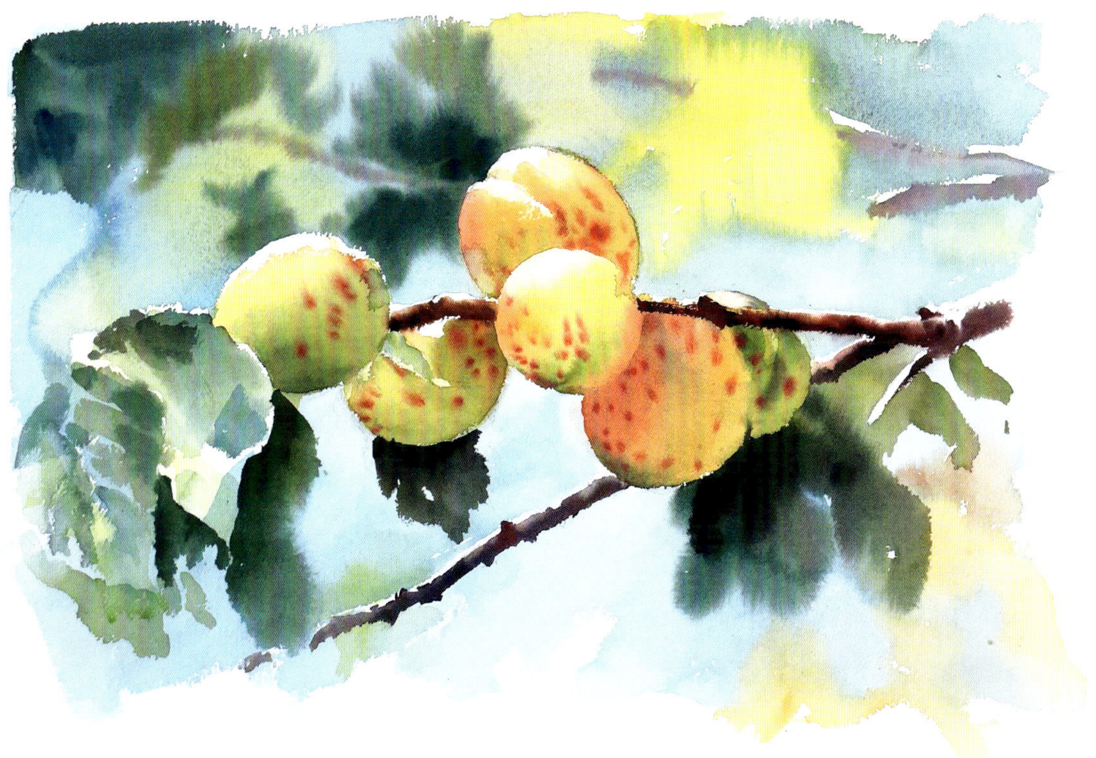

Plan Ahead

Because we have to leave light out, watercolours do require planning. If, for example, you want to include figures in a landscape, it is probably better to paint the people first, then bring the landscape in around them, so you know exactly where to leave out the highlights on heads, shoulders and bodies. Alternatively, leave an area within the landscape that is light enough in tone for the figures to be brought into without a conflict of value.

Although small highlights can be retrieved with white or opaque paint, they will never look as fresh as the untouched white paper highlights; it is undoubtedly the highlights as well as the fluidity of the pose that bring figures to life in a watercolour.

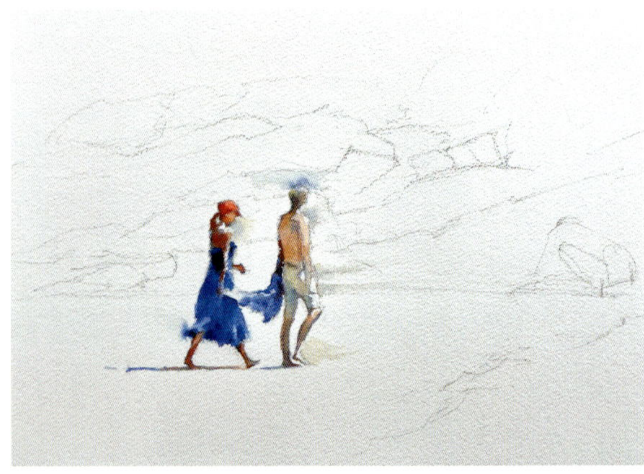

▲ I painted the people first. The light was coming from in front of them, so to preserve the thin slivers of light, I painted pale background tints around them as a message for the brush as to where to bring in the background later.

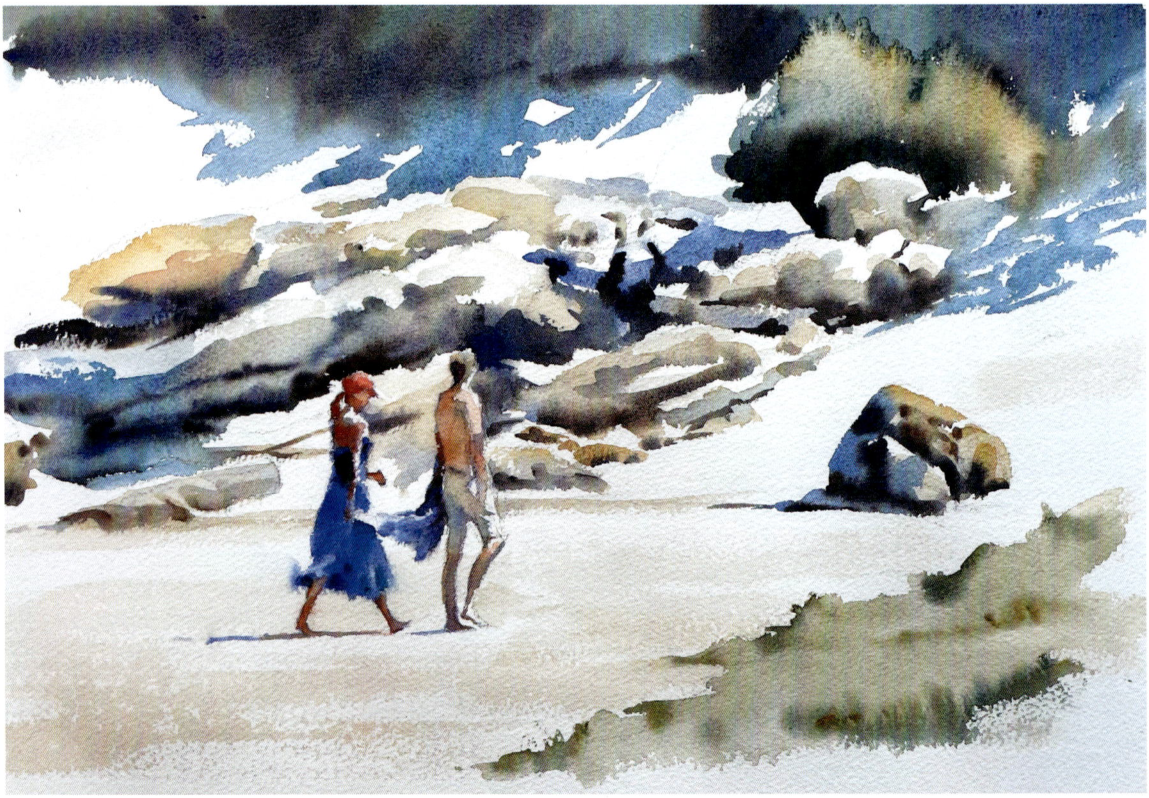

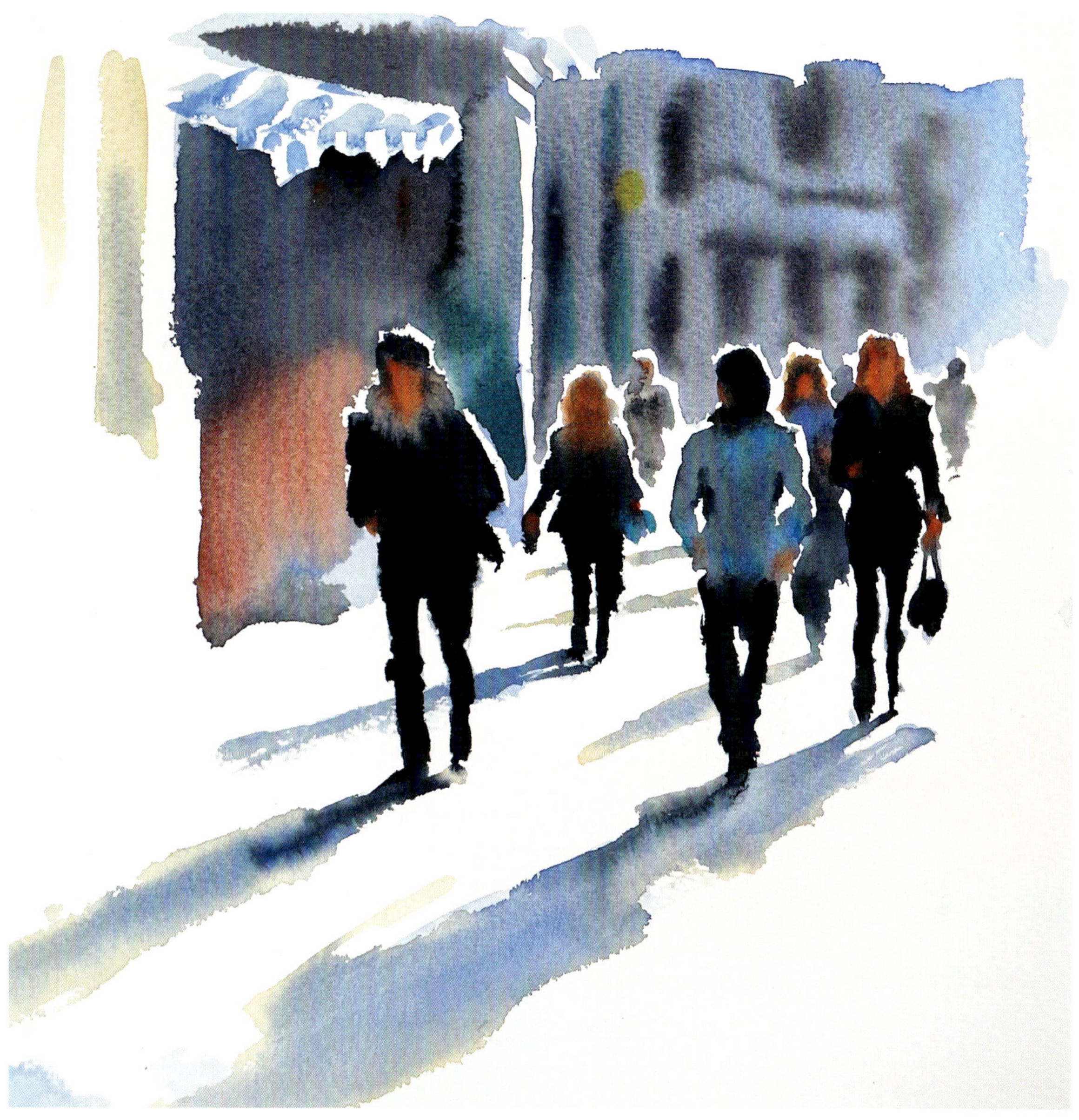

▲ **Sketch in Regent Street,**
28 x 28cm (11 x 11in)

The counterchange of the backlit figures against the buildings creates halos of light behind their silhouettes. By painting the figures first I could bring the background in around their heads and shoulders and imply the highlights so indicative of contre-jour by leaving slivers of white paper untouched around them.

◄ **Noordhoek Beach,**
30.5 x 43cm (12 x 17in)

When the landscape was painted around the figures, I contrasted darker tone against the lit sides (their fronts) and lighter tone against the shaded side (their backs).

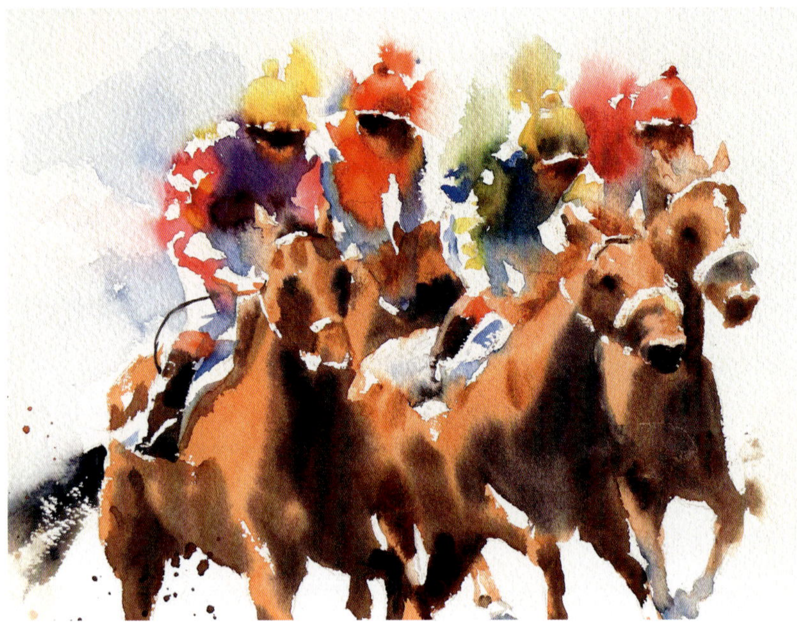

◀ In this painting, shown at a larger size on page 130, masking fluid was used to protect the small highlights and sparkle on the rein and bridle details and the white of the saddle blankets, allowing me to freely wash in the chestnut colouring of the horses.

Masking

To help preserve awkward, difficult or multiple highlights, masking fluid is a very useful aid. This creamy, colourless latex liquid helps watercolourists retain untouched paper as highlights and can be painted onto paper before painting, drying fairly quickly when not laid too thick.

To apply masking fluid, use cheap throwaway brushes or a dedicated applicator, as the gluey substance ruins watercolour brushes. Likewise, never start to paint over masking fluid before it is fully dry on the paper as the brush will pick up the latex within its hairs.

Masking fluid is a blobby substance, so it is worth painting the fluid as carefully as you can to create the most appropriate shapes for the highlights reserved, rather than just blobbing it on in a hopeful fashion. Once it is dry you can paint confidently over the dried masking fluid, knowing your untouched paper highlights are safely preserved underneath. Only when the painting is absolutely dry should the masking fluid be removed, either with a crepe or rubber eraser or by rubbing it off with the fingers. If paint has settled on top of the latex be careful not to smear it onto the paper as you peel it away.

The white paper shapes might look fine, or they might need some adjustment to make them more descriptive or less blobby. For this reason, remove the masking as early in the painting as you can to safely retain the highlights, then you can refine them naturally along with the rest of the painting. Choose colourless masking fluid so you can assess relative tone readily in relation to the temporary colouring of the masked highlights. Don't be surprised if you find yourself tinting some of the highlights at the end with a similar hue to the creamy masking fluid.

Avoid leaving masking fluid on the paper overnight, as it gradually seeps into the paper fibres over time and becomes harder to remove without tearing the paper. Likewise, heat causes the fluid to seep into the paper, so avoid using a hairdryer to speed up drying times in the studio and avoid painting under direct sunlight. Bottom line: peel the masking fluid off as early as you can.

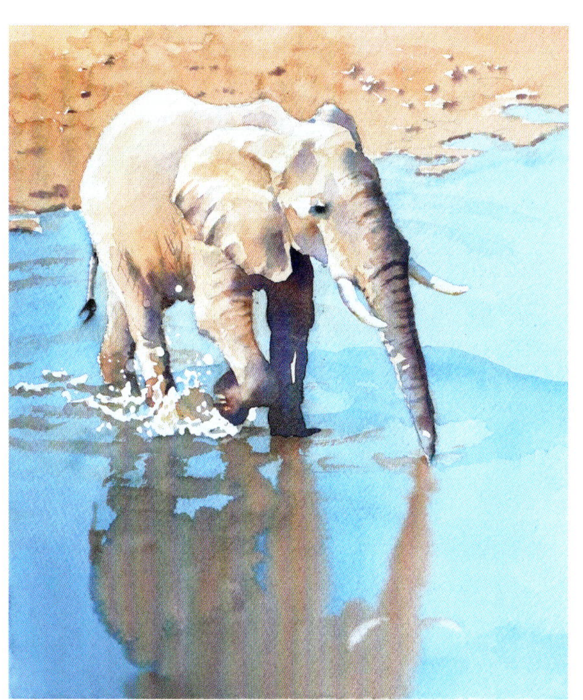

◄ **The Splash,** *38 x 33cm (15 x 13in)*

In order to confidently paint the broad wash of Prussian Blue for the water, both the tusks and the splash between the elephant's feet were reserved with masking fluid.

▼ **Still Standing,**
30.5 x 40.5cm (12 x 16in)

Masking fluid was painted down the lit side of the tree so the background hills could be freely painted over the top without having to leave out any difficult highlights. The masking was rubbed off before the tree itself was painted, once the background had dried.

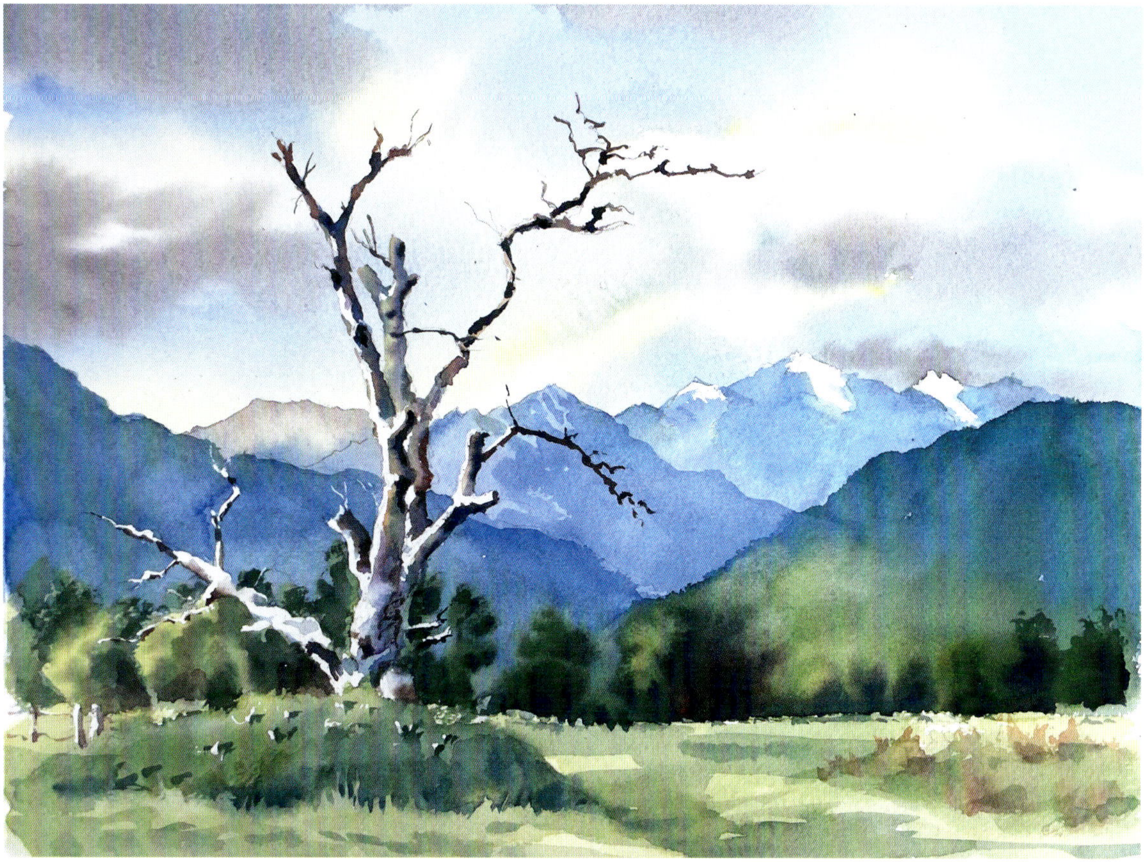

Wax Resist

Any product that repels or resists water will also resist watercolour; hence, white coloured wax can be used to retain white paper highlights in and on textured subjects. A white candle or wax crayon are ideal applicators: rub them onto the paper before painting to reserve light as a textural effect. Once laid, wax cannot be removed and the area covered will always repel watercolour, so be cautious: know exactly where the light is that you wish to preserve.

Due to its textural nature, wax resist is ideal for retaining light on rough surfaced subjects such as walls, rocks or ground, or on water to suggest distant waves. The rougher the surface of the paper, the more emphasis there is on the unevenness of the effect.

The lighter tone of mortar lines between bricks, the light catching on granite rocks, or the distant breaking of a wave are all subjects that can benefit from laying wax resist to protect the light.

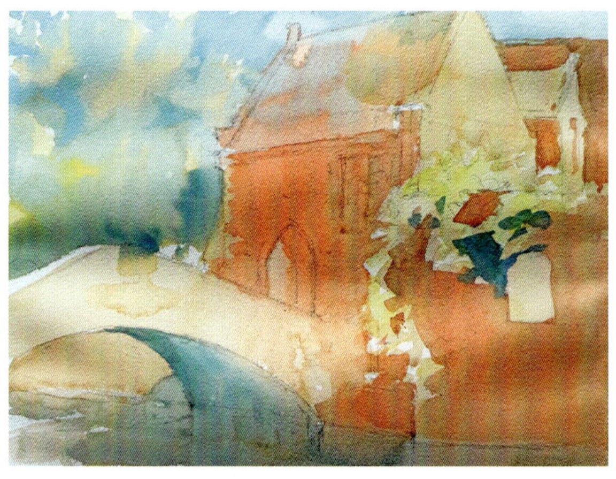

▲ **Lovers' Bridge in Bruges,** *30.5 x 40.5cm (12 x 16in)*
Since wax repels water, paint will not adhere to the paper where wax is applied, so I had to tint all the areas before applying the wax. I let the paper dry completely before rubbing on the wax resist.

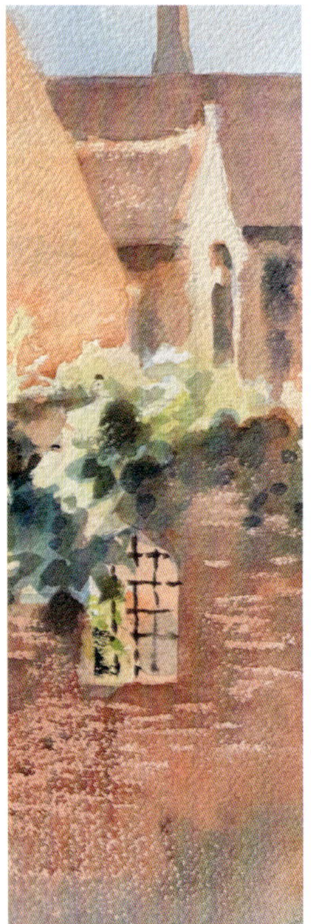

◀ The wax has been applied in short, linear strokes to give the impression of textured brickwork when the subsequent tint is laid on top.

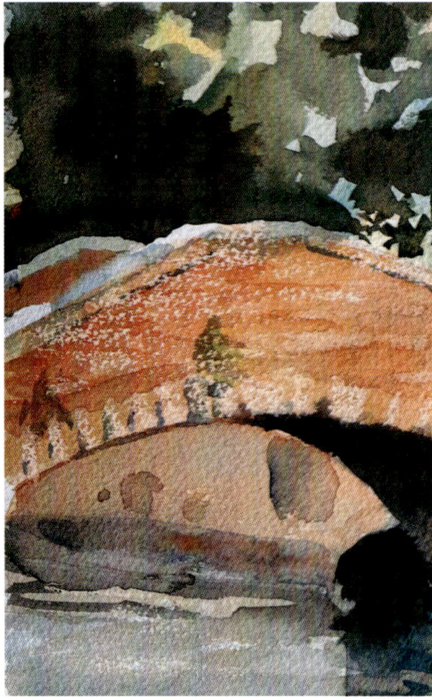

◀ White candle wax has been applied to the stone and brickwork on the bridge and painted over immediately with another wash of Red and Yellow Ochre.

▲ A second application of wax has been added to the bridge, to identify coping stones and brickwork in a lighter tone.

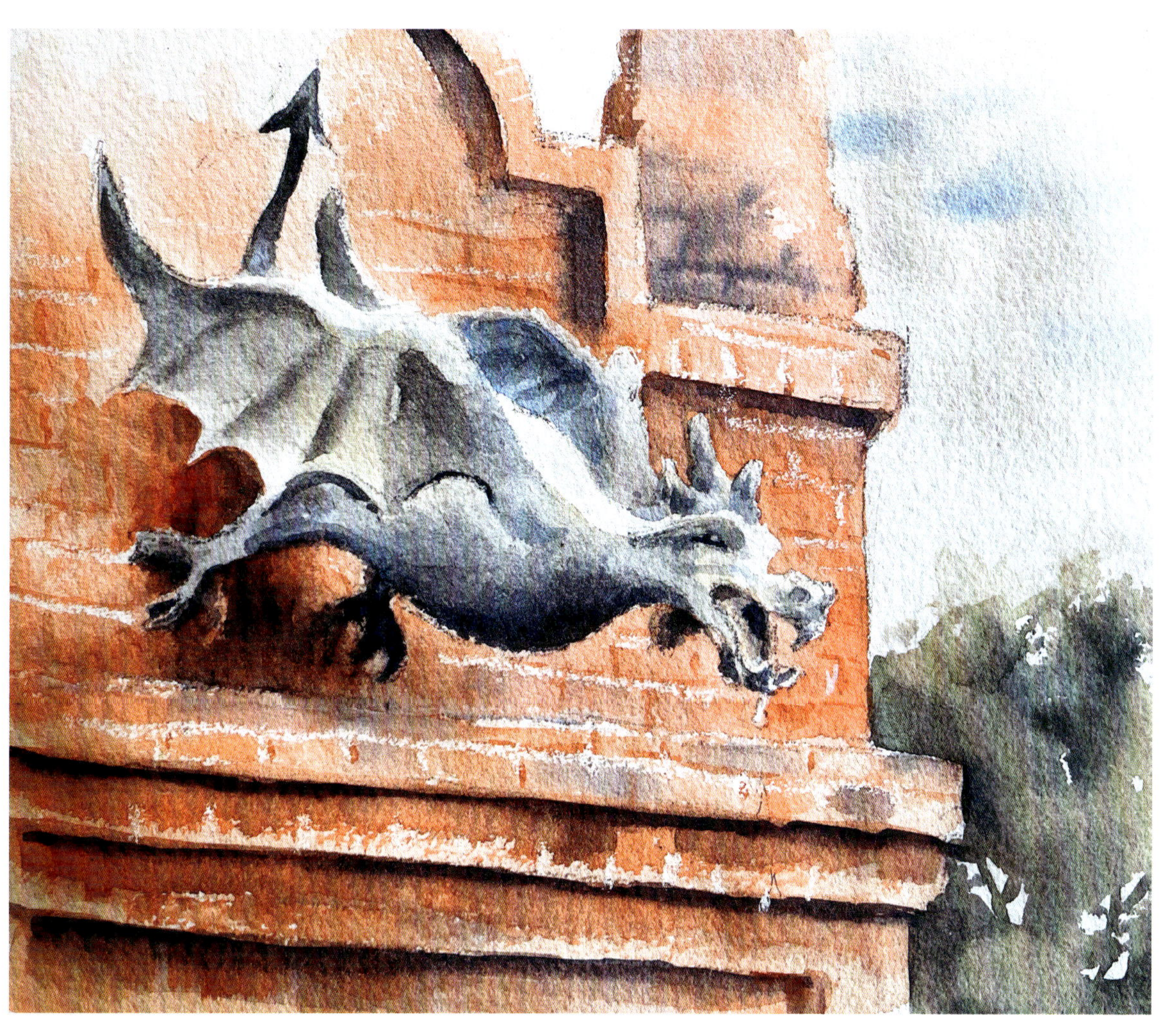

▲ **Gargoyle, The Rotunda, Dumfries House,** *20 x 25.5cm (8 x 10in)*

A wax candle was used to draw the mortar lines between the red bricks behind this gargoyle. You can see where the waxed line was not in perspective but could not be removed once laid.

Retrieval of Lost Light

The previous techniques are all useful ways to help watercolourists retain the precious light from the untouched white paper, but what if the light is lost, and highlights unintentionally covered by paint? Can light be restored or an overworked watercolour rescued?

There are some techniques that allow small highlights to be retrieved and larger areas of light to be restored to a greater or lesser extent, depending on the staining properties of the pigments employed. The rest of this chapter is devoted to rescue remedies.

All watercolour painters should recognize that sometimes it is better to abandon an overworked watercolour, especially if the method for retrieving the light may take some time to achieve its purpose. A watercolour is, after all, 'only' a piece of paper, and its value lies in the time spent. If more time is going to be spent trying to repair an overworked painting than it might take to paint from scratch, it is a better use of time to start again on a fresh sheet of paper. An abandoned watercolour is not a failure; it is all part of learning to paint. Once you accept this, no time is wasted.

If, like me, you hate wasting paper, any of the opaque media can make use of the abandoned sheet. Pastels, acrylic and gouache can all be painted directly onto the used paper, or you can seal its surface with a layer of gesso or even white emulsion paint, and make an appropriate surface for an oil painting.

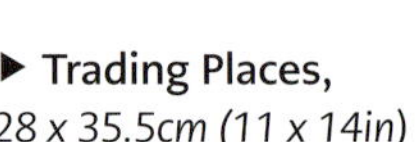

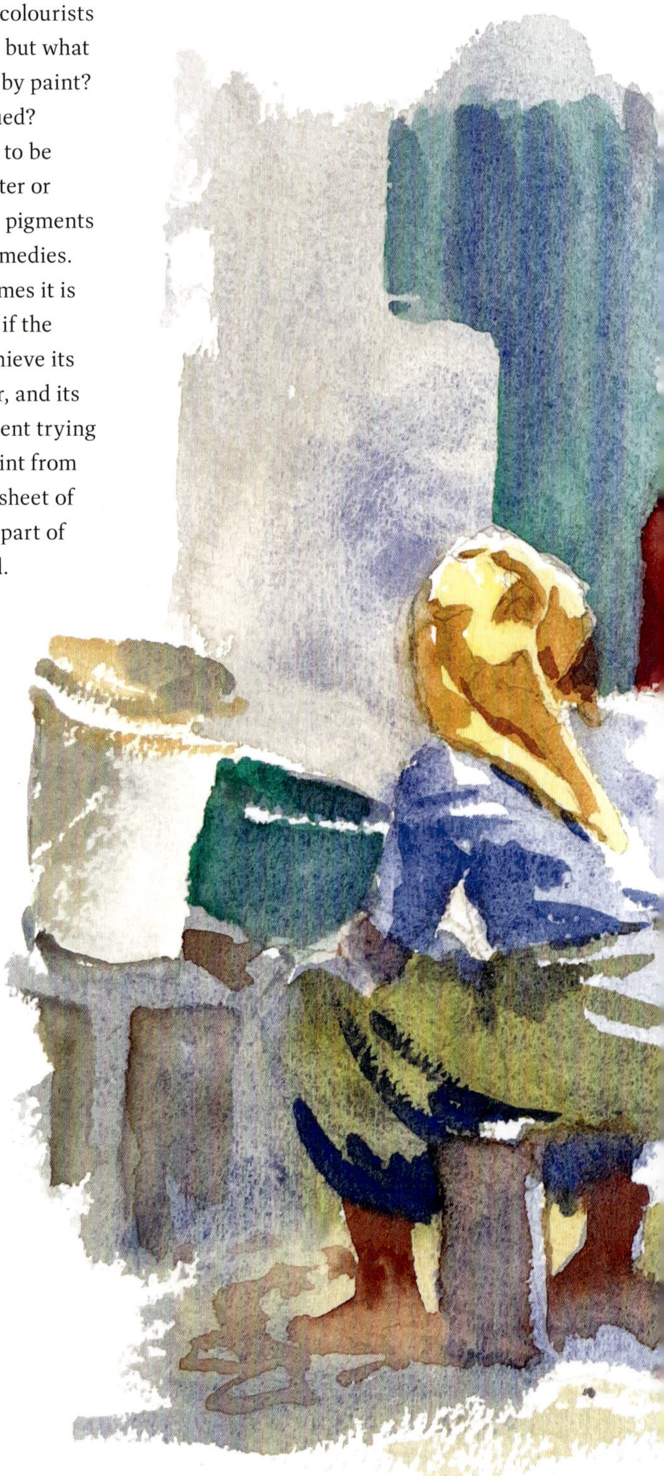

▶ **Trading Places,**
28 x 35.5cm (11 x 14in)
In the speed of painting this lively exchange, several highlights were lost and have been restored. Without the close-up details shown over the page I doubt you could tell where they are!

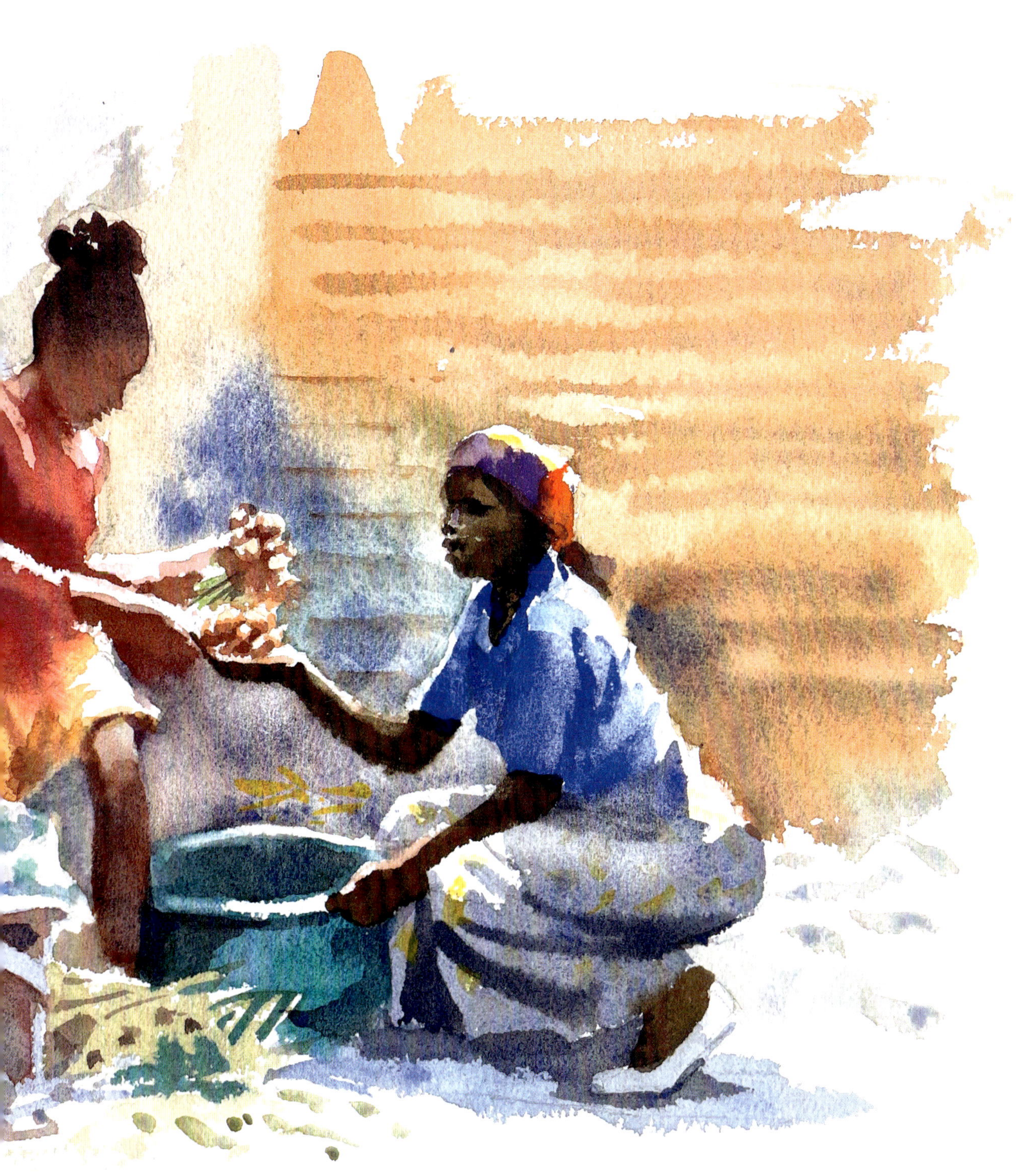

Scratching Off

When a small or linear highlight has been lost, it can be retrieved by scratching the paint off from the surface of the paper with a sharp blade to reveal the pristine white paper beneath. The grazed surface obviously gets 'damaged', and the affected area becomes like blotting paper, but this is an effective way of instantly restoring a crisp, bright highlight.

This technique is ideal for small or linear highlights, such as the sparkle on a glass or the wake behind a boat. It can be used on larger areas too: if the side of the blade is grazed carefully across a dark, flat wash, it can restore the glitter of light onto rough surfaces or backlit water, for example.

Scratching off should only be done at the very end of the painting. To employ this technique, use the side of the tip, or long side, of a clean, sharp surgical blade and draw it horizontally across the surface of the paper with sufficient pressure only to remove the paint from the surface of the paper, not enough to cut the paper. Hold the blade at an angle so the pressure is across the paper and not piercing into the surface. Make sure the paper is completely dry, as any dampness will cause tearing, as will a blunt blade. Practise the action on a used or abandoned watercolour first, or right at the edge of the painting, before you tackle the main event.

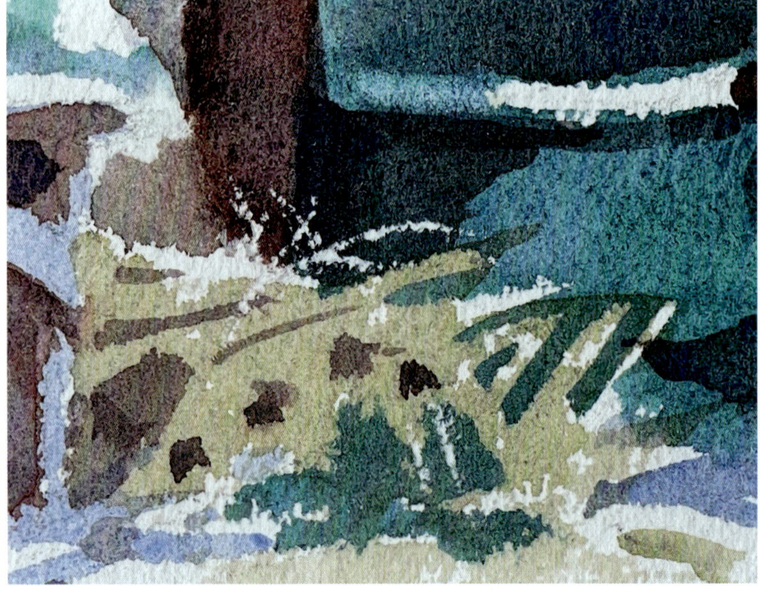

◀ In this detail from the painting on the previous page, the highlighted strands of straw have been scratched off with the blade of a scalpel to reveal the pristine white paper underneath.

▶ The highlight on the lady's right knee and the middle section of the highlight on the back rim of the basin are painted with Titanium White (the highlights on the straw behind are scratched off).

White Paint

In opaque media such as gouache, oil and acrylic, white paint is used to introduce light, whereas white paint is not normally required in watercolour because the white paper represents the light. White paint is, however, a useful colour for rescuing small lost highlights or to increase a colour's opacity.

Although watercolour paper is often a creamy white and white paint looks like a bright white, painted highlights never look as bright, crisp or clean as the untouched white paper. However, they come close when a rescue is needed and are ideal for small highlights or thin lines, such as balcony railings, the rim of a glass, or the halo around a silhouette. Use contrast to aid the highlight by setting it against a darker tone.

There are two main whites available: Titanium White and Zinc White (also known as Chinese White, so named in the 1830s after the whiteness of Chinese porcelain). Titanium dioxide, the pigment in Titanium White, is formed when titanium, a metal, combines with oxygen. This pigment is known for its superior brightness and opacity, making it the stronger, more opaque of the two whites, and also the warmer.

Zinc oxide, the pigment in Zinc White, is a compound formed by the reaction of the metal zinc with oxygen. It is more transparent, cooler, and more compatible with other pigments than Titanium White and therefore useful for subtle highlights, distant whites and glazing. As referred to earlier in the book (see page 34), the property of each white may be guessed from its name, titanium being the stronger, harder metal, and zinc the softer and more malleable one.

To restore a lost highlight, use Titanium White as concentrated as possible (you could even take it straight from the tube with the brush). If diluted, it will look very white while wet but less so when dry, so be prepared to apply more than one layer. Be careful not to apply it too thickly or with too many layers, or it may gain an unattractive sheen.

▸ The highlight along the lady's back has been widened on the shoulder with Titanium White paint, along with enhancing some of the folds.

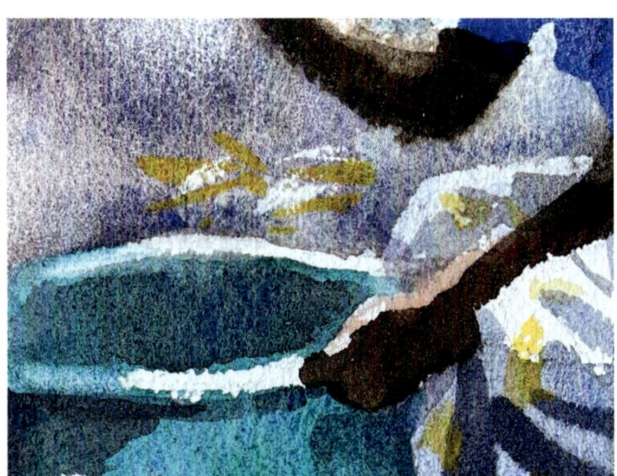

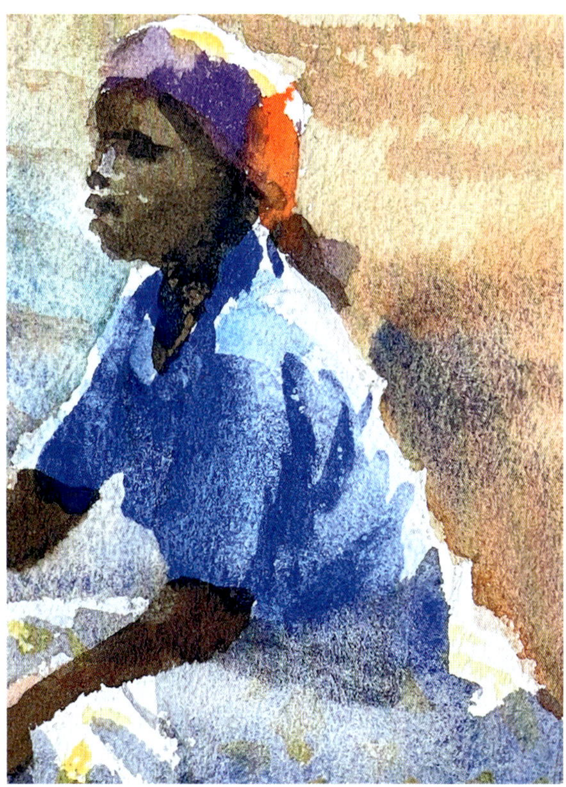

Lifting Off

Before white paint is added to a lost highlight, it makes sense to lighten the offending area as much as possible before introducing the clean white paint. The technique for this is termed 'lifting off', and was discussed in relation to the properties of non-staining pigments in Chapter 3 (see page 48). This process holds true for larger areas that need light or transparency restored. Although it is hard to retrieve pure white paper, if the paper is robust, and the position of the lost highlight allows you to rub a clean sponge with a little vigour, it is possible to remove a great deal of paint, especially on less absorbent papers. Some non-staining colours can be completely sponged off and washed off. Allow the paper to dry thoroughly before using again.

Most of the mineral and earth colours, and several of the metal colours, are non-staining to some extent, which means their pigment can be lifted and shifted to retrieve both large and small highlights, even though not restored to a pure white. Set a darker tone beside these lightened areas and they will look lighter by dint of contrast.

To create crisp edges to a lifted light, use the straight edges of stiff card or cut a stencil in the shape you wish to retrieve, place over the lost highlight and rub the paint off purposefully with a bristle brush or clean sponge, being careful to protect the rest of the painting. Repeat as necessary until maximum colour is removed.

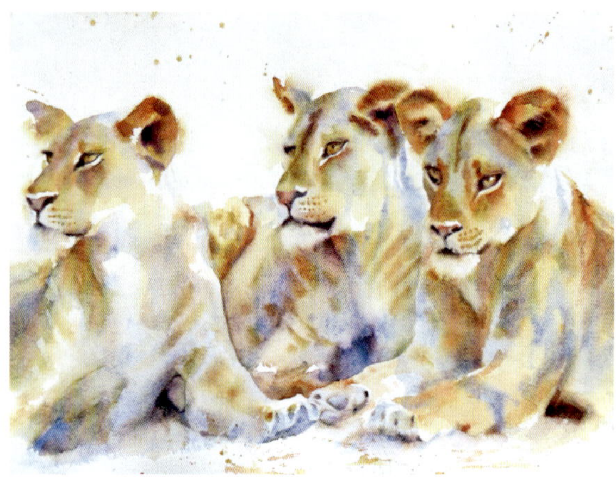

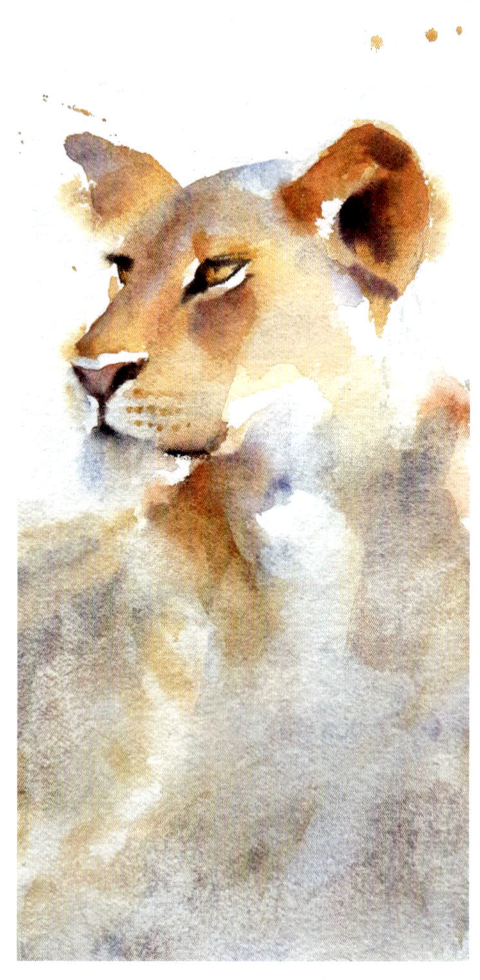

▲ **Wild Earth Colours,** *56 x 76cm (22 x 30in)*

▶ **Wild Lady,** *56 x 25.5cm (22 x 10in)*

I painted the three lionesses together but, unhappy with the body of the lioness on the left, I cropped the image to make two separate paintings. I liked the head of the lioness on the left and, having used mostly lifting colours (Cobalt Blue, Raw Sienna and Burnt Sienna), I was able to remove most of the body's colour with a clean, damp sponge. The Violet, however, is a staining colour and therefore still leaves a stain. (The other section of the painting can be seen on page 175.)

While filming *African Watercolours*, I painted a jackal with Ultramarine Blue and Burnt Sienna, but then, to show how easily lifting colours could be removed, I rubbed it clean away with a sponge, and the jackal vanished completely. I looked up at the cameraman: 'You did get that, didn't you?' Thankfully, the process was done in one take: sponging off works!

Failing everything, if the light is lost in the painting and it looks overworked and muddy, you can always rinse a good-quality paper under the tap. The non-staining colours will largely disappear, and the staining colours will leave their trace, allowing you to use the paper all over again once it is completely dry.

You will need to stretch the wet paper to prevent it buckling as it dries. The pristine glow of the paper may be sullied but you can use it as tinted watercolour paper instead, such as Turner used, and experiment with some of the bright opaque colours and increased tonal contrast to disguise the duller nature of the paper.

▼ ▶ Raw Power, Gravensteen Castle,
28 x 38cm (11 x 15in)

An overall wash of Raw Umber enabled me to establish a quick rendering of the massive walls of this famous castle in Ghent. Using a lifting colour allowed me to lighten the paler stonework details around turrets and ramparts, simply by lifting and dabbing a little of the Raw Umber with a clean, damp brush after the wash had dried, while keeping the wholeness of the painting intact.

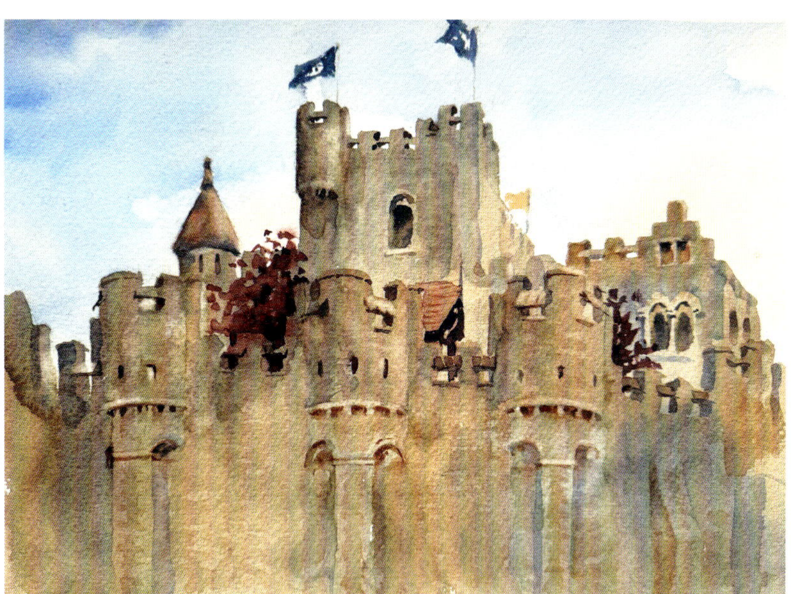

Before

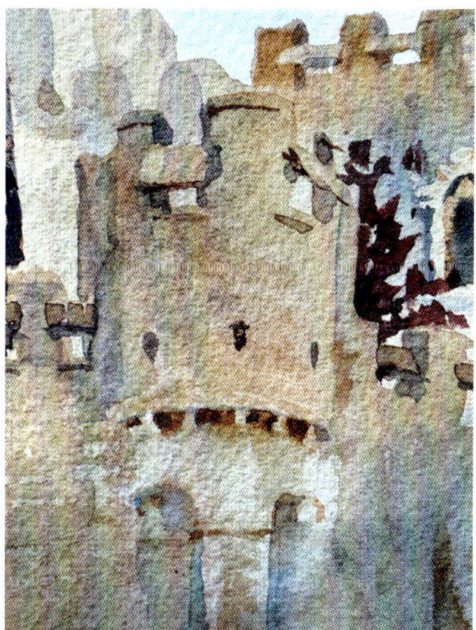

After

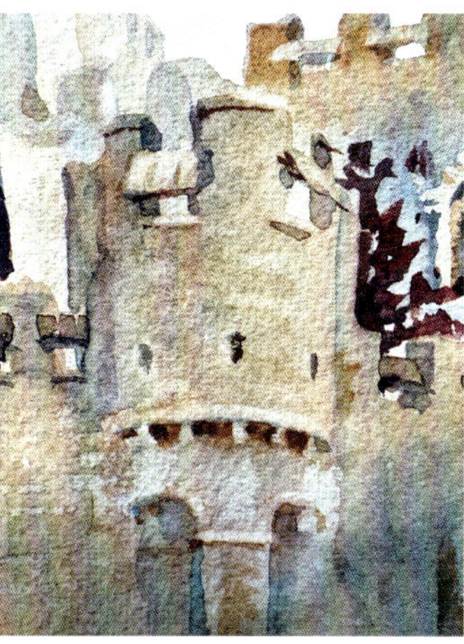

Distract or Disguise

If all else fails, and the light is lost and the painting looks dull, there is still a further course of action to turn to: that of distraction or disguise. For example, darkening the area adjacent to or surrounding the lost highlight will increase the tonal contrast and relative value, thereby 'tricking' the viewer into seeing the highlight as lighter than it is painted. This action may require increasing other shaded or dark areas to balance the tones across the painting. However, since the aim of a painting is to entertain and excite the eye, an increase in tonal contrast is likely to enliven the painting anyway.

Alternatively, if there is a suitable space in your painting, you can distract the viewer from lost light by introducing a new focus: a figure or an animal, for example. The human eye is always drawn to people, and especially movement, so adding active figures is a wonderful way to reinvigorate a flat or dull watercolour. If you feel nervous about where to place them, paint a couple of figures in different appropriate sizes on a separate sheet, cut them out and place them in different positions in your painting.

A figure will often have more impact positioned a third in from the left or right, rather than close to the edge, and may even work in the centre. It is easier to add a dark figure against a lighter background than to place a lighter figure against a dark area.

Choose an appropriate pose and suggest movement, which will add more interest than a static pose. Consider the direction of light: if the lighting comes from one side, you may need a sliver of light down the lit side. Neat Titanium White paint or scratching off are ways to make this fix.

Pause just before you add the figure, and check if there are other options. Would more figures be better than one, or could a landscape feature do the job better?

Practise the figure on a separate piece of paper before adding it into the painting with a minimum of brushstrokes, making sure to use colours already in the painting.

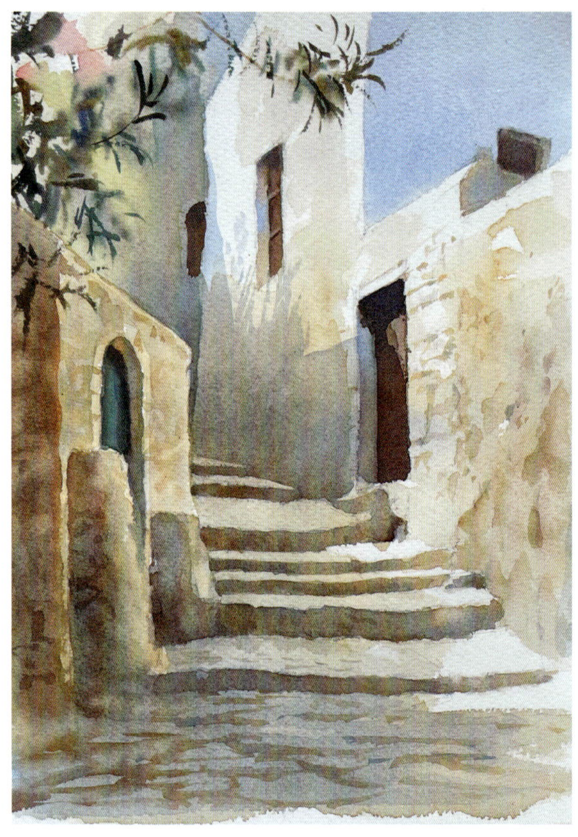

▲ This landscape looked a bit empty and lacked any storyline. I debated where to place a figure and chose the wide middle step, which would place the woman almost in the middle of the painting, against a mid-tone wall.

▶ The shadow on the wall meant the woman had to be painted in stronger tones to stand out. The black of her dress is a mix of the Cobalt Blue and Transparent Sienna already in the painting. I chose Light Red to bring out her skin tones, adding white paint to highlight her left-hand side. I added the cat as a balancing afterthought – together they give the painting a story!

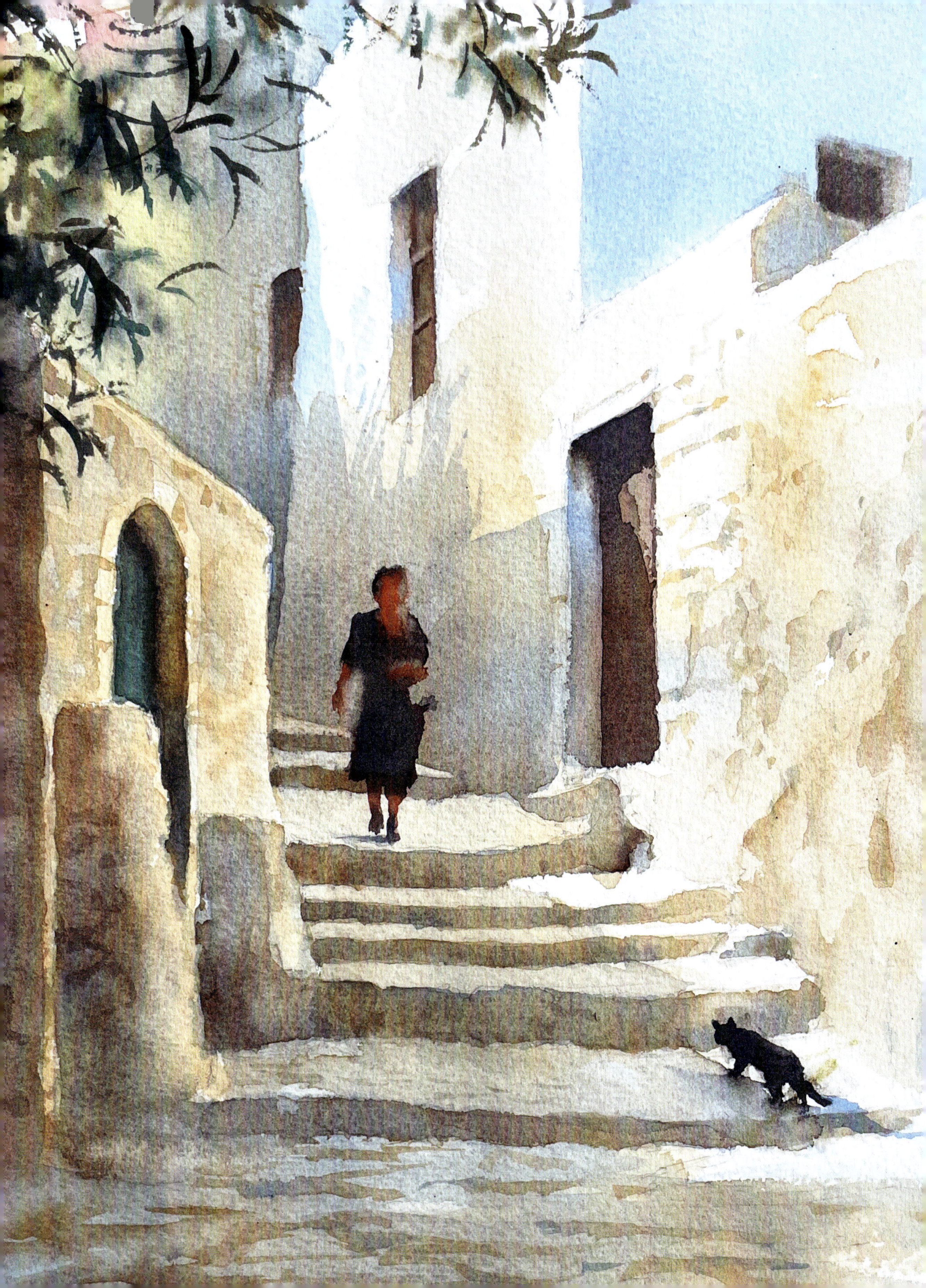

Practice, Practice, Practice

Reserving the Light

Since the aim in watercolour is to retain transparency and light, most watercolours are built from light to dark tones. Maximum transparency is found in the fewest layers of paint, especially with the darkest of tones and colours, so it is in our interest to reach the darks as quickly as possible. Follow the sequence used for painting this elephant in just two colours: Transparent Orange and Schmincke Violet.

Colours:

Transparent Orange

Schmincke Violet

Brushes:

19mm flat brush

Size 8 round brush

Size 10 round brush

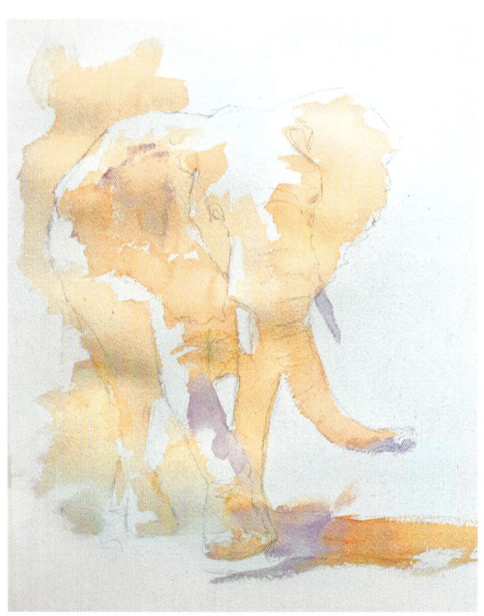

1 With dilute Orange and dilute Violet, I painted all the elephant, except where I wanted to retain white paper for highlights, using the broad strokes of a 19mm flat brush.

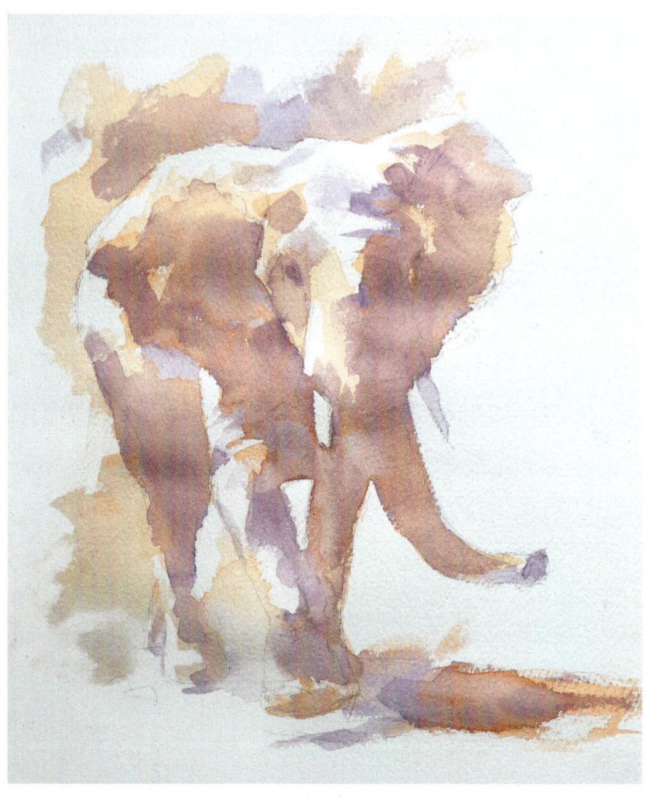

2 Over the first wash, which was still damp in places, I painted all the areas in shadow with dilute Violet, immediately establishing the form of the elephant.

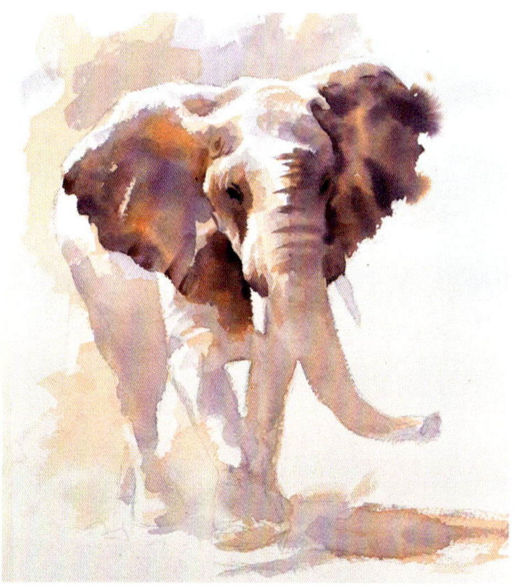

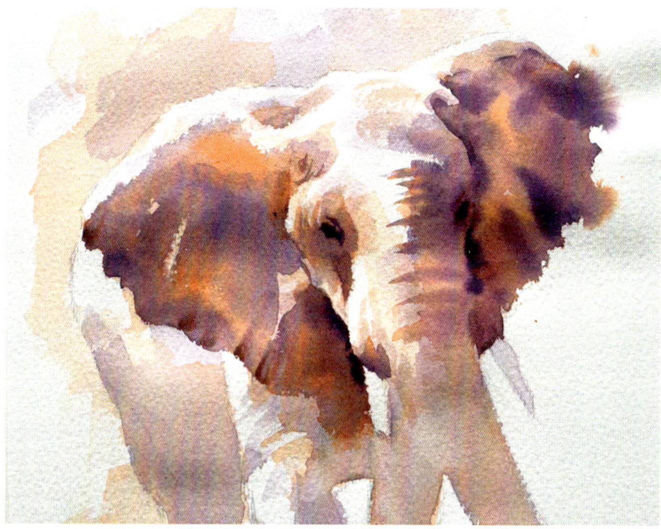

3 Even though both colours are highly transparent, because the painting's success depended on the intermingling between these two single-pigment secondary colours, I went straight to the finish, starting with the ears and head, bringing each area to conclusion with fully loaded wet into wet washes of concentrated pigment.

4 In this detail, you can see more clearly the mingling of the two rich, wet colours on the paper.

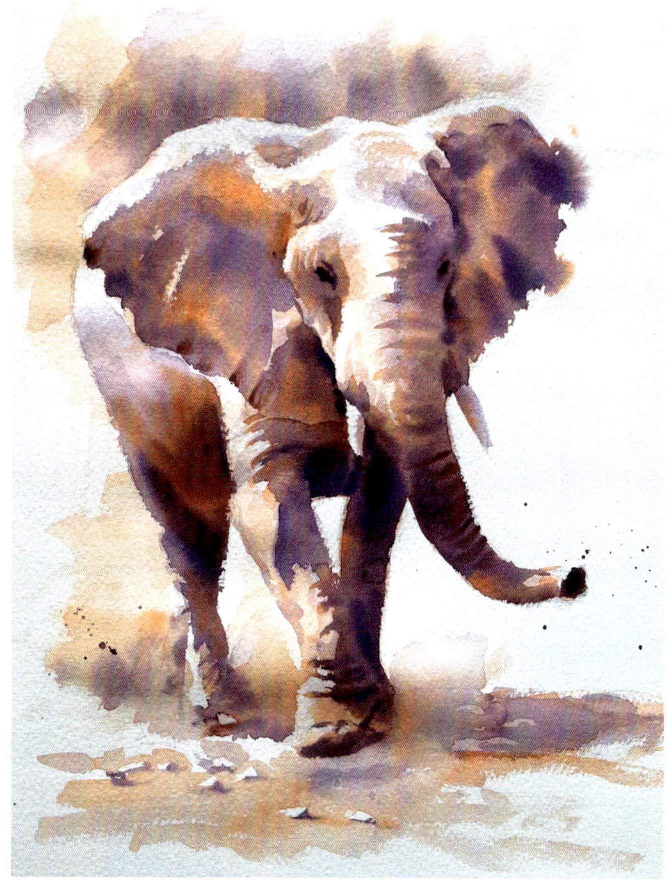

5 I carried the rich, deep colour through into the limbs and underbelly, mostly applying the pigment wet into wet, and using clear water to spread the colour beside the feet to create ambiguity caused by the dust.

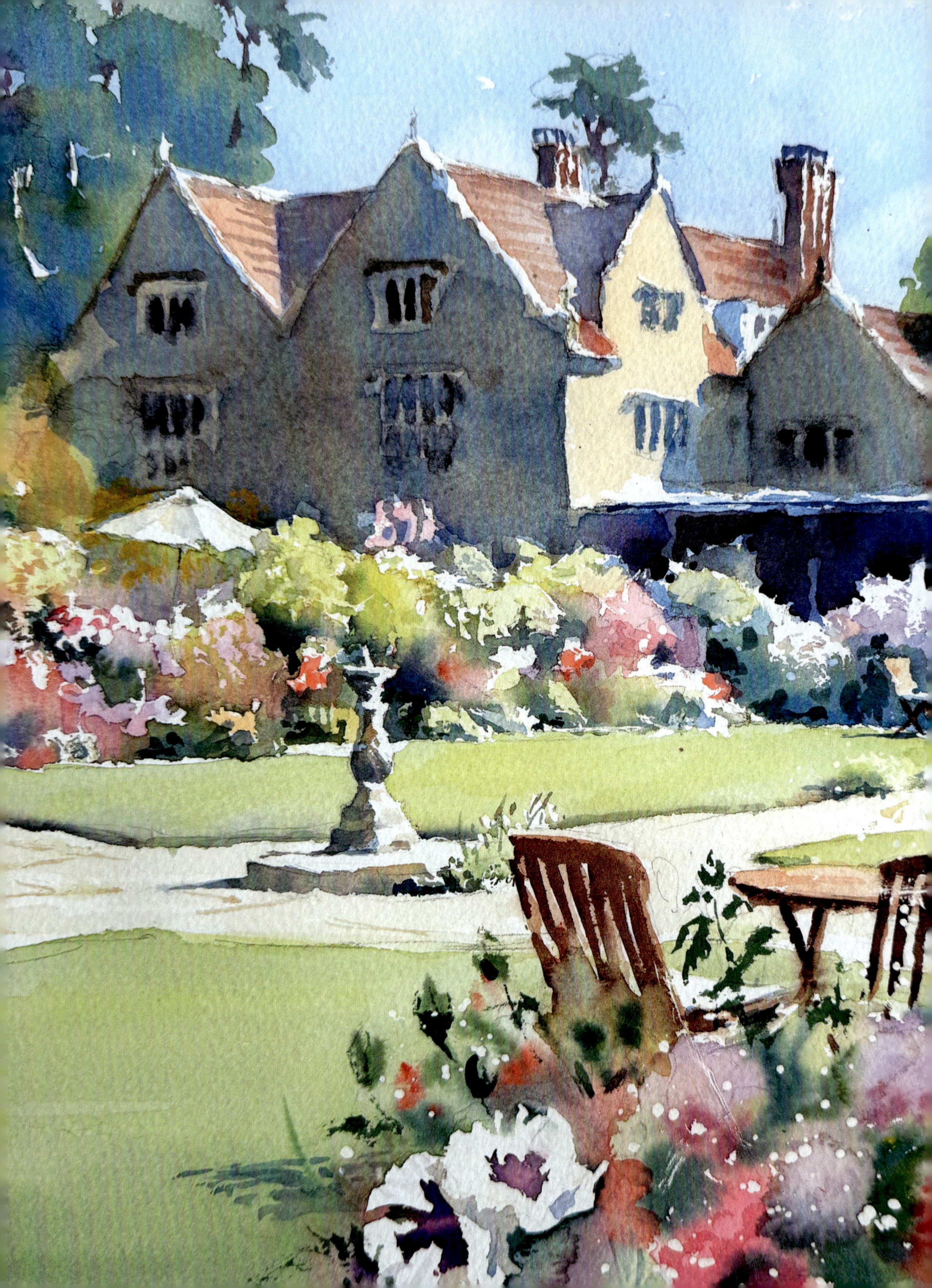

CHAPTER 8

Tackling Complex Subjects

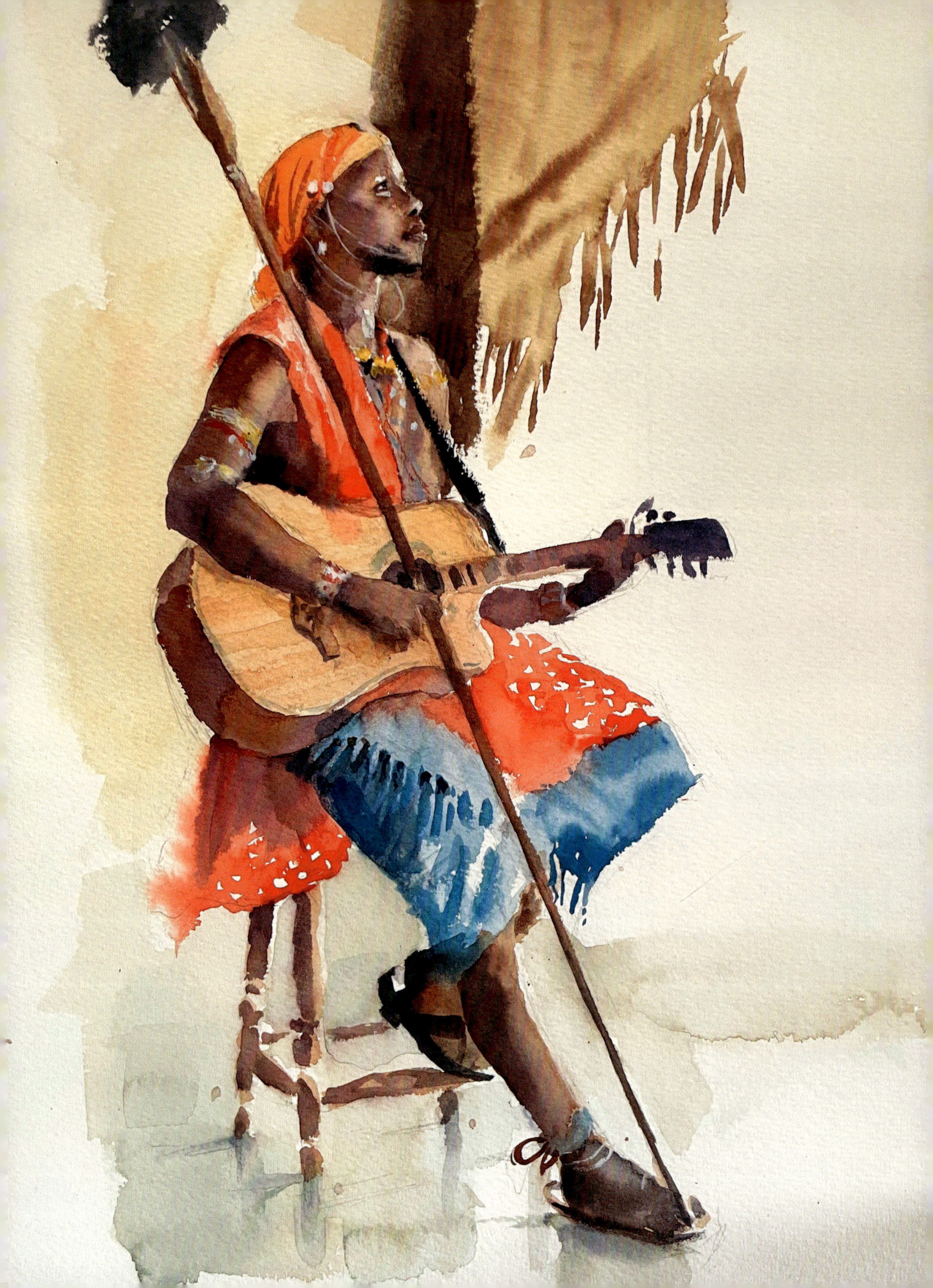

Challenging Subjects

Even though watercolour paintings can be painted quickly or over time, simply or with copious detail, complicated subjects are often avoided if they appear too daunting to tackle. Time constraints and changing light might make them seem too challenging to attempt. However, the fluid nature of watercolour and its suggestive brushmarks can simplify complex subjects into arresting paintings in fairly short timeframes. Recording the wonderful sights one sees with paint while travelling is reason enough to have a go. Complex architecture and intricate patterns should not be considered as too complicated to attempt, even if you end up just painting a small detail of the whole.

There is no subject unsuitable for a painting in the flat world of the watercolour: it is the pattern of light and shade, the shapes, colours and contours that make the painting work, not the subject, content or detail. This chapter will help you overcome the fear of tackling complex subject matter, so that elaborate architecture, decorative fabric and intricate patterns become a joy to paint.

◀ **Sakita Plays His Guitar,** *51 x 40.5cm (20 x 16in)*

The traditional Samburu clothing worn by Sakita presented complicated patterns and detail, and the time frame available was less than two hours. I drew more fully than usual, so I could be confident with applying looser brushwork. I painted the face first and worked downward, so if time ran out at least I had a portrait. I gave scant attention to actual detail, and the plan worked!

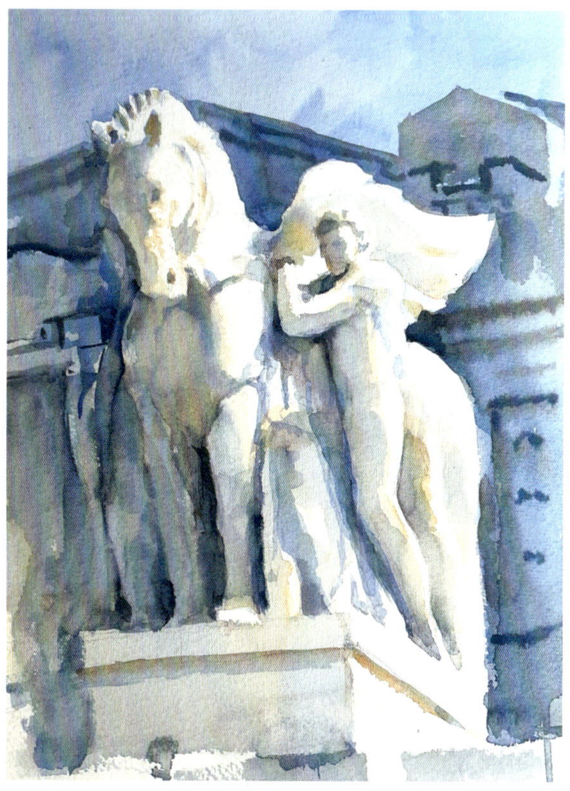

▶ **Pegasus detail, Milan Central Station,** *38 x 28cm (15 x 11in)*

Confronted with the whole facade of Milan Central Station, I chose to paint a sculptural detail on top of one of the columns instead, and positioned myself so it was lit from one side to make modelling the form easier.

Choose Helpful Light

A watercolourist can paint shade but not light, so a figurative subject becomes more suitable for painting quickly if the composition presents a pattern containing more shade than light. Complex subjects are easier to paint when the sun is shining because the light and shadow are more obvious and detail becomes obscured in both bright light and deep shade.

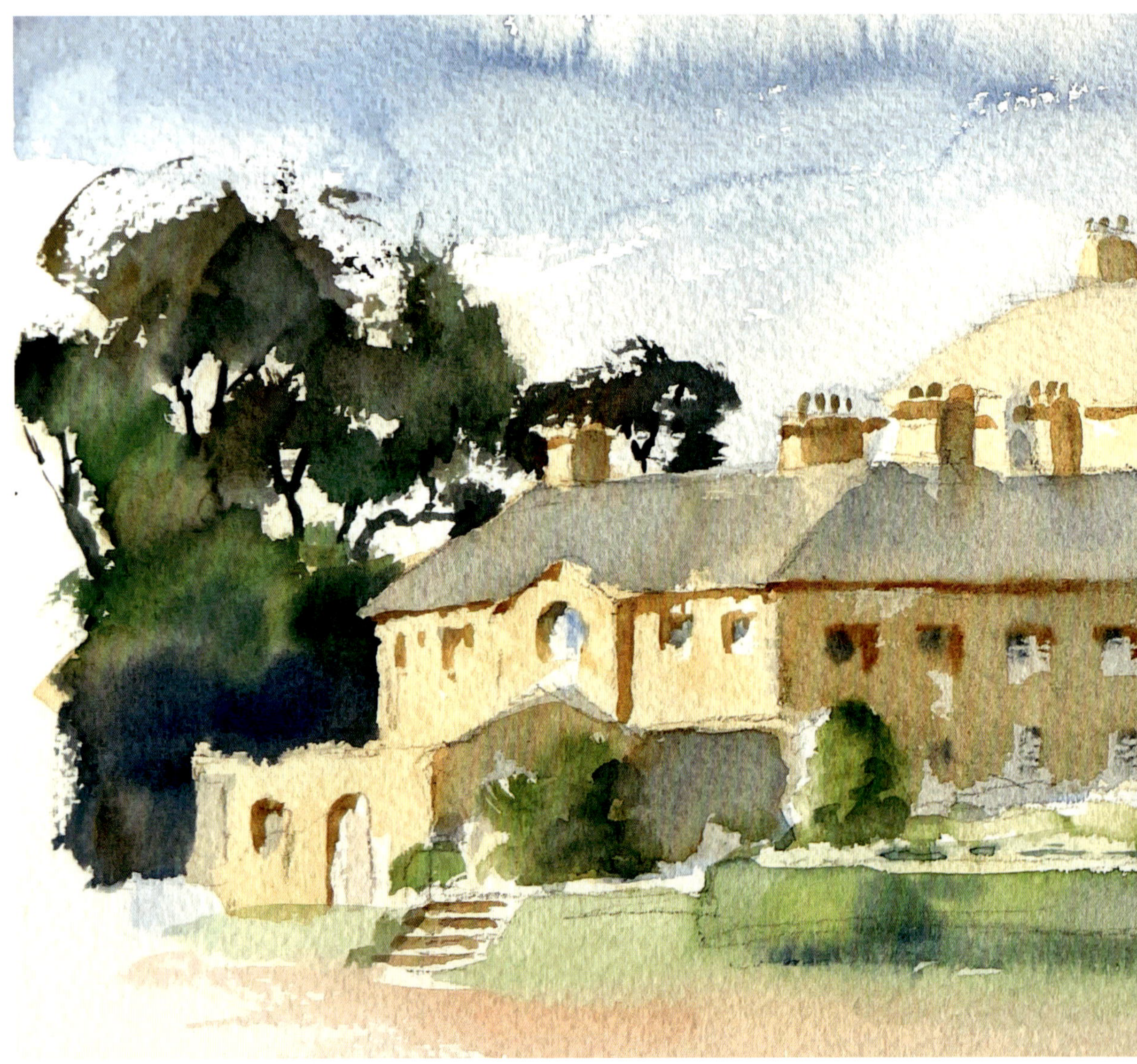

We cannot always choose the weather, nor the direction of light. However, we can apply logic regarding how to represent three dimensions on a flat sheet of paper, as the side facing the main source of light should receive more light than any faces turned away. If possible, choose an angle with an obviously predominant light on one side; this makes modelling form through the light, dark and mid-tone values much more straightforward.

▼ Quick sketch of Dumfries House, *18 x 45.5cm (7 x 18in)*

To paint this magnificent house, I waited for a brief sunny interlude. Then, with less than an hour to spare, I simplified the complex structure into its basic forms: rectangular faces, windows and roofs. With light on the west face and shade on the front, the warm and cool tonal counterchange provides enough visual interest, and little detail is required.

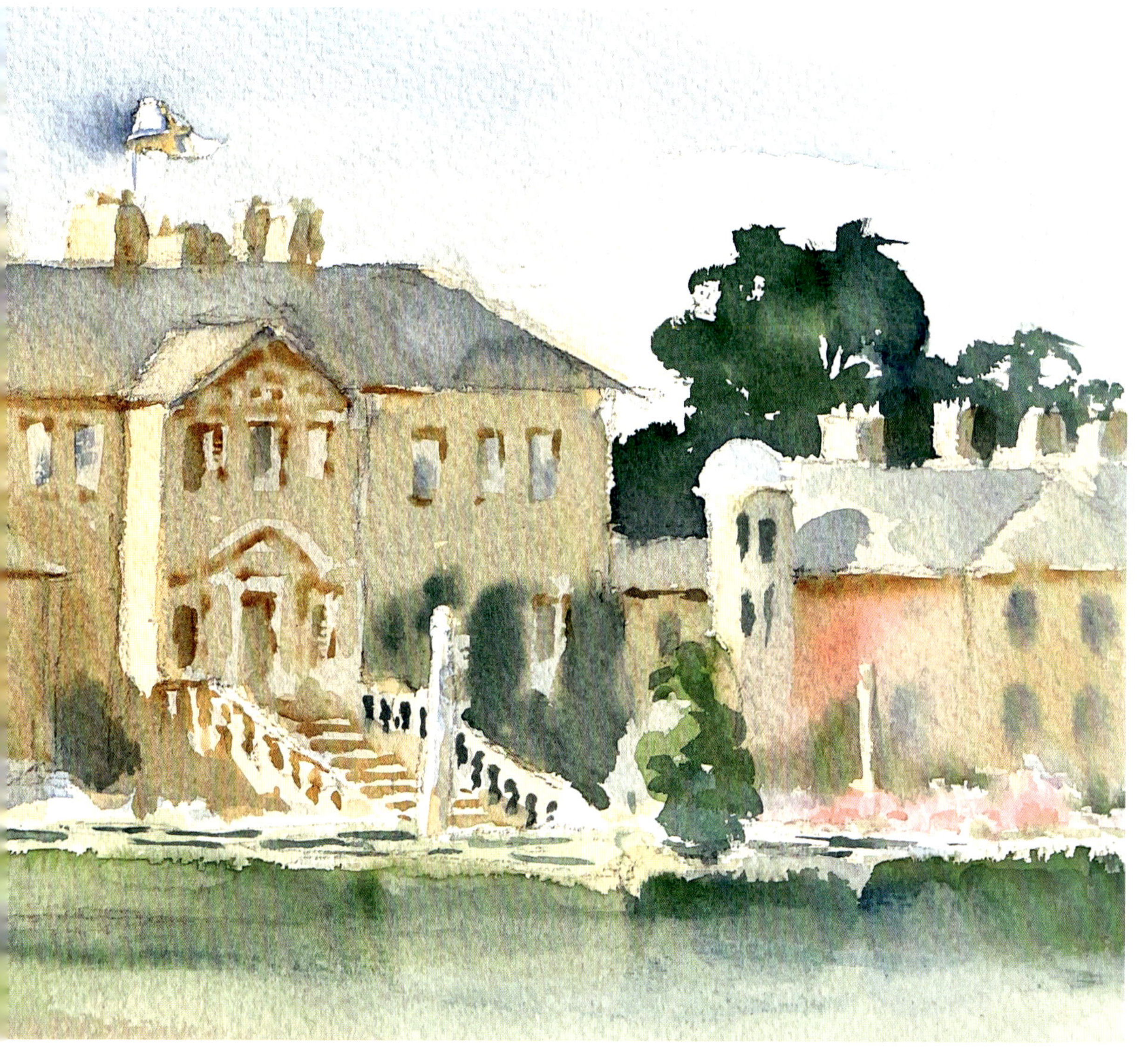

Form First

Think form first. Sort out the composition by simplifying a complex subject into approximate, basic geometric forms: spheres, cylinders, cubes, cones and pyramids. Thus, a cathedral dome becomes the top half of a sphere; a clock tower a cylinder; a spire a cone. Draw the rough structural form before thinking about the details covering the surfaces. You can add surface detail more precisely once structural form is in place.

Aim to paint what attracted the eye at first look, not what the eye notices after drawing the subject for half an hour. Apply logic: under a single source of light, the planes of a form facing the light will be lighter in tone than those not facing it. If you can see the top face of a form, since light generally emanates from above, that face is probably lighter than the side elevations. The planes directly facing the predominant light will be lighter than any of those turning away from the light, and the undersides will be darkest of all. Note, and know, from which direction the light is coming; you can place an arrow in the top corner to confirm. This is the key to getting the tone values to work and will enable you to finish the painting if the light changes.

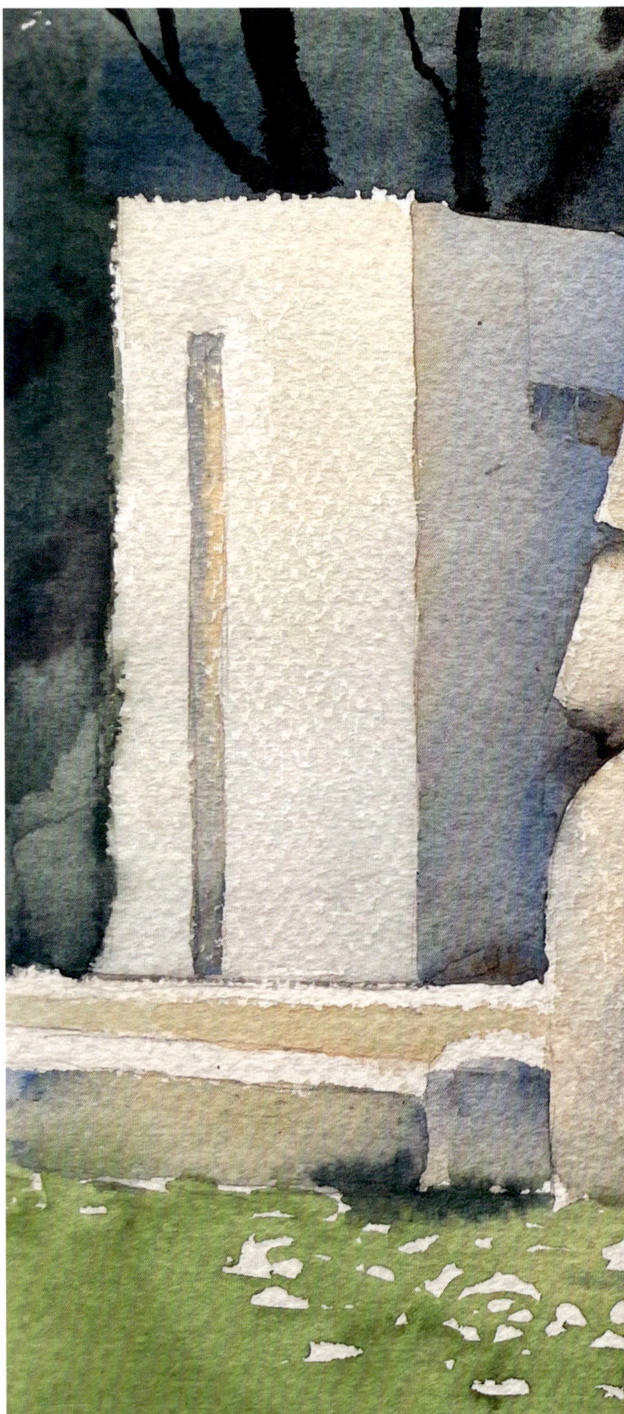

▶ **Mazzini Sculpture, Milan,**
28 x 38cm (11 x 15in)
I loved painting this modern sculpture. The form was obvious but the sunlight went in and out behind clouds, playing havoc with the relative tone, so I followed my arrow, with light coming from the left and the shadier sides facing right.

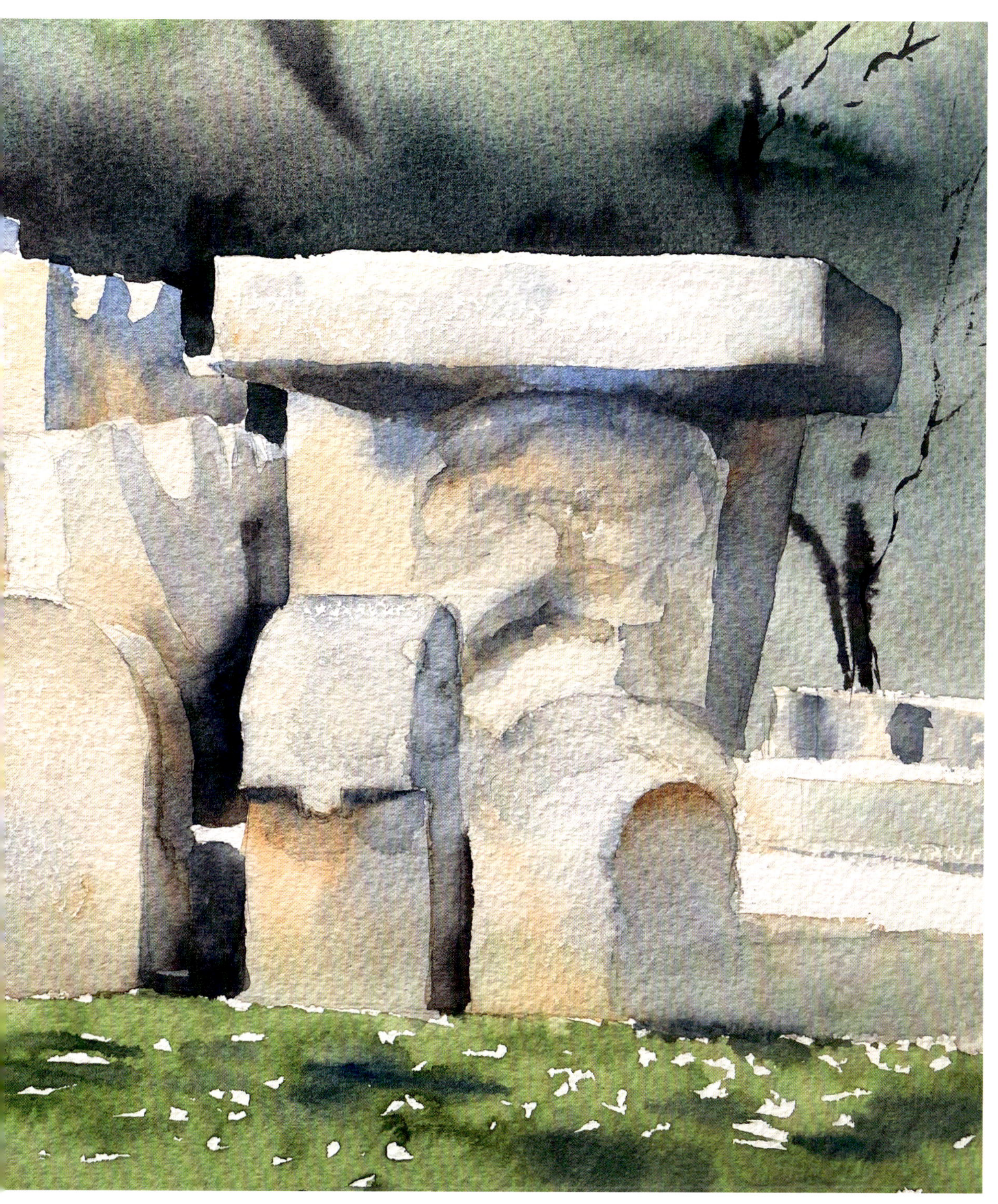

Lack of Perspective

Managing perspective is another challenge that can get aspiring painters into trouble, and may put them off even attempting to paint architectural subjects or complex views. Perspective will come into play if viewing a building or structure from an angle other than a frontal view. If the perspective of a building and the windows and doors are not aligned before starting to paint, it makes the painting much harder to pull together. However, this tricky element need not be so scary if there is a basic understanding of perspective and a seed of logic is applied.

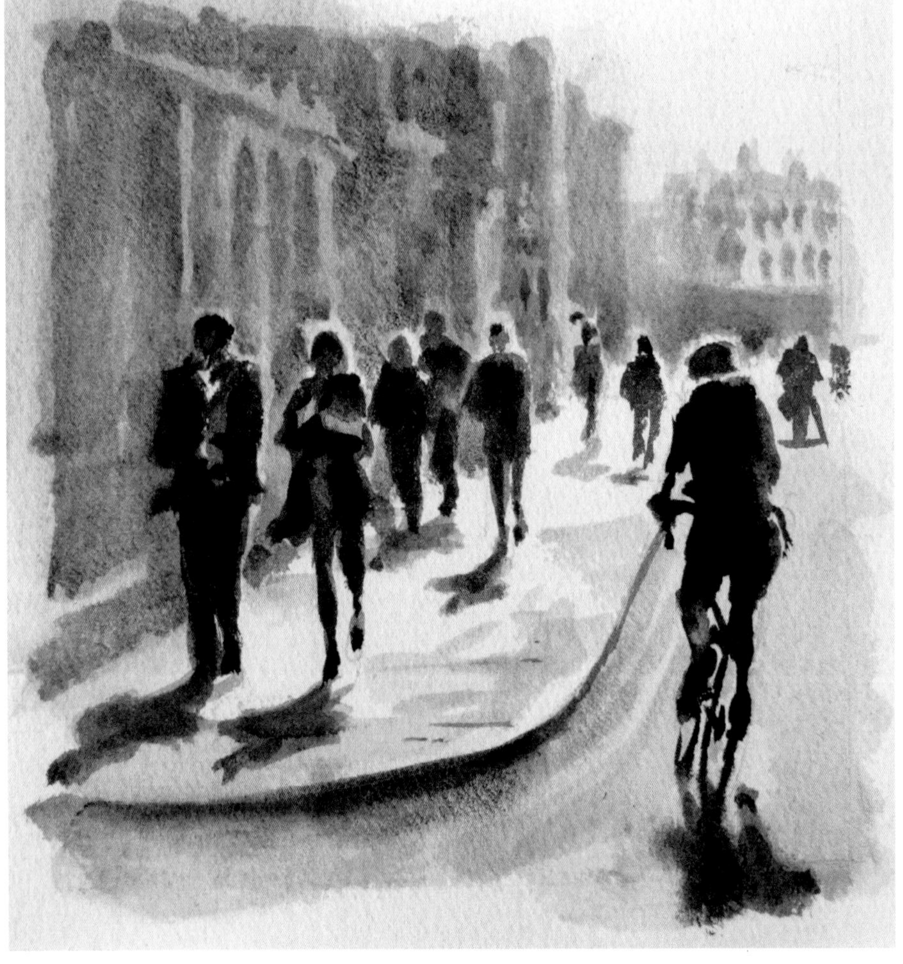

◀ When depicting space and depth in even a quick sketch, the basic rule of perspective comes into play: buildings and figures receding into the distance become smaller in scale.

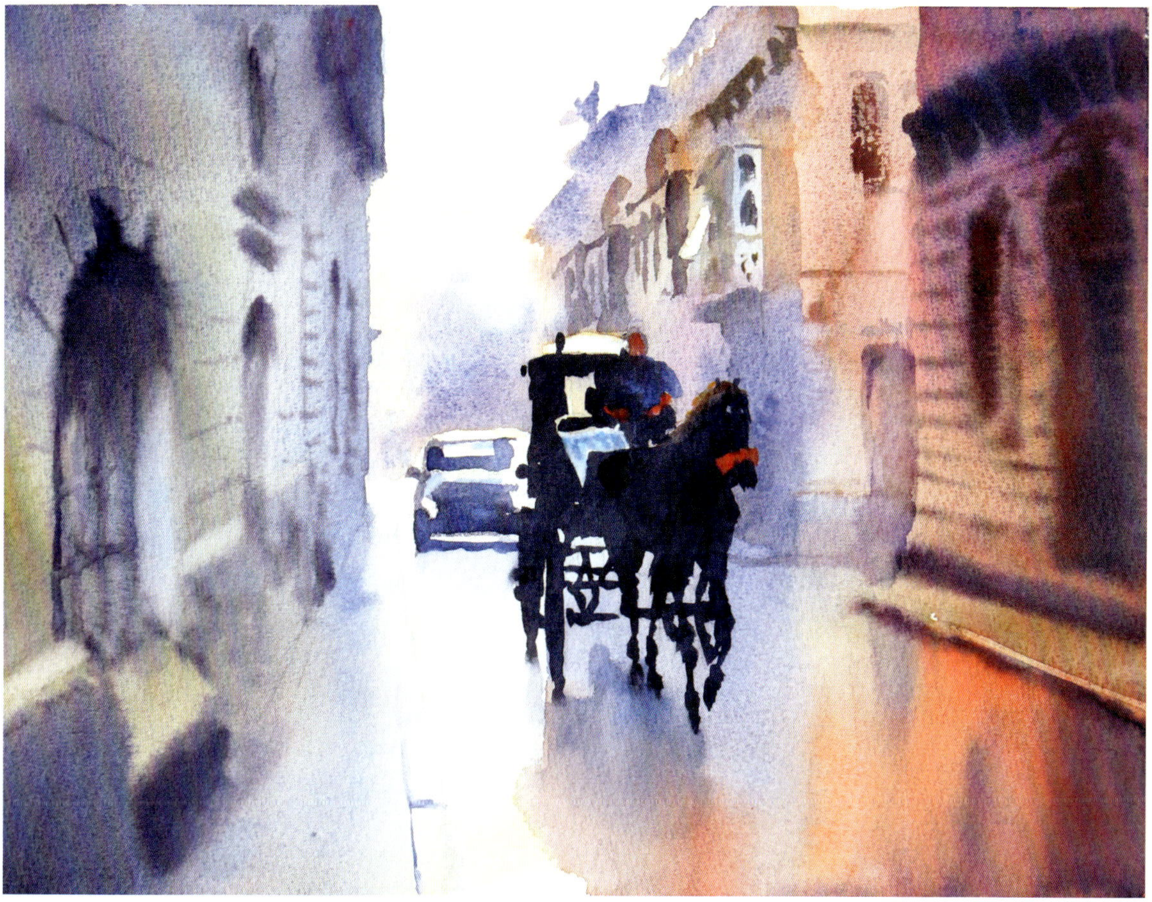

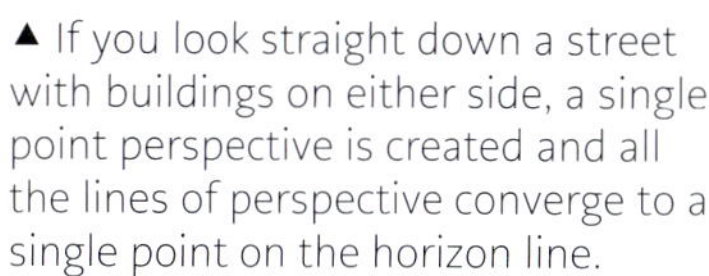

▲ If you look straight down a street with buildings on either side, a single point perspective is created and all the lines of perspective converge to a single point on the horizon line.

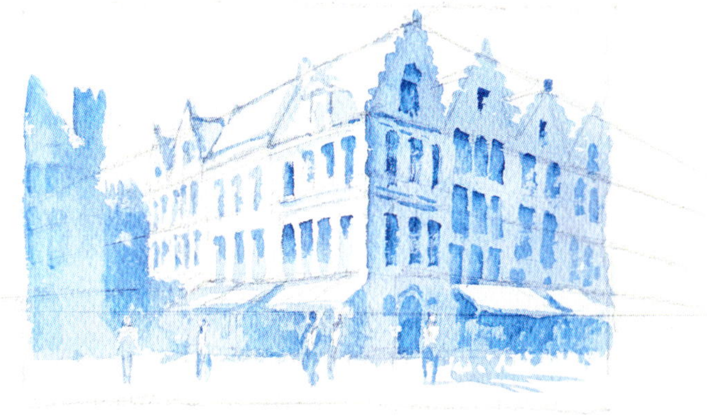

◄ When two sides of a building recede away from your viewpoint, there will be two vanishing points to the perspective. To compose the painting, draw a horizon line across the paper at eye level (likely the head/chest height of any figures), then trace the rooflines downward to meet at an imaginary point on the horizon (these vanishing points may be off the paper). Use these sloping lines to then find the perspective of windows, covings etc.

▼ Arco della Pace, Milan,
28 x 38cm (11 x 15in)
The lines of perspective have been carried from along the top and bottom of the columns, down to their vanishing point at the horizon (my eye level), which is the base of the arch. The surface detail is just a bunch of squiggly brushmarks!

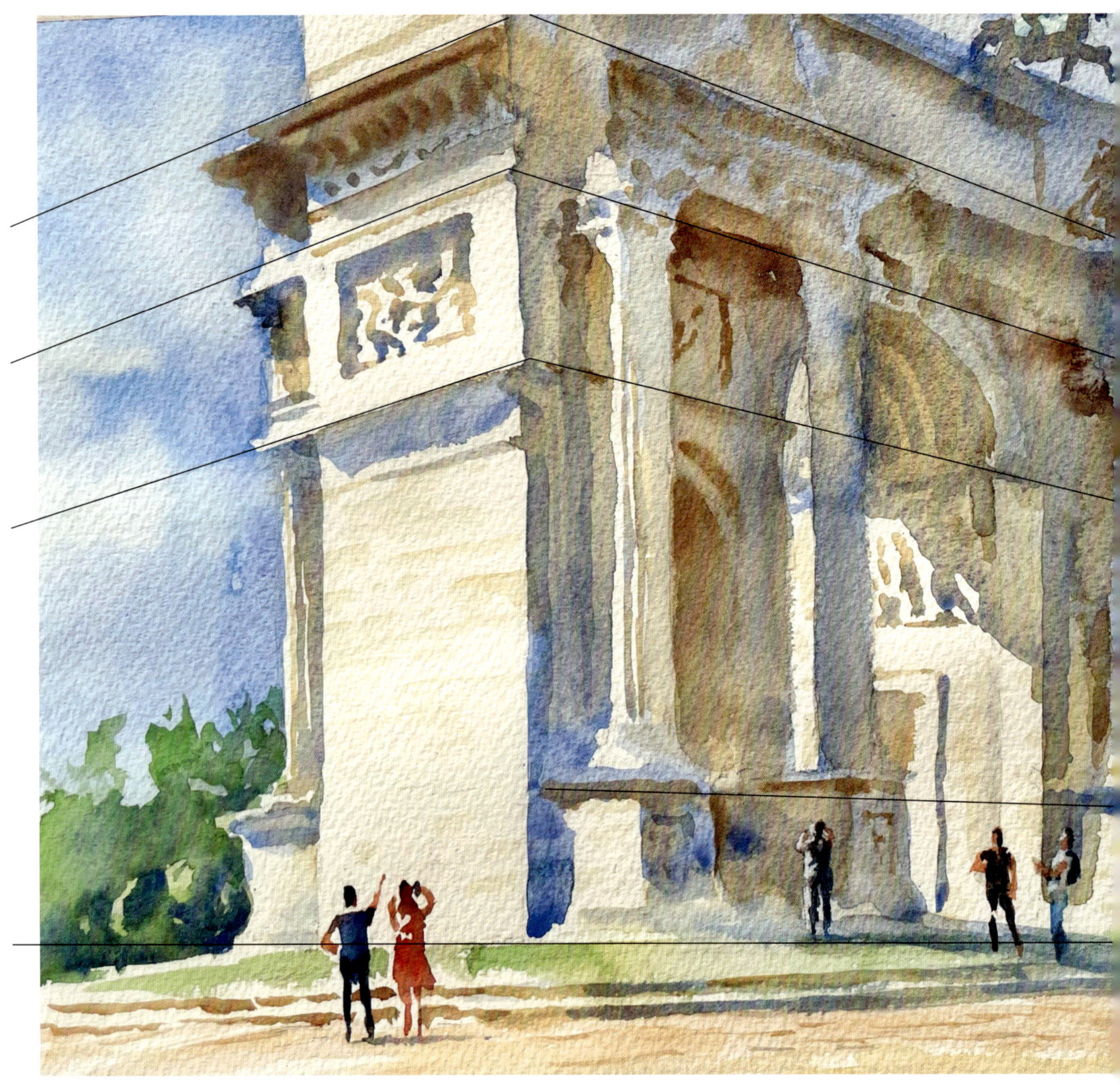

Perspective Made Simple

Remember, the horizon is always at your eye level, so you are in control of the horizon line. If a building's line, cornice or eave is above your eye level, the lines of perspective, called orthogonals, will angle downward towards the horizon line to what are termed vanishing points. The higher up the building, the steeper the angle; hence, the roof line is steeper than an angle drawn through window ledges at a lower level.

If you and the building are standing/sitting on the same level, the building line at ground level will fall below your eye level, so the perspective lines/orthogonals will angle upward to the horizon line, even if only slightly.

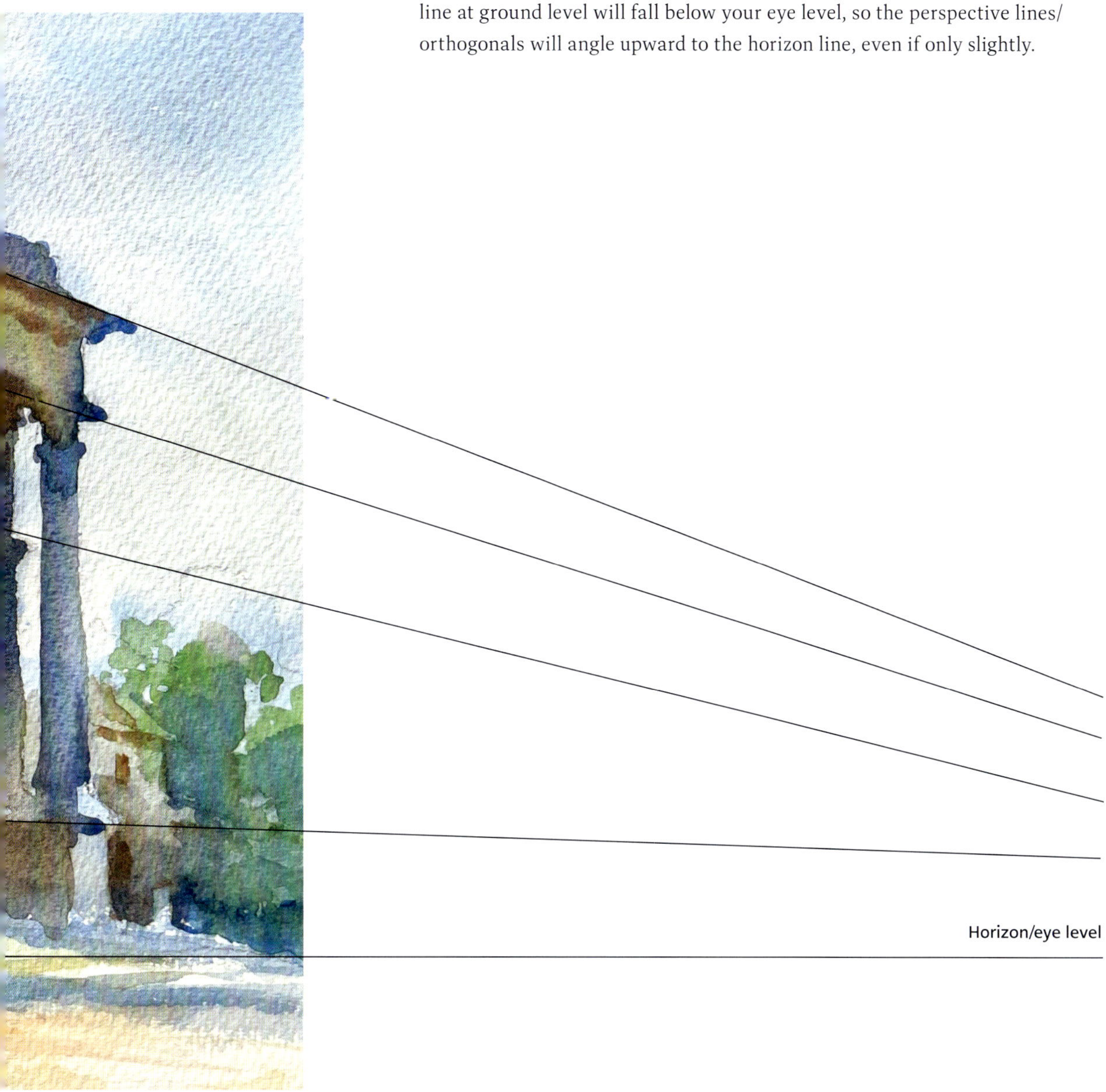

Horizon/eye level

The Picture Plane Window Pane

The flat surface of the painting is called the picture plane. To assess the angles of the orthogonals to be drawn on the picture plane, frame your view and imagine there is a window pane vertically in front of you. Hold your pencil level at a **horizontal angle** with an outstretched arm, pressed flat against the imaginary window pane. Look at all the sloping angles of the building lines in relation to your flat/horizontal pencil and guess the approximate angle – perhaps 15 or 30 degrees – to give yourself an idea of the angle of perspective. Orthogonals will drop from the top corner of a building in either direction down to the horizon, and angle up to the horizon from the bottom corner if viewed from above.

▶ This sketch of Rosary Quay was literally painted through a window. An outstretched pencil helped me find the perspective angles of the buildings. The superimposed lines represent the slope at which the pencil was angled relative to the horizontal. Remember, the pencil is held out as if pressed up against the glass, its point and end equidistant from me.

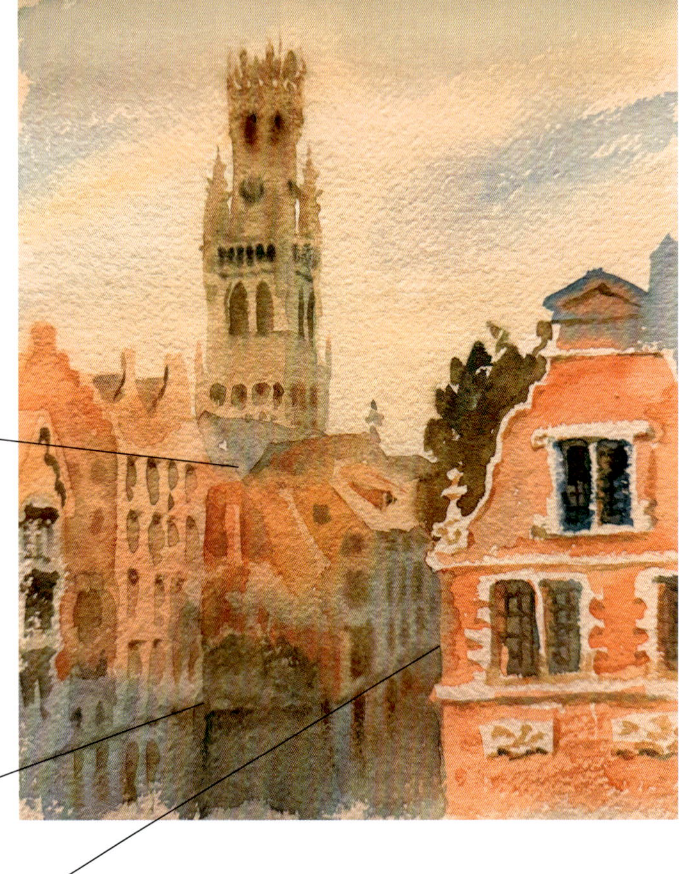

Perspective Tips

Many a time I have seen beginners actually make the perspective harder than it is in reality, by effectively lifting themselves above their subject and then looking down on it they attempt aerial perspective. No wonder they cannot work out the angles, neither could I! Unless you are actually looking down on the view from above, the perspective lines of the top of buildings will angle down to the horizon, not up. Even when painting figures, I see the same thing happening: instead of people gradually getting smaller behind those in front as they recede on the picture plane they are painted above each other, hovering in imaginary space!

The help is out there in front of your eyes – if you are standing to paint, your eye level will be similar to the level of the eyes on the figures you are painting (assuming they are of similar height): your eye level is the horizon. Figures further away will become smaller in relation to the foreground figures, the level of their feet rising higher on the picture plane as they recede, while their heads (and eyes) stay level with your own and each other's.

If you are sitting down to paint, the figures in the distance will shrink as they recede on the picture plane, with the level of their feet rising and the level of their heads lowering, because your seated eye level remains approximately level with their chest heights.

Only if you are looking down on the figures will they be assembled on the picture plane as higher than each other as they recede.

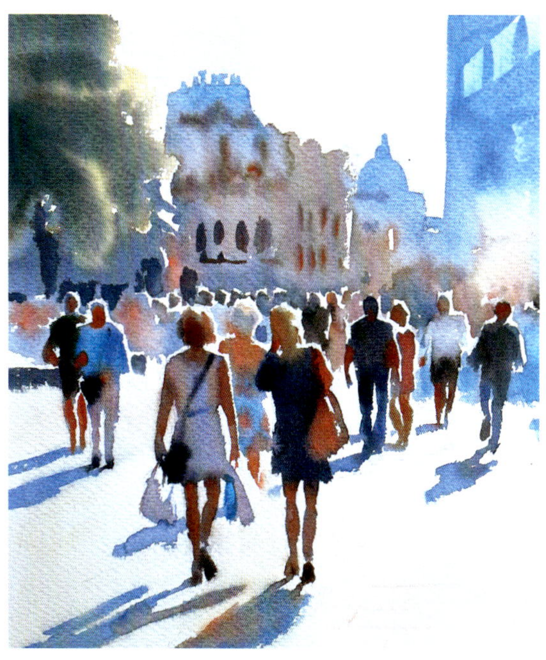

▲ **Loitering in Leicester Square,**
30.5 x 28cm (12 x 11in)

I painted this from a standing position. The figures in the background recede according to the laws of perspective, with their feet rising on the picture plane and their heads staying level with the horizon, my eye level.

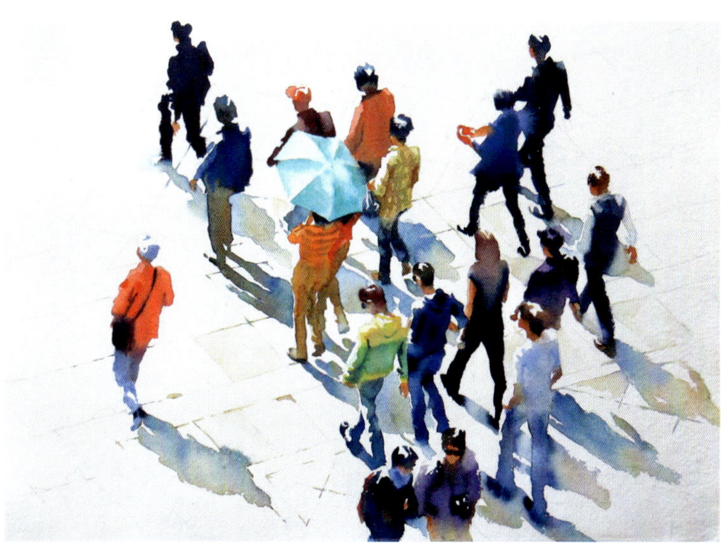

▶ **The Green Umbrella,**
56 x 71cm (22 x 28in)

The depth of field is very shallow in a view seen from above. There is no horizon line visible as my eye level is above the top of the painting/picture plane, and there is very little perspective to consider in terms of recession. However, as the figures are seen from above, their proportions are foreshortened.

Sequencing

All too often the desire to paint is strong but once the paper is in front of you, you cannot think how or where to begin. Watercolours are generally built from light to dark, so it makes sense to find a logical sequence for building your watercolour.

Start with pale initial stages that map in the main areas of colour and tone; this way you will keep in mind the whole picture. Keep your sketch fluid, working from your main interest outward, without worrying about details unless they are highlights that need reserving. See the composition as a pattern, areas of light, mid and future dark tones with a contrast of warm and cool hues. Lay out the major panels with pale washes, using broad, flat brushes, covering all except the highlights.

As areas dry, add in the broader details on top, and then later, the fine detail. This sequence helps complex subjects become far less daunting, prevents the painting becoming fragmented and bitty and keeps the integrity and harmony of the whole.

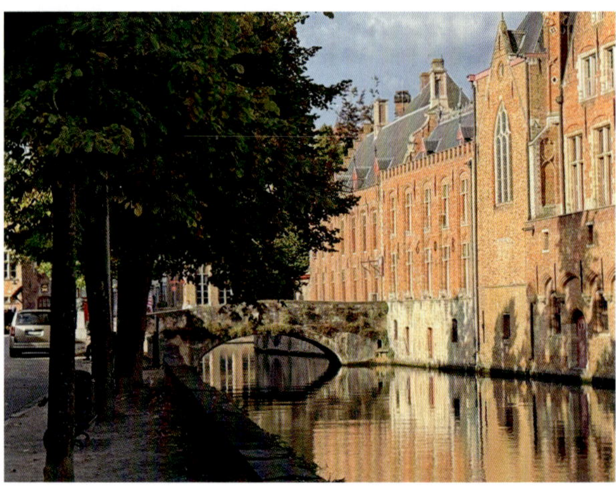

▲ The shapely bridge and glowing light along the walls of the canal caught my attention. I framed the composition in the photo between my thumbs and forefingers.

Colours chosen: Yellow Raw Ochre, Raw Umber, Red Ochre/Burnt Sienna, Ultramarine Finest (Blue), Sap Green.

Your watercolour is a new creation, not a copy of something that already exists in the real world: leave out whatever you wish, move trees, add people. You owe nothing, save the thanks for being an exciting inspiration!

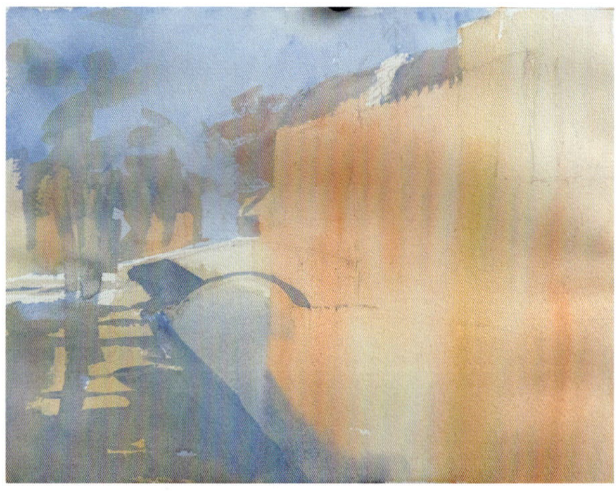

1 Over a minimal pencil sketch, I washed in Yellow and Red Ochre for the warm light on the lit walls, followed by Ultramarine Blue for the shaded side, the hue of the sky, the shadow cast across the bridge and the roofs.

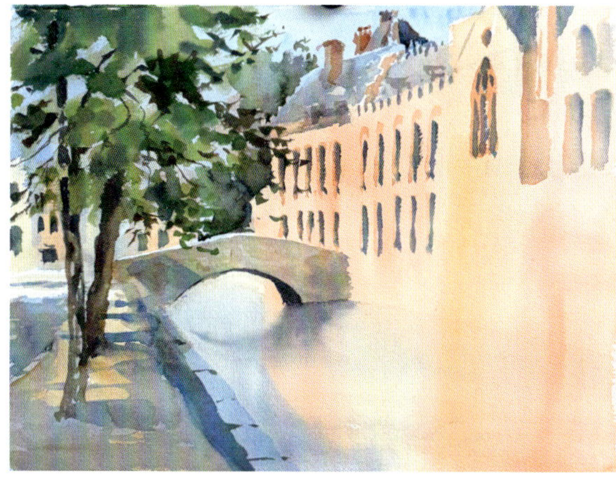

2 Being my focal point, I painted the bridge first. Then, following general perspective lines, brushed in the windows with narrow vertical strokes. I reduced the number of trees on the quay, and, blending a light, mid and dark tone of Sap Green mixed with Ultramarine, laid a large irregular wash with lively strokes and gaps of sky within the wash.

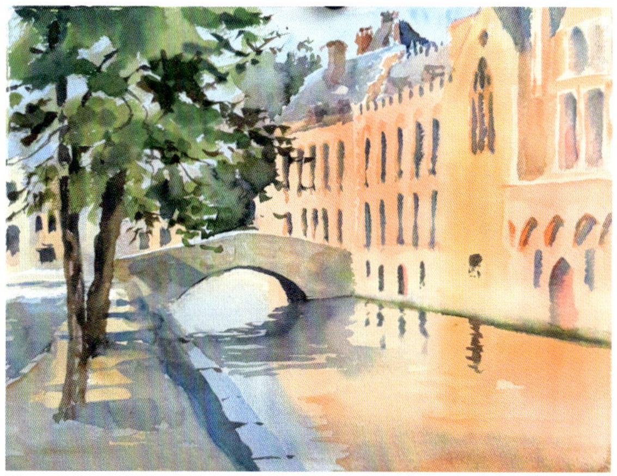

3 I painted the reflection under the bridge onto dry paper to define the edges and then softened the waterline area with a damp brush, brushing in a strong, dark line of Sap Green, and began the reflections of the windows.

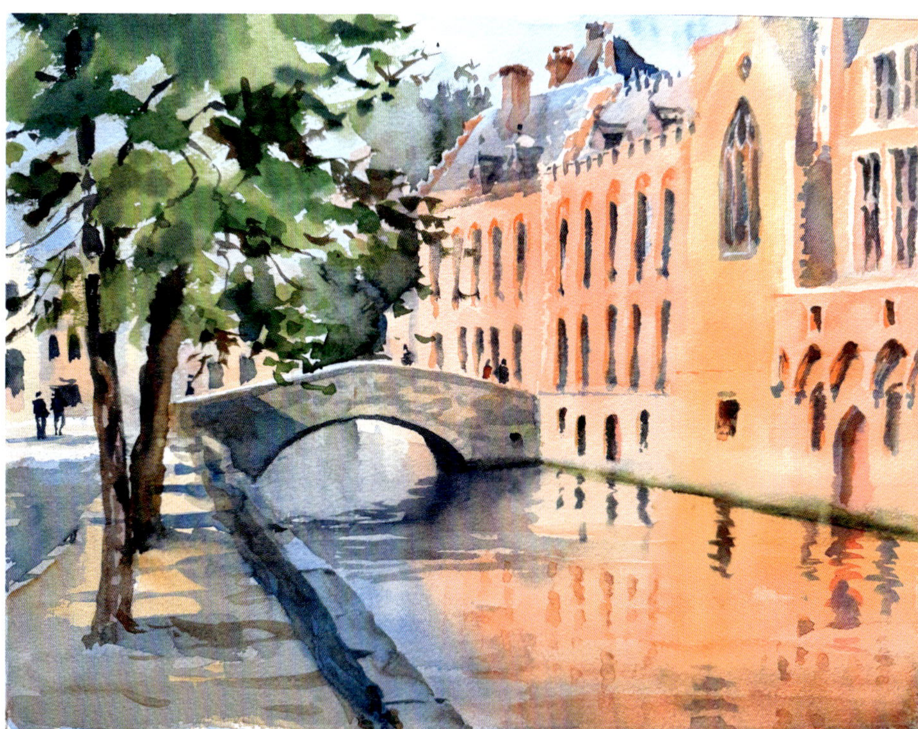

▶ **Rivers in Time,** *30.5 x 40.5cm (12 x 16in)*

With wiggly brushmarks I completed the reflections, darkened the wall of the quay, added detail to the roofline and bridge and punctuated the middle ground with a few figures.

Surface Detail

Decorative detail is another area that is very alluring to paint but can come with its own issues. Architectural detail is very interesting and can add a lot to your painting, but since form should be implied before the surface detail, it can be hard to work out how to leave out the highlights on decorative details and still wash in the general form. In these instances, surface detail has to be considered at the same time as you are building the structure, and this can be challenging. Usually, drawing is required to guide the brush around the highlighted areas.

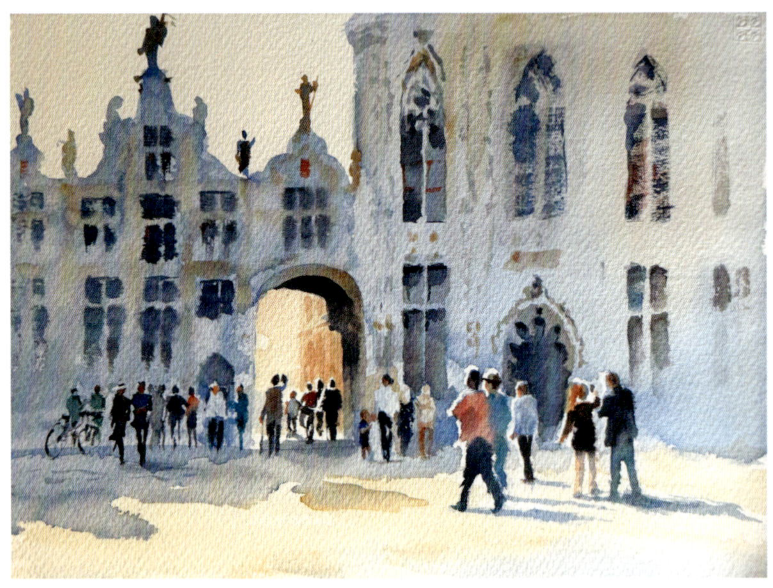

▲ **Sunlight in Burg Square, Bruges,** *28 x 38cm (11 x 15in)*
Multiple statues, reliefs and windows adorn the facade of the Burg in Bruges. Painting from across the square in the morning, the building was cast in shadow, so I painted a few people first, and then brushed in the building behind them. In this way I could paint a complicated subject simply, and without getting caught up in detail.

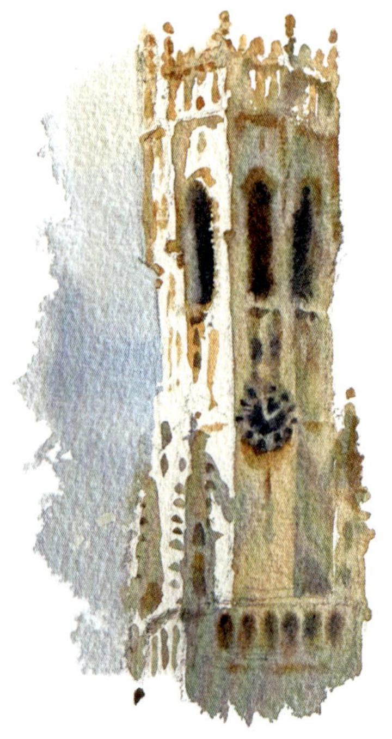

Suggestive Brushmarks

Decorative detail, such as arches and balconies, can also be simplified into suggestive brushmarks, effectively described by painting their shaded side or the shade they cast, rather than their structural intricacy. Loose, squiggly brushmarks can look highly descriptive and more lively than accurate, defined or measured detail, as shown in the tower to the left and with the roofline statues and figures above.

On the shaded side of a building, the detail can be represented more ambiguously still, with windows and complicated decorative features implied by wet into wet techniques. Paint the overall tone of the shaded side first and then, while still damp, touch in the neat, drier colour to represent the dark tones of windows, the shade cast from a cornice, or the features in a relief. There is no need to be afraid of detail when a quick squiggle can say so much, as can be seen in the arch on page 168 and the cathedral on page 133.

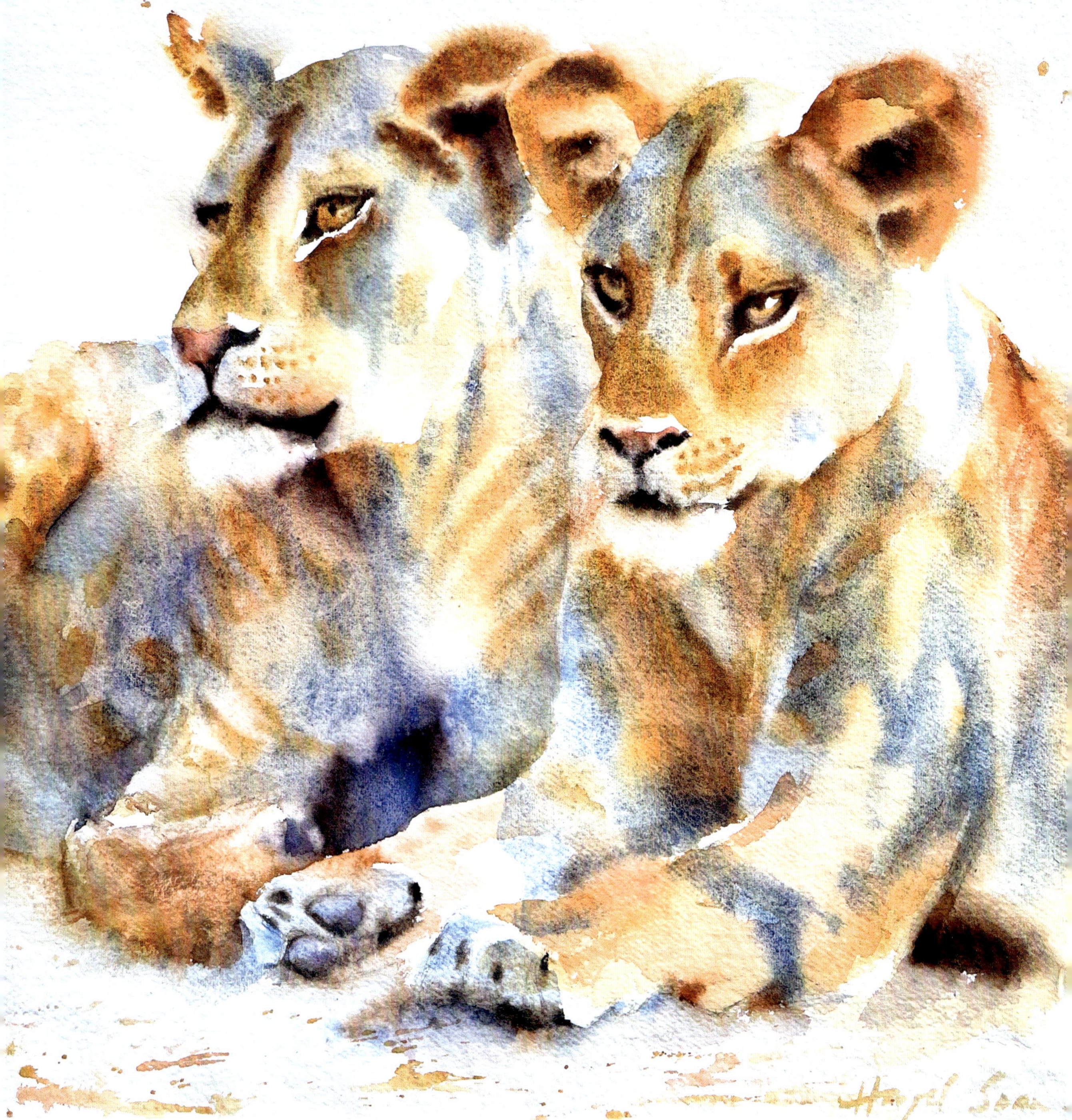

▲ **Sisters,** *56 x 51cm (22 x 20in)*

The ambiguity created by wet into wet blending allows for suggestion by default. Here the hair, claws, markings and facial details of the lionesses are actually quite loosely defined by the wet into wet technique, yet we have no trouble reading the suggestions as 'detail' in the painting.

Simplifying Windows and Doors

On the shaded sides of buildings, the numerous windows and doors can be suggested wet into wet to imply the detail, or made with dilute wet on dry brush marks delivered by a flat brush. On the lit facades, information is delivered wet on dry, with attention given to painting the shady areas, while tinting the lit areas. You do not need to tell the viewer everything about the construction of the building, most people are familiar with building facades and structures and will fill in scantily implied information with their own mind's eye - often a hint at the layout is enough.

▶ **Lake Como,** *38 x 28cm (15 x 11in)*

The many windows and doors in the building facades of this huddle of houses beside Lake Como were very complicated to work out, so I reduced their number and frequency and simply marked them in one above the other with the stroke of a flat brush, wet on dry.

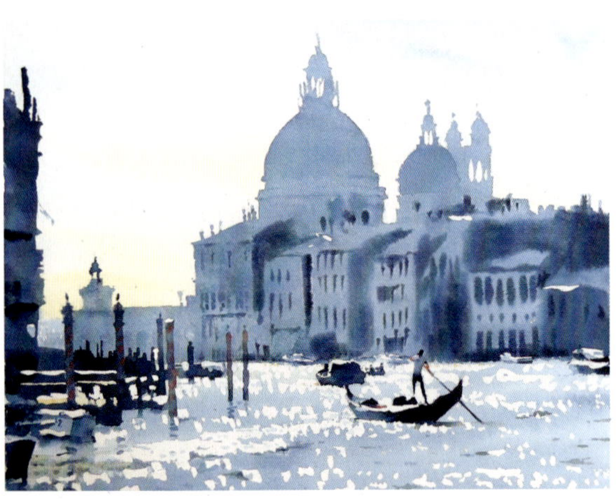

▲ **Glistening City,** *35.5 x 43cm (14 x 17in)*

In both of these paintings of Venice, the use of monochrome and masking fluid has greatly simplified the painting of a complicated subject. The windows in the Venetian mansions have been added wet into wet, with small amounts of concentrated Indigo to quickly render their facades.

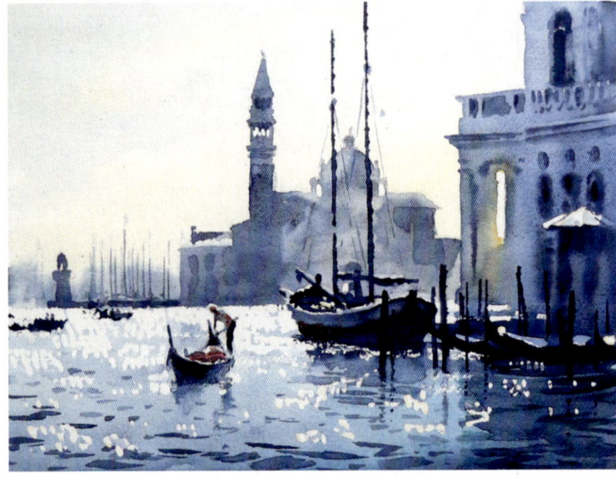

▲ **Venice in Indigo,** *30.5 x 40.5cm (12 x 16in)*

Suggestion is enough: the complex rigging, architectural details, many mooring poles, windows and balcony balustrade are suggested by just a few of their kind, brushed in with loose, irregular brushmarks.

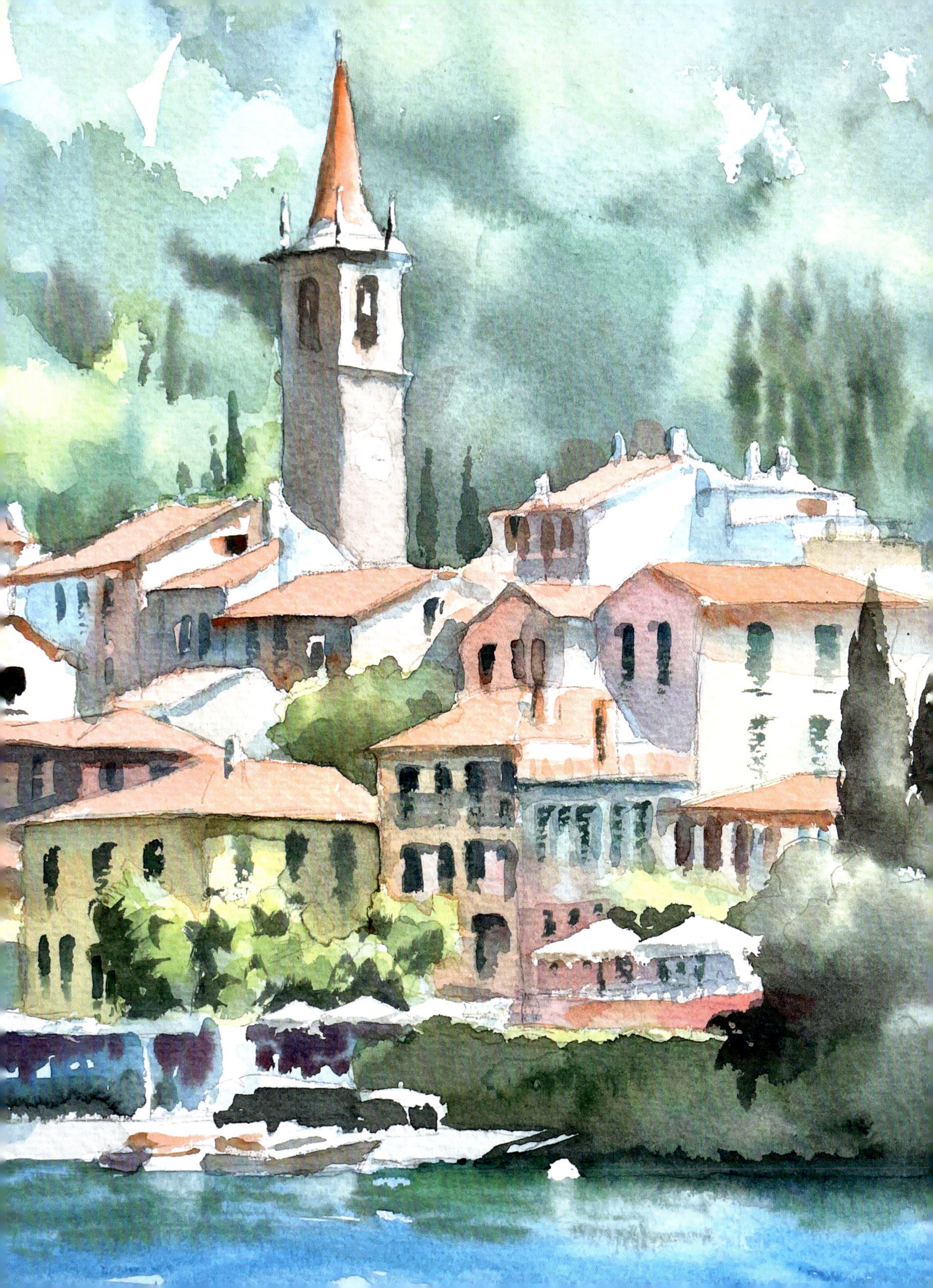

Convincing Figures

In the previous chapter, I talked about redeeming a dull watercolour by bringing a figure or figures into the composition, or using a figure or figures as a distraction from an errant passage of painting. Some readers probably sighed and thought, 'yes, good idea, but figures are so difficult'. You are not wrong: they can be. Painting figures comes with its own set of challenges, but the paintings here offer tips on painting convincing people as simply as possible.

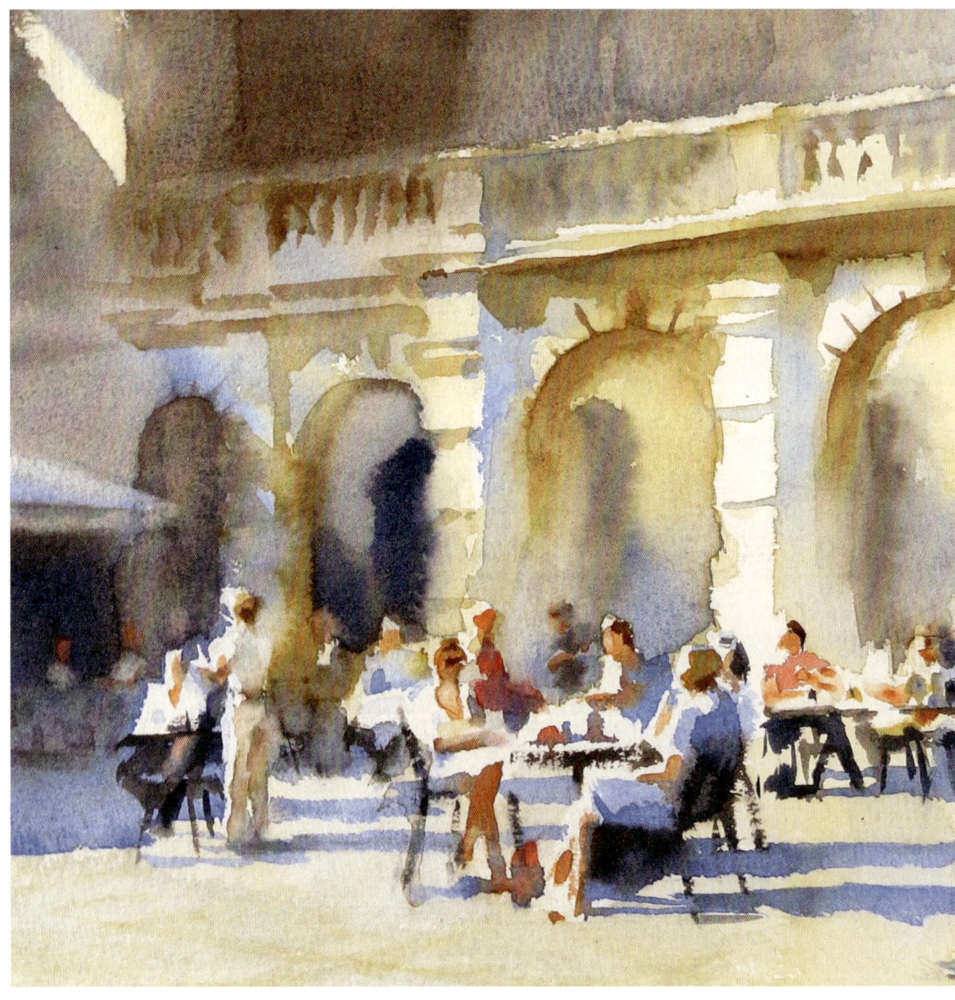

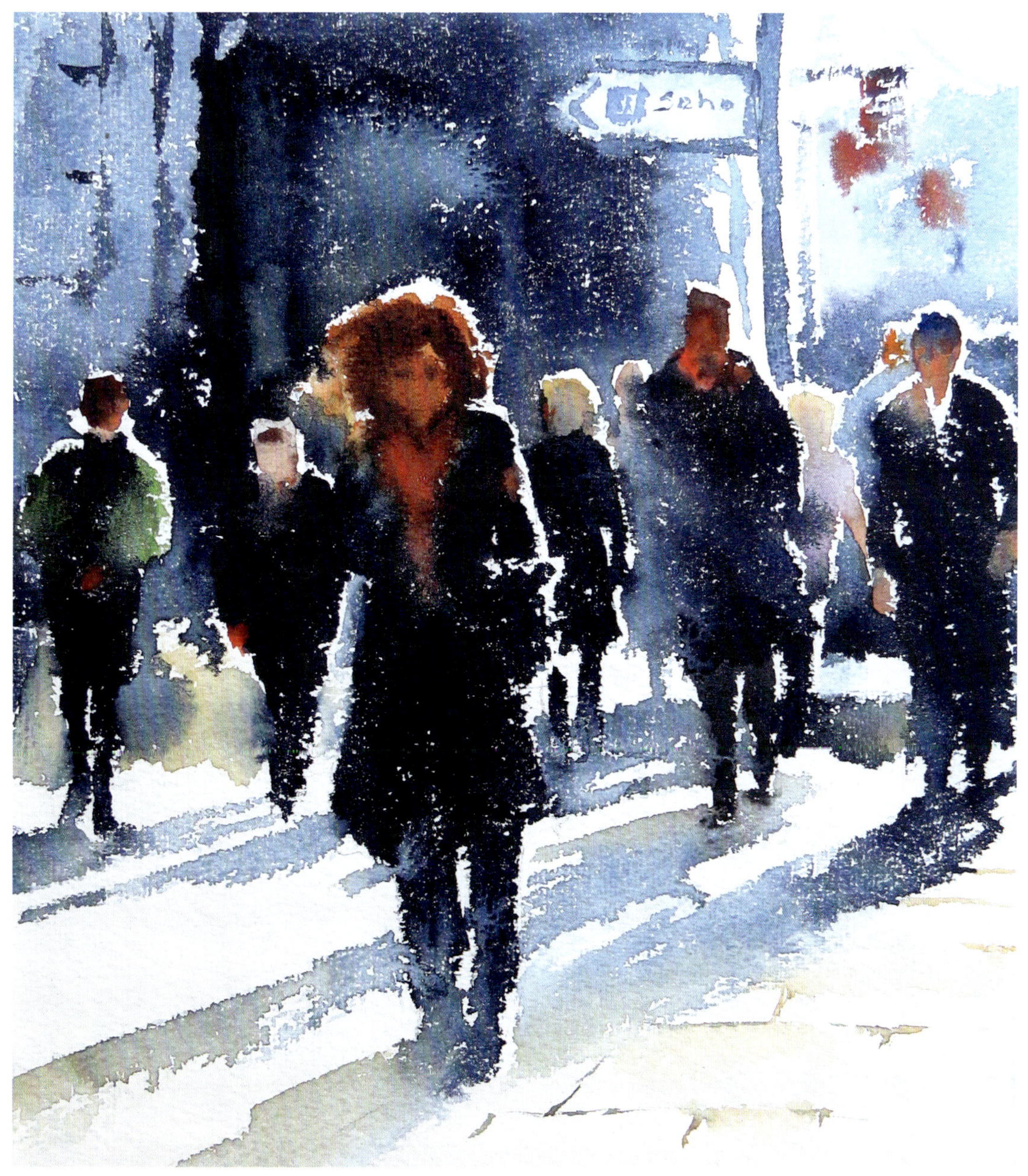

◀ **Cafe at the Royal Academy,**
25.5 x 25.5cm (10 x 10in)

People and architecture are complicated to paint, but by painting the shaded parts and leaving lit areas as white paper, watercolour can represent them as a few apposite blobs. Leaving out light and painting the shade is the key: it is the tonal values that make it work.

▲ **Snow Flurries,**
30.5 x 28cm (12 x 11in)

A bustling street can be represented by painting just a few of the people: a leading figure provides the focus, the rest are represented behind her, with pale oval heads set above blobby shapes edged in slivers of light.

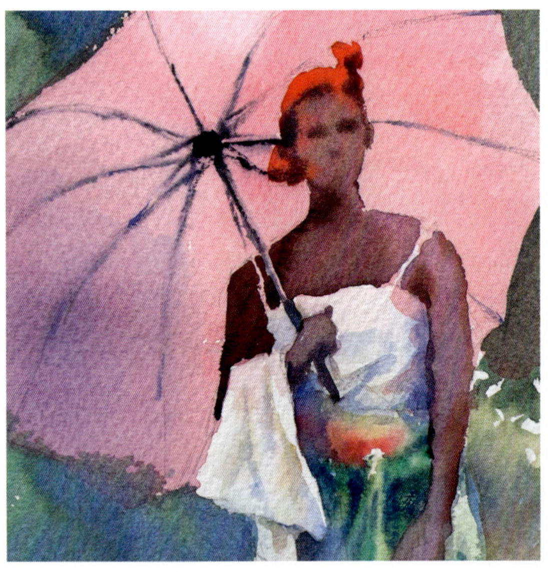

Tackling Portraits

Painting specific individuals is often assumed to be too complex a subject for a beginner watercolourist, but I say never shy away from painting portraits, however daunting. Having a live model pose for you, be it family, friend or stranger, is one of the greatest joys in painting. Do not worry about 'catching the likeness', just enjoy the opportunity to paint from life. You will always learn faster if you paint from life than if you paint from a photograph, so grasp the nettle whenever it is offered.

Set the light up in your favour. A contrast of light and shade is usually more exciting to read than an even light, so position your sitter with the light source coming from one side. Choose a three-quarter view, which makes it easier to paint the shape of the nose than a front angle, and brings the added attraction of an asymmetrical composition. Look at the spaces between the features as much as the shapes of the features themselves. Avoid adding lines and furrows unless they are the subject. Put a little more red into cheekbones and the tip of the nose to bring them forward. Place highlights in the eyes even if you cannot see any: this will bring a sparkle into the gaze. Paint the hair not through individual hairs but by painting the shadows cast between the strands and curls. In other words, see the hair as a mass, having three-dimensional form and structure, highlights, mid-tones and darks.

▲ **Pink Umbrella,** *15 x 15cm (6 x 6in)*

Just painting the shadows on the face was enough to suggest this lady's likeness under the shade of the pink umbrella.

▼ **Isoku,** *15 x 15cm (6 x 6in)*

Portraits can even be painted from the back view and still be an effective likeness of the model.

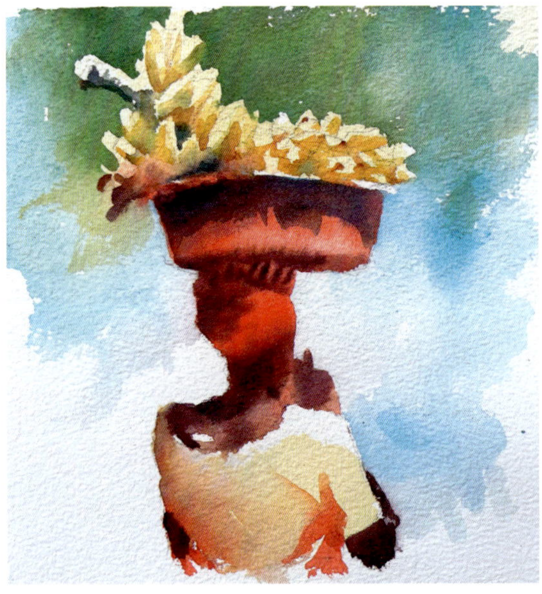

▶ **Sean,** *38 x 28cm (15 x 11in)*

I usually paint the eyes first – that gets the 'scariest' part done at the beginning – and as the pupils often contain the darkest tone, they help set the range of values for the rest of the painting. Plus, if I start to catch the likeness, I can usually recognize it earlier, and hopefully prevent needless overworking.

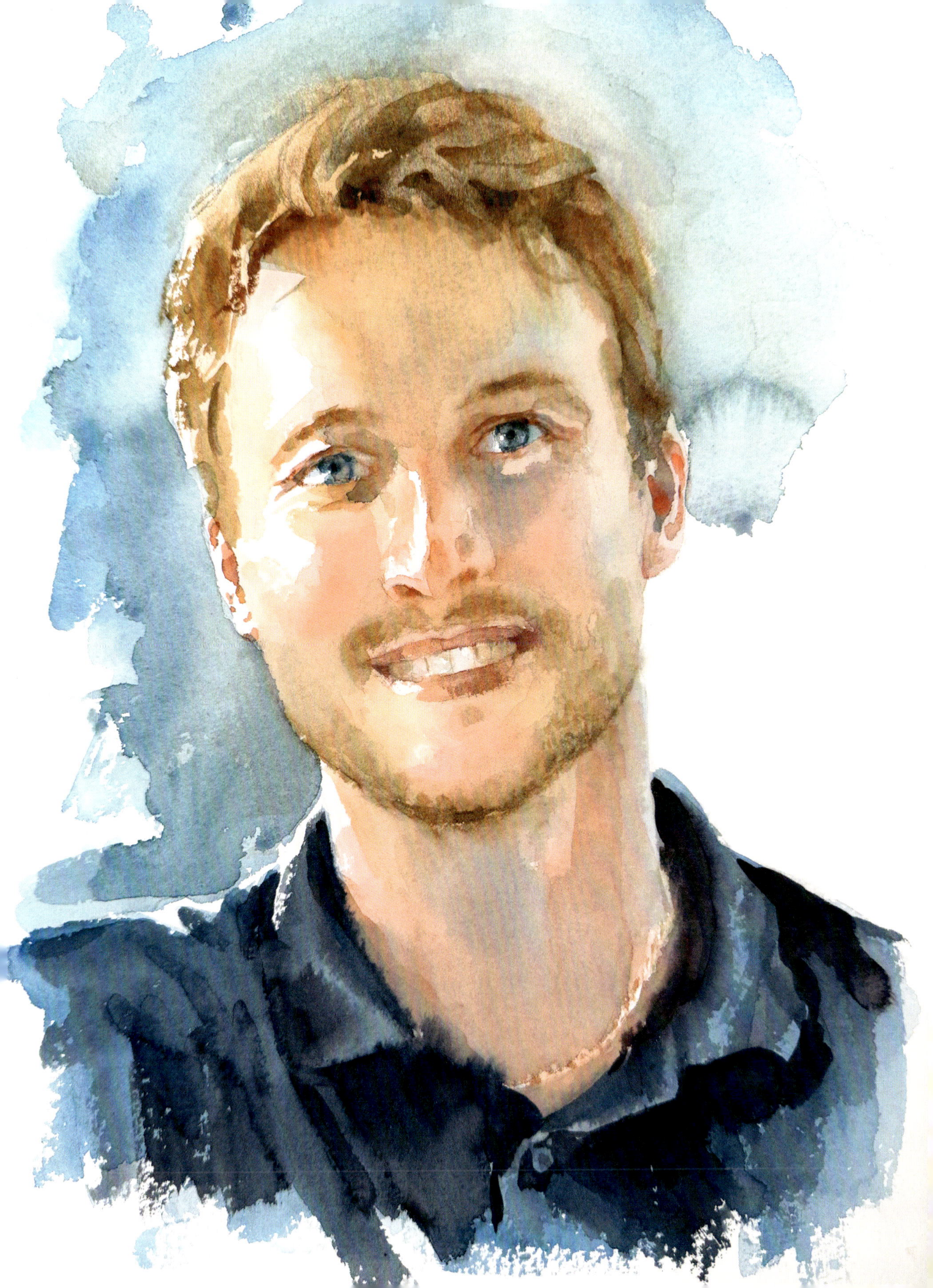

Practice, Practice, Practice

Divide the Painting into Manageable Sections

Few subjects are more colourful or complicated than a horse race, but complexity need not put you off painting anything: all you need is a method of approach that makes the sequence of painting manageable. Keep your eye on the whole, for therein lies the destination, and the image will not work if you see it in sections. However, that does not mean you cannot paint it in sections, for example from the middle outward or from one side to the other. But you must always start with the whole first: find pale hues that run through everything, for example a warm yellow for the light, a cool blue for the shade. Once you have bound the composition together in this way, you can go straight into more detail.

Colours:

Yellow Raw Ochre
Ultramarine Finest/Blue
Transparent/Burnt Sienna
Cadmium Red
Cobalt Blue
Viridian
Cadmium Yellow
Schmincke Violet
Alizarin Crimson

1 I drew the shapes of the horses and their jockeys with great care, paying particular attention to the spaces between things rather than the items themselves. I then protected all the highlights with masking fluid and allowed it to dry.

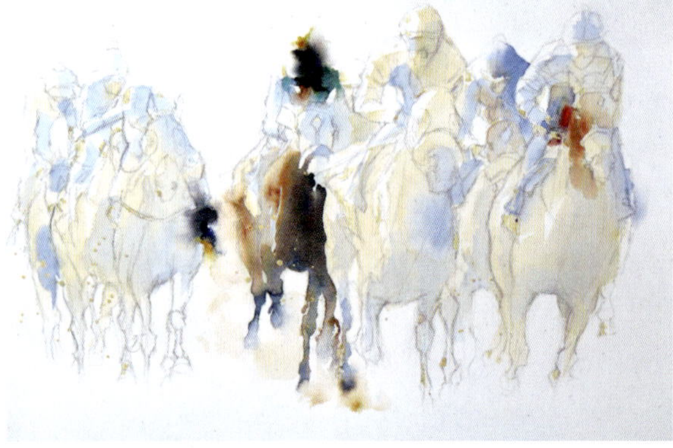

2 My first washes were a pale Yellow Ochre and pale Ultramarine Blue. Once I had noted and identified the main areas of light and shade, I felt more confident to paint each horse and rider in turn, starting from the middle.

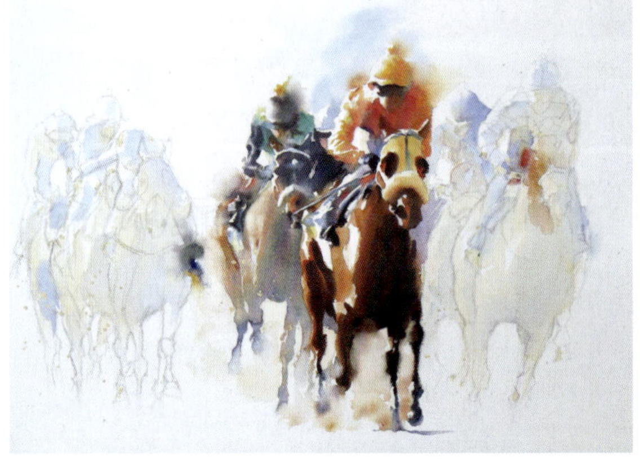

3 I now felt ready to go in more boldly with bright, strong colours and tones, blending colours wet into wet to imply movement and speed. Safe breathing spaces were found wherever I came up against a masked highlight. I rubbed the masking off as soon as the paint was dry.

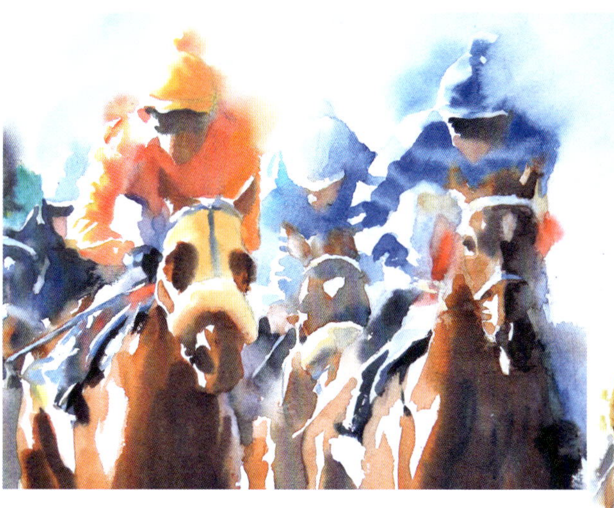

4 In this detail you can see the flow of the paint into dampened paper and into wet washes, and the contrast of this ambiguity with the sharp definition made by the unmasked highlights.

Brushes:

19mm flat brush

Size 8 round brush

Size 10 round brush

Size 12 round brush

5 Repetition is a strong persuader. By starting in the middle and then concentrating on the foreground horses, I was able to paint the rear horses and riders with much less definition, allowing the unmasked highlights to create the sparkle and jitter created by the speed of the action.

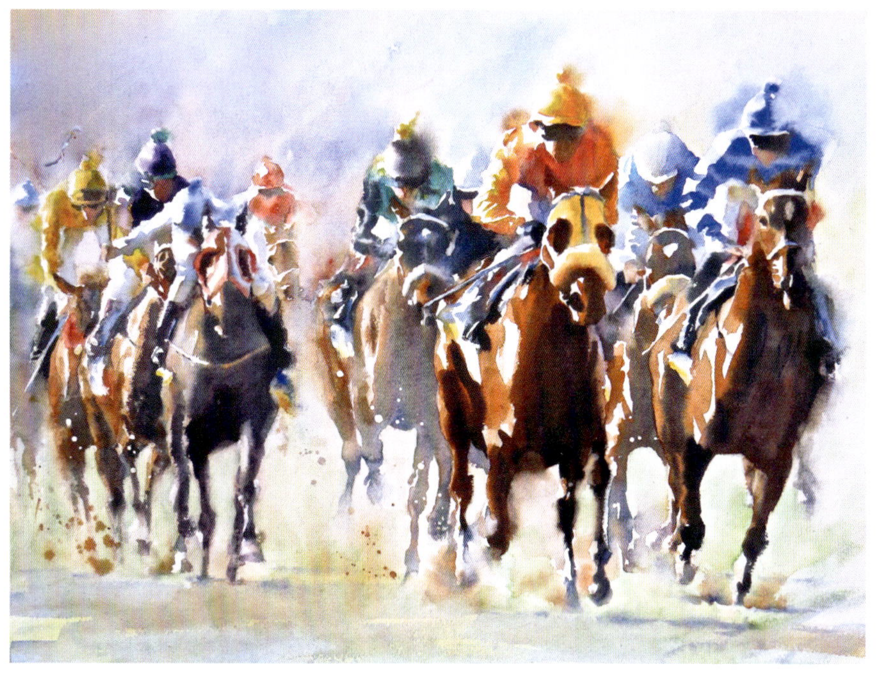

◀ **The Colours of Speed,**
56 x 76cm (22 x 30in)
I added additional jockeys in the rear to fill gaps, while I brushed in blue for the sky, shadows across the ground and a green haze for the turf. I couldn't resist indulging in some glorious splatter from a large brush for the clods of mud flung up by the thundering hooves. By dividing the subject into sectional areas, and yet keeping an eye on each section in relation to the whole, a complicated subject is rendered much more manageable to paint.

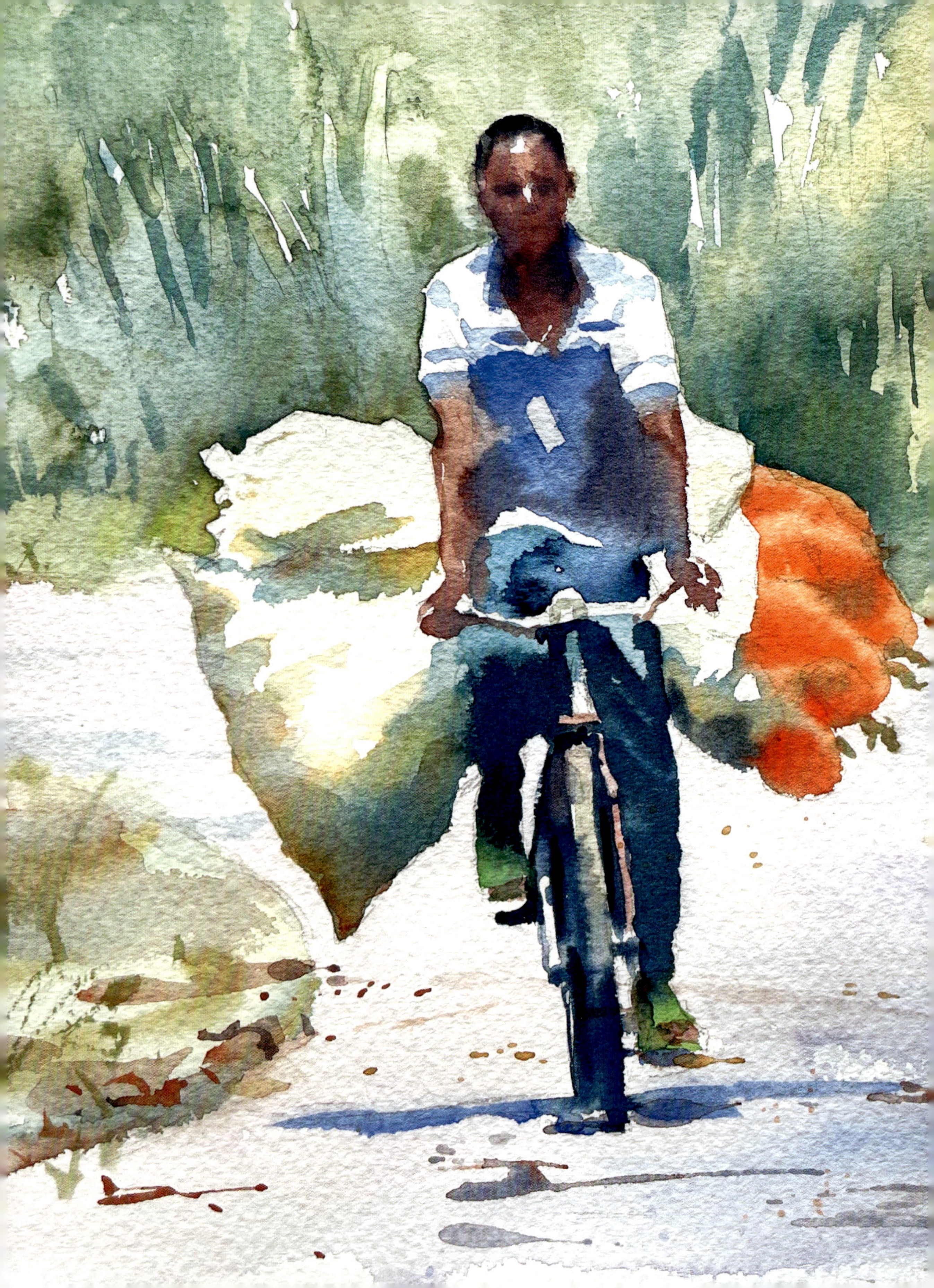

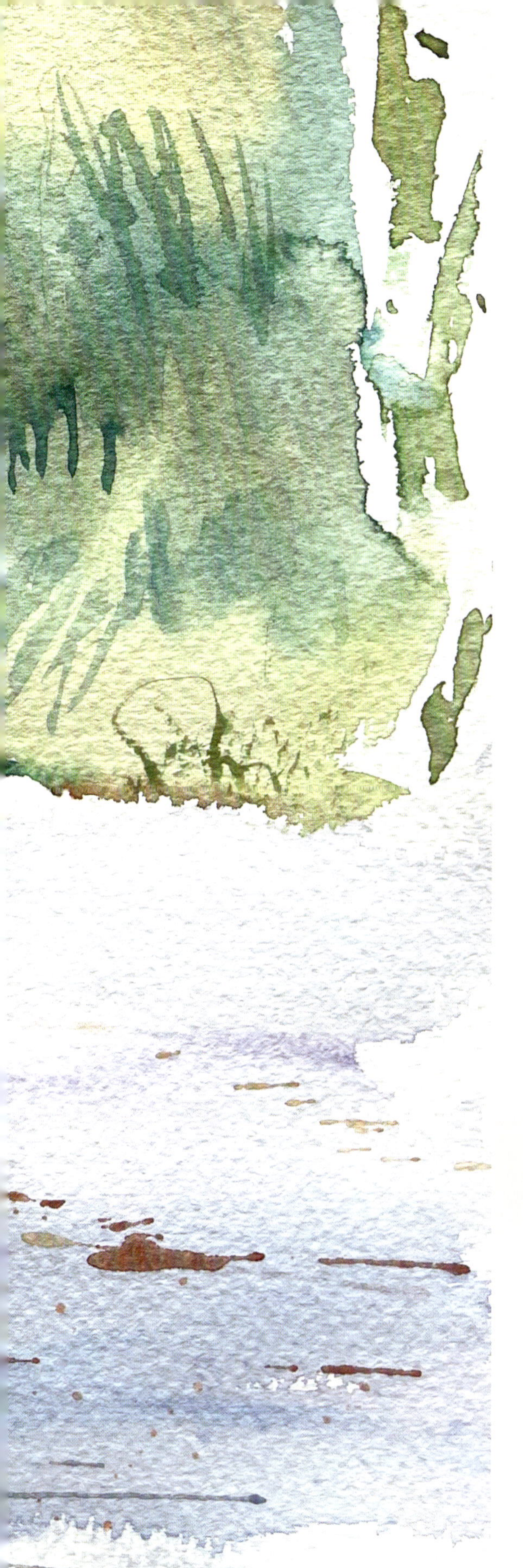

Epilogue

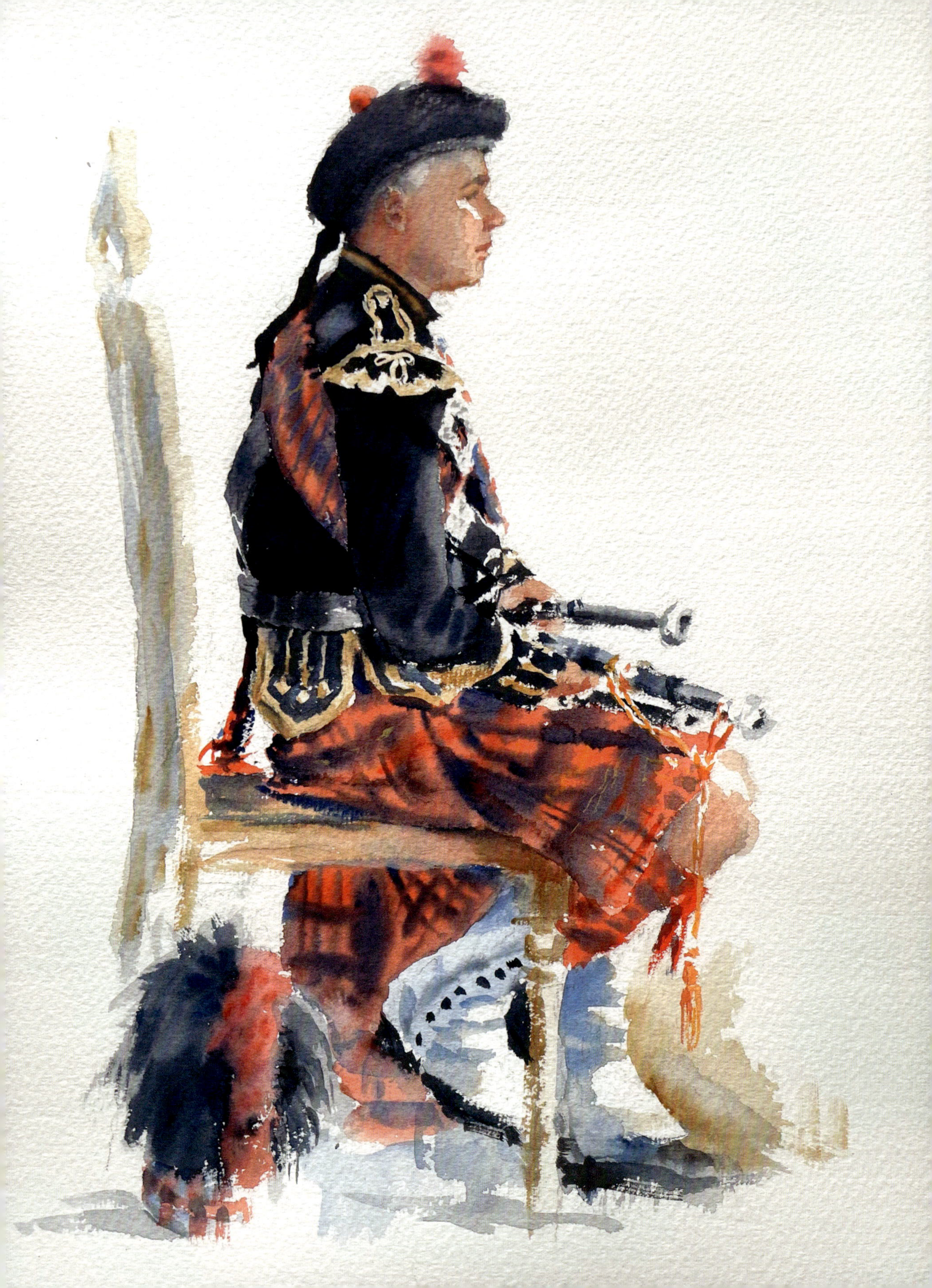

Art and Science

Being quintessentially a transparent medium, watercolour is reliant on the light reflected back from the white paper. Light is the key ingredient. In reciprocal fashion, much like the duality of light, watercolour painting beautifully mirrors the interplay between particles and waves. The pigment particles in watercolour are discrete, tangible entities, while the water carries them in waves, spreading and blending in fluid, wave-like patterns across the paper.

The magic happens as the water flows, spreads and creates gradients, pooling or evaporating, and the pigment settles, concentrating in specific areas or granulating in the paper's texture in obedience to gravity. This artistic process is a perfect blend of order and unpredictability, where the medium's nature does half the work, and your creativity guides the rest, creating something truly extraordinary.

There is something mesmerizing about watching the pigment spread outward across the white paper, and to witness it mingling with other colours in enticing new blends. The fine particles are too small to see individually, but it is worth considering how much they matter, as they reward the painter more fully when they are allowed to settle without undue interference and are not dragged back and forth across the paper or pushed into unhappy groups.

◀ **Highland Piper,**
51 x 40.5cm (20 x 16in)
This Highland Piper had a limited time to pose and presented a complex pattern of lights and darks, so it was necessary to find a shorthand way of describing the detail. Painting from life teaches you to make decisions about colour and tone far more quickly than if you take your subjects from photographic reference.

▶ **Cormorants,**
10 x 12.5cm (4 x 5in)
Birds are wonderful subjects for learning how to use the tip and body of the brush. Load and twist the brush to a tip in the palette for the beak, then press down for the body to widen the brush and release more paint.

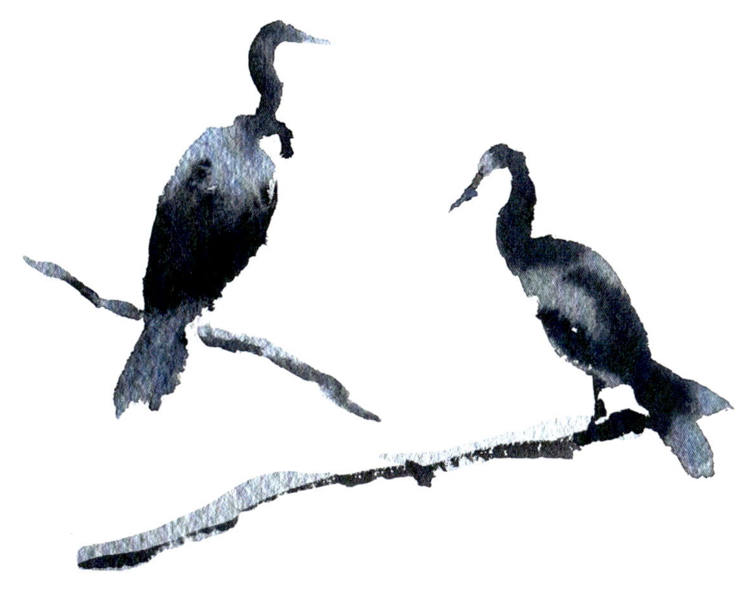

Is it Just a Piece of Paper?

Increased affinity with the watercolour medium changes the dynamic of painting. I aim to please the watercolour first, trusting it to deliver the freshness inherent in its nature as witnessed in the colours on the palette. Rather than using the watercolour to paint the subject, I use the subject to paint a watercolour. I have found the medium shows its finest when I put the medium's needs first: I respect the properties of the pigments, the fabric of the paper, and the purpose and versatility of each and every brushstroke. Instead of dictating my own terms and trying to cajole watercolour to do my bidding, I endeavour to keep the pigment and paper happy.

I have found watercolour to be the perfect marriage between art and science. Indeed, had Einstein taken up watercolour he would have had no problem accepting that causality and uncertainty can readily live in harmony. You can take that quantum leap too!

Understanding how watercolour works, knowing the properties of the pigments, and being more aware of the process helps conquer the fear and anxiety that hinders passion. With this book at your side, you will be able to avoid and correct the most common mistakes and have remedies ready for recovery, disguise or distraction, increasing your success rate while you discover the joy and freedom that comes from painting watercolour without fear.

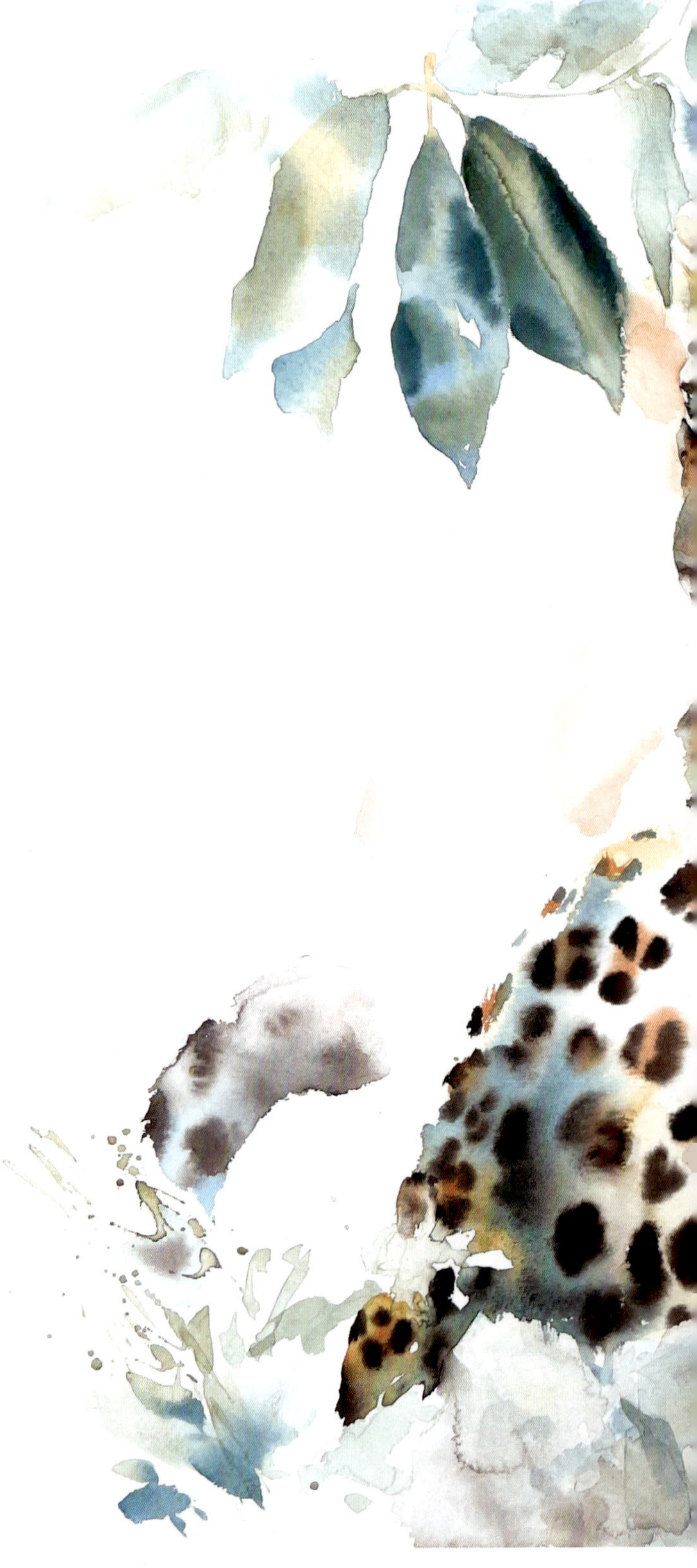

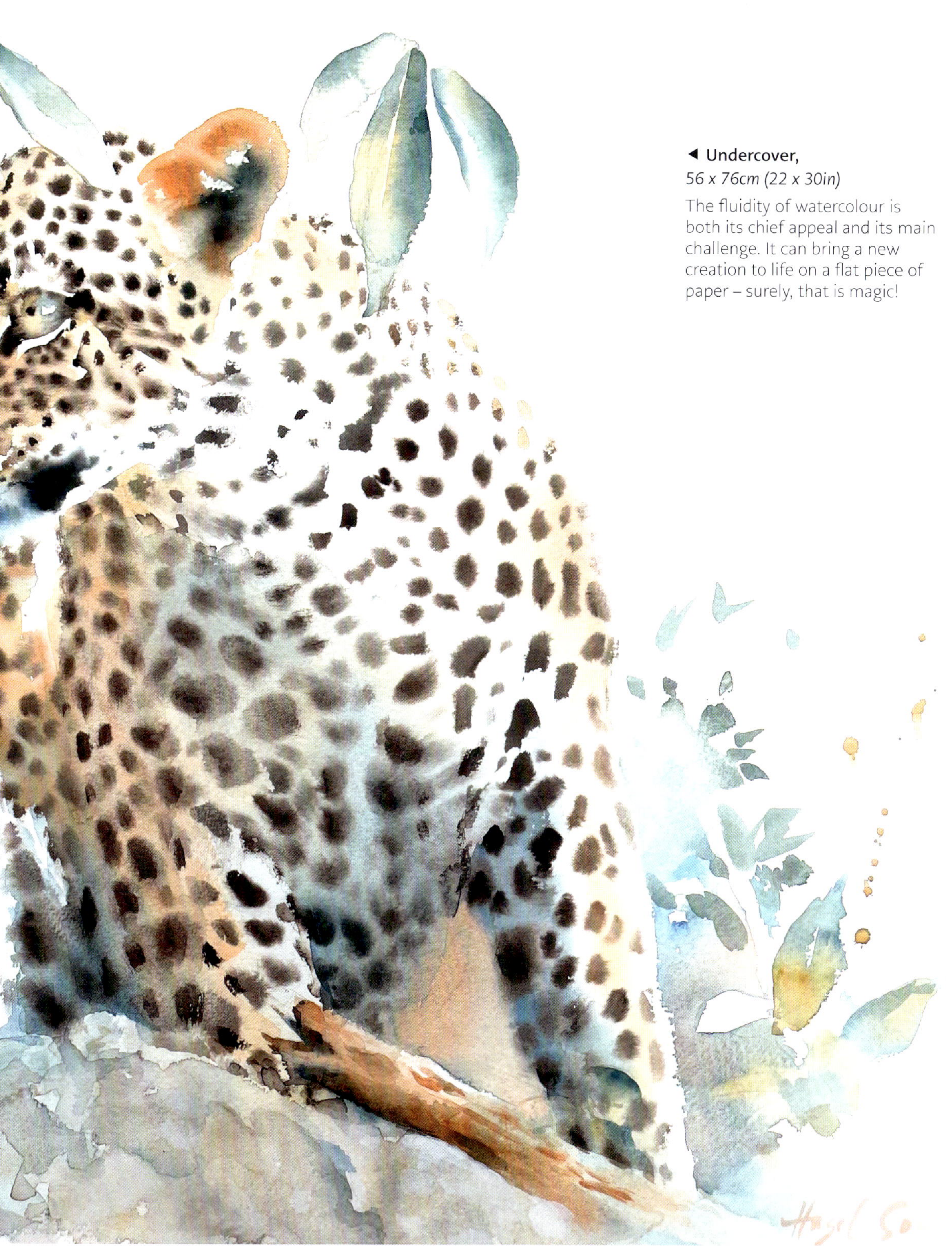

◀ **Undercover,**
56 x 76cm (22 x 30in)
The fluidity of watercolour is both its chief appeal and its main challenge. It can bring a new creation to life on a flat piece of paper – surely, that is magic!

Index

Acknowledgements

This is a book I have been wanting to write for a while, so my grateful thanks go first to my wonderful publishers, Batsford, and in particular to the Editorial Director, Nicola Newman, who said 'yes' when I asked for more pages! Bella MacConnol has been the perfect Editor. Just as with watercolour painting, there is a fair amount of angst while making a book, but her accommodating, swift responses to my emails, and the ability to prioritise when I was short on time are among her many talents, and my thanks go out to Bella for making the process feel seamless, and for taking the fear out of deadlines!

Huge thanks must go to the in-house designers, Eoghan O'Brien and Sanya Jain, and to Sally Bond, the freelance designer who has worked on several of my books. Once again, brilliantly, you have made the paintings as large as possible yet allowed them space to breathe, and given a clean, fresh appearance to the layout. Thank you!

Unlike painting watercolours, book production requires collaboration, and my thanks go to everyone involved in bringing this book into being and especially to Pete Rouse in charge of production. Many thanks also go to Everdien Bouwman for the photos of the Duomo demo on pages 132–133.

A watercolour artist benefits from the finest materials, and my thanks go to Schmincke, for making their consistently high quality Horadam Watercolours. I am proud to be an ambassador for their brand. For my brushes, I am grateful to Da Vinci for producing such fine sable brushes – like my paint, they are utter joy to paint with! I am equally thankful to St Cuthbert's Mill for their expertise in producing excellent watercolour paper: most of the paintings in this book are on their Saunders Waterford 100% cotton paper.

Books are meaningless without readers – the process is definitely two way! I am always touched when my followers take the time between paintings to tell me how much they appreciate my paintings and words, their support makes it all worthwhile.

Lastly, my thanks to my family and friends, their continued encouragement inspires me. They don't all read the books but they like looking at the pictures!

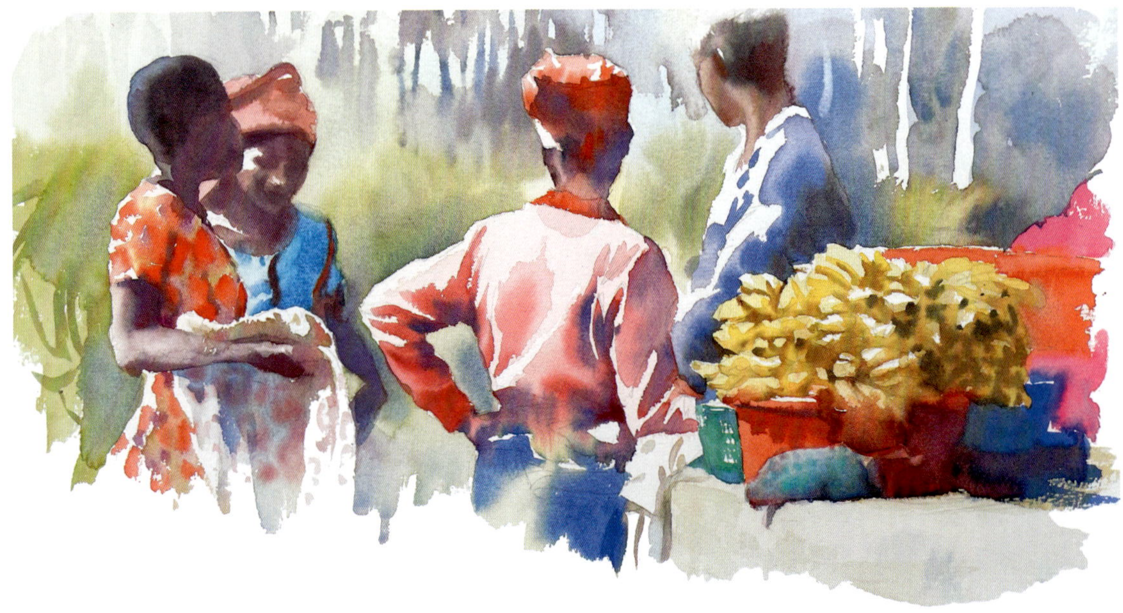